# CONSTRAINTS AND CREATIVITY

This book studies creativity in its own right in the search for a creativity science. If we assume that creativity can best be described by constraint theory, the complexity and paradoxes of creativity can be reduced by dividing it into manageable sections. The model is tested and evidenced by numerous historical cases of pioneering work within the three intellectual fields: science, art, and technology. The model guides non-specialists from the many disciplines studying creativity and demonstrates the first principles of creativity science. Going all the way back to Aristotle, the author makes the basic ideas of the original founder of creativity science accessible and up to date with current research.

FEIWEL KUPFERBERG is Senior Professor in the Department of Culture, Language and Media at Malmö University, Sweden, and Adjunct Professor in the Department of Sociology and Social Work at Aalborg University, Denmark.

T0381773

# CONSTRAINTS AND CREATIVITY

## In Search of Creativity Science

FEIWEL KUPFERBERG

*Malmö University*

CAMBRIDGE
UNIVERSITY PRESS

Shaftesbury Road, Cambridge CB2 8EA, United Kingdom

One Liberty Plaza, 20th Floor, New York, NY 10006, USA

477 Williamstown Road, Port Melbourne, VIC 3207, Australia

314–321, 3rd Floor, Plot 3, Splendor Forum, Jasola District Centre, New Delhi – 110025, India

103 Penang Road, #05–06/07, Visioncrest Commercial, Singapore 238467

Cambridge University Press is part of Cambridge University Press & Assessment,
a department of the University of Cambridge.

We share the University's mission to contribute to society through the pursuit of
education, learning and research at the highest international levels of excellence.

www.cambridge.org
Information on this title: www.cambridge.org/9781108813488

DOI: 10.1017/9781108884617

© Feiwel Kupferberg 2021

This publication is in copyright. Subject to statutory exception and to the provisions
of relevant collective licensing agreements, no reproduction of any part may take
place without the written permission of Cambridge University Press & Assessment.

First published 2021
First paperback edition 2023

*A catalogue record for this publication is available from the British Library*

*Library of Congress Cataloging-in-Publication data*
Names: Kupferberg, Feiwel, 1946- author.
Title: Constraints and creativity : in search of creativity science / Feiwel Kupferberg, Malmö University.
Description: Cambridge, United Kingdom ; New York, NY : Cambridge University Press, 2021. |
Includes bibliographical references and index.
Identifiers: LCCN 2020042225 (print) | LCCN 2020042226 (ebook) | ISBN 9781108839617
(hardback) | ISBN 9781108813488 (paperback) | ISBN 9781108884617 (epub)
Subjects: LCSH: Creative ability. | Creation (Literary, artistic, etc.)
Classification: LCC BF408 .K86 2021 (print) | LCC BF408 (ebook) | DDC 153.3/5–dc23
LC record available at https://lccn.loc.gov/2020042225
LC ebook record available at https://lccn.loc.gov/2020042226

ISBN    978-1-108-83691-7    Hardback
ISBN    978-1-108-81348-8    Paperback

Cambridge University Press & Assessment has no responsibility for the persistence
or accuracy of URLs for external or third-party internet websites referred to in this
publication and does not guarantee that any content on such websites is, or will
remain, accurate or appropriate.

# Contents

*Prolegomenon*

# Preface

This book is not meant to be merely another contribution to the 70-year-old discipline the psychology of creativity, nor does it pursue the problem of what creativity is and how it should be studied from the narrow point of view of any existing discipline or intellectual tradition that has studied some aspect of this complex and paradoxical phenomenon. The book aims at something different: to clarify the First principles of a science which studies creativity in its own right. It is a search for a creativity science from an educational psychology point of view. Like film studies, cognitive science and archeology, such a science has to be interdisciplinary in the sense that it draws upon a rich foundation of data studied by a huge number of intellectual traditions. Nevertheless, it represents a discipline of its own in the sense that creativity science has a distinct knowledge object which needs to be clarified. This basic view of science is very old. It goes back to Aristotle, the founder of the theory of First principles (the idea that methodological procedures have to be adapted to the nature of the knowledge object). But Aristotle, surprisingly, also identified the First principles of creativity science (the theory of the four causes).

Much has changed since Aristotle made his contributions. Creativity science has to be brought up to date. This is essentially what this book tries to do. For this purpose, starting by making a list of the most important unsolved problems of creativity science might be a good procedure: (1) How do we account for the complexity and paradoxes of creativity? (2) How and why are scientific forms of creativity (S-creativity) different from artistic and technological forms of creativity (A-creativity, T-creativity)? (3) How do we explain creative explosions in human history (H-creativity)? (4) Is nature creative (N-creativity) and what are the similarities and differences between problem solving in nature and culture? (5) How do we explain personal levels of creativity (P-creativity) within and across intellectual traditions? (6) Is there such a thing as geniuses, or should we instead look at levels of problem-solving capacity as learning roles (pioneers, professionals, novices)? (7) Are the motivations to engage in groundbreaking levels of creativity (pioneers, H-creativity) different from the motivations of professionals and novices? (8) Where does the problem-solving capacity of pioneers (P-creativity as H-creativity) come from in the first place and how is it to be explained? (9) What if any role does the protection of vulnerable versions or ideas play for the capacity to solve the trickiest type of problems (H-creativity), and how is the problem of protection solved in practice? (10) Is there such a thing as getting it right and does it matter if we generalize from successful or unsuccessful scientific, artistic and technological revolutions (S-, A-, T-creativity)?

A basic theoretical assumption of the book is that the best way to define and simplify the complexity and paradoxes of creativity is to foreground the role of constraints. In order to clarify the nature of these constraints, I have developed a theoretical model, consisting of five dimensions: I Types of constraints, II Levels of creativity, III Getting it right, IV Protection of vulnerable versions, V Structure of creative processes. Most of the book consists of elaborating this theoretical model or framework, referring to empirical cases I have collected over a period of 30 years, after I first became interested in the topic (Kupferberg, 1991).

The two main data sets I have drawn upon are (1) intellectual biographies of pioneers (P-creativity as H-creativity) within the three intellectual fields of science, art and technology (S-, A-, T-creativity) and (2) scientific disciplines in the making (discoveries of First principles in science, S-creativity as H-creativity). The choice of pioneers has probably been constrained by personal idiosyncrasy. The choice of disciplines has modeled itself upon the Enlightenment theory of knowledge as encyclopedic. Apart from film studies, cognitive science and archeology, I have studied or at least acquainted myself with a broad range of disciplines in the making in order to get an idea of what discovering the First principles of a science means in practice: mathematics, physics, chemistry, geology, evolutionary biology, primatology, sociobiology, molecular biology, economics, business economics, economic history, Soviet and East European studies, German studies, the psychology of creativity, neuroscience, educational psychology, pedagogy, sociology, cultural anthropology, cultural geography, architecture and design history, art history, literary theory, semiotics, psychoanalysis, medical philosophy and history, the philosophy of science, the history of science, the sociology of science, the philosophy of art (aesthetics) but also the engineering sciences, in particular materials science and computer science. Some of these studies go way back in my intellectual career, long before I became interested in creativity as an object of scientific study. Others were added as my idea that I was on to something which had not been done before deepened and made my search for a creativity science more focused.

The breakthrough came around 2016–2017 after reading Collins (1998) a magnum opus on the history of philosophy, a discipline I had begun to study at Stockholm university in the late 1960s after having abandoned a previous biographical project (Kupferberg, 1995b) to become a chemical engineer. Collins mentions the concept of "constraints" as a possible correction to the postmodernist "everything goes" (Feyerabend, 1975) theory. The concept of constraints fits into my previous interest in neuroscience (Kupferberg, 1995) plus Searle's (1996) and Hacking's (2000) critique of the weakness of "social constructionism". Combined with the alternative (Aristotelian and Darwinian) way to conceptualize creativity as a sociocognitive phenomenon which overcomes the nature/culture divide (Kupferberg, 2011, 2012c), I became convinced that the constraint theory approach is the best, most parsimonious theoretical framework for a creativity science (Kupferberg, 2017a).

Having independently arrived at a constraint theory approach, I discovered (P-creativity) that the pioneer of constraint theory (H-creativity) is John Elster (1983, 2000, 2007). The best definition of constraints appears in Elster (1999). Although that book is about emotions, the basic idea is the same: "We can try to explain the emotions . . . by identifying the conditions under which they tend to arise. The link between the triggering situation and the emotion has been viewed as largely conceptual, as causal and deterministic, or as causal but partly indeterminate. To illustrate the last approach, which is the one I've been taken here: When the suspicion that one's lover is unfaithful has been raised, the reaction might be to exaggerate it or to kill it" (Elster, 1999, p. 406).

This type of half-baked determinacy (constraints) is very common not only in human affairs. It can also be found in evolutionary biology (N-creativity). Why do some species become extinct whereas others survive in the "tree of life"? Strictly predictive models of the type we can find in physics (such as the law of gravity) are hard to come by. Nevertheless, it is possible to find more or less convincing explanations why, for example, the dinosaurs disappeared some 65 million years ago or how an ape-like creature was transformed into modern *Homo sapiens* within a time span of about 6 million years. One of the follow-up questions that a constraint theory approach to creativity science might help to clarify is if and in what sense Darwin's theory of evolution (N-creativity) can help explain

Darwin's own process of discovery (P-creativity, H-creativity, S-creativity). But there are also many other spin-offs such as what creativity science can learn from studies on technology (T-creativity), why science originated so late and why in ancient Greece, why science-based technology only became possible around 1600, why modern art has abandoned not only naturalistic paintings but painting as a medium, what we actually mean with a creative milieu, what role persons play in transformations of intellectual fields, etc.

The overall goal of creativity science is to (1) account for the complexity (Andersson & Sahlin, 1997) and paradoxes of creativity (Alperson, 2003); (2) not only test but also generate theories of creative explosions in human history (Strong & Davies, 2006/2011a, 2011b); (3) more generally to study the phenomenon in an objective, methodological manner (Montuschi, 2003). The five dimensions of the theoretical model or framework presented and elaborated in this book are meant to be an intellectual tool (Kupferberg, 2012b) or guide both for those who want to orient themselves in this seemingly chaotic field and those who want to study and analyze some chosen cases of creative processes in more detail, starting with person, work, tradition and moving on to other types of constraints. The book can perhaps best be described as an introductory textbook into the field of creativity science, a kind of impersonal teacher or mediated form of learning (Säljö, 2000; Kupferberg, 2013) of the type educational psychologists working in the cultural psychological tradition pioneered by Vygotsky (Wertsch, 2007) have discovered to be an economic/elegant or parsimonious cultural tool (Säljö, 2005). It can also help us to approach the core problem of educational psychology, how to bridge the problem of ontogeny, personal learning processes and discoveries (P-creativity) with the problem of phylogeny: pioneering work, intellectual revolutions or creative explosions in science, art and technology (H-creativity).

The logical structure of the book and what type of theory it seeks to falsify and why now follows. In order to become a scientific discipline, creativity science must identify the First principles of the discipline. But given that each discipline has its own First principles, the search for a creativity science might be enriched from how other disciplines managed to clarify their First principles (see Chapter 1). Such a comparison is helpful to identify a number of empirical patterns which creativity science can start its search from. One important discovery when comparing disciplines in the making is that what counts as valid data, method of interpretation or proof for one discipline does not necessarily count as valid data or proof for other disciplines (see Chapter 8). Valid data in practice tend to be adapted to the nature of the knowledge object. But the knowledge object might also sometimes have to be clarified. It cannot always be taken as given (see Chapter 7).

These methodological and conceptual concerns are at the heart of creativity science. Take the discipline of history. What is it that historians study and how? Professionally trained historians study literate societies and this legitimates the preferred method of historians (Thorstendahl, 1966), the critical comparison of contemporary texts found in archives. Contemporary texts are the type of data novices entering the discipline are trained to appreciate and regard as reliable and valid. But this type of data is of little value for archeology, the discipline that studies preliterate societies which at some point turned into literate societies. Until such transformations begin (as in ancient Egypt or Mesopotamia), such societies leave no texts to be compared. Hence, as a general rule (First principle), if we find texts, they must have been written long after the event. This is the reason why archeology, in order to become a scientific discipline, had to redefine its primary data from texts to artifacts (Trigger, 2003) and replace hermeneutics with stylistic analysis as its primary method of interpretation (Renfrew & Bahn, 2008).

Studying how archeology became a scientific discipline is interesting as it tells us how the unsolved "demarcation problem" (what makes science as science) can be solved in practice. Contemporary philosophy of science has given up on this problem. It has been declared to be unsolvable in principle (Laudan, 1996). But how do we know this to be an indisputable fact unless we have tested it in practice? Perhaps philosophers of science have arrived at this conclusion by using the wrong data and methods (see Laudan & Leplin, 1991/2007)? To get it right in science (Dimension III, Chapter 4) is not always possible for historical, professional or personal reasons, and this is where constraint theory is of help. Why did Aristotle believe that eels are reproduced by "spontaneous generation" (Rhill, 1999)? Why did he fail to discover the laws of fall (Renn, 2001) or solve the problem of the origins of species although he was very close to doing so, according to Darwin (Jones, 2001)? And how can we explain that Aristotle nevertheless, in spite of his many mistakes, did solve the "demarcation problem" at least in principle (the theory of First principles)?

As we know the discipline of archeology originated in Denmark between 1800 and 1830. But why precisely there and why around 1800? And why was it Christian Jürgensen Thomsen a successful businessman and amateur coin collector? Could the fact, noted by Charles Lyell, one of the two founders of geology (the other was the mining engineer James Hutton), in *The Ancestry of Man*, that Denmark for geological reasons had a rich source of data both to generate and test archeological theories, be part of the explanation? For this purpose, foregrounding the role of physical constraints (Dimension I, Chapter 2) and material cause (Dimension V, Chapter 6) might be helpful. But data have to be accessed and interpretations protected from premature death. This takes us to the problem of opportunity (Dimension I, Chapter 2) and helpers (Dimension IV, Chapter 5). Here Thomsen's successful career as a businessman which provided him with personal contacts in high circles with access to the Danish court might help us a little bit along the road. But this still does not exhaust the issue. How did Thomsen know precisely that stylistic analysis was the correct methodology, helping him to get it right (Dimension III, Chapter 4)? Here Thomsen's novice type of knowledge of numismatics (he happened to be an amateur coin collector), might provide the critical edge which explains why Thomsen could take the step from professional businessman to pioneering scholar (Dimension II, Chapter 3) in precisely this intellectual tradition.

In this case, the two data sets of intellectual biographies and disciplines in the making intersect. But this is not always the case: creativity science is also here to explain pioneering work in other fields such as art and technology. This raises a number of difficult and challenging questions for creativity science. Why is technological creativity (T-creativity) the type of creativity that is closest to nature (N-creativity) and why does science (S-creativity) appear so late in human records? For this purpose, we need to clarify the different rules of science, art and technology (Dimension I, Chapter 2).

Take Galileo and Picasso. If we are to believe Feyerabend (1975), the scientist Galileo essentially worked like the artist Picasso, breaking all the rules. But Galileo did not break the basic rule of science (to falsify theories by separating fact from fiction, Dimension V, Chapter 6). Nor did Picasso break the basic rules of art (evoking emotions by transforming facts into fiction). What Galileo did was that he collected the relevant data, interpreted them with valid concepts and adapted methodological procedures (problem-solving strategy) to the nature of the knowledge object (Dimension V, Chapter 6). This explains why knowledge constraints are critical for how scientific creativity works in practice (Dimension I, Chapter 2).

In contrast, the core problem-solving strategy of Picasso was the choice of techniques (Dimension V, Chapter 6). But in order to get it right,

Picasso had to consider the historical problem situation of French painting at the start of the twentieth century with the rise of American cinema as a threatening competitor (Dimension III, Chapter 4). A close analysis shows that what characterized these two art forms (one premodern, the other late modern) was ultimately the nature of physical constraints (Dimension I, Chapter 2). Feyerabend therefore managed to get nothing right.

Galileo managed to rectify Aristotle's basic methodological mistake (Dimension V, Chapter 6) projecting the laws of biology upon physics. But if this is indeed the case, how could Aristotelian physics be categorized as a science, as Feyerabend's colleague Kuhn claims? How could Aristotle be the pioneer of this discipline (according to Kuhn, Aristotle even anticipated Einstein)? Is Kuhn's simple sociological criterion, that politics, the predominance of one paradigm, is the only thing which defines what should be categorized as science, correct? Is scientific creativity not ultimately a type of problem solving? But in order to solve problems in a scientific manner we need to get the methodology (First principles) right. Kuhn's sociological theory of science is not more convincing than Feyerabend's.

But whereas Feyearbend's mistake was the belief that pioneers in science and art follow no rules, Kuhn's basic mistake was to project the peculiar logic of artistic revolutions upon scientific revolutions. Scientific revolutions evolve gradually, by overcoming one knowledge constraint after another (Kupferberg, 2017a; Dimension I, Chapter 2), artistic revolutions move both forwards and backwards just as planets do when seen from the Earth (Dimension V, Chapter 6). Naturalistic techniques evolve gradually over time but are once in a while abandoned and replaced by symbolic techniques, until naturalistic techniques are once again rediscovered, etc., a logic very similar to religion, see Max Weber's (1922/1964) sociology of religion.

Kuhn's basic mistake, that scientific revolutions follow the same pattern as artistic revolutions, has become the core principle of postmodernist theory (Lyotard, 1984; Schusterman, 2003). From a creativity science point of view though we also need to ask how and why Kuhn arrived at this misguided and misguiding theory of science. But for this purpose, we must be able to separate theories on or in science that manage to get it right and those that fail to do so. This is the very opposite of the "symmetry principle" recommended by David Bloor in *Knowledge and Imagery*. What Bloor fails to realize is that his methodological principle takes it for granted that Kuhn got it right when he claimed that scientific revolutions are not cognitive but exclusively sociological events. But this, as John Searle notes in *The Construction of Social Reality,* is itself a cognitive claim and has to be dealt with in a cognitive manner.

From this it does not follow that getting it right in science, art and technology does not entail sociological issues, but to understand what is social and what is cognitive and how the two are entangled, we must make a distinction between successful and unsuccessful scientific revolutions. A closer investigation of the intellectual origins of Kuhn's sociological theory of scientific revolutions, reveals that Kuhn for some reason chose to generalize his theories from an unsuccessful revolution. Copernicus' theoretical model in fact did not manage to get it right (Dimension III, Chapter 4). Hence the "symmetry principle" ultimately derives from a prototype which happens to use the wrong prototype (Dimension I, Chapter 2).

Falsifying incorrect First principles (S-creativity) is what pioneers in science engaged in the problem of "disciplines in the making" in practice do (Dimension V, Chapter 6). Pioneers in art (A-creativity) and technology (T-creativity) also do pioneering work ( H-creativity), but nevertheless they have different aims and use different types of problem-solving strategies. The best way to understand how this works is constraint theory. Constraint theory also helps us to reconstruct how and why Kuhn arrived at his false theory of S-creativity. But for this purpose we need to collect the relevant types of data (material cause, Dimension V, Chapter 6), (1) intellectual biographies and (2) intellectual traditions, in particular disciplines in the making (see Chapter 1).

Interestingly Kuhn's own method forbids the use of biographical data (called "anecdotic evidence") and the same applies to postmodernist theories of scientific and artistic creativity in general ("death of the author"). But as Carroll (1992/2008) noted, the idea of the death of the author is not a new methodology. It originated in literary criticism and aesthetics (the philosophy of art) where the methodological assumption of the "fallacy of intentions" (Wimsatt & Beardsley, 1954/1992) has been a governing doctrine (First principle) for a long time (cf. Beardsley, 1958; Gombrich, 1996; Dickie, 1997).

Studying archeology as prototype for a creativity science, might also help us to rethink the problem of creative explosions in human history (H-creativity). Paleolithic hunter-gatherer societies lived very close to nature (Cornwall, 1966). This could explain why technological creativity and the creativity of nature seem to be very similar, a recent discovery made both by scholars of engineering and evolutionary biologists (French, 1994; Dawkins, 1986/2006). It might also explain why technological artifacts happen to be the earliest form of creativity in the human record (Mithen, 1998; Gable & Poor, 2005). Art appears much later with the oldest art works being about 30,000 years old (Pfeiffer, 1982; Jensen, 2013). Science only appears very late, in ancient Greece 2,600–2,300 years ago. All these empirical patterns confirm that creativity is not contingent but constrained. The question is how these constraints work. For this purpose, the theoretical model presented in this book might be helpful. But the model can also help us to identify wrong ways to go about studying and explaining creativity. Falsification is the ultimate goal of all science and creativity science is no exception to this rule.

But science is also about clarification of concepts (Dimension V, Chapter 6, Hanson, 1956). Today we tend to take science-based forms of creativity ("modernity") for granted, but this is far from the case. Moreover, what is called "modernity" can be many things. Greek society for some reasons lacked science-based technology but was rich in science-based art (classical architecture, naturalistic painting and sculpture, and it also invented a new art form, drama). This raises the question why science-based technology (engineering science) was delayed for about 2,000 years. Without science-based engineering, there would have been no Industrial Revolution (science-based engineering functioned as a constraint of industrial development, an important creative explosion in modernity). How is this long delay to be explained? What delayed (constrained) it? And why was the pioneer of science-based technology/engineering science an Italian and why precisely Galileo? These are the types of questions creativity science is here to answer.

A new science originates when the time is ready for it and I believe the time has come for creativity science to be born. The psychology of creativity, which in contrast to postmodernism has not abandoned the scientific method, began in the late 1950s (Cropley, 2001) at about the same time as the birth of the computer (Isaacson, 2014/2015), cognitive science (Gardner, 1987), Crick and Watson's discovery of the structure of DNA (Ridley, 2006), but also the rise of primatology (van Lawick-Goodall, 1971) and sociobiology (Wilson, 1975/2000) as new and exciting disciplines. From a historical point of view, it seems as if the present time is a case of what Pfeiffer (1982) called a "creative explosion" (H-creativity).

Although psychological creativity research has done a lot to clarify the nature of creativity, the conditions of creativity, how to explain it (Sawyer, 2006 ) are still very much up for grabs. There might be many explanations why the psychology of creativity has not been up to the task. Psychology as a discipline is very good at studying cognitive phenomena or problem solving, the core of the content of creativity, but it lacks the competence necessary to analyze the sociological (historical and cultural) conditions of creativity. A constraint theory approach should be able to theorize the entanglements between context and content of complex and paradoxical problem solving. This is the ultimate reason (Mayr, 1998) why we need to move from the psychology of creativity to creativity science. The time is ripe for it. We live in an era of creative explosions, but we lack a theory which can explain both the present and the past (Strong & Davies 2006/ 2011a; 2006/2011b) from a creativity science/educational psychology point of view. Such an endeavor could not be more timely.

## Format of the Book

Regarding the format of the book and its expected audiences, most books on creativity are research monographs seeking to advance knowledge (Caves, 2000) of some special discipline other than creativity science and, if only for this reason, cannot function as a general introduction which, using the textbook format, seeks to outline the basic structure of the discipline, its knowledge object and guiding concepts, type of data it leans upon and methodology or First principles taking into account the overall aim of science, falsification. My two role models have been Lyell's *Principles of Geology* for the former purpose and Darwin's *On the Origin of Species* for the latter.

An introductory text needs to have a very clear and logical structure. This is best done if the structure can be described by a theoretical model which strikes a balance between simplicity and complexity. Novels are typically complex because casual chains (characters in action and interaction) are embedded in detailed narratives. Mathematical formulas are highly abstract and simple because so much information is crammed into a few symbols. Theoretical models (Wartofsky, 1968) lie somewhere in between. They combine detailed descriptions (stories) with simplifying concepts (formulas or schemes, see Gombrich, 1996). The way this works is exemplified in an abridged version of the theoretical model following immediately after this Preface and as an appendix to the introduction

Although aspects of the five dimensions that constitute the theoretical model I present can be found dispersed in the literature across a number of disciplines, they have never been gathered together in this economic and logical manner before, around the concept of constraints. The foregrounding of the constraint theory approach (Elster, 2000) is what makes this book different. But a theoretical model is basically here to serve as an intellectual tool. The idea is that the book should be of help to both students and researchers studying some selected historical case of creativity.

The book is meant to be read from beginning to end, but knowing how students often read books or how I myself have assigned chapters from books for reading, I have written the different chapters as self-contained, episodic "short stories" (compare the writing techniques of Selma Lagerlöf, who started her writing career after having trained and worked as a schoolteacher, see Edström, 2002). Moreover, the model can be used in many different ways. In principle a teacher, student or researcher can choose merely to focus on one dimension and ignore the other dimension or only focus on one aspect of a dimension and ignore the other aspects, although I would not recommend that. A better approach is probably to start with some aspect of one of the five dimensions, and work from there, by discovering other aspects either within the same dimension or another dimension. In this case, the richness of real cases and the complexity but also paradoxes of creativity as a conceptual phenomenon will be better balanced. The ideal approach is probably to start from the empirical end, select one biographical case, a pioneer in whatever personal, professional or historical problem situation and investigate that case in depth, using the theoretical model as an intellectual tool for interpretation of data.

My own interest in creativity originated in the mid-1980s, during a very stimulating year as an exchange professor at University of Wisconsin– Green Bay where I rediscovered art and literature. My first book on the topic was my Ph.D. thesis presented at Aalborg University in the mid-1990s. The book took on the problem of creativity in teaching and learning. My second book on creativity, published in 2006, explored the concept of "creativity regimes" which I had presented in an article for the Danish national journal of sociology (Kupferberg, 2003a). The idea for that book arose out of two projects, one on entrepreneurship studies and the other from a growing interest in film studies after a year as a guest researcher at Berkeley. My interest in the interesting similarities between N-creativity and T-creativity/C-creativity arose during the six years I functioned as editor of the *National Journal of Educational Research* in Sweden. My interest in artistic creativity has many sources but took off professionally during my 10 years in the department of Culture, Language and Media at Malmö University and then at the department of Artistic Crafts and design at Gothenburg University.

# The Theoretical Model

## Dimension I: Types of Constraints
1 Physical constraints
2 Prototypes or developmental constraints
3 Knowledge constraints
4 Rules of the game
5 Motivational constraints
   a pressure
   b pleasure
   c opportunity

## Dimension II: Levels of Creativity
1 Are children romantic geniuses?
2 Novices: participation as pleasure
3 Professionals: competitive pressure and transmutation of craft and judgment
4 Pioneers: opportunity as the regulative gene and the complexity of creative explosions
5 Is there such a thing as genius?

## Dimension III: Getting It Right
1 The principle of parsimony
2 Independent (re) discovery and convergent evolution
3 Co-evolution and the complexity of creativity
4 Problem situations and problem solvers

## Dimension IV: Protection of Vulnerable Ideas
1 Geographical isolation
2 Intellectual migration and teamwork
3 Skunk works
4 Confidants and working alone
5 Patrons, mentors and agents

## Dimension V: The Structure of Creative Processes
1 Material causes
2 Formal causes
3 Effective causes
4 Final causes

# Introduction

## Why Constraint Theory?

Creativity seems to belong to the broad type of phenomena which, like emotions, have causes or conditions but which can take different roads or have different outcomes. This is the basic reason why constraint theory might be a good place to start. Creativity is neither total order, nor total chaos (Simonton, 2007), but something in between, order in or through chaos. But to clarify how constraint theory can help us identify the First principles of creativity science, we need to collect the relevant data. According to Aristotle, a general First principle for all scientific work is for the researcher to get "intimate" with the relevant data (Anagnostopoulos, 2009). With "data" or whatever word Aristotle used, he meant not only raw data observed or collected by the researcher, but also data which had already been collected and interpreted by other researchers (the distinction we today call primary and secondary data was not that important for him). Having compared many intellectual biographies of pioneers (P-creativity as H-creativity) in science, art and technology (S-creativity, A-creativity, T-creativity) with a special focus on the discovery of First principles anddisciplines in the making, I became convinced of the soundness of Aristotle's approach. The core problem when it comes to data, is not whether they are primary or secondary but if the intimate knowledge gained by such data clarifies the nature of the knowledge object or not (compare Montuschi, 2003).

Let us say we want to understand how fiction works. The writer of a novel has to keep the reader coming back to the novel again and again, because of the many hours of intermitted reading (Elster, 2000) it takes to read such a work of art from the beginning to the end. This is an example of physical constraints (I.1), comparable to the geographical constraints Columbus faced when trying to reach China by sailing west. But where do novelists learn the techniques for writing novels if not from reading other novelists (prototypes, I.2)? In particular, first novels tend to have an easy identifiable role model. The way Jane Austen learned to write was to read and reread Richardson's novel *Pamela* which she knew by heart (see McKeon, 2010; Shields, 2002).

Physical constraints (I.1) also play a role when solving the problem of building musical instruments or how to reach an audience in a theatre. Physical constraints also constrain the aesthetic choices of architects. Building a house from straw or mud places different constraints on the architect than having bricks or carved stone at one's disposal. Greek architects mainly used carved stone for their monumental buildings. The fact that they had not yet discovered (knowledge constraint, I.3) the technology of making and using concrete (Kostof, 1985), might be the best explanation why they did not build arches and why Greek monumental buildings, only have columns and flat roofs (Hegel, 1970).

Greek, classical style (Le Corbusier, 1931/2017) also served as a prototype or development constraint (I.2) for other Greek architects. Building roofs in the shape of rounded arches the way the Romans did, was out of reach for the ancient Greeks because they did not know the building technique of using concrete to bind stones together (knowledge constraints, I.3). But this does not exclude the fact that Greek architects had intentions; they were designed by Greek architects, persons, and not merely by the Greek language as the "death of the author" theory would have us to believe. But there are other constraints as well such as rules (I.4).

Scientific theories basically aim at the falsification of previous theories, and this impersonal goal is the basic rule of science (I.4). But in order to gain social recognition for such an impersonal goal (struggle for priority, Merton, 1957), the scientific writer (Bazerman, 1988) must speak openly and take full personal responsibility for all the in principle impersonal claims made in the scientific work (scholarly article, academic book). The scientist cannot hide behind a fictive narrator or character (Booth, 1961/1983). Personal and impersonal elements are blended in both types of genres (Bahktin, 1986b), but in a complex and paradoxical manner.

Writers and artists in general basically investigate their own subjectively felt experiences (Cziksmenthalyi, 1996) but can easily hide the factual background by the impersonal techniques of fiction and/or art (compare Steffensen, 2017). Scientists or scholars play a game where one's own personal feelings are subordinated to the impersonal aim of falsification, but where the scholar is held personally responsible for the arguments or claims made by the author (as a rule one person when we are dealing with pioneering work). In neither case (science, art) is the author "dead" in the sense of irrelevant for analytical or interpretative purposes.

Only when we have come so far, do different types of motivations (I.5) become interesting. There are in principle three main type of motivations: pleasure (I.5a), pressure (I.5b) and opportunity (I.5c). The psychology of creativity has tended to vacillate between pleasure and pressure (intrinsic versus extrinsic motivations (cf. Amabile's, 1989,, 1996, 1997) dilemma, a problem solved by Czikszentmihaly's, 1988, 1994, 1999, dual theory of flow and social recognition as equally important motivations). Sociologists seem to ignore the role of pleasure and tend to start with problems of pressure (struggle for recognition, Honneth, 1992, accumulation of "symbolic capital," Bourdieu, 1974a, 1974b; "pressure to innovate." Lipset, 1979). Lately sociologists have also come to foreground the role of opportunity (Fuchs, 1994). Pressure and opportunity are often confused (cf. Bloor, 1976 and Latour & Wolgar, 1986) but should be regarded as analytically separate.

Opportunity is a critical motivational constraint (I.5c) which might explain one of the unsolved problems of creativity science, how pioneering work (H-creativity) in distinct intellectual fields such as science, art and technology (S-creativity, A-creativity, T-creativity) becomes possible (four of the best cases in science discussed at some length in this book are Jane Goodall, Jens-Jürgen Thomsen, Charles Darwin and Francis Crick and James Watson). This is the core problem of Dimension II (levels of creativity). There is much confusion in the literature on this issue. Educational psychology is mainly interested in the creativity of novices (II.2). Sociology as profession is committed to study the creativity of professionals (II.3) and only philosophers, historians of science, economic historians and archeologists have tended to be interested in studying the highest form of creativity, H-creativity or pioneering work (II.4).

The tendency of disciplines to specialize in relatively narrow areas, has provided us with a number of facts or data about creativity, but it has also blocked the evolution of a common theoretical framework and appropriate methodology to study this phenomenon (Gardner, 1988). But the phenomenon of specialization can be found not only in science (S-creativity), but also in art (see Dutch painting, Wright, 1978/1984, A-creativity) and technology (Marshall, 1890/1916,T-creativity). Interestingly functional specialization can also be found in nature (N-creativity). A case in point is Wilson's (1991/2001) description of the survival and reproduction strategies of cichlids in Lake Victoria. Specialization has the effect, as already noted by Durkheim (1893/1964), to reduce intra-species competition, but in science it also leads to problems of interdisciplinary communication (Bauer, 1990).

Most educational psychologists do not believe that studies of pioneers (II.4, H-creativity) are of any relevance for motivating children or novices. Novices are believed to be "geniuses" in their own right (II.1). But if children are geniuses, why does the natural curiosity of children tend to die as soon as they enter the school system (Dewey, 1917/1997)? Academic teachers, who in principle are professionals (II.3) teaching novices (II.2) at an advanced stage, where the task is to raise the problem-solving capacity (creativity) to the level of the professional (II.3, compare Schön, 1983; Flyvbjerg, 2001), tend to resent the idea of pioneers (IV.3) as well. In the history of art, pioneers are routinely categorized as "geniuses" (II.5). The latter concept has often recently been used for children who are believed to be "romantic geniuses" (II.1), but politically incorrect when applied to the highest level (H-creativity,II.4). Compare Bordwell & Carroll, 1996).

The best way to work around these difficulties might be to drop the emotionally or morally (Merton, 1976) ambiguous concept of "genius" (II.5) altogether and merely foreground four levels of problem-solving capacity: children (II.1), novices (II.2), professionals (II.3) and pioneers (II.4). There are several advantages with such a categorization. First of all, it foregrounds the role of problem-solving capacity as the core of the level of creativity and not mere motivation. Second it recognizes the obvious role of biological factors (II.1) but also foregrounds the importance of sociocognitive roles. One can become a novice anytime in one's life, as soon as one enters a new, subjectively unknown field. Moreover, it fits the empirical data of groundbreaking creativity (pioneering work) much better. Becoming a pioneer in practice means going through a biographical life transformation (Kupferberg, 1995b, 1998a, 2006a, 2010). But such transformations in practice begin when becoming a novice (II.2) and gradually moving to the level of professional (II.3) before moving to the role of pioneer (II.4). Cases in point analyzed in some detail in this book are Picasso, Matisse and Chagall in painting; Orwell, Hemingway and Plath in writing; Chaplin, Hitchcock and Bergman in filmmaking.

Let us assume that (1) creativity is essentially constrained forms of problem solving (Dimension I) and (2) that the ability to solve problems is distributed differently among individuals due to different degrees of problem-solving capacity or levels of creativity (Dimension II). This raises the problem of how and if problem solvers manage to arrive at the best possible or "correct" answers (Elster, 1983). Although educational theorists (including myself, see Kupferberg, 2009a) have been reluctant to talk about "correct" answers, it is difficult to imagine a science of creativity unless such a science provides us with correct or at least better answers than previous attempts (creativity as an end product of a process). Such a goal, the "advance of knowledge" (Kitcher, 1993) or the accumulation of a "body of knowledge" (Lloyd, 1991) is, in practice, a core goal of all scientific problem solving, including creativity science.

But what does this mean? Dimension III ("Getting it right") is an attempt to at least arrive at a preliminary answer to such an enormously difficult and highly contested problem. I have divided the overall category of "getting it right" into four subcategories: (1) parsimony, (2) convergent evolution or independent (re) discovery, (3) co-evolution or interdependent discovery and (4) problem solvers facing problem situations. I first stumbled upon the idea of "parsimony" when reading the chapter in Darwin's *The Origin of Species*, which deals with how bee colonies economize the amount of work necessary to build honeycombs. I later found that the concept of "elegance" often used in aesthetic appreciation (Zangwill, 2001) pretty much describes the same phenomenon (compare Pevsner, 1936/1991). I borrowed (prototype, I.2) the overall concept "getting it right" from John Elster (1983, 2000).

Arriving at a parsimonious solution is the core of getting it right (III.1) But how do we know that there is such a thing as getting it right in the first place? Here Dawkins' (2005) concept of "convergent evolution" has been of great help (III.2). The idea of interdependency or "co-evolution" (III.3) arrived from combining Abbott's (2004) theory of intellectual borrowing as a good heuristics of creativity in science, with Dawkins' (2010) fascinating examples of how this works in nature (including an "arms race" between species which I have used to analyze the relation between twentieth-century painting and Hollywood cinema).

Although getting it right is relatively easy to clarify in science (proven priority) and technology (parsimonious solutions), it becomes more tricky when it comes to art where originality can best be seen as inventing novel techniques of originality (Schiff, 1984). For this purpose I found Baxandall's (1985) distinction between historical, professional and personal problem situations a good intellectual tool (for a summary of the model for the purpose of educational psychology, see Kupferberg, 2018a).

Dimension IV, "Protection of vulnerable ideas" is basically a result of two types of empirical research interests I have pursued since the mid-1990s, the role of migration for scientific creativity (Kupferberg, 1998a, 2003b, 2010) and the creativity of immigrant entrepreneurship (Kupferberg 2002b, 2003c, 2004a), research supported by the Danish

Social Science Research Council and the European Commission. In both cases I found that novel ideas tend to be vulnerable at the start and must be protected in order to avoid premature death. Here geographical isolation (IV.1) often plays a critical role (Rudwick, 1996). The latter resembles the Galapagos effect, a core aspect of Darwin's complex (five-factor) theory of evolution (Mayr, 2004/2007).

But intellectual migration between disciplines (IV.2) can also function as a protection of vulnerable ideas as can "skunk works" (IV.3) a concept often used in entrepreneurship studies (Peters & Austin, 1985; Ketteringham & Nayak, 1986) as can the use of confidants (IV.4) among scholars (Gay, 1988; Browne, 1995, 2002). As I began to study artists (Kupferberg, 2012a) I found interesting similarities but also differences between these groups. A surprising discovery was that rules of the game (I.4) also seem to constrain the struggle for social recognition. The latter is dependent not only upon the creative mind (Gardner, 1993) but also upon patrons, mentors and agents (IV.5). Differentiating between these main types of "helpers" (Bruner, 1990) or "support systems" (Sawin, 1995/ 1997), can help clarify the detailed "mechanisms" (Elster, 2007) for how social recognition works in practice (intimate knowledge), a problem which has been poorly understood both in the psychology of creativity and the sociology of knowledge.

Having come so far, I to my great surprise, found that most of the four dimensions of the emerging field, creativity science, could be simplified even further by a fifth dimension which I call the "structure of creative processes." The latter is identical with the theory of the "four causes" originally laid out by Aristotle (Hankinson 1995, 2009; Lloyd, 1968), suggesting that the core of creativity science has existed for 2,300 years but that it has taken us so long to rediscover it (III.2).

Let us assume that creativity seeks to solve complex and paradoxical problems (Koestler, 1964; Bohm, 1998; de Bono, 1994, 2009; Boden, 1990; Weisberg, 1993, 2006; Popper, 1994b, 1999). For an educational psychologist as myself, what makes creativity interesting is that there is always a personal element (P-creativity) involved in this type of learning (H-creativity). But such creativity cannot be merely subjective. Objective aspects are also necessary, but how are the two aspects to be combined? This is the core problem that a constraint theory of creativity seeks to answer. It is important though not to forget the personal aspect along the road or we have missed the basic tensions, both cognitive and emotional, which makes creativity so interesting to study from the point of view of educational psychology. The two combined, P-creativity and H-creativity, is what creativity science is here to investigate and what this book is mainly about.

We can describe a learner as a "problem solver" who has become placed in a "problem situation" (III.4) attempting to "get it right." (III.1). But what does that mean in practice? For this purpose it is important not to forget that all humans or problem solvers do as nature does (Popper, 1999) we start with a problem situation. This method is different from Weber's method of Verstehen for the simple reason that Weber confuses "rationality" with "rationalization." Take the example mentioned in Sartre (1965). The French teaching system is highly meritocratic. In order to get the best teaching, up and coming teachers aspiring to the best jobs, compete among the best. One of Sartre's classmates later complained about the outcome of such a competition. How could he, a Frenchmen, have lost a competition for a post in French language to an immigrant? The problem situation is very clear: the best wins (rationality) and the loser's explanation of what happened is clearly a rationalization.

But to understand what make problem solvers rationalize, we need to start with the "problem situation" (Hacomen, 2000). The reason Sartre's schoolmate lost might have been that the immigrant was better motivated and had prepared better for the competition. The schoolmate was just too lazy. But there might be many reasons why some problem solvers are successful, and others are not. This has important methodological consequences if we want to say develop a science of creativity. Thus we need to ask why Aristotle, who was a highly successful pioneering scholar in many areas, got the First principles of astronomy completely wrong (Earth-centered universe, planets moving in perfect circles, gravity as a local force). And why did he believe that eels do not reproduce in the normal way, but come about by "spontaneous generation"? Why did he claim that the natural elements such as water, air, earth and fire were all "indivisibles."

The best way to approach such issues is to ask what in a problem situation constrained the problem. Take the case of Christopher Columbus (Bergreen, 2011/2015). In order to understand why he reacted the way he did (rationalized) when he discovered the previously unknown continent America, we need to look at him as an experienced sailor from Genoa (professional, II.3) who over the years had become strongly committed (Becker, 1951, 1960; Elster, 1979, 1983; Kupferberg, 1999b, 2000, 2002a, 2002b) to the idea or project to find the shortest way to China by sailing west. This bold idea could have cost him and his crew their lives, had he not stumbled upon a new and unknown continent after a month of crossing the Atlantic (physical constraint, I.1). Having grossly miscalculated the actual size of the Earth (knowledge constraint, I.3), Columbus believed he had indeed reached mainland China. He visited many islands and on reaching Cuba he tried to convince himself that it was part of that mainland. Grudgingly he had to give up that hope, after a mass of indisputable evidence (data, material cause, V.1) all pointed at the conclusion that Cuba was an island and not part of the mainland. Unwilling to give up his life dream, Columbus ordered everyone, from the highest officer to the lowest ship boy, not to tell the truth once they returned to Spain (rationalization).

Personal reality and objective reality (problem situation) might for several reasons fall apart. This is one of the reasons why solving problems can be very tricky and our reactions paradoxical. Why did Columbus not just admit that he had grossly miscalculated the distance been Spain and China from the start? One could just all well ask why the Germans kept on fighting foolishly or bravely, even after Adolf Hitler, their Führer, had given up and committed suicide rather than face the consequences of his political decisions as dictatorial leader for 12 years. Human intentions are very difficult to disentangle, but in order to understand what these intentions are, we at least need to acknowledge the importance of personal commitments (biographical projects, Kupferberg, 1995b) for how problem solvers tackle problem situations (III.4). The theory of the "death of the author" expects us to believe that such commitments do not matter, given that we are all mere "instances" of our national languages (Barthes, 1968/ 1977). But Thomas Mann also wrote in German and his book *Dr. Faustus* is certainly a very different book from *Mein Kampf.*

Columbus made no less than four journeys to the New World, but he never gave up his dream of one day presenting himself to the emperor of China. A study of his biography reveals the interesting biographical fact that Columbus already as a child (II.1) in the sea town of Genoa (physical constraint I.1), had modeled himself upon the hero of his youth, the pioneering traveler (II.4) Marco Polo. But Columbus also wanted to outdo his hero, traveling west rather than East. What stopped Columbus from reaching his goal was geography, a typical physical constraint (I.1). What kept him going was his role model or prototype (I.2), Marco Polo. But physical constraints and prototypes development constraints, do not always fall apart; they can also fit into each other. When Darwin sailed in the same direction more than 300 years later, knowledge of the physical constraints (I.1) of world geography (knowledge constraint, I.3), had advanced enough for him to know where he was going. Darwin also had a prototype (I.2) to lean on, Charles Lyell's three-volume work *Principles of Geology*, which for all practical purpose became his prototype (I.2)

Reading the book, helped Darwin (effective cause, V.3) to solve the scientific problem of the origins of species (S-creativity). The latter had remained unsolved since Aristotle tried but failed to solve it more than 2,000 years earlier (Jones, 2001). Darwin's problem-solving capacity as a pioneer (II.4) therefore depended not only upon the fact that he got the data (material cause, V.1) right, but that he had a theoretical model to compare with observed data collected during his five years of travel, the theory of "special creation" (role model or prototype, I.2). In his autobiography Darwin calls his book *The Origin of Species*, one "long argument," against the theory of "special creation."

In science most is impersonal, both the act of leaning on theories which one can learn something from (prototypes, I.2) and which one might end up falsifying (V.4). Barthes seems to have confused this type of impersonality with the problem of motivations (I.V) which certainly are personal. Writing novels are also personal in the sense that writers are strongly committed to the role of the writer (used in a different sense in Barthes, 1960/2000) but also problem-solving strategies. In contrast to scholars, writers (effective cause, V.3) do not approach problems from a methodological point of view (V.3). They learn the relevant techniques (Morell, 2004). The basic rule (I.4) of all art is to evoke emotions (final cause, V.4). Literary techniques are here to help writers accomplish this goal. This explains why writers of fiction use the technique of hiding behind a "narrator" (Booth, 1961/1983). One of the advantages of this technique is that it allows the writer fully to absorb his or her writing self into the world of the depicted characters (what sociologists call "role-taking").

Take the first-person character and narrator of *Lolita,* Humbert Humbert who is certainly not identical with the author Vladimir Nabokov. But from this it does not follow that author of the novel is "dead." Fiction like all art is often a masked way to describe a personal experience (Strauss, 1959; Bergman, 1959). Writing a novel can be described from a mere choice of prototype (I.2). It becomes merely a "formal cause" (V.2). Compare the theory of "art for art." Nabokov himself seems to have been strongly committed to this formalist theory of art (for a critique, see Carroll, 2005, 2010), but this as all creative choices had its reasons. Art is about emotions (Hjort & Laver, 1997) and it is here we should start. But whose emotions are we talking about? But Nabokov is cheating. There are so many professional resemblances between the narrator and the author (bookish professor of literature, knowledge of inner life of American motels, experience of driving cars on the vast road system of this continental-size nation) that we might be fooled to believe that writer and narrator are one and the same (Roper, 2015). In reality the character with whom Nabokov must have identified himself most strongly was the victim (Lolita) and not the predator (Humbert Humbert).

The biographical facts are the following: as a young boy in tsarist Russia, Nabokov had been seduced by a much older and dear uncle (Boyd, 1990, 1991). Having tried to write himself out of this dreadful memory, Nabokov finally found the form which best described the motives but also the rationalization of his uncle legitimizing how the uncle could allow himself to commit such a gruesome act of betrayal (mirror) without the readers of the novel ever suspecting its real, biographical source (masking). Nabokov wrote the novel while living in North America long after tsarist Russia had ceased to exist (change of historical problem situation, III.4). Nor was he a young boy but a professional teacher of Russian literature (change of professional problem situation, III.4). But all of these were devices, techniques (V.3), which allowed Nabokov, the victim, to better understand the rationalizations of the perpetrator by putting himself in the shoes of his dear uncle, disguised as a whimsical professor of literature suspiciously similar to the author's professional persona.

Misleading the reader was made easier by the framing of the novel as a confession made in front of a court. But fiction never seeks to tells the "truth" (Lamarque & Olsen, 1994). A novel is never an exact copy of biographical reality. Fiction writing is here to evoke or express emotions (the two are not necessarily identical, see Levinson, 2006, 2016; Carroll, 2010), by transforming facts into fiction (V.4). Creativity is paradoxical. But it is also complex. This is the reason we need to be very careful when we compare pioneering work in science, art and technology.

The book is structured in three parts. Part I, *In Search of Creativity Science*, consists of the introductory Chapter 1, "Disciplines in the making: What is science, what is creativity and how are the two related?" Part II, *Elaborating the Theoretical Model* consists of five chapters, each of which tries to deepen our understanding of how creativity is constrained. It can partly be seen as a critical test of the model presented above, partly as a way to clarify the guiding concepts (compare Torrance's well known theory of creativity as "elaborations"), partly as inspiration for readers to find their own examples or whatever type of problem within creativity science that interests them (the role of the reader). Here my work with art teachers at Malmö University and Gothenburg University during the years 2006–

2016 has been of great help. Part III, *First Principles of Creativity Science,* sums up the findings of the book. It is divided into Chapter 7, "Concepts and Knowledge Object" and Chapter 8, "Data, Methods and Constraints."

Chapter 7 argues that a combination of Darwin and Aristotle helps us clarify what it is creativity science is here to study (knowledge object) and what the guiding concepts should be. Chapter 8 combines Jarred Diamond's ideas of how to study complexity and paradoxes ("Anna Karenina principle," "natural experiments," "contrasting comparison") (Diamond, 1999, 2005/2011; Diamond & Robertson, 2010) with Elster's idea to foreground creative practices (Elster, 1983), given that self-presentations of creative minds are often unreliable for different reasons (Perkins, 1981 and Hackmen, 2000). This method is very similar to the one used by Weisberg (1993) and Gardner (1993). Both try to preserve the complexity of creativity but seem to avoid its paradoxes. Why did Aristotle, who was after all the founder of both creativity science and the theory of First principles as the core problem of S-creativity, fail to clarify the First principles of physics? Why did the solution to the problem have to wait until around 1600, and why was it solved by a person like Galileo?

Although Galileo's own method was a controlled experiment, from the point of view of creativity science, it can best be seen as a natural experiment, to be compared and contrasted with other natural experiments such as Picasso's process when painting *Les Demoiselles d'Avignon* around 1906/1907 and *Guernica* painted about thirty years later. Comparing the two types of pioneers helps us clarify how P-creativity is transformed into H-creativity across different types of intellectual traditions and fields (creativity regimes) but also why the type of constraints that make pioneering work in science art and technology possible is nevertheless constrained differently.

## Two Examples of Application (Galileo and Picasso)

The theoretical model I seek to elaborate in this book foregrounds different dimensions and aspects of the conditions that cause but do not determine (constrain) creative processes. One can in principle start with any of the five dimensions and include the other four as the analysis proceeds. Take the case of Galileo. Why did this effective cause (V.3) become the pioneer (II.4) both of the science of physics (S-creativity, Renn, 2001) and the core of engineering science and materials science (T-creativity, Petrosky, 1996)? A possible answer could be Galileo's dual training in mathematics and instrument building (overcoming knowledge constraints, I.3, combining rules of the game, I.4, intellectual migration, IV.2). Galileo's problem-solving capacity and motivation was partly derived from his professional knowledge (II.3). He was employed as a professor of mathematics at Padua university – but also from his novice knowledge as an instrument builder (II.2), originating from having observed his father at close hand (Galileo's father was a professional builder of musical instruments, see Naess, 2007). Apart from providing an opportunity (I.5c) for pioneering work (II.4), there also seems to have been another motivation for Galileo to engage in building instruments as a part-time business. Italian professors were poorly paid, forcing Galileo to supplement his income in order to support a family. This indicates that pressure as a motive (I.5b) was also present. But so was pleasure (I.5a) or Galileo would not have continued to do groundbreaking work in physics, astronomy and engineering (Renn, 2001; Ferguson, 2003; Petrosky, 1996).

A closer look at the motivational aspect of Galileo's pioneering work turns out to include all the three aspects (as in Darwin's case). But in order to understand the role of constraints here, we need to move beyond motivational factors and investigate the sociocognitive factors which constrained Galileo's problem-solving capacity as a pioneer (II.4) or effective cause (V.3), no "death of the author" here. Why did Galileo insist upon working in cosmology and in particular test Copernicus' model of the Earth as center of the planetary system? This was a very dangerous activity at the time and Galileo risked being accused of being a heretic which was punishable by death (Bruno was burned at the stake for this crime). In order to explain why Galileo took this risk (which almost cost him his neck, see Boorstin, 1985), personal motivational factors (pleasure) only take us so far.

Galileo (effective cause, V.1) must have felt constrained by the very rules of science (I.4) which is to falsify theories by providing logically coherent explanations which manage to separate data from fiction (V.4). Galileo's case can be contrasted with another pioneer (II.4), but in art (A-creativity). Galileo and Picasso were both problem solvers, but scientific and artistic problem solvers face different problem situations (III.4). Starting with the problem situation can be a good way to disentangle pioneering work whether in science, art or technology. Problem situations can in turn be divided into three main aspects: historical, professional and personal (Baxandall, 1985; Kupferberg, 2018a). Take Picasso's two most famous paintings *Guernica* and *Les Demoiselles d'Avignon,* mentioned above. As a problem solver, Picasso was placed in a problem situation (III.4). The two types of problem situations were not identical though. Before we look closer into these problem situations, we can start by categorizing the level of creativity in each case.

Picasso certainly needed time to solve the problems that he encountered when he painted *Guernica,* but these problems were relatively routine. They were of a professional type (II.3) and could be solved within five weeks. In contrast, it took Picasso a year to paint *Les Demoiselles d'Avignon,* reflecting that fact that the problems he was working with here were much more tricky. No one had done something similar before, and it was a pioneering work in progress. Given the relatively traditional form of *Guernica,* there was no need to hide the artwork in his studio for decades (skunk works, IV.3). On the contrary, it was eagerly expected and (mostly) praised for its aesthetic qualities (in clear contradiction to the former painting, see Penrose, 1958/1968).

From the point of view of level of creativity (Dimension II), Picasso was revolutionizing twentieth-century art when he painted *Les Demoiselles d'Avignon.* His role at the time was the pioneer (II.4) who struggled for social recognition of his pioneering work, making him strongly dependent upon helpers for the purpose of protecting vulnerable ideas (IV.5). Thirty years later his personally invented, easily recognizable style (O'Brian, 1976/2003) was seen as much less provocative, closer to the professional (II. 3) type of routinized problem solving (Carter, 2004). From the point of view of the structure of creative process (Dimension V), the "final causes" (V.4) of the two paintings were also different. *Les Demoiselles d'Avignon* was clearly aimed at an avant-garde audience, whereas *Guernica* was meant to be appreciated by ordinary workers. Although clearly an artwork, transformation of facts to fiction for the purpose of evoking emotions (final cause, V.4. rules of the game, I.4), *Guernica* was also meant to be a political statement. It was certainly not seen as merely "art for the sake of art" ("formal cause," V.2, see Barr, 1946).

Arnheim's (1962) study describes in detail how Picasso managed to "get it right" in the sense of finding an elegant and economic solution when painting *Guernica* (III.1). Given that the making of *Les Demoiselles d'Avignon* took much longer, and the novelty of the picture was far greater, identifying precisely how and when Picasso got it right might be more difficult, but not impossible. One clue might be the historical and professional problem situation that Picasso was facing as he started composing and painting *Les Demoiselles d'Avignon* (III.4). It so happens that the number of cinemas exploded in Paris in 1906, the year Picasso began the painting (Roe, 2015). The presence of a new and strongly competing art form (Danto, 1997) probably helped Picasso to "get it right" (III.1) in terms of the historical and professional problem situation in which the traditional art form painting stood at the time (III.4).

Picasso's individual contribution (Csikszentmihalyi, 1988; Gardner, 1993), helped inaugurate the avant-garde movements of the twentieth century (Stangos, 1974/1994) beginning with Matisse and the Fauvists (Barr, 1953/1976) but with roots back to Cézanne (Shiff, 1984). The closest competitor at the time, namely cinema (historical and professional problem situation, III.4) threatened to transform the profession of painting which Picasso had been trained in into a kind of prey to be hunted down and eaten by a superior predator (the Hollywood film studios). The painting can hence also be seen as a case of co-evolution of the arms-race type (III.3).

But there were also personal constraints related to Picasso's place in the Parisian avant garde (Roe, 2015). The presence of other avant-garde painters such as Matisse put Picasso under pressure (I.5b) to prove himself, plus the fact that he was a foreigner and spoke with a very thick Catalan accent according to Cowling (2002). But being in Paris also changed Picasso's professional problem situation (III.4), it provided him with the opportunity (I.5c) to walk around and see the rich art life (for a similar effect, see Chagall's first visit to Paris, discussed in III.4 and IV.5). A closer study of the making of *Les Demoiselles d'Avignon* (Richardson, 1996/1997) reveals that it was probably modeled upon two prototypes (development constraints, I.2), Ingres' *The Turkish Bath* and Matisse's *Le Grand Baigneuses*. In contrast the prototypes used in *Guernica* clearly originate from the Spanish cultural tradition (bulls, horses) but also from reusing personal motifs appearing in previous paintings by Picasso such as doves and the girl with the lamp (Cowling, 2002; Weisberg, 2006). But physical constraints (I.1) also play a critical role. *Guernica* is painted in gray. *Les Demoiselles d'Avignon* is dominated by pink and other garish colors which certainly provide them with very different emotional effects (V.4).

In order to clarify how Picasso got it right when painting the two pictures, we also need to take another type of constraint, rules of the game into account (I.4) which happen to be identical with the final cause of art (V.4). As noted by Elster, "emotion. . . is an important element in all art. Emotion is elicited in readers, listeners and viewers by formal as well as substantive aspects of works of art" (Elster, 1999, p. 197). Exactly what type of personal emotions (problem situation, III.4) Picasso sought to express in *Les Demoiselles d'Avignon* is still very much under debate (Green, 2001) but using forms (formal cause V.2) that were very different from the ideals of beauty (Zangwill, 2001) dominating the classical and naturalistic French tradition (Barr, 1953/1976; Greenberg, 1961/1965) was one of the things that made *Les Demoiselles d'Avignon* a provocative, shocking work of art even for the French avant garde at the time (Olivier, 1935/1982).

What is striking when we compare Picasso's and Galileo's cases is the predominant role of opportunity (I.5c), and not merely pleasure and pressure (I.5a, I.5b) but also the need to protect vulnerable versions, where factors like geographical isolation (IV.1), intellectual migration (IV.2), skunk works (IV.3), confidants (IV.4) and helpers or support systems (IV.5) play an important role. A closer look at Galileo reveals that he too had helpers. In the beginning of Galileo's career Venice (Padua University was under the administration of Venice) was a helper. Later, with Galileo's rising reputation in Europe, the pope and his advisors in Rome became Galileo's main patrons, mentors and agents.

From a helper (Bruner, 1990) or support system (Sawin, 1995/1997) point of view (IV.5) there is a striking similarity between Galileo's case and Darwin's case. *On the Origins of Species* critiques the geological theory of "special creation" written by Charles Lyell, the founder of geology (Darwin carefully read the three volumes of *Principles of Geology* during his five years voyaging with the *Beagle*). The awkwardness of critiquing his own mentor in public might have been an emotional and not merely a cognitive factor which might explain why Darwin procrastinated in publishing his book, despite encouragement from Lyell to do so. Only the threat of losing his scientific primacy (Merton, 1957) to an unknown rival, Wallace, finally made Darwin change his mind (Browne, 2002). In spite of these complications the fact is that Darwin worked in secrecy (skunk works, IV.3) during his voyage on the *Beagle* but also during the long period (more than 20 years) when Lyell was one of his confidants (IV.4).

Like Darwin, Galileo was also well aware of the fact that his new patron, mentor and agent, after he moved to Rome, was not particularly happy about Copernicus' theoretical model. Although the model preserved the fiction that celestial phenomena such as planets move in perfect circles (which explains why Copernicus' alternative model to Ptolemy's was hopelessly complicated and impossible to understand for laymen), Copernicus did get something right (III.1): the fact that the center of the planetary system happens to be the Sun and not the Earth.

This theory went against the teachings of the church, which meant Galileo had to tread carefully. The way Galileo tried to solve this dilemma was to present a scientific argument as if it was a theatrical play (confusing rules of the game, I.4), a drama with a protagonist and antagonist (Bruner, 1990), engaged in a dialogue between representatives of two opposing theories. As we know this artistic form did not fool his enemies, Galileo was forced to admit in public that he had been mistaken. But he was only put under house arrest and could continue his scientific studies, as long as he stayed away from actively promoting Copernicus' theory. This suggests that the risks he took were relatively small and that his main helper, the pope, continued to protect him (IV.5).

Nevertheless, the teaching of the pope was not science. It was religion which follows the rules (I.4) or rhetoric. Then as now, learning rhetorical tricks was at the core of most of the humanistic professions (such as the law, the church and politics). In contemporary Western societies, best described as "late modernity" (Giddens, 1990, 1991), these traditional humanistic professions still function, in spite of the role of science. Moreover, new professions which use rhetoric as professional tool have evolved in marketing, media but also the arts. But rhetoric is neither science nor art. The point about rhetorical devices from a scientific point of view is that they appeal to emotions (as do art) but also to the lack of patience and intimate knowledge to be able to follow a complex argument expected from scientific audiences (Rapp, 2009). Rhetoric is not science. It is not concerned with facts and intentionally confuses fact and fiction, in order to function as oratory and not falsification, the aim of science.

In this book I have largely avoided discussing rhetoric, a special type of productive knowledge (Anagnostopoulos, 2009), unless it has a direct influence upon theories of science, art and technology. Most of my efforts have been devoted to clarifying the complexities and paradoxes of creativity. Why did Aristotle make the mistake of projecting biological laws upon physical laws? Why did Kuhn make the opposite mistake of treating scientific revolutions as if they were governed by physical (cyclical) laws? Why did Popper confuse the problem-solving strategy of science (methodology) with the problem-solving strategy of nature and technology (trial and error)?

## The Role of the Reader

Although there is no such thing as the "death of the author," this does not exclude that there is such a thing as the role of the reader. The best description of this phenomenon can be found in Umberto Eco's works on semiotics (1979) and literature (1984, 2002). What Eco basically suggests is that each reader (as each student in a classroom) brings with her biographically unique experiences and personal knowledge interests to the text (compare Pierce's 1991 concept "the interpretant" and Eco, 1979). What Pierce and Eco suggest is that no text will be read in exactly the same way by individual readers (for a similar theory in educational psychology, see Marton et al. 1984/1986; Marton & Booth, 1997). Nevertheless there is not an endless amount of correct readings which are constrained by the "fictive facts" found in the work of fiction (Eco, 2002).

The pedagogical idea of writing an introductory textbook on creativity science is that the model in combination with the many cases or examples illustrating it should help readers ask themselves in what way a constraint theory approach of the type mentioned in the book might be of help for the type of problem the reader happens to be interested in, given the level of problem-solving capacity (Dimension II) and type of intellectual field (I.4, Dimension V). One of the scientific pioneers which helped me clarify the dual problem of what makes pioneering work possible more generally and how First principles of sciences are discovered in practice, was the founder of archeology, Jens-Jürgen Thomsen. Why Thomsen (Trigger, 1989; Jensen, 1992)? How do we explain that a Dane became the founder of archeology ("effective cause," V.1, pioneering problem-solving capacity, II.4)?

Part of the explanation seems to have been easy access to the primary data (material cause, V.1). Denmark for geological reasons (physical constraints, I.1) had a very rich collection of archeological artifacts (Lyell, 1863/1970). We can also call this the "historical" problem situation (III.4) facing this problem solver. There was also a professional aspect (II.3). Preliterate societies had been studied by "archivarian scientists" who had been trained in analyzing texts. But texts did not exist in preliterate societies, hence such professional knowledge was of little use. Thomsen was an amateur coin collector (novice, II.2) and as such used to comparative stylistic analysis of things (artifacts), precisely what was missing (personal knowledge). There was also another personal factor, the "opportunity" (I.5c) given to him by the Danish king to build what would become a National Museum situated at the royal palace in Copenhagen (Jensen, 1992). These factors combined explain why precisely Thomsen managed to get it right (III.1), but they do not prove that he was a genius. This is the reason why I regard the genius category (II.5) as redundant for creativity science. The category of pioneer (II.4) will do the job.

The skills and attitudes (Fleming, 1969) of this problem solver ("effective cause" V.3) in combination with access to a unique database ("material cause" V.1) help us explain why Thomsen managed to find the core concepts ("formal cause" V.2) necessary to falsify the strongly text-oriented intellectual tradition of "archivarian science" ("final cause," V.4). This new science was called "archeology" after the identification of its primary data ("material cause," V.1) and the identification of the correct data coincided with or rather constituted (Searle, 1969, 1996) the distinctive step that led to this new science. Foregrounding artifacts meant rejecting texts as primary data ("material cause," V.1) and hermeneutics with stylistic analysis ("formal cause," V.2) for the purpose of falsifying theories of relevance for the knowledge object of archeology ("final cause," V.4). It was because Thomsen ("effective cause," V.3) could fill this sociocognitive function ("getting it right," III.1) that he became the pioneer of archeology (II.4).

But this means that Thomsen in practice solved the "demarcation problem" (what makes a science a science), although twentieth-century philosophy of sciences has ended giving up on this theoretical problem, declaring it to be impossible to solve (Laudan, 1996). But perhaps the inability of twentieth-century philosophy of science to solve the "demarcation problem" might be found in the discipline (philosophy of science) itself and in particular the "Copernican revolution" of Kant (Beardsley, 1966/1967). Kant's "analytical philosophy" has strong roots in the intellectual tradition, which goes all the way back to Plato (Russell, 1957). Although Aristotle was Plato's student and learned much from him (Lloyd, 1968; Collins, 1998), the two types of philosophies are very different. This was also recognized by Darwin who probably would not have discovered evolutionary theory without a thorough training in empirical Aristotelian philosophy of science, probably mediated by his teacher (role model or development constraint, I.2 and mentor, IV.5) at Cambridge, the combined empirical historian and philosopher of science, William Whewell (Sloan, 2009; Laudan, 1981a; Whewell, 1984, 1989).

# PART I

# *In Search of Creativity Science*

# CHAPTER I

# What is Science? What is Creativity and How Are the Two Entangled?

## Science, Art and Technology

In order to clarify the First principles of creativity science, we must first know what science is and why science is different from both art and technology. Most attempts to explain creativity get stranded, because they are unable to solve this fundamental issue. Take cognitive science. This relatively new discipline (Gardner, 1987) assumes that scientific (theoretical) thinking is built into the human brain. But this cannot be right. The ability to learn language quickly (Pinker, 1995) is indeed built into the human brain (Pinker, 1997/1999) but not theoretical, conceptual thinking. If it were, how do we explain (1) that scientific thinking appears so late in the human record (compare Hegel's apt metaphor "Owl of Minerva") or (2) that children have great difficulty understanding mathematical thinking and concepts in general? Even small children understand what emotions are and how such emotions can best be expressed symbolically (compare the joy of a young boy who has just discovered that a broom can be used to imitate riding a horse, see Vygotsky, 1995), but it takes many years of hard work to understand how scientists think (Vygotsky, 1999).

The favorite example often used to prove that scientific thinking is hardwired (Donald, 2001) into the human brain is the hunting practices of African tribes (Boyd & Silk, 2003). But the fact that African hunters sit down and formulate hypotheses of how far ahead or close the male hunters are to the hunted animal is not yet science as Carruthers (2002) claims. Hunting techniques are cases of practical thinking, like technology in general (R. Laudan, 1984). It should not be confused with theoretical thinking, knowledge for its own sake (Kline, 1953/1987; Rihll, 1999), which is very different.

Science, in the sense of theoretical thinking, appears very late in human history: 2,300–2,600 years ago in ancient Greece. In contrast, the creative explosions in technology coincide with the birth of modern *Homo sapiens*

100,000–200,000 years ago (Oppenheimer, 2003). This creative explosion might have been the result of another creative explosion, the birth of moral thinking, which historically has tended to take the form of religion and is centered upon burial practices (Jensen, 2013). Respect for the dead is the core of moral thinking and it can already be found among the Neanderthals, our immediate ancestors (Papagiani & Morse, 2013). What the Neanderthals seems to have lacked was articulated language (Donald, 1990, 2001; Wilson, 2012). This evolutionary advantage might explain why the Neanderthals were able to imitate the technology of Cro Magnon, but do not seem to have left any traces of art.

Cognitive science is not the only science which has failed to clarify what science is. Some postmodernists claim that there is no such thing as a scientific method. Pioneering scientists like Galileo essentially work like artists. They break all the rules (Feyerabend 1975). But from a closer look, this is incorrect. Galileo became a pioneer of physics (Renn, 2001; Darling,2006) and engineering science (Petrosky, 1996) and made some important discoveries in astronomy (Biagioli, 2001; Shapin, 1996) precisely because he was keenly aware of the different rules of science and technology and moreover was knowledgeable about the chiaroscuro techniques of how to create light, darkness and shade (Shapin, 1996).

Kuhn does admit that there are such things as rules of science (Hacking, 1982), but like Feyerabend he rejects that the aim of science (V.4) is to falsify theories. Instead he opts for a "taxonomic solution" (Hacking, 1995), a view of science which is strikingly similar to Linnaeus' argument in *Systema Naturae* (Frängsmyr, 1983). Kuhn's theory of revolutions is usually presented as a theory of change of "paradigms" (Agassi, 2002; Andersen & Fayé, 2006) which have no rational or logical reasons. So why choose one paradigm instead of another? A possible reason according to Kuhn might be that younger generations tend to be less conservative than the older generations (Martindale, 1990). Hence scientific revolutions become ultimately political or rhetorical phenomena (cf. Shapin & Sheffer, 1985 and Latour, 1984/1993).

A core claim in Kuhn's theory of scientific revolutions is that pioneers of science such as Copernicus do not engage in puzzle solving. Only normal science does that (Kuhn, 1959/1977). Scientific revolutions are not cognitive (logical) but psychological, linguistic or political events (social constructions). From a linguistic point of view scientific, revolutions represent loss or gain of meaning. This is because languages are incommensurable (untranslatable). Kuhn obviously confuses scientific disciplines with art forms. Given that novices entering a discipline in order to become

professionals need to learn the First principles and these are as incompatible with each other as history and archeology (or geology and biology),
disciplines tend to be incomprehensible to each other from a communicational point of view (Bauer, 1990). But art is here to evoke emotions
which is an everyday type of experience and easy to understand. What
different art forms do is to use different techniques (V.3) to evoke or
express simple emotions (bodies in space, characters in action, see Lessing,
2008) in order to get it right (III.1). It is these distinct techniques, based
upon physical constraints, that make art forms incommensurable in the
sense of difficult to translate with loss or gain of meaning (Baxandall, 2003;
cf. Josephson, 1941/1991; Seger, 1992).

## Disciplines in the Making

One of the reasons Kuhn failed to solve the demarcation problem, what
makes a science into a science, was that he used the wrong prototype (I.2).
The Copernican revolution was not a successful revolution because it
lacked parsimony. The number of ad hoc hypotheses necessary to "save
the facts" (Ferguson, 2003) made his model look as contrived as Ptolemy's.
What we need to do to get out of this trap is to make a list of successful
disciplines in the making. For such a list to be representative in the
analytical sense, we need some criteria of selection. Our sample should
include disciplines which managed to solve all the three critical aspects of
First principles.

1) What are the relevant (primary and secondary) data?
2) What methods of interpretation can help us analyze such data?
3) What is the nature of the knowledge object?

A preliminary list of such groundbreaking or pioneering work in science
could include for example:

- Empirical philosophy of science (Aristotle)
- Physics and materials science (Galileo)
- Economics (Adam Smith)
- Archeology (Jens Jürgen Thomsen)
- Geology (James Hutton and Charles Lyell)
- Evolutionary biology (Charles Darwin and Alfred Wallace)
- Business economics (Alfred Marshall)
- Relativity theory (Albert Einstein)
- Physical chemistry (Linus Pauling)

- Structure of DNA (James Watson and Francis Crick)
- Cognitive science (Noam Chomsky and Jerome Bruner)
- Computer science (Many)
- Continental drift (Wegerner and tectonic plates)

Several preliminary empirical patterns emerge from this list:

1) In all the cases but one, the revolutions were successful through falsification of previous theories. The only exception was computer science. But computer science is not a theoretical but a practical science. It belongs to engineering or technology. Engineers are not so much interested in concepts as they are in designing prototypes that work and hopefully work better than previous versions (I.2, see Petrosky, 1996). Successful pioneers in science are successful in the sense that they falsify theories. Kuhn must have been looking at the wrong cases. As philosophers tend to do, he chose paradoxical and complicated cases, but this is probably not the best method.

2) All of these falsifications but one, Einstein's theory of relativity, were unintended. But this goes against Popper's argument that falsification has to be intended. Einstein did revolutionize the discipline of theoretical physics, but he originally trained at a technical college intending to become a teacher and later worked at an engineering patent bureau (Darling, 2006; Isaacson, 2008). Although modern technology has been science-based since Galileo's discovery of materials science (Petrosky, 1996), and teaching became science-based somewhat later (Kroksmark, 2003), both teachers and engineers are basically interested in practical problem solving (R. Laudan, 1984). They are not interested in problem solving for its own sake (Vincenti, 1990/ 1993; Weber & Perkins, 1992). Scientists are here to falsify theories, and for this purpose they need to separate facts from fiction. Engineers and teachers are here to create facts (V.4). They want to change the world and not merely explain why things are as they are (Shields, 2007/2004).

Marx called himself a scientist, but his last thesis on Feuerbach reveals that he was unhappy with the scientific attitude to the world. He wanted to approach it as an engineer or teacher would. Communism has sometimes been called a kind of engineering of the human soul, which might explain why it has attracted both dissatisfied intellectuals and highly intelligent, dissatisfied workers (Skvorecky, 1984). Einstein in contrast had increasingly become unhappy about remaining in a practical profession. He had gotten a job at the Swiss Patent Office with the help of a friend (networking, weak ties, helpers, IV.5), but wanted to start anew. Looking for an opportunity (I.5c), he looked at an intellectual field close to his own training in teaching physics and mathematics, theoretical physics, which did not depend on practical problem solving at all but worked by different rules (I.4).

When Einstein started to investigate his possibilities, he found that the discipline was in deep crisis. Indeed, the crisis began soon after Newton launched his theory of gravity as a universal and notably local face (Bohm, 1998). A number of unsolved problems (anomalies) had appeared. Having been trained to solve problems from a practical point of view, Einstein set himself the task of solving these unsolved theoretical problems one by one, saving the most difficult task, Newton's theory of gravity, as the last problem to be solved (Darling, 2006). He succeeded and the result was a new discipline: relativity theory.

This discipline is not about subatomic physics but about the universe (cosmology, see Levin, 2002/2003). The two knowledge objects are very different. Einstein's quarrels with Heisenberg and Bohr ("God does not play dice") simply reflect this indisputable fact and corroborate Aristotle's 2,300-year-old theory on scientific methodology. It also corroborates Elster's (1983) claim that to be creative is to try to get it right (Dimension III).

But artists are here to transform facts into fiction, not to create facts (V.4). Jules Verne imagined what it would mean to travel to the moon or live in a submarine. He was very successful because he had worked as an artist (fiction writer, effective cause, V.3) using techniques as his core problem-solving strategy. Jules Verne had neither the competence (II.3) nor the type of helpers (IV.5) necessary to accomplish such feats. His patrons were his readers, his agent was his publisher and his mentors were probably previous fantasy novels he had read, although he was certainly one of the pioneers of this particular sub-genre (science fiction).

As noted by Baxandall (1985), both engineers and artists basically solve problems in the intended rather than the unintended manner. The main difference is that engineers solve practical problems of great concern for the human species, which from the beginning have to fight against powerful natural forces. One of these forces (strong gales) forced the Tay railway bridge in Scotland to collapse. There was evidently something wrong with the design (V.2). A new engineering firm was hired and the new Tay bridge was built. This time the new construction turned out to be successful. Although the leading engineer of the firm which took on the job (Baker) did not know in advance what they would end up with, he had the failed version to start from and improve (design), which gave his work a clear direction from the start (V.2). In a similar way artists always start from prototypes, which for them are compositions. This and the rules, evoking emotions by transforming facts into fiction with the help of problem-solving strategy techniques, explains why artistic creativity belongs to the category of intended rather unintended discovery. This might seem surprising given that modern artists seem to produce paintings which look spontaneous (Shiff, 1984), for example by making them look childish (Scholz & Thimsen, 2008), but this is not how it works in practice. Artistic creativity is strongly controlled from beginning to end (cf. Jørgnsen, 2011).

The fact that the most difficult problem in theoretical physics was solved by a person who had been trained as a teacher and worked at an engineering patent bureau, both of which tend to approach problem solving in an intended manner, might explain why Popper (who also had been trained as a teacher) throughout his life insisted that falsification in science had to be intended. Generally it is not. Einstein's falsification of Newton was an exception. Popper's idea was to use this example to solve Hume's problem of the fallacy of induction, but he ended up making the same mistake. Wegener did not intend to discover continental drift nor did the geophysicists and geochemists who discovered tectonic plates. Thomsen did not take on the task from the Danish king with the intention of falsifying what at the time was called "archivarian science" (Trigger, 1989). It was clearly an unintended discovery. The pioneers of computer science usually started with clear intentions, but computer science is a practical and not theoretical science. It belongs to the realm of technology and not science in the strict sense. Thus, just like Kuhn, Popper ended up generalizing from an unrepresentative prototype (I.2) with the important difference that Einstein's revolution belongs to the category of successful revolution. This might explain the basic attitude of the "Popperians," the feeling of optimism or belief (Ziman, 1996) that science will ultimately get it right. Knowledge does advance, although gradually (Kitcher, 1993; Miller, 2006; Deutsch, 2012).

3)    One of the falsifications, made by Darwin and Wallace, belongs to the relatively rare cases of independent discovery. Merton in his theory on "multiples" (se III.2) argues that this phenomenon, far from being rare, is very frequent in science, but this is false. Merton confuses normal science (II.3) with pioneering work in science. The important

difference between the two is that whereas professionals take on small problems and in principle already know the answer, pioneers solve very tricky problems where there does not seem to be an answer until the pioneer, to the surprise of everyone, proves that there is. Other rare cases could be Mendel and de Vries (Mayr, 1982) or Leibniz and Newton (Boorstin, 1985).

What is interesting here is to explain how this phenomenon, independent discovery, although rare in science (but very frequent in nature, see Dawkins, 2005), is possible. It certainly goes against "contingency" theory and suggests that scientific problem solving must ultimately be constrained (Kupferberg, 2017a). But this raises the question of the nature of these constraints and how they are to be conceptualized, which is the core theoretical question of creativity science. For this purpose, foregrounding (1) the types of constraints that have to be overcome (Dimension I) (2) the problem solver (pioneer, II.4; effective cause, V. 3) in order to (3) arrive at a parsimonious solution (III.1), "Getting it right" (Elster, 1983 ) is helpful. Complex and paradoxical problem solving cannot be the result of mere imaginative play (II.1) where there are neither constraints (contingency theory) nor a creative mind (death of the author) as postmodernist theorists claim (Krauss, 1986).

Although postmodernist theory tends to reject Kant's (1790/1997) idea of art as "genius," a closer look at Kant's theory of aesthetic judgment (1790/1974) reveals that what Kant actually meant as genius was the presumed total "freedom" of the artist. In contrast with practical judgments, which are utilitarian, the artist does not have to prove that personal creativity serves any practical purposes. In contrast to scientists, who work in a systematic manner gathering and interpreting data, the artist is completely free (for a similar argument see Kahnweiler, 1980). Although postmodernists have rejected the "genius" argument, Kant's fundamental idea of art as freedom in the sense of contingency has been retained. The question though is whether this is correct. Kant's definition of art neglects the critical role of (1) physical constraints (I.1) or material causes and (2) rules (I.4) or final causes (V.4). Kuhn's theory of art as genius also ignores (3) the important role of opportunity (I.Vc) for doing pioneering work in art, (4) what it means to get it right in art (Dimension III), and how vulnerable versions of pioneering art works in the making are protected (compare biographies of Matisse and Picasso), etc.

The only thing recognized by both Kant and postmodernist theorists of art is the role of prototypes (I.2). But for Kant this was seen as proof of artistic genius. For a postmodernist philosopher of art such as Krauss, this proves that the very idea of an avant garde in the sense of pioneering work (H-creativity) in art is a myth. But this is often the case with one-factor theories. They suffer from what philosophers call "underdetermination" (Latour, 1987; Laudan, 1990). One of the reasons why the problem of evolution could not be solved before Darwin was precisely the predominance of such one-factor theories (vitalism, use, gradual change etc., see Mayr, 1982). A complex, five-factor theory (Mayr, 2004/2007; the Anna Karenina principle, see Chapter 8) was necessary to convincingly falsify existing creation theories.

4)  Psychologists of creativity have a tendency to present pioneering work as a result of structures of the human mind or brain (Gardner, 1993) or of sole persons (Weisberg, 1993), but pioneers are persons who are never fully alone. Darwin (person) and not his brain spoke with Fitzgerald and sent lots of letters home about his discoveries (Burkhardt, 2008). After he started to work on what was to become *On the Origin of Species*, he had five secret confidants apart from the fact that he contacted a large number of authorities to check the facts in areas where he lacked specialist knowledge (*On the Origin of Species* is full of references to such personally addressed sources). Crick and Watson shared the same office (Watson, 1968/1996), during the time the two worked secretly ("skunk works" IV.3) on solving the "problem of the century" (Ridley, 2006); Bruner and Chomsky frequently met at Harvard, and out of these conversations, a new science, cognitive science, was born (Gardner, 1987).

Not surprisingly, close cooperation played a crucial role in the evolution of computer science (Isaacson, 2014/2015), but it also seems to play an important role in the arts, with one exception, writing. In order to understand why, we need to look closer at the different functions of support systems in the arts. Whereas support systems in the fine arts (painting and sculpture) tend to be highly personal, support systems in novel writing tend to be impersonal. Filmmaking seems to combine both. Part of the reason might be that the best way to learn how to write fiction is to read novels, which is best done alone. This in turn is because novels take a long time to read, which points at the role of physical constraints for different art forms (I.1):

5)  A few of these significant contributors might possibly be called geniuses (II.5), but most individual contributors though can best be

described as pioneers (II.4 cf. Kupferberg, 2006a, 2006b). But if the creativity of the pioneer is a sociocognitive phenomenon, then the professional (II.3) and novice problem solver (II.2) must also best be defined as sociocognitive roles (Schön, 1983; Flyvbjerg, 2001). When the problem solver (III.4, V.3) manages to solve the problem in a relatively economic and elegant manner (parsimony III.1), the solution arrived at functions as a prototype (paradigm I. 2) for professional problem solvers. They in turn function as intellectual role models for novices (Collins, 1998), defined as would-be professionals in the process of entering a new profession and the discipline legitimating that profession (Abbott, 1988; Kupferberg, 1999b).

Pioneers hence function as prototypes (I.2), having arrived at the correct First principles first. This provides both professionals and novices with something to start with. Professionals basically apply the First principles discovered by pioneers (Kuhn's "normal science") and only those problems which can be solved by such First principles. Seemingly unsolvable problems or "anomalies" are routinely ignored. Novices in a sense repeat the relatively chaotic learning processes of pioneers (Kuhn 1977, 2000; Kupferberg 1995c, 1996a, 1996b, 1999c, 2006c), but in this case someone (the professional teacher) already knows the correct answers in advance and guides the novices into a process of learning until these correct answers are thoroughly understood (cf. Bruner's 2006b theory of "scaffolding").

Sociology has had little difficulty in conceptualizing such intended, institutionalized forms of learning. Teachers are categorized as professionals or at least "semi-professionals" (Etzioni, 1969). They function as mentors (not agents, IV.5) guiding novices through highly institutionalized "status passages" (Strauss & Glaser, 1971).The fact that pioneering work is not institutionalized and pioneers tend to follow more irregular careers, might be one reason why the sociological discipline has had great difficulty in recognizing this category (compare the apt concept "law of small numbers," see Collins, 1998). But there are other reasons as well. Another intellectually inhibiting factor or "knowledge constraint" (I.3) has been the Weberian sociology of knowledge tradition which tends to reduce knowledge and creativity to existential issues (Merton 1968a, 1968b) ignoring the constraints of creativity (dimensions I, II, III, IV, V).

But there is also the more general tendency among trained professional sociologists to identify the "social" with mere interpersonal relations ("working together," see Becker 1982), ignoring the fact that working together is usually mediated (Latour 1998, 2005; Kupferberg, 2008a,

2008b, 2009a, 2009b, 2009c, 2013). This can be easily seen in a classroom. Teachers give the class texts to read for preparation. They use artifacts such as chalk on the blackboard. They talk and interact with students (performance) and sometimes they use calculations. These mediated forms of the social are hence integrated into the "presentation of self" of the teaching professions (Kress et al., 2001; Kress & van Leeuven 2001, 2006) Mediated forms of the social function as sociocultural tools (Säljö, 2000, 2005) and clearly constrain creative processes. But if these mediated forms of the social already exist at the lowest level of problem solving (novices and professionals) they must also fundamentally shape the groundbreaking creativity of pioneers as well.

6) All the pioneers above profited from what we could call intellectual "borrowing" (Abbott 2004) or used prototypes (I.2). Cognitive science modeled itself upon the core idea of computer science: that machines can "think" in the sense of solving complex problems. But if computers can think, the human brain must also be able to think in the sense of solving similar problems. It cannot be a "black box," the First principle of behavioristic psychology (Säljö, 2000). Evolutionary biology modeled itself upon the idea of geological time, a result of Hutton's groundbreaking discovery (Repcheck, 1993/1999). But where did Darwin get the idea of "common descent" from? Here we need to draw on another prototype, Linnaeus' *Systema Naturae* (Frängsmyr, 1983). Common descent is very similar to Linnaeus' idea of a hierarchy of species (compare Richars, 2009; Wilson 1991/2001). Such intellectual borrowing is very easy to make within the same discipline or intellectual tradition (compare Tycho Brahe's "compromise formula," see Ferguson, 2003), which certainly does not fit Kuhn's theory of incommensurability. They are much more difficult to make if we move between disciplines (the problem of incomprehensibility).

But intellectual borrowing does not always require that we meet our "teacher" in person. Aristotle's huge cultural impact on Western thinking (Nisbet 1969/1970) is based upon reading of "texts," which is the most imported type of "mediated" form of the social or "cultural tool" (Wertsch, 2007; Säljö, 2005) not only in science but also in fiction and religion, which might explain why some scholars such as Bloor (1976) have great difficulty in distinguishing these very different intellectual traditions. Books are similar in terms of physical constants (I.1). Reading books quickly become a lifetime habitus and tends to produce the "bookish" type of personality. But priests, novelists and scholars are nevertheless three very different occupations. This can be best understood via the method of contrasting comparisons (see Chapter 8). First principles always matter in science.

7) Prototypes (I.2) clearly function as constraints for scientific creativity (compare the two cases of Kuhn and Popper). But in order to understand how this works, we need to take into consideration that prototypes can be accessed from outside the discipline itself, say by intellectual migration (IV.2) or personal knowledge (III.4). The founder of geology, Charles Lyell, borrowed ideas from archeology (Lyell 1830/2009, 1863/1970), Darwin and the founders of evolutionary biology, in turn borrowed from geology (Wilson, 1972). The discovery of DNA, which led to the new discipline of molecular biology (Olby, 2009), can be seen as a cross pollination of physical chemistry with ideas from physics and ornithology (Ridley, 2006). Such cross pollination or intellectual borrowing often triggers pioneering work in science (Koestler, 1964), technology (Wiener, 1993) and art (Josephson, 1940/1991). Cross pollination also exists in nature (the transformation from simple prokyarotes to eukarotes, with complex nuclear cells, might have been the result of such cross pollination, see Mayr, 2002 and Margulis & Sagan, 2003). In contrast to cross pollination in the strict sense, intellectual borrowing is a more or less conscious processes and this might explain why Darwin's theory of evolution alone (N-creativity) cannot fully explain his scientific discovery (S-creativity, Gardner, 1999). A more complex theoretical model is necessary (Anna Karenina principle, Chapter 8).

8) A closer look at disciplines in the making might also reveal other interesting empirical patterns which need to be accounted for theoretically. Without the discovery of the First principles of geology by Hutton and Lyell (Laudan, 1987), the later discoveries of continental drift and tectonic plates as the mechanism explaining the former (Andréasson, 2006; Oldroyd, 2009) would have been impossible (knowledge constraints, I.3, co-evolution, III.3). Groundbreaking scientific discoveries tend to lead to new, previously unimagined problems which call for new solutions (Deutsch, 2012). This observable empirical pattern indicates that at least scientific creativity can indeed be explained (Sawyer, 2006). But what does scientific creativity mean in the first place? Why does the creativity of technology tend to imitate the creativity of nature (Dawkins, 1986/2006; French,

1994)? And how do we account for the fact that artists seem to be constrained not only by commitments to certain techniques (prototypes, I.2) and rules (I.4) but also by physical constraints (I.1) which turn out to be distinct for different art forms (Lessing, 2008; Hegel, 1970; Elster 1983, 2000)?

## Problems and Disciplines

As noted above, Aristotle's theory of First principles foregrounds three core problems for an intellectual tradition to become a science: (1) empirical data, (2) conceptual methods of interpretation (theoretical framework), and (3) clarification of the nature of the knowledge object. Different disciplines face different problems. In the case of archeology, the knowledge object (3) was unproblematic (preliterate societies). The core problems were empirical data (1) and methods of interpretation of data (2). In other cases, such as chemistry, the most difficult (complex, paradoxical) problem was to clarify the nature of the knowledge object. This took a very long time (more than two millennia). The problem was in fact only solved after 1900 when Linus Pauling clarified that (1) molecules are what chemistry studies (neither natural elements as Aristotle believed, nor atoms, the belief shared by Lavoisier and Dalton; see Goodman & Russell, 1991) and (2) molecules can in turn be divided into inorganic and organic molecules. (3) X-ray crystallography made it possible to discover that both types of molecules are crystallized, but the design principles of such crystals are very different (Pauling, 1947/1988); (4) the best way to explain how this works was the theory of strong versus weak molecular bonds, a discovery made possible by borrowing ideas from quantum mechanics (knowledge constraints, I.3, co-evolution, III.3; intellectual migration, IV.2), see Goertzel & Goertzel, 1995).

In both cases (Thomsen, Pauling, effective cause, V.3), intellectual biographies seem to be the best, most parsimonious data to start with (material cause, V.1). But for such data to make sense we must make a distinction between successful and unsuccessful scientific revolutions. But precisely this procedure is forbidden by the "strong program," the First principles of Bloor's (1976) sociology of science. But this First principle, as we have seen, is based upon an intellectual prototype (I.2), Kuhn's argument that scientific revolutions are sociological rather than cognitive phenomena. But Kuhn's sociological theory of scientific revolutions was in turn based upon the Copernican revolution, which was an unsuccessful rather than a successful revolution.

But why was Copernicus' revolution unsuccessful? In order to answer this question, we need to identify the knowledge constraints (I.3) that astronomy had to overcome in order to clarify its First principle and arrive at an economic and elegant answer (parsimony, III.1). But this can only be done retroactively. Kuhn in his preface rejects such a method of retroactive reconstruction as scientifically invalid. Here he refers to the critique of "Whig history" by Herbert Butterfield. But Butterfield does not mention the problem of "Whig history" at all in his history of science (Butterfield, 1957/1965). The problem he seeks to explain is why scientific revolutions tend to take such a long time. Why could Aristotle not discover the First principles of physics? Why could he not solve the problem of the origins of species?

Methodologies have to be adapted to the nature of the knowledge object. Different knowledge objects raise different type of problems. A science or discipline starts with identifying the type of problem this science or discipline is here to solve. Political history obviously studies other problems than the history of science, the history of architecture, the history of art, the history of the novel, the history of technology, etc. This is the reason we need to take the rules (I.4) of distinct creative regimes (science, art, technology) but also other forms of constraints seriously.

## Disciplines and Constraints

Having identified what scientific creativity is (disciplines in the making) and what makes it possible (constraints) we can now begin to look closer at those disciplines which traditionally have tended to study creativity or some aspect of this tricky phenomenon such as the psychology of creativity, the sociology of knowledge, the philosophy of science, aesthetics, the economics of technology, archeology and evolutionary biology. Most sociological and psychological theories have tended to overemphasize the role of motivation as have neo-classical economic rational choice theories (I.5). Sociologists are trained to foreground pressure (I.5b), mainly struggle for recognition. Psychologists prefer to look for pleasure (intrinsic motivation or flow) and rational choice theories look for opportunities, presumably shaped by value hierarchies, preference structure and sometimes precommitments also (Elster, 1979, 1983). For a creativity science to be possible, a more complex theory, foregrounding the overall role of constraints, with motivational factors as only one among many constraints, is necessary in order to account for both the complexity and paradoxes of creativity.

Although we will have to wait until Chapter 7 to clarify the exact nature of the knowledge object of creativity science, so much is clear that merely foregrounding one aspect of creativity is not creativity science. Take the humanities that are divided into a number of disciplines, some of which study some artistic form of creativity (A-creativity) often by foregrounding the problem of communication of meaning or language (Scholes, 1981, 1982). For the language aspect see Carter (2004) and Pope (2006). But if creativity starts in nature (N-creativity) we also need to ask how non-humans communicate (a major discovery of sociobiology, see Wilson, 1975/2000, 1980). Being trained in the humanities is to take pride in one's knowledge of how novels are composed, the role that color plays for modern artists, the aesthetic effect of volume and light for architecture, discovered by Greek architects and rediscovered (III.2) by the pioneer of architectural theory and teaching, Le Corbusier (Weber, 2008; Le Corbusier, 1931/2017). Moreover, we have to account for the fact that birds did not need spoken or written language to solve the tricky problem of calculating longitude (Tudge, 2008), although humans certainly did (Boorstin, 1985). How did birds manage to solve this tricky problem, millions of years before humans? This is a paradox, but creativity science is here to solve such paradoxes.

Spoken language might be an important source of human creativity, but so are texts, artifacts and calculations. Abstract calculations were born with geometry and in turn made both Greek science and classical architecture possible. Bloor's (1976) argument that mathematical knowledge is contingent is clearly wrong (the critical role of geometry for the birth of science also undermines Latour's 1993 claim that we have never been modern). Galileo's clarification of the First principles of engineering science (materials science) relied upon an even more advanced form of mathematics than geometry: algebra. So how can the history of mathematics prove that scientific advance is contingent as Bloor claims? Is it not a historical fact that the absence of algebra functioned as a core knowledge constraint (I.3) for science-based technology in Greek society, but for some reasons not for the arts, which went through a creative explosion at the time? These are the types of problems we need a creativity science to explore, and, hopefully, explain.

What is interesting from the point of view of the theoretical model is that geometry clearly functions as a role model or prototype (I.2) for Greek science (Rihll, 1999) but for two different reasons. For Plato the perfect forms of geometry, which could be calculated precisely, functioned as role models for Plato's idea of ideal forms (later to become "formal cause," V.2) in Aristotle's model of the structure of creative processes. But geometry also functioned as role model for Aristotle's First principles. Geometry is based upon the intellectual operation of proof, but in order to make such a proof work, one needs to start with some basic assumptions (Kline, 1953/1987) which are doctrines, but not necessarily myths as Bloor (1976, 1999) claims. Myths are fiction (such as the fiction that Columbus had indeed landed close to mainland China). The problem is that fiction is structurally similar to myth (transformation of facts to fiction, compare Nabokov's novel *Lolita*). If science really had modeled itself upon myth, it would not have advanced much. If we look at political history, it only became a science when it accepted that this was not the role of history as science. The role of history as scientific discipline was to separate facts from fiction (V.4; compare the early versions of Swedish history writing, see Henrikson, 1963/1988).

Postmodernist contingency theory based upon Ferdinand de Saussure's theory of languages is itself constrained in the sense that it is based upon certain assumptions, most of which turn out to be false. It is indeed possible to study language as it is used in everyday life (compare speech act theory, pioneered by Austin, 1975 and Searle, 1996), the system of signs and signification (la langue) only provides us with a partial truth of how languages work. Moreover, Saussure's contingency theory of the system of signs or signification is based upon a synchronic analysis. Saussure's life project was to supplement this static, synchronic theory of signs with a diachronic or dynamic theory. Unfortunately, he died long before he completed this intended project (biographical fact). To base a theory of language upon Saussure is the same as cutting off the limbs and head of a pig and declare that what is left tells us the truth about this particular species.

Saussure's theory of language as a system of signification rests upon the further assumption that phonemes (combinations of sounds) are the most elementary forms of language. Such phonemes are in turn combined into words. But since phonemes are different in different cultures, the relation between words and things become contingent according to Saussure. Thus, what an English speaker calls "dog" (for the abstract referent or category of dogs, see Scholes, 1981), can be represented by many "words" such as "sobaka," "chien," "hund," etc. This is the reason why language systems are in principle "contingent" according to Saussure. But this cannot be right. If my mother was Russian and my father French, there is a great probability that I will call a dog "sobaka" or "chien" rather than "dog" or "hund." My everyday language use will be constrained and not contingent.

Children are born with (Pinker, 1995) the capacity to pronounce all possible combinations of sounds (phonemes), but gradually, during the first six months of a child's life, they tend to become reduced to the few combinations used by the mother usually embedded in a local culture such as "Chinatown" in San Francisco or "Södermalm" in Stockholm (Crystal, 1987). Apart from role model (the mother, I.2) physical constraints (I.1) restrict the choice of language. A baby cannot crawl far away from its mother and this creates an excellent learning environment. The role of physical constraints can also be illustrated by the late discovery of the thousands of languages found in the jungle of previously unexplored New Guinea (Diamond, 2012). The impregnability of the terrain of the island and lack of modern means of transportation (knowledge constraints, I.3), created similar physical constraints, which helps us explain why there were so incredibly many local languages within a relatively small area.

This short overview of how different disciplines have gone about trying to make sense of human creativity, provides us with two important lessons. All disciplines are ultimately constrained in the sense that they always start with some basic assumptions (First principles), including Saussure's discipline which claims that there are no constraints, and claim that languages are contingent. The fact that all disciplines are constrained also helps us to understand why there is no creativity science. Specialization has its advantages, such as making discovery more effective, but it also has intellectual costs. Disciplines are problem-solving machines, but the type of problems such machines are here to solve are very different. Harvesters are good and effective to fill magazines with corn, but they are not built for roads, where they are a nuisance. They will sink to the bottom if we try to use them as ships and they will not become airborne no matter how hard we try.

## The Role of the Pioneer

In the psychological literature on creativity (see in particular Simonton's works) the concept of "genius" is sometimes used in order to categorize the type of problem solver I have chosen to call "pioneer." There are three main reasons why I prefer the concept of pioneer. One is that the word "genius" tends to surround the problem of doing pioneering work in a chosen field with too much mystique. Even the highest forms of creativity can and should be explained, which is one of the reasons we need a creativity science. The other main reason is that motivation can best be described in terms of constraints. A talented painter such as Marc Chagall no doubt felt pleasure when painting (this was easy for him, he learned quickly), but becoming a pioneer is just as much or more constrained by opportunity. Moreover the very ambition of becoming a pioneer might also be felt as a pressure (I.5; compare Matisse's biography).

The third and most important reason why I have abstained from talking about geniuses in this book is that it is mainly a biological category. Pioneers play a social role by taking upon themselves the cognitive task of solving tricky problems. Some rare individuals seem to be endowed with extraordinary talents from birth (Gleick, 1993; Isaacson, 2014/2015). This in combination with early stimulation does allow us to classify some very exceptional individuals as geniuses (II.5; Mozart could probably be placed in this category, see Solomon, 1995). But does one have to be a genius to become a pioneer (II.4)?

An interesting case is Shakespeare whom I hesitate to call a genius. His dramas are mainly rewritten versions of previous works (prototypes, I.2, Bate, 1997/2008). The emotional ambivalence and intensity (Beardsley, 1958) of his plays can best be reexplained by combination of several factors (see Chapter 8). One could be the feeling of "magic" (Bergman, 1989; Martin, 1978) which a well-written play can achieve in the special context of live theater. This points at the importance of physical constraints (I.1) for emotional effects. If we want to understand why and how Shakespeare managed to get it right (III.1) other factors have to be drawn into the analysis such as existing prototypes (I.2, the strong tradition of Elizabethan drama), the historical problem situation (III.4, tensions between a Protestant court and some aristocratic families secretly celebrating Catholic Mass, see Strong & Davies, 2006/2011b), patronage and agency from both groups (IV.5) but also his father who paid for his education, his many mentors both at school and when he started as an actor (IV.5), his professional problem situation (III.4) working not only as writer but also as an actor and producer, but also his personal problem situation (III.4) both as an absent husband and father who cared more for his role as financial provider than the emotional needs of wife and children, but also a son who betrayed the family tradition.

If we look at the motivational constraints (I.5) we find pleasure (I.Va), which can best reexplained by his rhetorical skills which he learned at school (he was well educated and was certainly not an autodidact from which the myth of Shakespeare's "genius" probably derived). He worked hard at school and used most of what he learned as artistic capital all his life. We know little of Shakespeare's life after he left Stratford-upon-Avon (Ackroyd, 2005/2006), but his sonnets indicate he must have had some aristocratic patrons who might or might not have celebrated the more colorful Catholic Mass (according to Strong & Davies, 2006/2011b) and saw theater as a compensation for the more gray and biblically oriented Protestant services. It also seems that there was a strong resentment against dull services in Shakespeare's household. Thus his father probably had to pay fines for not regularly attending Protestant services (Bate,1997/2008). These factors might explain some of the topics that return again and again in Shakespeare's dramas (treachery, suspicion, opportunism, but also filial alienation and disturbed communication (best expressed and evoked in Hamlet). But such disloyalty and betrayal were probably handled with utmost secrecy ("skunk works" IV.3), but also called for confidants (IV.4). All these factors should be included when we went to account for the groundbreaking creativity (II.4) of Shakespeare.

Other cases in my sample confirm that we can do without the category of genius. Darwin confessed that he was a slow thinker (Sulloway, 1996). Picasso showed very little talent in painting as a small child in spite of immense stimulation (Penrose 1958/1968; Richardson 1991/1992; Cowling, 2002). Sylvia Plath's transformation to pioneer was unexpected and can best be explained by a deep emotional and professional crisis very similar to her first failed suicide attempt (Bredsdorff, 1987; Stevenson, 1989). Neither Crick nor Watson seem to have been exceptionally talented (Watson, 2001; Olby, 2009). In order to explain why the two managed to get it right (III.1) when solving the "problem of the century" (Ridley, 2006), foregrounding knowledge constraints (I.3), the opportunity factor (I.Vc), the historical problem situation (III.4) and factors related to protection of vulnerable ideas (Dimension IV) plus access to data (material cause, V.1) might be helpful.

Einstein (Isaacson, 2008) was no extraordinary achiever in school (Hermann 1996; White & Cribbin 1993), and moreover he found some of the advanced mathematics (vector theory) necessary for his equations very difficult and had to ask for help from colleagues (Darling, 2006). The main reason Einstein became a pioneer seems to have been his early training at the Swiss Federal Polytechnic School and time spent at the Swiss Patent Office (see Isaacson, 2008). This in combination with Einstein's close immersion in state-of-the-art theoretical physics (intellectual migration, IV.2) in this particular case between intellectual fields with very different rules (I.4) and problem-solving strategies (trial and error versus methodology. V. 3) seems the best explanation of how and why Einstein managed to prove Newton's theory of an ether to be fiction. The dual nature of light (wave and particle) explained how gravity can travel in empty space (Elster, 2007).

But the role of the historical problem situation (III.4) needs to be taken into account as well. Newtonian physics was in deep crisis at the time. Indeed, it had already been so when Newton discovered the general theory of gravity (Bohm, 1998), given that Newton could not explain how gravity could work over distance. It lacked an explanation of the "mechanism" involved (Elster, 2007) and it was by providing this mechanism that Einstein managed to get it right and solve the problem (III.1).

Both teachers and engineers in contrast to scientists basically work in an experimental, trial-and-error way (V.3), but they usually also know what they want and their intentions are relatively clear from the start. They are not out to falsify a theory but to adapt previous solutions to new conditions (V.4, Petrosky, 1996). It was probably this essentially practical attitude to science that helped Einstein to solve the anomalies that had accumulated in physics since Newton (Darling, 2006). But Einstein's intentional falsification, the prototype (I.2) of Popper's theory of intended falsification, seems to be an exception to the rule in pioneering work. Darwin had no intention of falsifying Lyell's theory of "special creation" when he embarked the *Beagle*. He did not even know that the theory existed and was a novice (II.2) in the discipline of geology when he left England in December 1832. He was an acclaimed professional (II.3) when he returned, but he only became a pioneer (II. 4) much later and in a different discipline (a case of intellectual migration, IV.2, which started with geographical isolation, IV.1). The trial-and-error model does indeed work for technological creativity, which might be the reason why the concept "genius" is rarely used here (compare Baldwin, 1995).

Summarizing, so far, the concept of genius (Gleick, 1993; Miller, 2000,) is redundant for creativity science and should be replaced by the categories: novices, professionals and pioneers. Novices (II.2) are in the process of entering a given field, tradition or discipline. They have not yet mastered the routinized forms of problem solving which characterize professionals (Schön, 1983; Lave & Wenger 1991; Flyvbjerg 2001). Routinized forms of problem solving (II.3) work with objectively and subjectively well-defined problems (Abbott, 1988, 1995). Novices work with subjectively ill-defined but objectively well-defined problems (Kupferberg, 1995c, 1996a, 1996b, 1999c). Pioneers take it upon themselves to solve problems which are both subjectively and objectively ill-defined (Abbott, 2001a, 2001b, 2004; Collins, 1998).

## Why Novelty and Originality Are Neither Necessary nor Sufficient for Defining Creativity

Dimension III, "Getting it right," somewhat surprisingly arrives at a definition of creativity as product, which does not lean upon novelty or originality as either necessary or sufficient criteria of creativity. The essence of creative problem solving is getting it right. The question this chapter raises is what getting it right means (parsimony III.1). How we know this to be a fact (convergence. III.2), what makes this possible (co-evolution III.3) and how the actor of successful problem solving (Koestler, 1964) can be analyzed in detail (problem situations and problem solver, III.4). This makes Kuhn's prototype Copernicus much less interesting and as we have seen completely misleading. Pioneers do solve tricky problems and this is what they are here for (cognitive aspect). But they certainly do not do it alone (sociological aspect). Recent sociological theory has completely misread the problem but for this purpose we need to be more circumspect over what prototype (I.2) to choose to model our thinking on.

The problem, from a creative science point of view, is to clarify why precisely this pioneer managed to get it right (retrospective analysis). In order to clarify these issues, we need to define what we mean by parsimony (III.1). It can best be described as simple, economic or elegant solutions. Some aesthetic theorists have tried to define what elegance means (Zangwill, 2001), but theories of parsimony are rare (compare Elster, 1983, 2000). What should be emphasized is that parsimony is not only an aesthetic quality. It is an economic quality as well and as such it can also be found in nature (compare Darwin's discussion of the geometrical shape of honeycombs in *On the Origin of Species*). But parsimony is also constrained by physical constraints and prototypes (I.1, I.2), knowledge constraints (I.3) and rules of the game (I.4) as well as motivation factors (pressure, pleasure and opportunity, I.5).

How do we know that parsimony is the best definition of creativity as product and not novelty or originality? For this purpose, we can start by looking closer into the phenomenon of independent (re) discovery (Merton, 1961/1973, 1963/1973a, 1973b) or convergent evolution (Dawkins, 1986/2006, 2005), elaborated in III.2. Why is it that scientists sometimes arrive at almost the identical solution to a given problem, although unaware of each other? Parallel phenomena can be found in technology (see Isaacson's 2014/2015 close study of the evolution of computers). Similar cases in archeology are the geographically independent transitions from hunter-gatherer societies to Neolithic societies (Pfeiffer, 1977; Diamond, 1999) and independent inventions in metallurgy (Killick, 2000).

Whether there is such a thing as independent discovery in art history is a trickier issue. Something resembling the impressionist style can be found in early Chinese painting (Lin, 2006; Anzhi, 2006), but given that knowledge of similar Japanese painting influenced the French Impressionists

(Honour & Fleming, 1982/1984), the evidence is indecisive. Braque and Picasso are usually seen as inventors of the collage principle (Rubin, 1989), but collage or "montage" as Brecht called in in his avant-garde scenography (Schumacher & Schumacher, 1978) is the editing principle of movies, invented by Porter, an engineer working at Edison's studio (Jacobs, 1968), which makes it a case of imitation based upon prototypes (I.2).

Convergent evolution in nature, can, as Dawkins notes, basically be explained by physical constraints (I.1). There is only a limited variety of basic ways to beat physical laws, such as building an eye, flying, designing a functioning radar system, etc. In order to understand such biological phenomena such as the high speed of predators and prey or the mutual adaption of insects and plants (or birds and flowers), co-evolution (Dawkins, 2010) is the best, most parsimonious description of how to get it right or finding the best possible solution. As noted by Dawkins (2005), the capacity of animals running for their life and/or food for themselves and their young is very similar to the military arms race among nations preparing for war (conflict). But co-evolution in culture can also take other, more peaceful forms (cooperation). An interesting case of co-evolution is the evolution of "modern" painting. Rather than studying it in a purely "intrinsic" or "autonomous" manner (Greenberg, 1961/1965; Luhmann, 1995/2000) it can best be seen as an example of the "arms race" with the film industry as a competitor or "prey" threatening this art form with extinction (Danto, 1997; Roe, 2014/2015).

In order to understand how getting it right and arrival at parsimonious solutions work in practice, a good strategy is to foreground how problem situations constrain problem solvers (III.4) The concept "problem situation" was invented or discovered by Karl Popper (O'Hear, 1982; Hacomen, 2000; Miller, 2006). As noted by Popper (1999), the physical (I.1) and development constraints (I.2) of problem situations on problem solvers seem to guide them in in getting it right even when there are no conscious intentions (which can be seen as a reply to Gardner's 1999 argument that Darwin cannot explain Darwin). Such unconscious or pre-conscious constraints seem to transcend the nature- culture divide. An apple tree turns out to be a very skillful problem solver, adjusting the falling of ripe apples to the seasons, which in turn requires some complex chemical mechanism (Popper 1999; compare Elster, 1999, 2007). Such knowledge probably evolves gradually, by overcoming knowledge constraints (I.3), indicating yet another parallel with Darwin's theory of evolution. In contrast, rules are man-made and conscious (Searle, 1969), which indicates the limits of a Darwinian explanation of Darwin (compare Gabora, 2005).

Baxandall (1985) argues that the model of problem situations and problem solvers (III.4) can help us solve the problem of artistic intentions and the role they play for artistic problem solving. As bridge builders, painters face certain problems that need to be solved. This is a clear intention. The psychological motives for solving a problem are in principle irrelevant. It could be pressure (I.5b), pleasure (I.5a) or opportunity (I.5b). Brunichelli and Michelangelo often worked on commissions (patronage, IV.5) which provided them with opportunities (I.5c) to build the two most famous art works in Florence and Rome (Welch, 1984; Honour & Fleming, 1982). No doubt pressure (I.5b) of some sort (say financial) played a role as did pleasure or flow (I.5a). In all cases of pioneering the core issue from the point of creativity science is what tricky problems are to be solved, such as how to best translate biblical texts into the dual constraints of pictures and architecture in the Sistine Chapel. Problem situations are objective and constrain the problem solver (III.4), whether he or she possesses human forms of language and consciousness or not.

Whereas the psychology of creativity tends to overemphasize the role of consciousness for problem solving (Gardner, 1999), most aesthetic theories claim that intentions are worthless in art criticism ("the fallacy of intention," see Wimsatt & Beardsley, 1954/1992; Beardsley, 1958; Dickie, 1997). But this is not a convincing argument (Elster, 1983; Carroll, 1992/2008). We cannot ignore intentions if we want to know how artists manage to get it right, but nor do we need to assume that all intentions are fully conscious to the degree of being critically reflected. This assumption is often taken for granted in contemporary educational psychology (Perkins, 1995). Interestingly, Perkins has presented convincing evidence of the opposite in a previous work (Perkins, 1981), suggesting that pedagogical rhetoric can function as cognitive pressure on empirical scholars, tempting them to avoid the most challenging problems.

Intentional constraints are often of what Elster (2000) calls "self-imposed." Elster's own favorite example, the use of improvisation in jazz, indicates though that there must be some more objective constraints working here as well. Why is improvisation so important in jazz? And why did this technique decrease in importance when EPs were replaced by LPs (Elster 1983)? The former is trickier to answer and the latter points to the role of physical constraints (I.2).

A possible explanation can be found in Becker (1966). An amateur jazz musician who trained to become a sociologist, Becker found a social tension between the expectations of "light" music by audiences (final cause, see V.4,) who merely want to be entertained, the "squares" (novices,

II.2), and the need felt by professional musicians (II.3) to show what they are capable of for other, professional audiences (V.4). The problem situation is completely different in art. Here painters, in particular pioneers (II.4), are encouraged by professionals (II.3), in reality support systems (IV.5) – an elite of connoisseurs consisting of wealthy art collectors, owners of galleries, critics and curators and avant-garde artists working as art professors or mentors (Steffensen, 2017) – to ignore the hopelessly retrograde taste of the squares (lay audiences, novices, II.2). We, the elite are in power here. We decide what is good taste and not (avant-garde artists and connoisseurs traditionally see themselves as a kind of cultural aristocracy or Nietzschean supermen, high above the slave mentality and vulgar tastes of the manipulated and conservative masses (see Boundas & Olokowski, 1994; Due, 2007).

But even avant-garde artists might sometimes ignore such elite audiences and paint for broader audiences (squares). A case in point is Picasso's *Guernica* (Arnheim, 1962). Like a good novel (Kundera, 1987), the painting probably has something to say both to connoisseurs and mass audiences. As noted by Cowling (2002) the painting uses figures which refer both to public and private symbols, recognizable in Picasso's earlier works (prototypes, formal causes, V.2,) of interest for the connoisseur. But these are not the prime audience here (final cause, V.4). The title of the painting "anchors" it (Barthes, 1964/1977) in something recognizable, an event in the Spanish civil war. Picasso's choice of symbols which were clearly embedded in Spanish cultural and religious tradition (bulls, horses, the Madonna and child) moreover supports rather than confuses or provokes the intended audience (the supporters of the Republican government).

But the painting would probably not have felt emotionally right (III.1) if Picasso had failed to solve what is in a sense a mere "formal" choice (V.2), the placement of the bull. Picasso struggled with the compositional problem for weeks, making five different overall compositions. Only the last composition allowed Picasso to get it emotionally right in the sense that moving the bull from the upper center of the painting to the upper left and hence also allowing for the horse to rise up in agony and become a symbol of the will of the Spanish people to keep on fighting for the Republican cause (Beevor, 1982/1989). The mere change of composition transformed the feeling of cynicism and hopelessness, which was precisely what the bombing had aimed at, to pity and hope, the core emotions of dramatical narratives, which was precisely what Picasso's audience expected and the Republican government had commissioned him to do.

## The Vulnerability of Novel Ideas

As noted by a number of scholars working in science, art and technology, parsimonious ideas which are seen as novel, tend to be vulnerable at the start and risk premature death if not protected somehow (Peters & Austin, 1985; Grosskurth, 1991; Penrose, 1958/1968) until they are robust enough to be presented in public (for a psychological theory and attempted strategy to solve this problem, see de Bono, 1994, 2009). How is this task, the protection of vulnerable ideas, solved in practice? Darwin's conversion from convinced "creationist" to convinced believer in evolution (Eriksen 1999) seems to be a case of the role of geographical distance protecting vulnerable ideas in science (IV.1). As noted by Rudwick (1996), this strategy was not consciously intended. It was transformed into a conscious strategy a few years after Darwin returned home and settled in a small village (Downe) a day's journey from London (Desmond & Moore, 1992; compare Kupferberg, 1998a).

The conditions of Darwin's discovery also contain elements of intellectual migration (IV.2) in particular his growing knowledge of the newly emerging discipline of geology (Wilson, 1972; Laudan, 1987). There are also clearly elements of skunk works (IV.3). His first book (Darwin 1839/1989), based on his voyage in the *Beagle*, reveals almost nothing about his conversion from a creationist to an evolutionary thinker during the five-year voyage (Eriksen, 1999). After Darwin returned home, he spent more than 20 years working on his theory (Gould, 1996), making it presentable for inherently skeptical audiences (Merton, 1942/1968; Butterfield 1957/1965; Wild 1992). As Freud (Gay, 1988), Darwin also confided in selected knowledgeable persons during the long period (IV.4) in order to get all the details right in the most parsimonious way possible (III.1). These confidants functioned as critical "soundboards"(Abbot, 2004) for the clarification of Darwin's emerging ideas. Confidants should not be confused with teamwork (IV.2), which is something else (compare the case of Crick and Watson).

Like most pioneers, Darwin not only had helpers (IV.5): patrons (his father), mentors (first the biologist Henslow and later, after his return to England, the leading geologist Lyell) but also agents (his publisher Murray and his "dog" Huxley), although Huxley played a very marginal role in the social recognition of Darwin's pioneering work (this comes out best when comparing Darwin, a scientific pioneer with Picasso). Patronage also plays an important role in technology. Although the most active risk capitalists also tend to function as both mentors and agents of the innovator (Heller,

2020), the bulk of investors (shareholders) are passive and should hence best be categorized as patronage (Isaacson, 2012).

Protection of vulnerable ideas in technology (Kirton, 1989) can take many forms such as toll barriers and trade wars between nations, patents acquired by companies or individuals in the process of establishing a firm (entrepreneurs), and generous research grants (often by the military in times of hot or cold wars or arms races). Protection of vulnerable ideas in science is less institutionalized and the system of anonymous referees and scholarly journals probably tends to protect fewer original ideas more than they protect radical scientific thinking (compare Ericson's 1999 critique of Csikszentmihalyi's somewhat uncritical system model of how groundbreaking creativity is recognized).

In contrast originality and novelty is expected by patrons, mentors and agents of modern art, as long as they obey both the general rules of art (evoking emotions, V.4) and the distinctive problem-solving strategies or techniques (V.3) of twentieth-century art such as abandoning naturalistic forms of representation (primitivism), incomprehensibility (art intended for support systems, IV.5 rather than lay audiences, compare the film industry), colonization of other art forms such as theater (for performative art, see Goldberg, 2004), etc. Although the support system of avant-garde painting is today clearly functionally differentiated (Luhmann, 1995/2000), this was not necessarily the case in earlier periods when pioneering art collectors such as Kahnweiler and Peggy Guggenheim took upon themselves several of these roles (Fitzgerald, 1996; Richardson, 1996/1997; Sawin, 1995/1998; Dearborn, 2005/2006). In contrast, publishers of fiction usually only play the role of agent (and hence tend to function mainly as gatekeepers rather than helpers, V.5, see Coser et al. 1982).

The combination of patronage, mentors and agents also seems to work differently in painting and filmmaking. Private patrons seem to be the rule in the early career of pioneering painters (best illustrated by the case of Chagall, see Wullschlager, 2008). In filmmaking the huge costs make personal patronage impractical, and institutional patronage is the only realistic option (Bergman, 1959, 1989; for the case of *Fanny and Alexander,* see Donner, 2009). There are also differences between European and American films (Dale, 1997). In the former the state plays a heavy role both as patron and mentor, leaving agency to the film studios. In the classical Hollywood, the major film studios combined all the three roles (Mordden, 1987), but with the rising costs (partly due to the role of agents who have driven up the costs of "stars"), studios can no longer afford to function as patrons of filmmaking. The major studios have shrunk and have been incorporated into huge conglomerates from the media and technology industries (King, 2002). This does not exclude the fact that studios still function as mentors and agents, although they have lost some of these functions as well to film schools and independent agent bureaus for talent (McDougal, 2001; Rose, 1995).

The best, most well-researched study on the role of protection of vulnerable ideas for discovery might be the case of Crick and Watson's discovery of DNA. All the five factors constraining the protection of vulnerable ideas are clearly present. Geographical isolation (IV.1) is a relative phenomenon. It can be manifest by a university campus close to Russell Square in the center of London or a number of research and teaching establishments in a smaller city such as Cambridge (compare the Cavendish Laboratory). The role of more or less geographical isolation is rarely mentioned by geographers such as Andersson (1985) and Florida (1992).

These geographers have foregrounded the concentration of minds as a core factor of creative milieus, but this neglects the need to protect vulnerable ideas, which might take many forms, among them distance to "normalizing" professional communities. The reason Harvey chose Padua to make his anatomical investigations which revolutionized the understanding of how the heart works (Boorstin, 1985) might have been access to human corpses, transported secretly (skunk works, IV.3) to the medical building by an underground channel (personal observation, FK). One of the reasons why the skyscraper was not invented in New York but in the younger city Chicago (Condit, 1964), might have been the lack of an established architectural profession (Hall, 1999). There were many reasons why the American film industry relocated to the west coast (escaping legal action from the engineering firms owning the patents, lack of trade union control over wages and work hours, longer sun hours, etc.), but one of the reasons the creativity of this new film colony exploded, apart from stunning natural features (Brownlow, 1979; Robinson, 1996), might have been the geographical distance from the "normalizing" financial control center and mass audiences in the north east ( French, 1971).

Crick and Watson's discovery is a clear case of both intellectual migration and teamwork (IV.2). Crick had trained as a physicist (Olby, 2009) and Watson as a zoologist (Watson, 2001) before they moved into physical chemistry (and later microbiology). Moreover, the two shared an office (teamwork) at Cambridge (Watson, 1968/1996) as they were intensely but also secretly (IV.3) discussing these issues (V.2), hiding them from everybody, including their boss Lawrence Bragg and their foremost competitors

(Wilkins. Franklin and Pauling) that they were up against. After almost two years it turned out that they had during this time been secretly pre-committed (Elster, 1979) to solve the "problem of the century" (Ridley, 2006), making this a clear case of skunk work (IV.3, see Watson, 1968/1996; Judson, 1996/2013; Maddox 2003; Goertzel & Goetzel, 1995). This concept has mostly been developed by business economists studying entrepreneurship (Peters & Austin, 1985; Ketteringham & Nayak, 1986,). In contrast to Darwin (Browne, 2002), Crick and Watson only confided (IV.4) in each other and their "teamwork" (IV.2) also functioned as a soundboard.

### Back to Aristotle

Dimension V, the structure of creative processes, adds an even deeper level of how constraints work in creativity, allowing us to simplify the high complexity of creativity (Andersson & Sahlin, 1997). For this purpose, resurrecting Aristotle's theory of the "four causes" (Hankinson, 1995, 2009) might be a good, parsimonious conceptual tool. Aristotle's theory of the four causes on a more fundamental level helps us to conceptualize how creative processes in general are structured and why they are con-strained the way they are. Science is here to falsify theories, by separating facts from fiction (final cause, V.4). For this purpose, science uses meth-odology as a problem-solving strategy (V.3), clarifying concepts (V.2) and collecting data (V.1). But such data have to be adapted to the nature of the knowledge object. This is the reason why knowledge constraints (I.3) are critical for how science evolves.

In contrast, art is here to evoke emotion as well as transforming facts into fiction (V.4). This explains why the core problem-solving strategy of art is choice of techniques (V.3), why artists' work processes foreground issues of composition (V.2) and why the material cause of art is not data but material, something it shares with technology (V.1). This in turn explains why physical constraints are critical if we want to understand the origins of artistic revolutions. Martindale (1990) believes that stylistic revolutions can best be explained by the simple psychological mechanism that novelty wears of quickly and has to be replaced by something new to avoid boredom. This might explain the long series of artistic revolutions in the twentieth century, but it does not explain *Les Demoiselles d'Avignon*.

The best explanation might be the physical constraints of the fine arts compared with cinema. Painting and sculpture are both bodies in space, which can be taken in at one glance. In a movie one at least has to sit to make these 90 minutes a pleasurable experience. There is little pleasure in standing in front of a painting or sculpture for 90 minutes, unless the act of looking at the work of art is transformed into something completely different. This was and is the objective problem situation of the fine art of the twentieth century. It puts pressure (I.5b) on twentieth-century artists to solve precisely this type of problem, but it also provides them with an opportunity (I.5c and given the chance they might even find pleasure (I.5a) in it).

# PART II

## Elaborating the Theoretical Model

# CHAPTER 2

# Dimension I: Types of Constraints

## Illuminative Cases and the Problems of Selection

In the following five chapters I will seek to elaborate the theoretical model. Although the basic methodological considerations of the choice of types of data and method (contrasting comparison of natural experiments, borrowed from Jared Diamond, prototype, I.2) will be discussed more in detail in the concluding chapter, I should say something here about the problem of selection. From the point of view of pedagogy or personal discovery (P-creativity), cases should be selected for their illuminative value. I have mainly chosen to use artistic forms of creativity (A-creativity) to illuminate the concepts of physical constraints. In contrast I have chosen the creativity of nature in order to illuminate the role of prototypes. All art historians and literary theorists agree that prototypes play a critical role for the creativity of painters and writers of fiction (indeed this discovery is sometimes used are an argument for the "death of the author," see Krauss, 1986). What is surprising is that nature does the same. Indeed this critical discovery ("common descent" or "three of life") is what provided Darwin with the solution to the problem of the origins of species. Evolution is basically gradual transmutation of previous forms (Mayr, 1998, 2002).

In order to illuminate rules as constraints, I must provide examples from all the three creativity regimes (A-creativity, S-creativity, N-creativity). Motivations addresses a somewhat different type of creative logic which is more fully described under Dimension II, how personal creativity (P-creativity) is transformed into significant contributions (H-creativity, creative explosions). The reason that the motivational factors are placed under Dimension I is to foreground the fact that motivations function as constraints. Here I have been more lavish in my choices and have followed more closely Diamond's method of contrasting comparisons of natural experiments, mainly because the problem of method has been much discussed in the psychology of creativity.

The role of motivation for creativity can best be illuminated by Darwin's scientific biography. Darwin's discoveries were made possible by the opportunity (I.5c) to join HMS *Beagle* (Browne & Neve, 1989), an opportunity that can be compared with the offer to Latour to enter the Salk Institute to do field work (Latour & Wolgar, 1986) or Crick and Watson's employment at the Cavendish Laboratory (Watson, 2001; Olby, 2009) or Picasso's move to Paris around 1900 (Richardson, 1991/1992) or Chagall's similar move a decade later (Wullschlager, 2008). But there was also a great element of pleasure (I.5a), (compare his letters home, in Darwin, 1898/1958). Darwin probably also felt pressure (I.5b) from home to prove himself to his father who had financed the trip (Keynes, 2003) and his fiancée whom he hoped to marry after his return (Desmond & More, 1992).

The role of opportunity as motivational constraint has consistently been missing in psychological research on creativity (which also tends to confuse intentions with motivational factors). The motivational factor opportunity is a "transitional form" in the sense that it bridges the cognitive core of creativity (problem-solving capacity) and sociological factors. It explains why creativity can best be studied as a sociocognitive problem. The cognitive aspects are foregrounded in this chapter (Dimension I) and Chapter 4 (Dimension III), the sociological aspects in Chapter 3 (Dimension II) and Chapter 5 (Dimension IV). Chapter 6 (Dimension V) tries to show how the two can be combined (sociocognitive approach).

To treat creativity as a sociocognitive phenomenon means to investigate how successful problem solving (getting it right, Dimension III) comes about in practice. Whereas the sociological method is inadequate for studying this aspect, the attempts of psychologists to combine motivational factors with cognitive factors have not managed to solve the problem either. Where does the problem-solving capacity of creative individuals come from? Whereas the first generation of creativity research foregrounded something they conceptualized (V.2) as the "creative personality," this First principle was abandoned in the late 1980s (Sternberg, 1988; Boden, 1990; Gardner, 1993; Weisberg, 1993). But where do motivational factors come in here?

Theories foregrounding motivational factors such as Amabile (1982, 1988, 1996, 1997, 1998) had great difficulties in accounting for the problem solving of the creative individual due to her tendency to reduce motivational factors to intrinsic motivation, a form of pleasure (I.5a). Csikszentmihalyi's "systems model" of creativity (1988, 1994, 1996, 1999) tried to solve the problem by combining pleasure (conceptualized as "flow") with pressure (I.5b) conceptualized as social recognition from the field, an idea borrowed from the sociology of Bourdieu. None of the two models foregrounded the role of opportunity (I.Vc). Simonton's explanation of Darwin's "genius" (1999a, 1999b) does not seem to take the opportunity factor seriously either (compare Simonton's weak contribution to an anthology on the role of cities for enhancing both the motivation and problem-solving capacity of creative minds in Andersson et al. 2011).

## Physical Constraints

Material causes (V.1) in science basically consist of data. But the criteria for choosing the correct data (Getting it right, Dimension III) is objectively constrained by the nature of the knowledge object (V.1), the core of Aristotle's theory of First principles (Dimension V). This in turn might explain why cognitive constraints (I.3) are critical for the logic of scientific revolutions. Art in contrast starts with materials which is a kind of physical constraint (I.1). This might explain why such physical constraints are critical for the logic of artistic revolutions. A case in point is architecture. First of all architecture is strongly site-specific (Graham, 2003). The Parthenon would certainly have given off a very different impression or evoked other ambivalent and intensive emotions of mass, volume and light if it had been placed somewhere else than on the top of Acropolis (this intuition is confirmed by the fact that the present building is only a shadow of its ancient glory). Physical constraints (stone) probably also constrained the chosen classical style. The Romans also used stone, but they had discovered the technique (V.3) which allowed them to build rounded arches (Kostof, 1985).

According to some historians of architecture, stylistic choice is also constrained further by subjective, aesthetic preferences. Thus, architecture tends to follow very different ideals (Pevsner, 1945/1990), either the ornamental or decorative style or the opposite, the functional or classical style. Ruskin's (1853/2001) aesthetic ideals leaned in the former directions, whereas Le Corbusier leaned more in the classical direction (Cinqualabre & Migayrou, 2015). I prefer to see these as two different prototypes (I.2) closely related to matters of composition (V. 2) but the fact that we find only these two basic prototypes indicate that there are deeper, basically physical constraints which we need to consider (compare Dawkins' 2005 concept "convergent evolution," III.2).

The role of physical constraints (I.1) plays a surprisingly important role in order to understand how artistic creativity (A-creativity) is constrained in practice (as noted by Elster, 1983, studying artistic practices is a better strategy than interview data, for a similar insight see Perkins, 1981). It is a physical fact that novels can only be appreciated by intermittent reading (Elster, 2000). In contrast the emotional effects of a painting are present already at short glance. A movie lasts about 90 minutes and is usually consumed during one sitting. A stage play tends to be somewhat longer but is over and done with during an evening's entertainment. The much longer time it takes to read a novel allows the writer to invite the reader into the inner, invisible thoughts of characters (McKeon, 2000; Holquist, 2002), but it also forces the writer to make such characters vivid and memorable (Culler, 1975/2002). This can best be done by techniques (V.3) that show the protagonists engaged in action which involves both protagonists and helpers (IV.5). But the author must also create suspense, which is done by withholding strategic information from the reader (Zalewski, 2009). This element of suspense should preferably be created from the start, say by giving a hint of the outcome or "destiny" of the main character or characters (Eco, 2002), but such techniques of anticipation have to be repeated endlessly to keep the reader on their toes (Barthes, 1966/2000). Professionals (II.3) do this routinely (Giddens, 1984, 1990; Kupferberg, 1996b; Carter, 2000), pioneers (II.4) invent new techniques (V.3), compare Symons (1987) and Lee (1996).

The problem of what makes art forms distinct is briefly touched upon in Kant's *Kritik der Urteilskraft*, a book which basically repeats Kant's general philosophy and has very little to say about artists' practices. The section on art forms is 14 pages long out of a book almost as long as Darwin's *On the Origin of Species*. In contrast the great bulk of Hegel's three volumes, about 1,500 pages long, *Vorlesungen über Ästhetik*, systematically compares different art forms with each other. Interestingly, physical constraints are one of the recurrent themes of the tree volumes. Thus, in Volume II, in a long chapter on the classical architecture of the ancient Greeks, Hegel mentions several physical constraints which an architect needs to consider and which in turn inform aesthetic choices. Some of these physical constraints are clearly related to the natural environment. In the Nordic countries of Europe, where there are often storms and powerful winds, roofs tend to be sloping to serve as protection against bad weather. In the Mediterranean countries the core problem is protection against the strong sun which would explain why roofs tend to be flat (Hegel, 1970, Vol. II, p. 314).

Whatever solution chosen for whatever reasons, the basic structure of all houses can be divided into three main components. The carrying part, the carried part, and the surrounding part (tragene, getragene, umschliessende). This again leaves the architect with yet another basic choice, whether the aesthetics of the house should strive for breadth (typical for Greek, classical architecture, see Kostof, 1985) or for height (typical for the medieval Gothic cathedrals, see Gimpel, 1983). Let us say the architect choses breadth. Here the architect can choose to leave the walls open or closed. The Greeks chose the former option, using columns as the carriers of the roof. Whatever the reason (such as closer connectedness with nature or indifference to storms and winds, mere protection from the sun), the result was a type of building dominated by flat roofs (getragene) and columns (tragene). This left little room for ornaments (umschliessende), which might explain why the columns themselves became increasingly ornamental (Doric, Ionic, Corinthian style) but also why a lot of aesthetic energy was spent on ornamenting the entablature (Kostof, 1985, pp. 765–766).

As noted by Hegel, classical architects, who quickly became experts on the construction of columns, mainly by stone, another physical constraint, soon noted that some perceptual peculiarities in the human eye made columns look thicker when they were too close to each other. In order to make them look slender or lean, they had to be placed at some distance. This points to the role of techniques as the core problem-solving strategy of artists (V.3) but also the role of final cause of art, which is to evoke emotions of some kind (V.4), which could be for example "calm" (an important emotion for Matisse) or feelings of "unity" and "harmony" (an important notion for the Greeks, compare Aristotle's *Poetics*), but hardly "movement." For this purpose sculpture or paintings probably work better (Barr, 1953/1976; Dondis, 1973).

Another point made by Hegel in his discussion of architecture was that the columns had to be thicker in the middle in order to look straight, from the point of view of the human eye (Hegel 1970, Vol. II, p. 322). Such techniques (V.3) illustrate the deceptive aspects of art noted by Plato in *Ion* (Cahn & Meskin, 2008), and one of the reasons why Plato wanted art banned from the republic. As noted by Gombrich (1996, 1997, 2000), the "illusory" function is constitutive for all visual or plastic arts. What is called "naturalistic art" is also illusion. A canvas (material, V.1) is flat but naturalistic patterns are there to make them full of life (Lopes, 1996), which requires inventing or learning techniques (V.3) that create the illusion of three dimensionality (fact into fiction, V.4). As noted by Berenson (1930/1960), the Italian Renaissance painters were pioneers (II.4) in this area, particularly the painters of Florence had a gist for finding ways to create the illusion of tactile qualities (touch, mass, volume,

light and darkness, etc.) on a flat surface. The painters in Venice specialized in the shimmering effect of color, which Berenson regarded as a
secondary type of technique (later rediscovered by Cézanne and Rothko).

The Cubists strived for the opposite. They intentionally abstained from
upholding the illusion of three- dimensionality in paintings. The ideal was
a completely flat and lifeless surface (Greenberg, 1961/1965). The Cubists
also abandoned the idea that a painting had to use traditional materials
(V.1). Braque seems to have been the first to replace (expensive) oil paint
with much cheaper types of industrial paint. In a next step, this abandonment of previous techniques (V.3) led to the use of other types of material
(V.1) such as bits of wallpaper or pages from magazines. These new
techniques served as prototypes (I.2) for coming generations of avant-
garde artists (from Duchamp to Warhol). But the idea of mixing such
different materials on the canvas ("collage") was probably inspired by the
basic technique of making movies, editing (Brecht's "montage" also used
this prototype, V.2). In both cases we are dealing with a kind of co-evolution
of artistic creativity (III.3).

Picasso later abandoned Cubism and invented new techniques (V.3)
aimed at making paintings look like sculptures (compare the massive
bodies in his "neo-classical" period, see Cowling, 2002). But the Cubists
also invented new techniques which aimed to obliterate the distinction
between painting and sculpture. Sculpture was modeled (I.2) upon the
techniques of Cubist paintings, and began to look like Cubist pictures, flat
and bereft of volume (guitars, guitar players), a case of intellectual migration (IV.2). This in combination with new techniques using unusual
material (V.1) led Picasso to experiment with other materials such as iron
instead of stone. Given that iron has a physical quality which makes it able
to stand on its own, this in turn (physical constraint, I.1) allowed for a new
the type of sculpture which created space and volume without mass and
with lots of light, giving sculptures an architectural quality (this idea was
followed up by the Danish sculpturer Robert Jakobsen, who learned the
new technique in Paris, see Højsgaard, 2001).

Using iron in this way, to create empty space, completely eliminated
the ideal or aim of naturalistic sculpture. Instead being of life-like,
sculptures were made as lifeless or "machine-like" as possible. This
indicates the presence of an extra-artistic constraint entering the machine
age of the twentieth century (a case of co-evolution, III.3). Such co-
evolution can also help explain the Futuristic and Constructivist movements in art (A. Moszynska, 1990). The Constructivist movement was
particularly strong in pre-fascist Italy and post-revolutionary Russia

(Honor & Fleming, 1982/1984, but this "machine" aesthetics also clearly influenced Le Corbusier (1931/2017), one of the pioneers (II.4) of twentieth-century architecture (Lampugnani, 1963/1986).

The paradox is that whereas Le Corbusier's machine aesthetics can be seen as a rediscovery of classical Greek or naturalistic architecture analyzed in great detail by Hegel, Cubism was essentially a return to the strongly Symbolist style of painting and sculpture characteristic of ancient Egypt (Honour & Fleming, 1982/1984). Michelangelo's rediscovery of these naturalistic techniques (V.3) can be seen both in his painting and sculptural forms (Stone, 1961). These techniques aimed precisely at making depicted or sculptured bodies "come alive," either by the illusion of movement, such as a discus thrower caught in the midst of a violent effort with muscular tensions and cringed body (see the commentary on sculpture by Matisse in Barr 1953/1976) or by an illusion of human skin concealing tense muscles and tendons (Honour & Fleming, 1982/1984). Both techniques require close observation of the human body. For the Greeks the dressed female becomes important (Honour & Fleming, 1982). For Renaissance sculpture (Stone, 1966) the naked male body becomes even more alive by borrowing the newest scientific methods (V.3) for observing corpses (another case of co-evolution, III.3). The new anatomical methods of observation had been pioneered by the medical faculty at Padua University, which for this reason became a center of medical research (support system, IV.5), attracting medical scholars from all over Europe. The main reason seems to have been Padua University's ability to protect vulnerable ideas within medical research, mainly by gaining secret access to (skunk works, IV.3) and exchanging confidential knowledge (IV.4) about corpses, the core data (V.1) of medical research. Geographical migration (IV.1) also led to groundbreaking work in medicine, in particular Harvey's discovery that the heart functions as a kind of machine or pump (Boorstin, 1985). Paris eventually took over the leadership in medical research at the beginning of the nineteenth century for somewhat different reasons. At this time standardized access to corpses had become the norm and Paris had become the "city of cadavers" (Dierig et al., 2003).

## Prototypes and Development Constraints

The second type of constraints, prototypes or development constraints (I.2), happens to be the core idea of Darwin's theory of evolution (common descent, see Mayr, 2004/2007). Vertebrates and crustaceans are two basic choices in the evolution of animals and such original or prototypical design (V.2) constrains all later transformations of species (Dawkins, 2005). In a similar way the limbs of mammals tend to be homological (Mayr, 2002; Ruse, 2006). The basic structure is the same, although the anatomy of such limbs can take many different forms which are adapted to the physical environment (the finlike limbs of whales living in the sea, the loose skin between the prolonged thumb and first finger of bats allowing this species to fly, hands and feet made for climbing in trees among chimpanzees, etc.). The role of prototypes for the evolution of human creativity (culture) can best be seen by studying the history and development logic of technology (Basalla, 1988; Petrosky, 1996; Vincenti, 1991/1993), although prototypes certainly also influence science (paradigms, disciplines, traditions) and the arts (compare the nude body, landscapes and myths in painting and sculpture, etc.).

Prototypes play a predominant role in the film industry, in particular Hollywood movies, which, at least since the 1920s have been dominated by one and the same aesthetic formula (Maltby, 1994): action-packed movies, exotic environments ("production value") and boy meets girl. This is probably best explained by the fact that the Hollywood movie industry can best be seen as a hybrid creativity regime, combining traits of technological and artistic forms of creativity (Kupferberg, 2006a, 2006b). As an art form, Hollywood movies transform facts into fiction and evoke emotions. As a technological industry, Hollywood constantly adapts to conditions of survival and reproduction of this peculiar industry (V.4). A case in point is Billy Wilder (Sikov, 1998). When he arrived in Hollywood in the 1930s his typically European "pessimism" fitted the predominant mood of American film audiences. Gradually, though the natural "optimism" of American society rebounded, Wilder's career slowed down until he was unable to make movies anymore. As noted by Fleming (1969), geographical and intellectual migrants (IV.1, IV.2) bring both attitudes and skills and both have to be right (III.4) for successful creative careers.

For avant-garde artists (painters and sculpturers), this is not a new discovery as Krauss (1986) claims but rather a case of independent rediscovery (III.2), compare (Josephson, 1941/1991). In contrast to de Vries, Krauss was too busy promoting her discovery (agency, IV.5) to search for possible obscure predecessors (obscurity in science might reveal lack of erudition in the field of languages). But rather than conceptualizing (V.2) the obvious role of prototypes in all art forms as a proof that artistic creativity is constrained, she opted for the postmodern First principle of contingency. For this to work, Krauss had to comply with another First principle of postmodernist theory, the death of the author, precisely the opposite of Aristotle's theory of the structure of creative processes, which does not work without the assumption of effective agency (V.3).

Both Matisse and Picasso had a predecessor, Cézanne's technique for reducing bodies to simple geometrical forms (compare Plato's ideal types). But this does not make Fauvism and Cubism identical. Matisse combined Cézanne's rediscovery of Plato's concept of ideal form for the purpose of composition (V.2) with the Symbolist use of color in religious art, redis-covered (III.2) by Gauguin (V.3) as his two main prototypes (I.2). As noted by the naive, autodidactic painter Henri Rousseau, both he and Picasso were "primitivist," but the early prototype for Picasso was the lifelessness of human bodies depicted in the purely symbolic Egyptian art (first depicted in *Les Demoiselles d'Avignon*). In contrast to science where independent rediscovery among pioneers is relatively infrequent, this seems to be the rule among artists. Picasso probably learned this technique by close observation of Iberian stone statuses and African masks.

African masks had mainly magical purposes (to scare off evil spirits and gods, compare Weber, 1922/1964). From the point of view of material cause (V.1) they could be made of anything available – wood, straw, feathers, etc. – an idea marginal to the Cubists but made into a main technique (V.3) by Duchamp, Art Pauvre, the Jackson Pollock branch of the Abstract Expressionists, Andy Warhol, etc. But Picasso also seems to have been constrained by another prototype (I.2), French Symbolist poetry (Picasso's two closest friends, François Jacob and Guillaume Apollinaire were Symbolist poets, see Richardson 1996/1997). French Symbolist poetry was in turn modeled upon German Romanticism in literature (Abrams, 1953).

German Romanticism represents what Hegel identifies as the third major type of artistic style, which can best be conceptualized (V.2) as expressive art, foregrounding the emotions of the creator (effective cause, V.3). There is a lot of anger in *Les Demoiselles d'Avignon* but also a lot of naughty humor. The strange and repelling noses of the two women to the right in the painting were in fact modeled upon (transformed form fact to fiction) upon his Afghan hound Kazbek, as a "commentary on the dog nature of women." As we know Duchamp built his whole career upon this single idea of art as a form of naughty humor (Tomkins, 1996). Given that pedagogy is a kind of exaggeration of the didactic (Ryle, 1949/2000) aspect of all science (getting it right presented as Ready Made First principles rather than as hard to come by, discovered and rediscovered First princi-ples), it is perhaps not surprising that the far too complex discoveries of Picasso were replaced by Duchamp as the preferred pedagogical prototype in art schools. This for some reasons only happened in the 1960s (Chaplin, 1994), which points to the need to look at changing problem situations as well when trying to define what "getting it right" means (III.4).

But the "expressionist " style also had its own history. It influenced such painters as Vincent van Gogh who mainly used the techniques of brush work (V.3) and the color yellow (material cause, V.1) to express the explosion of feelings which eventually drove him to commit suicide (Stone, 1934/1987). From the point of view of Weber's (1922/1964) sociology of religion, this act could be seen as an ultimate sacrifice, aimed to pacifying the gods, whose anger van Gogh for some inscrutable reasons had failed to soothe with his previous acts of penitence (being too lazy and forced to give up a privileged career as an art dealer, failing to function as a lay preacher, before trying to become a painter).

In the case of Edvard Munch, the other major expressionist (Prideaux, 2005), the overwhelming feeling is sadness, probably a result of mourning a sister who died at an early age. Whereas these feelings of mourning were at the start expressed in a mainly naturalistic, vivid style, as if he wanted to keep the memory of his recently dead sibling alive, the sad act of mourning is in his later works replaced by a strongly symbolic style, similar to the Egyptian style. A possible explanation provided by Weber's sociology of religion could be that the Symbolist expression of emotions was a kind of magic aimed at seeking to control the evil spirits. The memory of his dead sister had begun to haunt him and he needed to protect himself from being overwhelmed by such tragic memories and get on with his own life.

There are also elements of mourning the dead in Picasso's "Blue Period," resulting from the suicide of a close friend from Barcelona who had recently shot himself with a pistol in a dramatic scene in a Paris restaurant, after having missed killing his former lover. But in Picasso's case the style of these paintings is Mannerist, a version of baroque painting (elongated figures, see Gombrich, 1966). This style is very strong in the Spanish classical tradition (compare El Greco, the prototype for Spanish Mannerism). Picasso's "Rose Period" preserves the Mannerist style (also visible in Matisse's later paintings, the two were rivals and engaged in a kind of arms race, III.3) in the sense of composition (V.2) but does express a very different mood, symbolized by the choice of a very different color (material V.1). This makes Picasso's sudden transformation as the leading pioneer of twentieth-century art into something of a mystery, a problem I will return to later.

Expressivist art rarely exists in its own right but is usually combined with either naturalistic or symbolic art. But whatever combination is chosen, modern artists like previous artists use role models. Gauguin modeled his most famous painting, *Who are we, where do we come from, where are we going?* on Pui de Chavanne (Shackelford & Frèches-Thory, 2004). Gauguin's symbolic use of colors in the painting of Jacob struggling with the Angel Gabriel also has a mainly expressionistic purpose (Cachin, 1992). In contrast to, say, Nabokov, Gauguin seems to have had strong pedophilic longings, which he masked in his later paintings of brown-skinned Tahitian nudes (Mathews, 2001; Danielsson, 1965).

Given that techniques (V.3) make up most prototypes in art (I.2), choice of prototypes might also be indirectly caused by physical constraints. Architecture is perhaps the most physical of all art forms and this might explain why change in architectural style has historically tended to have an immediate impact (co-evolution, III.3) upon the style of the other visual arts such as painting and sculpture (Honour & Fleming, 1982). Twentieth-century art forms (not only visual arts) in contrast seem to have been dominated stylistically by the aesthetics of Hollywood movies (Robinson, 1996). The dreamlike quality of the Surrealist style was explained by pioneers such Dali as an effect of Freud's theory of the unconscious (Gale, 1997). But this is deeply problematic, given that the surreal effect was intentional, whereas the unconscious works unconsciously (Freud, 1938, 1968, 1977). The dreamlike quality of movies, which started with Méliès' film art (Ramsey, 1924/1964) is a better explanation of the origins of Surrealism (perhaps Freud's theory of dreams and the unconscious were inspired by movies as well).

The impact of film as dominating art form in the twentieth century is a problem of its own (co-evolution, III.3) which needs a separate investigation. Artistic revolutions are highly complex and paradoxical phenomena (compare the problem of explaining the origins of a painting such as *Les Demoiselles d'Avignon*). And how do we explain such a phenomenon as Jackson Pollock's "action-painting" (Meecham & Sheldon, 2005)? In all these cases though, prototypes (I.2) played a critical role, although for various reasons which need to be clarified. Prototypes are only one of many possible constraints which need to be disentangled in each concrete historical case.

One conspicuous aspect of twentieth-century art is the homelessness (Berger et al. 1973) of modern art, its abandonment of its own media and attempt to colonize other media such as poetry, sculpture, theater, film, popular culture, architecture and commercial art (Danto, 1997; Dickie, 2000). This phenomenon is strikingly similar to the survival strategies of reindeers as this species migrated north at the end of the last ice age

(Jensen, 2013) and can best be explained by investigating the impact of the rise of new media such as photography and film. The invention of photography (Edwards, 2006; Sontag, 1977) functions both as a pressure (I.Vb) and an opportunity (I.Vc). Both these aspects are prominent in the artistic career of Matisse (Spurling, 2009). Photography also functions as a prototype (I.2) for the Impressionists, making the act of painting into a more pleasurable (I.Va) experience. Compare the idea of "painting quickly" (Brettell, 2001) outdoors.

But painting fast outdoors (physical constraints, I.1) had other unintended effects upon the creative practices of painters. Photographs were much closer to everyday life and armed painters with the possibility of painting motifs in a more "spontaneous" manner (Thomson, 2006) in the sense that the composition (V.2) of the painting did not have to be as obviously organized or rigorously conventionalized as in academic painting where the rules of composition but also "framing" of the painting were very strict (Shiff, 1984).

But Impressionism was not a single style. It "transmuted" as species under protection (Dimension IV) tend to do. Manet's paintings still work with the basic technique of chiaroscuro, value or the distinction between light and dark (Wilson-Bareau, 1991/1995; Aristides, 2016). The innovation of Manet becomes visible when we contrast his style with French Renaissance artists such as Poussin. Following the basic techniques (V.3) of chiaroscuro, Poussin attempted to create a gliding or gradual effect between light and dark. Manet rejected this naturalistic effect by choosing the technique of strong contrast (the role of electricity in bars which Manet frequented, might have something to do with this aesthetic preference; in this case co-evolution, III.3 in combination with physical constraints, I.1 should be included in the explanation). The new technique of abandoning the gradualist effects to the chiaroscuro technique might have functioned as a prototype (I.2) in the sense of transitional form, compared with the post-Impressionist Cézanne. The difference between Manet and Cézanne is that Cézanne ended up abandoning the chiaroscuro effect all together and replaceed value with hue:

> Cézanne believed that "there is no line... there are only contrasts. The contrasts are not given by black and white, but by the sensation of color." In other words, nature was perceived immediately as contrasts of color, from these relationships of hue, any pictorial order of shape or modelling would follow as if automatically... Denis observes that even in the background areas, Cézanne's canvases reveal the scintillating pattern of contrasting colors." The entire canvas is a pastry where each color *plays* separately

and yet mingles in sonority in the ensemble. The characteristic aspect of Cézanne's painting derives from the juxtaposition, from this mosaic of separate tones gently merging one into another. "As a result of this technique, "the perspective planes disappear."" (Shiff, 1984, p. 123)

Cézanne's complete abandonment of chiaroscuro (value) for the brilliance of colors (hue) on the one hand represents a rediscovery (III.2) of the Venetian painters, but whereas they, as Berenson (1930/1960) noted depended on the naturalistic tradition, Cézanne departed from this tradition, by using Manet as prototype (I.2). Cézanne also used simple geometrical forms to solve the problem of composition (V.2). Both stylistic changes were part of what has been called Cézanne's "gaucherie" or return to "primitivism."

The return to "primitivism" of Late-modern paintings is somewhat of a paradox. One explanation could be to see it not as a "regression" but a way to protect the "craft" of the artistic profession. The new competitor photography was based upon modern, science-based technology. In contrast, painting has traditionally been a craft just as design was before 1900 (Pevsner, 1936/1991). Given that painting imitated photography (quick painting, spontaneous motif, rather than arranged composition, etc.), it needed to distance itself from association with this modern technology and this is where gauche or "primitivism" (Walther, 2005; Lynton, 1981/1989; Rubin, 1984) might be a good sign or symbol of why art was still different from modern technology. Compare the opposite strategy, machine aesthetics which on the contrary tried to model itself (prototype, I.2) upon late-modern technologies of rapid transport on trains, in cars, on boats and in the air. As noted by Thompson (2006), Duchamp's Readymades can perhaps best be seen as an attempt to make this alternative strategy a laughing stock (using Picasso's naughty humor in *Les Demoiselles d'Avignon* as his prototype).

What is called "primitivism" is not a logically coherent but ambivalent phenomenon. According to Shiff, Cézanne invented a new "technique of originality." By "unifying and repetitious patterns contrasting warm and cool colors that seemed to suppress, supplant, or simply supersede a differentiating chiaroscuro," Cézanne wanted the painting to look as if it had been painted in a spontaneous, unlearned manner, as if by a child. The reality was the opposite (paintings controlled by clear intentions): "His use of color *appeared* naïvely expressive, spontaneous. But it could also be seen as *signifying* the natural and the spontaneous" (Shiff, 1984, p. 123).

In a sense, Cézanne renewed Kant's theory of art as genius and gave it a novel and easily recognizable form (parsimony, III.1) which made it easy to use as a prototype (I.2). The first Late-modern painters, Matisse and

Picasso, saw the value of this particular prototype. Both recognized their intellectual debt to Cézanne, "the father of us all" (Richardson, 1996/ 1997). Learning techniques (V.3) help painters, filmmakers (compare Gottlieb, 2002) and fiction writers achieve their unique voice (Engdahl, 1994/2005) or style (Ross, 2003). But what does this mean in practice? Personal style can be studied on different levels. We can look at the evolution of single art works, the evolution of the art works of a single artist or the evolution of a single motif in art history. The best study which combines all the three levels is Ragnar Josephson's historical study of art (see Kupferberg 1995c, 1996a, 2013).

One of Josephson's many discoveries is that artists tend to reuse motifs (figure in compositions, V.2), which function as prototypes (I.2) for later works (compare his analysis of Leonardo's works). A similar strategy of parsimony (III.1) can be found in Picasso's works (minotaurs, doves, the female nude), in Paul Klee's works (birds, fishes), in Marc Chagall's works (cows, goats, severed heads, religious motifs). But reusing the same motif can also be a strategy to make the paintings more recognizable, which makes life easier for both private collectors, mentors and agents (IV.5, compare Greenberg, 1961/1965).The easily recognizable motif provided a common language for the different roles of the support system just as Newton's theory of gravity provided a common language for the ruling classes in England and promoted the first industrial revolution founded on science-based technology.

Recurrent motifs can be seen as central for the form or "composition" of an artwork (V.2) but such recurrent motifs can also function as symbols for a basic feeling which the artist seeks to evoke (Final cause, V.4). Not always successful, thus Matisse often tried to express the feeling of calm, but evoked very different emotions among art audiences (Spurling, 2009). There have been different attempts to explain the evolution of such recurrent motifs/easy recognizable signs of personal style, but whatever explanation we arrive at, biographical data (V.1) is probably the most parsimonious (III) from a creativity science point of view. Robinson's (2001) study of Chaplin's early movies reveal that the figure of the tramp evolved slowly and hesitantly. It was not a stroke of genius as Chaplin claims in his autobiography (1964). Bergman's two autobiographies (1989, 1990) are more reliable, but are nevertheless strangely silent about his early attempts to make it as a writer (Koskinen, 2002), or how this might have influenced his style of film writing (Koskinen & Rhodin, 2005).

Hitchcock constantly told the story of his incarceration in a police cell as a boy as the reason why he made the type of films he did (Taylor, 1978;

Truffaut, 1983/2017). It is far more plausible though that he borrowed this central motif as an apprentice in Germany (Gottlieb, 2002; Friedman, 2015). The "whom can we trust motif" becomes stronger and stronger over the years, perhaps culminating in *The Birds* where the feeling of paranoia becomes a threat to the whole human race by the rebellion of a normally shy species which usefully avoids human contact unless kept in a cage (the film starts as a meeting with a stranger in a shop in San Francisco selling caged presumably innocent birds which most certainly present more danger).

The remake of *The Man Who Knew Too Much,* originally shot in Weimar Germany in the 1920s, reveals where and from whom (problem situation and problem solver, III.4) Hitchcock learned how to make films which symbolized this motif (Gottlieb, 2002; Friedman, 2015). A similar feeling can be found in Fritz Lang's films, which Hitchcock knew intimately from frequenting German cinemas, but it can also be found in many of Brecht's plays from the same period (Schumacher & Schumacher 1978). The main difference between the two versions is that Hitchcock had exchanged the support system (IV.5) in between. This gave him access to the professional knowledge, technology and financial resources of Hollywood that allowed him to concoct an even more emotionally intensive story. In both versions, an innocent child is kidnapped and held as hostage in order to prevent the parents worried out of their wits from revealing a planned murder of a top diplomat. The most important difference between the two versions was that the two sets of parents were played by world famous movie stars. This made it much easier (parsimony, III.1) for movie audiences to identify with the bereaved parents and their dilemmas and accumulated fears.

Choice of prototypes in art is ultimately constrained by physical constraints though. In order to analyze these constraints in arts, a good method could be to identify types of cultural tools or mediated forms of the social (Kupferberg, 2013). Some art forms are primarily made out of texts (novels, plays, poems). Other art forms are made out of artifacts (architecture, sculpture, painting), some of which are less mobile (some sculptures are very heavy, almost like buildings, others, frescoes and friezes cannot be removed without removing walls). Theaters are more complex. They are both buildings (architectural artifacts) and use props (mobile artifacts), but for a live performance to work there also have to be actors and audiences and the physical interaction between the two is what produces the "magic" of the performance. Theater as an art form (Bentley, 1968) basically has a performative quality as do musical performances.

Films are tricky. From one point of view they are clearly artifacts (film, projector, projected images on a canvas). But they depend upon live actors performing in from of camera (performance plus artifacts). They are first shot under supervision of a director (effective cause) and later edited with the help of a machine (artifact). But they are usually based upon texts (novels), theatrical and musical performances but for a much larger audience (calculations). Theater and film are both constrained, but in very different ways. Theater audiences have to sit still. Only actors are allowed to move. In contrast, film has abandoned this physical constraint by the invention of the mobile camera (Arnheim, 1957).

## Knowledge Constraints

The third type of general constraints, knowledge constraints (I.3) and how they are overcome, is probably best understood by studying the history of science. Why did Aristotle believe that eels were reproduced by the "spontaneous generation"? Why did Galileo and not Aristotle manage to clarify the First principle of physics? Why did Darwin fail to independently discover Mendel's laws? Why could Linus Pauling and Rosalind Franklin not solve the "problem of the century" (Ridley, 2006), the structure of the DNA? Why was this task solved by two newcomers to the field, Crick and Watson (Watson, 1968/1996; Olby, 1974/1994; Crick, 1988; Maddox, 2003; Goertzel & Goertzel, 1995; Judson, 1997/2013)?

These are indisputable facts, but according to Popper's theory of science there is no such thing as indisputable facts (1998). But this cannot be correct. It is retrospectively (the Owl of Minerva) an indisputable geographical fact that there are such continents as North and South America with Central America and the Caribbean islands between them. The point is that such indisputable facts have first to be discovered and established. For this purpose, we need to separate fiction from fact. Art works in the opposite direction. Because the final cause or aim of art is to evoke emotions, art tends to transform fiction into fact (V.4). This transformation of fiction into fact is the essence of "rationalization," a core aspect of Weber's sociology of religion and possibly the ultimate conceptual source of the current confusions in the sociology of knowledge (the strong program of Bloor and the Dadaism of Bruno Latour).

Take the case of Columbus. At the time Columbus set out to find what he believed to be the shortest seaway to China, by sailing west, the actual size of the Earth was disputed. Columbus, probably because it served his purposes, chose to believe the most optimistic calculation, which later turned out to be completely wrong (fiction). Nor did he know that there was huge continent blocking his way and that he would only be able to reach his goal by sailing around it. Columbus manipulated his diaries in order to support his beliefs that he was close to mainland China (rationalization). Before and after his next three voyages, he held stead-fastly to his claim that what he had discovered could not possibly be a new continent but that he was still very close to mainland China. Both the claims and the fact that he was not are indisputable facts. So how can there not be indisputable facts?

In order to understand how Popper could makes such an elementary mistake we have to introduce the third form of knowledge. Popper correctly identified the final goal of science to be falsification (separation of fiction from facts), but he confused aim and procedures. The problem-solving strategy of science is methodology, not trial and error (V.3), which is the preferred problem-solving strategy of the engineer (but also nature and teachers). Indisputable facts are uninteresting for engineers. Technology is here to create new facts (V.4) or more generally practice knowledge. Columbus as Bergreen (2011/2015) shows was a highly skilled sailor who could master the worst possible storms and navigate in unknown waters. What he did in reality was to show that it was possible to reach this new and previously unknown continent. He created a new fact just as the Americans did when they landed the first man on the moon. This was indeed an impressive fact, but this is technology not science (compare the successful building of the new Tay bridge which could resist the strong gales in Eastern Scotland, described in Baxandall, 1985).

Technology is here to create new facts (V.4). This is because technology just like all living organisms constantly needs to adapt to changing physical environments over which they have no ultimate control but nevertheless want to survive and thrive (reproduce) as all living species are programmed to do. Science in contrast is here to falsify previous theories such as Newton's explanation of how gravity of distance (the theory of the "ether") is possible. Einstein's discovery of relativity theory (that gravity is a form of energy traveling with the speed of light) made the fiction of the "ether" unnecessary, just as the discovery of tectonic plates made Wagener's speculative explanations of how "continental drift" is possible unnecessary.

Creating new facts also requires knowledge, preferably scientific knowl-edge, nevertheless the aim is different and so are the problem-solving strategies. Popper's (1999) claim that "all life is problem solving" is no doubt correct, but from this it does not follow that scientists and engineers work in the same way (compare Berger & Luckman's descriptions of engineering as essentially "tinkering"). From a formal point of view, engineers transform "designs," whereas scientists transform "concepts" (V.2). Weber in his sociology of religions also talks about the role of "concept," but this is confusing. Religious belief systems are rationalizations (Elster, 2007) intended to evoke emotions, although of a special kind. This explains why they have the same formal structure as art; they are "compositions" (V.2). Religious beliefs reflect the concerns of religious communities, not merely the religious professions (magicians, priests and prophets) as Weber tends to claim.

As Weber noted, the appearance of prophets represents the hidden form or "rationalization." Prophets only appear in those cases when there is only one almighty and omniscient God (monotheism) with whom the religious community has struck a bond of mutual obligations (covenant), typically in the Jewish religion. As Weber reminds us, Christianity is not a strictly monotheistic religion. Jesus is not seen as a prophet but as half-god, half human, ideas widespread in the Mediterranean at the time. Such "idols" had no place in Mosaic law, which precisely institutes the idea of a covenant between God and humans. Weber's tendency to foreground the self-interests of the religious professions (religion is ultimately an economic phenomenon according to Weber, and this might explain why he devotes a chapter on the sociology of religion in his economic sociology, Wirtschaft und Gesellschaft) is strikingly reductionistic (economistic) and reflects a basic weakness in his thought.

Science is neither art nor technology. Technology creates new facts and art transforms facts into fiction. In contrast, the job of science is to separate facts from fiction (false beliefs). The fictive fact that organic molecules are much too small to constitute life (historical problem situation, III.4) functioned as a knowledge constraint (I.3) just as Newton's "ether." It delayed the discovery of DNA. Researchers for a long time also believed that such molecules had to be composed of many molecules, stitched together somehow. Later on, the belief that such a relatively simple molecule as DNA could not possibly be the core of life constrained the correct understanding of life, until Avery provided proof of the fact that it did. But this proof or evidence remained disputed for some time (historical problem situation). Even Crick, who together with Watson was to solve the problem some years later, was very skeptical of Avery's discovery from the start (Olby, 1964/1994).

But knowledge constraints can also take the form of knowledge interests (Habermas 1968a, 1968b). But what are knowledge interests and where do they come from? For Habermas, knowledge interests originate in the sciences which are conveniently divided into the natural sciences, the social sciences and the humanities (compare Hastrup, 1999). Whereas the humanities are interested in communication, the natural societies are interested in control and the social sciences are interested in human emancipation. But this cannot be right. The natural sciences are not interested in "control," but the engineering sciences are. Habermas confuses science with technology (compare Gouldner's, 1976 critique). The natural sciences as all sciences have a theoretical and not a practical purpose. They are interested in falsification which is their "final cause" (V.4).

But in order to become sciences, the natural sciences need first of all to clarify their First principles. A closer view of the natural sciences reveals that this is far from easy and it might take a long time (often thousands of years). This is because the precise nature of the knowledge objects of the natural sciences are highly complex. What is matter and how is it constituted? What are physical laws and how do they work in practice? Why are physical and biological laws not identical? One of Darwin's most important methodological discoveries was that physical laws are repetitive or cyclical (compare the idea of the rock cycle, the core concept, V.2 in geology). Darwin had to find other concepts to prove that biological laws function differently (such as "speciation," the separation of species with "common descent").

Knowledge constraints also explain why disciplines have great difficulties in communicating with each other (Bauer, 1990). This type of communicational constraint has been excellently analyzed by Nicolas Luhmann (1987). Compare his concept of "autopoiesis." Luhrmann's mistake is that he tends to project this phenomenon upon the way society works, just as Aristotle projected biological laws upon physical laws and Lyell projected physical laws upon biological laws. But what might be difficult to communicate between disciplines can be overcome by individuals. It is true that Lyell, the founder of geology, had great difficulty in understanding Darwin's biological theory of evolution, but Darwin, who had trained himself in both disciplines (personal problem situation, III.4), had managed to overcome this interdisciplinary knowledge constraint (I.3). So had Crick and Watson who became pioneers of the new discipline molecular biology because of their different intellectual backgrounds (intellectual migration, IV.2). Both Pauling and Franklin were basically physical chemists. Crick trained as a physicist (Olby, 2009) and did not hesitate to use the routine problem-solving technique of testing "bold conjectures" as a way to speed up the process of falsification (Collins,

1998). Watson had trained in zoology (Watson, 2001) and instinctively knew that in biology everything comes in pairs. He could therefore easily identify Pauling's elementary mistake.

Knowledge constraints ultimately also explain why there is no creativity science. In order to clarify the First principles of creativity science, data and methods (Chapter 8) have to be adapted to the nature of the knowledge object (Chapter 7). But all disciplines studying creativity are only interested in one tiny aspect of the problem. For Bohm (1998), an episode in the history of physics, Newton's discovery of gravity as "universal" force, serves as a prototype (I.2) for all forms of creativity. For Popper, Einstein's intended falsification of Newton's theory of the "ether," based upon the problem-solving strategy of the engineer (trial and error), serves as the prototype for scientific creativity. For Kuhn, Copernicus' failure to find a parsimonious model, which could reduce the number of epicycles in Ptolemy's model from +80 to zero (it is an indisputable fact that Copernicus' model only reduced the number of epicycles to +30, see Kline, 1953/1987), served as prototype for the falses theories (1) that there is no such thing as "falsification"; (2) that scientific revolutions do not solve tricky problems, only "normal science" is interested in problem solving; (3) scientific revolutions are sociological and linguistic phenomena and merely replace one type of language with another (taxonomic solution, incommensurability).

The problem with the "autopoiesis" as Luhmann noted is that "disturbances" hardly affect systems (disciplines) at all. This is because disciplines are problem-solving machines, programmed to solve certain type of problems of interest for this discipline (compare Habermas' concept "knowledge interests"). Economists in so far as they study creativity are mainly interested in technological creativity. Most of the humanities (including aesthetics, a philosophical subdiscipline) are concerned with either linguistic or artistic forms of creativity. The creativity of science has mainly been studied by philosophers, historians and sociologists of science, the first with a main focus on pioneering work or scientific revolutions.

Only the psychology of creativity has been concerned with a more general theory of creativity, but psychology is here to study individual problem solving. The problem is that in order to understand what makes pioneering work possible, we need to cast a much broader net and let it sink to the bottom of the ocean. Sociologists make the opposite mistake. They assume that individuals do not count, only institutions do (this is the core idea of the concept "social construction of reality," see Berger & Luckmann, 1966). Bourdieu's concept of "intellectual fields" and "symbolic capital" comes somewhat closer to the knowledge object of creativity science (Chapter 7). The problem with Bourdieu's method of theorizing (Swedberg, 2012), is that the core of creativity, sociocognitive problem solving, is ignored.

What Bourdieu calls "rules" of say art (1995) are merely forms of social recognition. They have nothing to do with whether pioneering artists like Picasso and Hitchcock, for example, were both able (capacity) and willing (motivation) to engage in solving complex and paradoxical problems within their chosen art form (painting and filmmaking). Nor is Bourdieu interested in the fact that these two models or prototypes (I.2) of avant-garde art and popular art have co-evolved (III.3), where one is threatened by extinction by the other art form. Nor has the concept of "rules" of art as used by Bourdieu had anything to do with the "final cause" (V.4) of all art, to evoke emotions. Nor is Bourdieu interested in the core of the problem-solving strategy of artists, techniques (V.3).

Bourdieu's concept "rules of art" has nothing to do with the aesthetic type of problem solving in which artists are constantly engaged (Elster, 1983). What this misleading concept (V.2) describes are the different strategies of publishers of fiction (the "literary field"), those who either specialize in publishing avant-garde books for small audiences but with a hopefully long lifespan or commercial publishers who prefer to publish bestselling novels which give immediate profit. Such choice of publishing strategies no doubt contributes to the accumulation of symbolic capital of writers of fiction such as James Joyce or Agatha Christie. The problem is that it tells us very little about the aesthetic techniques of these writers (V.3), nor the type of problems situations faced by problem solvers (III.4).

In the case of James Joyce the final cause (V.4) or audience are professional writers, interested in a pioneering writer's experimentation with new techniques of writing, art on art (Ellman, 1959; Magalener & Kain, 1955/1990; Burgess, 1990). In the case of Agatha Christie, the final cause (V.4) was the audience of lay readers, who were mainly interested in the pleasure of reading a good, professionally composed work of fiction (Thompson, 2007/2008; Morgan, 1984/2017). Agatha Christie can best be categorized as a good and solid professional writer (II.3). She continued in a typically English tradition pioneered long before she began a profes-sionally successful career as a writer of detective novels (Curran, 2016). Joyce was a pioneer (II.4) exploring new techniques of fiction (Symons, 1987).

Interestingly perhaps the predominant model for studying creativity in contemporary psychology, the Gardner-Csikszentmihalyi model (Gardner,

1987; Csikszentmihalyi, 1988) has more or less uncritically modeled itself (prototype, I,2) on Bourdieu's clearly non-cognitive model of intellectual fields and symbolic capital with the important difference that in this model pioneers do make significant contributions to the intellectual field (called domain, see Gardner, 1993). But this leads to a strangely disjunctive theory of creativity which assumes that the problem solving of the pioneer is exclusively cognitive rather than sociocognitive and that the problem of social recognition can be studied as an autonomous field, logically separated from the intellectual domain.

But this cannot be right. Intellectual domains and social fields are in practice strongly integrated. This can best be seen by studying the role of support systems for artistic careers (V.5). Such support systems can conveniently be divided into patrons, mentors and agents. The type of support that James Joyce received, where the publisher functions as patron, is highly unusual in literature which normally addresses huge lay audiences and not small elite audiences as in twentieth-century painting (Rauterberg, 2007). In order to live off writing as profession, the writer needs to create his or her own audience, who have become "fans" hooked on reading novels from this particular writer (see Svedjedal, 1999; Edström, 2002). Some great writers such as George Orwell and Saul Bellow only managed to achieve such professional success late in life and in the meantime had to support themselves with other forms of income such as journalism (Crick, 1980) or teaching (Lederer, 2015).

The dependency of novels as genre on mass or lay audiences, explains why novels from an emotional point of view have the final cause (V.4) of evoking what Aristotle identified as the core dramatic emotions of "pity and fear." This final cause functions as one of the basic rules or constraints for novels (I.4). These basic rules in turn constrain the choice of aesthetic techniques (V.3), rules for the use of suspense (Zalewski, 2009), originating in the physical constraint (I.1) of intermittent reading (Elster, 2000) and "vraissemblement" (Culler, 1975/2002) which derives from the need to extinguish the distinction between facts and fiction (V.4; Lamarque & Olsen, 1994; Eco, 2002). In contrast, science is here to separate fact from fiction (including moving from disputable to indisputable facts, where this is possible).

## Rules

Distinct rules of the game such as the rules of science, art, technology (I.4) still play a crucial role as constraints for creativity, in spite of the claims to the contrary by recent sociology of science (Bloor 1976, 1999; Barnes, 1982; Barnes et al. 1996; Latour & Wolgar, 1986; Latour 1984/1993). Although science and technology have increasingly come much closer together, to the degree that it is almost impossible today in solid state physics, for example, to identify what is science and what is technology (Rosenberg, 2010), this only means that the analytical task of categorizing and explaining in an era of "hybrid modernity" (Kupferberg, 2003a, 2007) has become more difficult. From this it does not follow that the difference in the training and tasks of engineers and scholars (scientists) has ceased to exist as prematurely claimed by Latour (1987, 1993).

The Nobel committee in Stockholm has probably contributed to this conceptual confusion by awarding Nobel prizes in physics to pioneers within the branch of scientific instruments (von Hippel, 1988) which is basically engineering. So is computer science (Isaacson, 2014/2015). But this only proves how difficult it is to "get it right" (Dimension III), whether in science, art or technology, all of which tend to be submerged in rhetoric, which in Late-modern societies have become science-based as well (business marketing, political spin doctors and possibly also art criticism, see Greenberg, 1961/1965 and Danto, 1997). Rhetoric or oratory (Aristotle, 1984b, 2152–2269) is a kind of fake science, in so far as it appeals to lay audiences who lack the patience or disciplined training to follow a complex argument (Rapp, 2009) and fake art in the sense that it seeks to evoke emotions that lack sincerity or authenticity (Kupferberg, 2003a; Tolstoy, 1898/1995). Compare Fest's two-volume biography of Hitler (1973/2014a, 2014b).

Most of the confusion of the role of rules derives from Popper's confusion of the final cause of science (falsification, V.4) with the problem-solving strategy of technology (trial and error, V.3). But once we renounce falsification as the final cause of science (V.4) and rule (I.4) anything becomes possible as Feyerabend (1975) claimed. In order to clarify Popper's, Kuhn's and Feyerabend's mistake, a good strategy might be to study the problem-solving strategies of artists, which turn out to be based neither on trial and error, nor on scientific methodology but techniques (V. 3). For a good description see Morell (2004) to be compared with the current confusion in sociology (Becker, 1997, talks of sociological methodology as "tricks of the trade," hence reducing methodological issues to techniques, the problem solving strategy of artists).

But nor are techniques mere "conventions" as Goodman (1976, 1978) argued. On the contrary, the choices of artistic techniques (V.3) are constrained (Elster, 1983, 2000). Painting as all art is constrained by the final cause of all art, to evoke emotions (V.4), but as an art form painting is also fundamentally constrained by physical facts (I.1) such as (1) paintings in contrast to fiction can be taken in at one glance (Lessing, 2008); (2) canvases in contrast to sculptures are flat, which means that mass, depth and volume (tactile qualities according to Berenson, 1930/1960) are illusions, the result of deceptive techniques; (3) the images painted are necessary static, hence movement can only be indicated, for example by the technique (V.3) of imbalance (Dondis, 1973). Painting cannot show characters in action. But moving images are also phenomenally illusions or deception, only because the human eye can only take in so much movement (up to 16 pictures per second, physical constraint, I.1, which is why the first movies, "flickers"(Robinson, 1996), went for this calculation, see Ramsay, 1926/1964).

Conventions do change. The Stanislavsky method, according to which artists should seek to evoke emotions among audiences by imagining being placed in a situation which brings forth similar feelings as the ones the playwright has tried to evoke and express in the play, is relatively new. We do not find it in Greek drama, where actors appeared on stage with masks and where the Chorus commented upon the ongoing drama. The type of techniques preferred by twentieth-century artists (Richardson, 1991/1992; Spurling, 1998/2000, 2009; Wullschlager, 2008; Helfenstein & Osadtschy, 2017; Scholz & Thomsen, 2008; Prideaux, 2005; Sweetman, 1995; Steffensen, 2017) are clearly also different from previous periods. But this does not prove that such changes are contingent, nor that the basic rules of art have changed. The rules of art are still to evoke and express emotions, not to falsify theories (V.4) and for this purpose choice of appropriate techniques, and not methodologies (V.3) is what we should look for. All art is a form of pretense (Walton, 1990), but the form of such pretense is usually constrained by physical constraints. Painters routinely use colors on flat pictures, which are inherently static. Hence we would expect these constraints to reappear among, for example, twentieth-century painters who do not use canvases, brushes, color, etc., but other types of materials (V.1) to produce their compositions ( V.2). Compare Teresa Beecroft's installations, commented upon in Kupferberg (2017b).

Such "colonizations" of other art forms by contemporary avant-garde artists (painters) illustrate a core idea of this book. Physical constraints (I.1) and prototypes (I.2) together with rules (I.4) constrain choice of techniques (V.3) but not in any deterministic sense. Take theater (live performance on stage). Chinese theater is more epic than dramatic, a theater foregrounding spectacle (Wickham, 1985/1992; Schumacher & Schumacher, 1978). But the two, drama and spectacle can also be combined as in the Elizabethan theater (Strong & Davies, 2005/2011b; Ackroyd, 2005; Bate, 1997/2008) or they can diminish the element of spectacle and focus on the element of drama as Greek classical drama (Hegel, 1970) or modern, naturalistic drama (Sprinchorn, 1982; Gottfried, 2003).

In order to understand stylistic changes, whether on a historical, professional or personal level (III.4; Ross, 2003), Hegel's distinction of three major types of stylistic constraints – symbolic, naturalistic (classical) and expressionist (romantic) – is a good parsimonious thinking tool. Whereas foregrounding physical constraints (I.1) of different art forms helps us to understand better the role of professional techniques (V.3) for making the strongly emotional world of the human species (Elster, 1999, 2007; Frijda, 2007) come alive (Why do actors use different techniques from fiction writers, painters, sculptures, architects etc.?), the three major types of stylistic approach (prototypes, I.2) help us to understand better changing historical constraints (problem situations, see III.4).

Richardson's (1991/1992) detailed study of the type of training Picasso received in the art schools of Spain (his own father in Málaga, the art academies in Barcelona and Madrid) reveal that a simple technique (V.3) for solving the compositional problem (V.2) of "proportion" critical for naturalistic representation, was to start by making simple geometrical figures such as circles, triangles, squares, etc. Cézanne's mature style of painting constantly refers to this simple, geometrical form (Harris, 1982). Here the aspect of professional training (II.3) dominates. In contrast, Chagall's more "narrative" techniques (V.3) to solve problems of composition (V.2) can probably best be explained by both his historical and personal situation (III.4) as a Jew in tsarist Russia in a city dominated by Russian Orthodox churches (Chagall, 1922/1965). Chagall's choice of professional techniques (V.3) had a clear "Russian" dimension. In fact they were modeled upon Russian icons as a prototype (I.2) which seek to objectify the core idea of Orthodox belief, the presence of Jesus the savior in the world, by the compositional (V.2) technique (V.3) of simultaneous narrative threads, a prototype (I.2) re-used again and again in Chagall's mature works (Makarius, 1986/1988).

## Motivational Constraints: Pressure, Pleasure and Opportunity

Marc Chagall's artistic career is a good example to illuminate and elaborate upon the last type of constraints, which are factors of motivation. Motivation is basically a question of career choice, professional commitments and a search for identity (Eriksen, 1968/1882, 1970; Hughes 1964; Becker, 1953, 1960; Kupferberg 1995b, 1999b, 2012a). Individuals in Late-modern societies, in contrast to middle or early industrial modernity, typically the type of society that Jane Austen describes in her novels (see Johnson 1991), are in principle free to choose their own careers and shape their own self-identity (Giddens, 1991; Beck 1992). But the choice of careers in Late-modern, highly individualized societies (Simmel, 1964) cannot be reduced to a "social construction" (Berger & Luckmann, 1966) for two reasons.

First of all in Late-modern societies, career choices are made by individuals and not groups or institutions (I became strongly aware of this fact when studying the contrasting case of East German biographies before and after unification, see Kupferberg, 1995b, 1998b, 1999a, 2000, 2002a). Moreover such career choices are made with great uncertainty, forcing individuals to become "entrepreneurs of their own lives" (Hughes, 1964; cf. Kupferberg 1996d, 1997, 1998c, 2001a, 2002b, 2014b). In Chagall's case this professional uncertainty increased as he became engaged to Bella Rosenberg (personal situation, III.4).

There is a class aspect here (Bourdieu, 2000). Given that Bella's parents had a much higher social status than his own family of origin, Chagall felt under *pressure* (I.Vb) to prove himself capable of supporting a family before the two could be properly married (Wullschlager, 2008).This motivated him strongly in his work, in particular as it led to a several years of physical separation, Bella living in Moscow and Marc in Paris. It was only when his artistic reputation had earned him a growing market both in Paris and Berlin, that Chagall felt that the he could now return to Vitebsk in triumph to claim his bride to be (Helfenstein & Osadtschy, 2017). When the couple reunited in Vitebsk in the spring of 1914, three years had passed since they had last seen each other.

Although artists do tend to be influenced by their physical environment (I.1) – this is clearly visible in Chagall's works made both before and after his first years in Paris (1911–1914) – Late-modern ("romantic") artists are basically preoccupied by their own feelings, which at the time were mainly feelings of uncertainty about his combined professional and personal future (III.4). The artistic problem for Chagall was how to express this uncertainty and evoke sympathy for the artist-character among the art audience of the artist's plight. Here the Paris years (Chagall, 1922/1965) presented an *opportunity* (I.5c) to learn and experiment with many of the formal styles (techniques, V.3) offered as prototypes (I.2) by being phys-ically close (physical constraints, I.1) to the paintings found in the studies and sometimes exhibited by the avant-garde artists of Paris. In particular, the Fauvism of Matisse and the Cubism of Picasso and Braque, the two dominant art movements at the time (1911), were important for Chagall's transformation from professional (II.3) to pioneer (II.4) and in this sense functioned as an opportunity (I.5c).

Traces of this intellectual influence (prototypes, I.2) are clearly visible in many of Chagall's paintings from this period, in particular the distorted perspective, the flat surfaces but also the coded language, forcing the art audience to look long and closely at the surface to decipher the meaning of the painting (Wullschlager 2008, pp. 125–148). Physical access (I.1) to these new styles clearly represented a historical, professional and personal (III.4) opportunity (I.5c) for Chagall to find his own, personal style.

> No academy could have given me all I discovered by getting my teeth into exhibitions, the shop windows. Beginning with the market-where for lack of money, I bought only a piece of cucumber - the workman in his blue overalls, the most ardent followers of Cubism, everything showed a definitive feeling for proportion, clarity, an accurate sense of form, of a more painterly kind of painting, even in the of second-rate artists. (Chagall, 1922/2018, p. 98)

This motivation relieved or compensated for the strong pressure (I.5b) he must have felt, both due to the "rational" type of uncertainty of his artistic career and the accompanying "emotional" uncertainty of his marriage prospects. For some reason, Chagall in his autobiography tends to belittle the importance of opportunity and completely ignore the role of pressure. What he foregrounds instead is the *pleasure* factor (I.5a), in particulate the excitement of artistic life in Paris.

Pressure and lack of pleasure are contrasted at the center of his narrative about 1921–1922 during another uncertain period of his life in Russia. At this time, he was married and had a child. The problem situation (III.4) had changed and the personal responsibilities following from this new social role must have weighed hard on him, in particular as it stopped him from doing the type of work that gave him great pleasure (similar motives are clearly present in Gauguin's biography as he decided to leave Copenhagen, to which he had moved with wife and children and return to Paris, see Sweetman, 1995 and Gauguin, 1956). Chagall laments that he traveled everyday between Moscow where he worked as a scenographer for a Russian theater and a small town outside Moscow where his wife and child waited for him.

Chagall's autobiography, written relatively early in his career also foregrounds the important role memory plays in his artistic work. Although Chagall did hire live models from time to time, most paintings are made from memory. This choice was imposed upon him given the geographical distance between the painter and his live model, Bella (physical constraint, I.1). All these biographical factors are important in order to explain the origins of Chagall's unique, highly personal style compared with other avant-garde artists. The core idea that paintings should tell an easy recognizable story or drama (narrative dimension), cannot merely be explained by his Jewish family background. Rothko, a pioneer of the "color field" school of the Abstract Expressionists (Harrison, 1994) also had a Jewish family background. But at the time Rothko entered the scene, the historical and professional problem situation (III.4) had changed. Chagall happened to be in exile in the USA at the time when the New York school evolved (Sawin, 1995/1997), but his personal style had at this time become recognizable and professionally successful. There was little temptation to change style. The time and place an artist enters the role as a "novice" (II.2) clearly matter for the choice of personal style or techniques (V.3).

Why did Chagall choose to become a painter? All career choices in late modernity are in principle uncertain or risky (Kupferberg, 1995b; pressure, I.5b). A possible way to ascertain that one is on the right track might be that working in this particular intellectual field brings joy and intensity (pleasure, I.5a) to the individual, possibly because the task is neither too difficult, nor too boring, which means it is challenging but nevertheless relatively easy to get it right (compare Vygotsky's "zone of proximate development," see Kroksmark, 2003). Most novices make a number of blunders and need constant instruction but also correction to go on trying (Bruner, 2006a, 2006b). For others it comes relatively easy because working in this area routinely creates moments of flow (Csikszentmihalyi, 1996). But some careers might be difficult to pursue although they give the individual great pleasure/feeling of flow. This is where help from the outside (opportunity, I. 5c, but also helpers, see IV.5) becomes critical. Without such opportunities and support systems, even highly talented individuals might give up prematurely.

The model seems to work for Chagall's choice of career as an artist. His first teacher, Pen, was a relatively successful artist with a similar Jewish background as Chagall. Pen had settled in Chagall's hometown Vitebsk and opened an art school. This no doubt presented a huge opportunity (I.5c) for the young Chagall, who had artistic inclinations but had not yet settled for a career as an artist. After a nervous visit accompanied by his mother, Chagall was accepted as a pupil at Pen's school around 1905. His teacher must have seen that drawing came easily for Chagall (pleasure, I.5a). This type of motivation (pleasure) seems to be the main motivation for novices (II.2). From Pen, Chagall, who was but a talented novice (II.2) at the time, "received the solid classical art education, organized along academic lines – lessons in drawing, plaster casts, copying drawings, working with a model, depicting a still life from nature – that was the bedrock from which all the revolutionary Russian modernists, from Kasimir Malevich to Wassily Kandinsky, went their own ways." This was because they all started by learning the basic techniques of art, "Exact reproduction of nature, mastery of drawing, rhythm and propor-tion." Techniques (V.3) can only be learned from prototypes (I.2). Such learning naturally comes easier if the teacher is a good professional (II.3), which seems to have been the case. Chagall "learned the basics of his craft easily and quickly from the patient, enthusiastic, nurturing Pen, who empathized passionately with his pupils" ((Wullschlager, 2008, p. 45).

Chagall's solid early training as a novice (II.2) clearly influenced his transformation from mere professional (II.3) to pioneering artist (II.4). Take the case of Chagall's famous paintings of Jews and rabbis. From Pen, Chagall had received a thorough training in Rembrandt's techniques and motifs. Rembrandt serves as clear role model (prototype, I.2) for these paintings. But access to this prototype has been mediated by Pen as mentor (IV.5). Although Pen himself never had the ambition to become a pioneer (II.4) but merely a professional artist (II.3), as an art teacher Pen nevertheless helped foster a pioneering artist by helping Chagall to take the step from novice (II.2) to professional (II.3). But without profes-sionalism there can be no pioneering work (for the case of Sylvia Plath, see Bain, 2001). This is why Chagall's mentor-learned (IV.5) problem-solving capacity is present in his original work. Pen had "acquired an impeccable mastery of traditional techniques but showed neither originality nor a desire to be modern." He derived his style from a painstaking allegiance to Rembrandt whose works, first encountered at the Hermitage's out-standing collection, he copied endlessly and from the realism of the Russian Peredvizhniki (Wanderers) group" (Wullschlager, 2008, p, 43).

Chagall continued his studies to professional artist at several art schools in St. Petersburg in 1908 and arrived in Paris in 1911. His main reason for leaving was that he wanted to continue his studies with the even more successful, world famous St. Petersburg artist Léon Bakst, whose art school Chagall had attended for about a year. Bakst was at the time moving away from avant-garde art, to become a scene decorator for Ballets Russes and probably feared that his highly talented pupil would become a formidable, unwanted competitor, if he, the master, invited his pupil-apprentice to join him in Paris. But, in spite of his attempts to discourage his best pupil

from following him to Paris Chagall went there anyway in the spring of
1911. One of his many Jewish art patrons (IV.5) in St. Petersburg,
belonging to the leading circle of liberal members of the Duma, Maxim
Vinaver, volunteered to pay for Chagall's journey to Paris as well as provide
him with a monthly grant of 125 francs for the purpose of studying art in
the French capital (opportunity, I.5c). Paris had at this time become the
unsurpassed center of the art world (Hall, 1999).

Chagall's breakthrough years as a major artist seem to have started
during the years he spent in Paris (1911–1914). As indicated in
Chagall's autobiography, the opportunity (I.5c) to come to Paris gave
him great pleasure (I.5ca), although he was completely quiet about who
gave him this opportunity (patrons, mentors. IV.5), nor does he mention
the personal pressure (I.5b; III.4 ), the need to prove himself worthy of
marrying Bella. Nevertheless it was Vinaver's (patronage, IV.5) offer to
finance Chagall's travel and stay in Paris in combination with what he had
learned from his mentors Pen and Bakst (IV.5) that provided him with this
lifetime opportunity (I.5c) comparable with Henslow's role as both mentor and agent promoting Darwin's chance of a lifetime to sail on the *Beagle*
(see Browne & Neve, 1989).

Chagall in his self-presentation *My Life*, claims that he learned nothing
from either Pen or Bakhst, presumably because he was unable to receive
instruction and help from his main mentors (IV.5), This might be true in
an emotional sense (Chagall was very sensitive to criticism). Nevertheless
Pen's deep understanding of Rembrandt's techniques are clearly visible in
Chagall's many paintings of rabbis. The time spent with Bakst was not in
vain either. Indeed Chagall's transformation into one of the leading
colorists of the twentieth century probably derived from Bakst (mentor,
IV.5) but also the prototypes (I.2) which Bakst's students copied from,
although they only understood the full meaning of this pedagogy later
(compare Wertsch, 2007 and Barr, 1953/1976).

> Announcing that Gauguin, Matisse and Maurice Denice were the artists of
> the future, Bakst led students towards a modern internationalist idiom,
> where they could find their own form of expression in a spirit of intellectual
> independence. To simplify form, enhance color, and liberate brushwork
> were the goals. Still lives were composed of simple crude, objects. Models
> were chosen for their unusual silhouettes, and beautiful ones were not
> invited. Students painted on rough, coarse grained canvases such as sack-
> cloth, used carpenter's glue for the ground and wide brushes (narrow fine
> ones were banned to achieve sweeping strokes and a thick paint surface). To
> retain freshness of expression, underpainting and preparatory drawings were

discouraged; colour combinations above all were emphasized. So were a certain monumentality. Bakst had made his name as a set designer in Paris and had his doubts about the future of easel painting, dreaming rather of a decorative style harmonized with architecture. (Wullschlager, 2008, p. 113)

But Chagall's transformation from professional (II.3) to pioneer (II.4) cannot be explained merely by support systems (IV.5) and motivations (I.5a, I.5b, I.5c). The historical, professional and personal problem situation of a Jew who had been born and grown up in Vitebsk (physical constraints, I.1) also play an important role. The personal unique combination that constitutes Chagall's creativity (compare Koestler, 1964) is indicated by Chagall himself in his autobiography: in the beginning it was the shock of the new that impressed Chagall. "It was as if Russian art had been condemned by fate to follow in the wake of the west ... Here, in the Louvre, before the canvases of Manet, Millet and others, I understood, why my alliance with Russian art had not worked. Why my very language is foreign to them" (Wullschlager, 2008, pp. 96–97).

Over time though, disillusion with such a formalistic view of art set in. As noted by many other artists, Chagall's type of "primitivism" was close to Matisse's "Fauvism" where the use of color techniques (V.3) play a critical role (Whitfield, 1967/1994; Barr 1953/1976). Chagall's preference for the use of color had also been noted by his previous mentor (V.5) Bakhst, whom Chagall met in Paris "your colors sing" (Chagall, 1922/1965, p. 101). Bakhst's view on color was very similar to Cézanne's and the Impressionists. "Hue" was more important than "value" (the core idea of chiaroscuro technique (V.3) for both emotional and aesthetic effect (V.4), "Art is only contrasts...I have a taste for intense color and I have tried to achieve a harmonious effect by using colors which contrast with each other rather than a collection of colors which go together ... Bright, pure color is the natural taste" (Wullschalger, 2008, p. 113).

Having been convinced of his own strengths and that he had something to contribute by his previous mentor (IV.5), Chagall's first, overenthusiastic appreciation of the formal experiments of Cubism changed as he became less and less impressed by French art.

Let them choke themselves with their square pears and their triangular tables. . . . perhaps my art, I thought, is a wild art, a blazing mercury, a blue soul leaping up on my canvas. And I thought: Down with naturalism, Impressionism and realistic Cubism. They cramp me and make me sad. All the questions are brought up again – volume, perspective, Cézanne, Negro Art. Where are we going? What is this age that sings the hymns of too technical art and makes a god of formalism? (p. 105)

Perhaps it was not as simple as a linear theory of progress in art assumes. "Russian painters were condemned to be pupils of the west; they were, I think, rather wayward pupils, by their very nature. The best Russian realists' shocks when compared with the realms of Courbet. The most authentic Russian impressionism is puzzling when compared with Monet and Pissarro...I love Russia" (Wullschalger, 2008, p. 97). Matisse when he first came to Russia (Spurling, 2009) to meet his patron (IV.5), Schuchkin (Barr, 1953/1976), was also attended by the "primitivist" power of Russian icons. But it was Chagall who understood that this tradition had solved a problem that he had been working on for a long time: how to replace the classical linear narrative dominating the western religious tradition, where a narrative is structured by time. In Russian icons, narrative threads are co-existing in memory, which was precisely Chagall's solution to the problem of modern art. A case in point is Golgotha from 1912.

> In place of a canopy enclosing the central events, the scene of action is framed by a series of secondary scenes fitted together that fail to provide a clear narrative structure. The simultaneity of action and the eschewing of precise localization of the individual events defines the structure of the pictorial presentation The spatial setup makes it impossible to locate the setting, and the relationship between interior and exterior is ambiguous... a strategy inherent in icons in which temporal sequences are blurred. (Schellewald 2017, p. 111)

But would Chagall have rediscovered the strength of the Russian tradition of non-linear narratives had he not been prepared to appreciate the "hue" technique (V.3) from his mentor (IV.5) Bakst? "Uninterested in naturalistic accuracy, he [Bakst] rated a painting according to the tone and texture, tensions and dialogues, among the colors; he encouraged simple drawing and forbade black outlines, because they interrupted the flow between colors" (Wullschlager, 2008, p. 113). Bakst's influence on Chagall confirms the complexity and paradoxes of creativity and why one-factor theories do not work (compare the Anna Karenina principle, see Chapter 8). It also falsifies the idea of the "death of the author." One of the core weaknesses of Barthes' theory is that it is modeled upon the myth of the French writer, dedicated to this one language, the French language of which writers are presumably mere "instances" and where life (personal needs) is in complete service of art. But artists are mere humans. They are vulnerable, have private lives, move often between different cultures and might even change profession.

Per Kirkeby was vulnerable from the start of life, but also highly privileged at the same time (Steffensen, 2017). His father married beneath his social class, his parents were atheistic communists, his grandparents were strongly religious. The marriage was unhappy and Kirkeby had great difficulties at school, learning to read very late. His original choice of career, to become a geologist, can best be seen as a way to get away from the tensions of home (pressure, I.5b) but also a form of physical constraint (I.1; a similar longing to get away can be found in the autobiographical novels of Martin Andersen Nexø, Aksel Sandemose and Karl-Ove Knausgaard). Kirkeby started his career as painter after returning home from a summer's field work in Greenland, to which he returned several times later. Geological and physical constraints (I.1) of landscape far away from "home" and "family" are strongly present as motifs and composi-tions, V.2, in Kirkeby's paintings (see Morell, 2004). After his return, Kirkeby discovered the pleasure (I.5a) of painting. He applied and was accepted by an experimental school of painting in Copenhagen (opportu-nity, I.5c).

Kirkeby ended up having children with and marrying women who were much stronger than him psychologically. They constantly humiliated him in front of their friends and professional colleagues. His tremendous success as the most rewarded and commissioned artist in post-Second World War Denmark and Scandinavia (Tøjner, 2008; Gohr, 2008) did not make Kirkeby any happier but more unhappy and vulnerable as a person. His art was in a sense what saved him from going insane and committing suicide (like his mother, the first woman in his life through her own example (prototype, I.2). She demonstrated that no woman, not even mothers, can be trusted (Steffensen, 2017), the basic but hidden motif mirrored and masked in his art. In contrast, the avant-garde film maker Lars von Trier uses his film art as a way to take revenge on a mother who failed to understand the simple truth that children cannot educate themselves. They need mentors (IV.5) and prototypes (I.2) to model themselves upon (Schepelern, 2000).

Matisse is another example which tells us how this works in practice and how support systems (IV.5) in practice constrain motivational constraints. Matisse decided to become a painter rather late in life. He had spent a year in Paris studying law and started a career as legal clerk, which he regretted, and begged his main patron (IV.5), his own father (a professionally successful merchant in Bohain-en-Vermandois, the center of the textile district in north-eastern France – physical constraints, I.1), to let him have the chance of becoming a professional artist (II.3).

This would take many years and without his father's reluctant patronage (IV.5) Matisse would never have become the Matisse we know from intellectual biographies about this pioneering avant-garde painter. He, together with Picasso, paved the way for the likes of Duchamp and conceptual art. The two changed or transformed the historical and professional problem situation (III.4) for professionals (II.3) but also novices (II.2) entering the profession mostly but not exclusively via traditional art schools. For this purpose, biographical data are of great value.

Why did Matisse become a pioneer (I.4)? Matisse's vocational choice did not come unprepared; he had found pleasure (I.5a) in painting long before he opted to make it his vocation. At the start he was mainly encouraged by his mother (as Chagall) and he had also been taught by local teachers. Arriving in Paris at a relatively late age, he found himself demoted to the role of the early novice (II.2), a life stage he had already been through and had not expected to have to go through again. Pleasure (I.5a) was suddenly transformed into pressure (I.5b) to prove himself. Coping plasters and copies of art works were not what he needed in this stage of his learning process. What he wanted and what Paris could offer was the Louvre, and the opportunity (I.5c) to study the original masters. He had come to Paris expecting to take the last steps in the transformation from novice (II.2) to professional (II.3) and was reduced to the position of a child (II.1) taking the first step to become a novice (in this case being introduced to the techniques of art. V.3). This probably led to a crisis of identity (see Dimension II), which in turn functioned as a pressure (I.V.2) to innovate. Once again the complexity and paradoxes of creativity need to be foregrounded.

# CHAPTER 3

# Dimension II: Levels of Creativity

## Are Children Romantic Geniuses?

In order to study levels of creativity we need to reject two myths, the myth of genius (II.5) as a necessary condition of pioneering work (II.4) and the opposite myth of children as romantic geniuses (II.1). The myth of children as romantic geniuses entered pedagogy with Rousseau's book *Émile ou de l'education,* although it can probably be traced back to Plato's dialogue "Menon" (Kroksmark, 2003). We should separate this myth from the core problem of education: why is it that the natural curiosity of children tends to die when they start school, a problem already noticed by Dewey (1917/1997) and which led him to suggest that schools (Dewey, 1902/2000) should try to imitate the problem-solving strategy of nature, trial and error, the root of Dewey's "pragmatist" approach. Dewey also had some interesting things to say about art (1934/2005), in particular its "holistic approach" (science is analytical; art on the contrary is inter-disciplinary and helps us make visible the elements of drama in human life, including intellectual careers) but Dewey's influence on how schools think has been diminished by a lack of clarity. Like Popper, Dewey tended to reduce scientific methodology to trial and error (V.3), see in particular Dewey (1917/1997).

Looking for pragmatic solutions is typical of the way nature routinely solves problems, but this is not how science works. This indicates that rigorous scientific types of thinking have to be postponed and it should not by imposed upon young minds but introduced gradually. Scientific thinking is unnatural and it is not programmed into the human mind as cognitive science assumes (Gardner, 1983, 1993; Carruthers, 2002). Precisely these assumptions also might explain why the natural curiosity of children tends to die when they start school. The theory of children as romantic geniuses legitimates a type of problem-solving strategy (V.3) which is unnatural. It is not the case that the methodological thinking of science is hardwired into the human brain (compare Vygotsky's carefully controlled experiments, reported in Vygotsky 1999).

Vygotsky was not as critical of Piaget as is often assumed. On the contrary, his data confirmed Piaget's basic discovery, that children have great difficulty thinking in terms of scientific concepts (V.2). This comes out most clearly in mathematics (Rothenberg, 1977). Piaget's very detailed studies (Kroksmark, 2003) have during the last decades been strongly attacked for widely underestimating the inherent capacity of children to think like advanced or abstract mathematics does (concepts such as space, volume etc.). These abstract concepts only need to be made concrete, and the problem is solved, at least from a pedagogical point of view (Bruner, 1960/1977).

But this precisely avoids the problem discovered by Piaget. Why do children have such difficulty thinking in terms of abstract concepts? Bruner in his attempt to renew educational philosophy (Bruner, 2006a, 2006b) tried to overcome Piaget's hesitation about the capacity of young children to learn abstract mathematics by combining it with Vygotsky's theory of the "zone of proximate development" or "scaffolding" as he called it. But this is avoiding the core of the problem. Scientific thinking is not pro-grammed into the human mind or brain. The brain is a practical and an emotional problem-solving machine. It is not a theoretical problem-solving machine (compare the critique made by the sociological phenomenologist Alfred Schutz, 1971–1973).

But not only did Vygotsky prove the theory of romantic genius in the field of abstract mathematics to be wrong. He entered the psychology of creativity from the psychology of art (Vygotsky, 1971). Having studied art works and artistic practices in great detail (he wrote his Ph.D. on *Hamlet*), Vygotsky realized that although children have a natural inclination to express emotions by simple symbols (compare Arnheim's, 1962 example of a tree with hanging branches which a child instinctively recognizes it as being "sad"), professional artists use techniques (to express and evoke emotions and such techniques have to be learned). In particular natural-istic techniques of representation aimed at making pictures "come alive" (Lopes, 1996; Nobel, 2001) seem to be the most difficult to learn, which might be the reason why children tend to give up relatively early when trying to draw and paint in an naturalistic style (Vygotsky, 1995).

Strangely children tend to be natural actors. A wonderful example of this is a boy holding a broom between his legs, pretending to ride a horse (this example is the prototype, I.2 for Walton's, 1990, 300-pages-long philosophical investigation of the meaning of make-believe). But as noted by Stanislawsky, what is natural for children is unnatural for grown-ups, which is why long training is required to become a professional actor. One of the reasons is the problem of self-awareness (Stanislavsky, 1944; Giddens, 1984) which tends to set in around puberty when the self-identity of individuals in modern societies tends to develop (Eriksen, 1968/1982). Another reason might be that the number of societal roles which the child can imitate is rather limited at the start and the number of significant others is small. To reach the level of the "generalized other" takes many years (Mead, 1934/1967; Giddens, 1993). Given that the fundamental emotions of children have been shaped by the limited number of significant others, there might be an emotional block which has to be overcome, and this is where professional techniques (V.3) for overcoming this emotional barrier become important and the first hurdle to overcome in training to become a professional artist (Stanislavski, 1967; Chekhov, 1953/2002; Hodge, 2000).

Solving problems in the arts is more natural from the point of view of the way the human brain works, due to the important role that emotions play in human life (Elster, 1999, 2007; Frijda, 2007). Nevertheless artistic techniques for evoking and expressing emotions also have to be learned in genres such a poetry, where ancient myths and symbols have to be consciously used and referred to (Tafdrup, 1991/1997; Kroll, 1976/2007). This makes the relation between art and emotions (Hjort & Laver, 1997; Langer, 1948/1958, 1953/2008) much more complicated than in everyday life where more or less instinctive body language is enough (Darwin, 1872/2009), independently rediscovered (III.2) by Goffman (1959). But film has also profited from this innate problem-solving capacity of the human mind. The film camera made it possible to get close enough to the human face to simulate the "behavioristic" type of communication (Müller, 1996) which starts right after birth of the human child.

Such emotional, unmediated communication is indeed spontaneous. In contrast what is called "primitiveness" in modern art is highly conscious and planned, the idea is to "give off the impression of spontaneity" (compare the "technique of originality," V.3, mentioned by Shiff, 1984). This element of planning can already be found among the earliest art forms, the Paleolithic cave paintings. Not only were they highly naturalistic (Hauser, 1979) and technically sophisticated (Honour & Fleming, 1984) they must have been planned carefully in advance (why they were placed in caves which were difficult to access and had to be illuminated to be seen at all, see Pfeiffer, 1982).

Most probably these cave paintings were only to be seen during special rituals (Lewis-Williams, 2002). This "ritualistic" element has been an important aspect of modern art (compare the drip paintings of Jackson Pollock, Edward Lucie-Smith, 1999, and Beuy's Coyote performance at MoMA in New York). The performative type of Primitivism was invented by the surrealists and transplanted to New York by exiled artists (Sawin, 1995/ 1997). The exiled artists functioned as prototypes (I.2) for the New York school of art (a kind of intellectual migration, IV.2 by transmission, see Coser, 1984), Another type of "Primitivism" has been the attempt to imitate children's art. But such art has been made by professionally trained artists and could not have been made by children. Compare Klee's remark "if my works sometimes produce a primitive impression, this 'primitiveness' is explained by my discipline, which consists of reducing everything to a few steps. It is no more than economy; that is the ultimate professional awareness. Which is to say, the opposite of real primitiveness" (Scholz & Thomsen 2008, p. 98).

As noted by aesthetic philosophers and art historians (Hegel 1970; Gombrich 1996) "symbolic" forms of representation come naturally for children. Even a three-year-old can easily draw four round circles, as symbols for a car (Kress 2000). More advanced symbols such as the Egyptian way of depicting the human body (Gombrich, 2000) such as the face in profile, upper body shaped as a triangle, both feet in the same direction and both showing the inner side of the foot (which is contrived and physically impossible, facts into fiction, V.4) are in contrast based upon techniques (V.3) which have to be learned (novice, professional, II.2, II.3). But before they can be learned they have to be invented or discovered (P-creativity as H-creativity in the realm of A-creativity), which is the job of the pioneer (II.4).

Professional acting is also based upon certain techniques that have to be learned such as abstracting from or ignoring the "fourth wall," the presence of a live audience and the technique (V.3) of going into a character by remembering similar experiences in once own life. Neither abstract mathematics, nor professional acting, nor naturalistic or complex symbolic art, is built into the human brain. Both scientific method and artistic techniques (V.3) have to be learned and this is the reason we have the categories novices (II.2) and professionals (II.3). But before they can be learned they have to be discovered, which is what pioneers (II.4) are here for (sociocognitive role) and why one of the First principles of cognitive science (that both science and advanced art are built into the human brain, see Gardner, 1993) cannot be right.

This does not exclude another First principle of cognitive science, the idea that if programmed machines can think so can human brains (this served as falsification of the First principle of behaviorism, see Gardner, 1987). The confusion probably comes from the second important and valid discovery of cognitive science, the programmed capacity of children to learn human language. This second First principle is the only reasonable explanation why spoken language is learned so quickly during the first three years of life (Crystal, 1987; Pinker, 1995; Vygotsky, 1999).

Bruner's critique of Piaget's studies on the great difficulties that children have in learning mathematics, seems to be based upon a projection of this prototype (I.2) of natural learning upon more advanced forms of learning which are a result of culture (C-creativity) rather than nature (N-creativity). Bruner was one of the two founders of the discipline "cognitive science" (Gardner, 1987). Cognitive science can best be seen as a "unique combination" (Koestler, 1964) of two main ideas: (1) the basic idea of computer science (Isaacson, 2014/2015), that programmed machines can "think" in the sense of solving complex problems and (2) Chomsky's discovery of a "universal" grammar, built into the human mind. This discovery was later confirmed by more recent discoveries of the natural, easy, spontaneous way that children learn spoken language. But there might be a third source of the idea of children as romantic geniuses namely the turn to Primitivism in modern art (painting). Compare Picasso's claim that he spent the last part of his life learning to paint as a child.

This reflects the fact that autobiographical data of artists are rarely reliable. They should be seen more as presentations of self which might vary with context (Kupferberg, 2012a). Klee's factual account is an exception to the rule and probably reflects the fact that Klee worked for many years as an art teacher at the Bauhaus. In this case, Klee's factual account has been confirmed (independently discovered, II.2) by growing academic interest on Klee's life and work. An important belated discovery (Owl of Minerva) was that Klee's Primitivism was both intended and a result of professionally learned techniques. His "new combination of formal simplicity and illustrative story telling" was grounded in

> Klee's long-term revalidation – though not imitation – of children's art. His watercolor *Landschaft der Vergangenheit* is an autobiographical testimony of his imaginary regression into childhood, since it harks back to a landscape watercolor he had painted at age eleven. Klee enriched his watercolor technique through a multitude of innovative groundings and pigments which enhanced effects beyond the technical means of the medium.

Hence most of his new watercolors could not be mistaken for children's work, however childlike they might look. (Schuster, 2008, p. 44)

The turn to Primitivism reflects the historical and professional problem situation of twentieth-century avant-garde painters (III.4), but a closer look at pioneering twentieth-century painters such as Matisse, Picasso, Klee and Chagall, confirm that this technique was a result of a long process of searching to renew painting by returning to or rediscovering (III.2) techniques which had been invented much earlier. These techniques (V.3) were neither "spontaneous" nor "primitive" they were planned and complex. But although professional concerns were no doubt driving forces, some avant-garde artists such as Dadaists and Surrealists were probably also enraged by the brutalities of the First World War. The Spanish Civil War was also immensely brutal, but on an interpersonal level (mass executions, rapes, torture, etc. see Beevor, 1982/1999). *Guernica's* description of human suffering by impersonal machines paradoxically underestimates the cruelty of what humans can do against humans (another case of facts transformed into fiction, V.4). Chagall's combination of naturalistic, symbolic and expressive forms of representation are, although surreal or magic, much closer to actual truth (imprisoned and impoverished Jewish life in tsarist Russia; the plight of the Jewish people being crucified again and again as a repetition of what the Romans did to countless rebellious Jews before one of them was posthumously made into a demi-god born under miraculous circumstances, although the irony of it probably escapes Gentile art lovers).

Art is here to evoke and possibly express emotions, but emotions are always ambiguous, which is reflected in art. Pioneering German artists after the Second World War, most of whom came from East Germany (Walther, 2005) probably combined political disillusion with the "workers' and peasants' state" with the shame of post-Hitler Germany. Regression to the presumed innocence of childhood might have provided a special motif for the return to Primitivism of this generation (historical problem situation, III.2). Younger generations tend to look differently at the immediate past than older generations (Feuer, 1969).

Nevertheless, the basic assumption of this book, that artistic revolutions are ultimately triggered by physical constraints (I.1) seems the most plausible. Take the Danish Artist, Peter Severyn Krøyer (Hornung, 2005), who entered the art world when it was still dominated by the naturalistic tradition. Krøyer had as little freedom to choose as contemporary artists who all model themselves upon Duchamp's Readymades (conceptual art). Art is about techniques (V.3), but novel techniques have first to be discovered or as seems to be the case of twentieth-century art, rediscovered (III.2). But this does not make pioneering work less of pioneering work. Becoming a pioneer (H-creativity) is still a process of personal learning or discovery (P-creativity). The theory of the child as romantic genius is not very helpful in clarifying how this is possible. Constraint theory is a much better theory to start with.

### Novices: Participation as Personal Responsibility

Creativity works on different levels and functions differently in different situations in life. Take the role of novice. Children and youth, the favorite topics of educational theories (Illeris, 2007), are not the only type of novices. In Late-modern societies adults might even be put in the problem situation of the novice. The Swedish pioneer of drama, August Strindberg in his play *A Dream Play,* illustrates these common experiences of everyday life in late-modern societies by the nightmare of an officer, who suddenly finds himself sitting behind a desk in a classroom. Hans Christian Andersen, the great Danish fairy-tale writer, literally experienced such a humiliating situation when he was placed in a classroom in Copenhagen among schoolmates who were far below his age. Sixteen million East Germans experienced a similar feeling of degradation when they found that most of what they had learned not only in school but also in their professional lives were of little value (Kupferberg 1998b, 1999a, 2002a).

Neither cognitive science, nor the theory of social construction, helps us capture the problem situation of this type of novice experience, which can best be seen as a sociocognitive phenomenon. According to constraint theory, we cannot make precise predictions since humans as life forms have a choice. This is confirmed by the case of German Democratic Republic (GDR). The East Germans tended to react very differently to the shock of having one's past suddenly and unexpectedly devalued (Markovits, 1995). Generational but also professional and political factors led to very different forms of adaptation (Wensierski, 1994; Kupferberg, 1995b).

Being put in the sociocognitive role of the adult novice does not have to be felt as offensive or insulting to the self-dignity of individuals though. It depends upon the biographical context. Interviews made with young nurses (Kupferberg, 1999b) (defined as having finished their training less than ten years before the time of the interview) revealed the opposite of the experience of middle-aged East Germans (Kupferberg, 1998b). This might be due to age because novice nurses in Denmark start working part time during training, which usually starts in their early twenties, immediately after or a few years after their high school exam (*studentereksamen* in Denmark). This means that most student nurses are in the same age cohort (20–25). The younger starting age might help explain why this group of adult novices reacted differently from the East German group. Although the experience of the student nurses was often frustrating – strong status awareness reflecting the high prestige of surgery and maternity clinics and the low prestige of psychiatric patients and the elderly; lack of time to attend to the personal needs of patients; shift work and anti-social hours, etc. – such frustrations were seen as "side-bets" (Becker, 1960), the price an individual had to pay as part of the long-term commitment to the chosen profession (compare Becker's 1951 study of Chicago School Teachers).

Another possible reason why the role as student nurse was not felt as humiliating or degrading as in the case of the GDR (Engler, 1999; Dahn, 1999) was that the type of work done by the student nurses (novices) was seen as valuable for society. The personal ability to solve unexpected problems met in the new professional role, provided feelings of self-worth and importance, precisely the opposite to the personal experience of the East Germans (Glaessner, 1993; Schmitz, 2005). A third difference can be conceptualized as a different type of "pedagogy" (Kupferberg, 1999a). Student nurses were from the very start put in the situation of the "legitimate periphery participant" (Lave & Wenger, 1991) typical of the master-apprentice type of teaching and learning (compare Nielsen & Kvale, 2000). This more self-confirming role of student nurses, where the novice is made part of the community of practice from the very start, was also typical of the pedagogy at Aalborg University (Kupferberg, 1995c).

One of the ideas of problem-based learning is that for learning to be felt as a pleasurable experience (I.5a), novices should be invited into the craft and judgment (skills and attitudes) of the discipline or profession from the very beginning. Rather than having to wait until the end of practical training to write a thesis (typical for teacher education in Malmö where I worked for some years as a professor of education), the idea at Aalborg University was that students should try to do independent research from the very start of their higher education (Kupferberg 1996a). Although far from unproblematic – the new situation also created frustration and uncertainty – the main educational goal, to keep curiosity alive, was nevertheless achieved (Kupferberg, 1996b, 1999c, 2006c).

What this suggests is that the core problem of unification of the two Germanies from a both pedagogical and creativity science point of view was the lack of feeling of participation in the ongoing experiment. An important aspect of the feeling of being part of the process, legitimate periphery participation found among the student nurses, was the feeling of being made personally responsible for solving problems of the type nurses routinely encounter in work (being made into "effective cause," V.3, rather than the opposite "death of the author"). Thus, one nurse who had worked in the psychiatric ward, related an incident with a young female patient, whom she had taken for a walk outside the protected area. Suddenly the patient stopped and pointed at her feet, claiming that worms were crawling out between her toes. Rather than engaging in an argument with the patient, the student nurse embraced the patient physically, thus reassuring her emotionally that someone cared for her as person. Having waited for the patient to calm down, the student nurse pointed at the patient's feet and said, "Look. There are no worms! Can you see?"

For some reasons personal responsibility seems to be the key to the creativity of the novice. To be given personal responsibility to solve a problem in real life is a sign of trust. One's helper (mentor, V.5) believes that one is up to the task, which probably strengthens one's self-worth and generates more confidence. Moreover, working with a problem close to real-life problem situations (III.4) makes the novice (II.2) feel that this is relevant for their future. It is not a waste of time. I am not doing it merely to please the teacher but for myself, my own future career. Third, being given personal responsibility probably also strengthens the long-term commitment of the individual to this career (Becker, 1951, 1960). The person begins to see it as a long-term investment and is hence better prepared to cope with inevitable frustrations, uncertainty, humiliation, etc., tied to the inevitable pressure (I.Vb) involved in the struggle for recognition (Honneth, 1992).

Fourth, personal responsibility probably also increases the amount of patience necessary to solve more complex problems (Amabile, 1989). Fifth, a series of successful problem solving, confirms that the novice has achieved the right combination of skills and attitudes necessary for successful problem solving (getting it right, III.1). "I can do it," which most certainly is a good feeling. Working with these type of problems gives rise to feelings of pleasure (I.V.a). "I like this, I want to do this, I have found my niche in life, I do not have to search in complete darkness anymore for a meaningful job or profession."

## Professionals: Competitive Pressure and Transfer of Skills and Attitudes

Modern teaching is mostly about motivating novices by making learning a pleasurable (I.5a) experience (an important and possibly critical aspect of keeping curiosity alive). As novices enter the profession a new element appears which is held down or repressed during the period of education. Here everyone is in principle treated as equal. Although each individual is given a grade or mark for his or her level of personal achievement (demonstrated level of problem-solving capacity), modern pedagogy tends to emphasize the "communistic" aspects although in another sense than science where knowledge ideally should be available for everybody free of charge (Merton, 1942/1968). "Communism" in a pedagogical context means that pupils or students should look upon themselves as "comrades." They are basically equals and should stick together and help each other rather than caring only for their own self-interests. This "communistic" aspect comes out very clearly in the pedagogy of the GDR, where the individual aspect was completely suppressed; this caused a lot of problems not only for school teachers but for all persons who had been shaped by the GDR school system when the country collapsed (Dudek & Tenort, 1994; Kupferberg, 1996d). In a sense, the GDR can best be described not as a dictatorship of the proletariat but as a dictatorship of the teaching profession (Kupferberg, 2002a).

There might be other types of reality shocks. How do academics cope with the uncertainties of changing career orientation and start to become self-employed. This was the basic problem of a project, based upon the biographical method, that I pursued with the help of student assistants at Aalborg University on academic entrepreneurs with a background in the humanities and social sciences (reported in Kupferberg 1996d, 1997, 1998c, 2001a). Having first planned careers in academic teaching and/or research, these young professionals were forced to rethink their previous life planning or biographical project, entering a new world with different values, norms and rules (I.4) closer to the business world. This change of life planning was imposed upon them. They did not do it voluntarily and there was a strong element of pressure (I.5b). The problem situation (III.4) in which they found themselves was not what they had planned for and they were forced by circumstances to engage in a process of unlearning and relearning which involved looking for new role models (I.2). What was interesting was that the previously learned personal knowledge, skills and attitudes, were not completely abandoned but rather transformed or "transmuted" (the concept Darwin uses in his evolutionary theory).

Some of these transitions were more chaotic than others, but in all the 10 cases studied strong competition or overcrowding of the labor markets (problem situation, III.4) played a critical role. It is important to stress though that this objective factor was, from a subjective point of view (P-creativity) only experienced or discovered gradually, step by step (Kupferberg, 1997). It was emotionally hard because it was regarded as an abandonment of a previous biographical project (investment plus commitment). Although rational in the economic sense of self-interested (Weber's basic definition of rationality is modeled upon neo-classical economics, with Marshall as prototype, I.2, see Parsons, 1938/1968), there is also a strong emotional or moral component in such personal commitments. Loyalty to a long-term commitment is a sign of virtue, disloyalty a sin. This explains the need to legitimize the choice to change commitments retroactively. The way this was done was to downplay the elements of opportunity (I.5c) and pleasure (I.5a) and foreground the element of pressure (I.5c). I had to do it. I had no choice (the moral aspects of abandonment are excellently described in Ebaugh, 1988).

### Change of Life Plans as Gradual Process

Most of the respondents were at the start reluctant to change life plans and uncertain if they had made the right choice. A typical case was a woman in her mid-thirties. She had planned to become a teacher in foreign languages (French and German), but having tried for seven years to get a foothold in teaching at a Danish "gymnasium" (advanced high school), she accepted a job offer from a private firm producing water beds as language consultant. What she was not told was that the domestic market for water beds in Denmark had collapsed and that the new business strategy was to expand the market to countries south of the border. This was why they needed a language consultant. But the new business strategy failed. After a year the firm went bankrupt.

The chief engineer of the waterbed firm, came up with a solution. He offered her co-ownership of a "virtual firm" basically reaching for the high value end of the market, offering to design water beds and night tables on commission from private customers (V.4; compare the business strategy of painters and architects in the Renaissance, see Welch, 1984, but also Le Corbusier's regular clients, see Weber, 2008). She told the interviewer that had she been given this offer a year earlier, she would most certainly have declined, but having taken the first step, the next step did not seem as daring or drastic. This type of life planning fits Luhmann's (1994) argument that choices made under conditions of uncertainty, create their own constraints further on in individual careers. This might or might not be an independent rediscovery (III.2), given that Hughes (1964) had arrived at a similar theory 30 years earlier (cf. Mendel and de Vries, see Mayr, 1982).

This evolutionary (step-by-step) pattern was typical for most of the respondents although there were some interesting variations. Thus, an architectural historian in his forties who held a research position at the National Museum in Denmark, lost his job because of imposed savings from the state. He had to be inventive (pressure, I.Vb) in order to secure his income and managed to apply for funding from the EU. This made it possible for him to do the same type of pleasurable academic research (I.5a) but as a freelance researcher living off grants rather than full-time employment (opportunity, I.5c).

A third type of passages to entrepreneurship mainly found among ethnic entrepreneurs in Denmark were highly chaotic and presented stories of personal "sacrifice" in order to support the family but also gain some self-respect in the eyes of the local ethnic minority community. Among female ethnic entrepreneurs the theme of "autonomy" was much more prevalent (Kupferberg, 2003c, 2004a). Overall, the "pressure to innovate" (Lipset, 1979) was a predominate motive. But pressure (I.5b) combined with a undue problem-solving capacity can also lead to highly successful forms of entrepreneurship and sometimes to pioneering work (a case in point might be the Hollywood movie moguls, see French, 1971; Gabler, 1988; Kupferberg, 2002b, 2006b).

An interesting and somewhat deviant case was a teacher of psychology. She had always dreamed of becoming a self-employed Freudian, psycho-therapist, presumably because this type of work gave her great pleasure (I.5a). What she was waiting for was the opportunity (I.5c), in the sense that she had to postpone this professional transition until she had built up a reputation (IV.5) solid enough to attract the number of clients necessary. In the meantime, she had to find other jobs within her professional competence, such as teaching psychology at Danish gymnasiums. This element of opportunity can also be found among the Hollywood immi-grant entrepreneurs in the personal transformation from professionals to pioneers (Dick, 1997; Kupferberg, 2002b) but also in Chagall's biography (1922/1965; Wullschlager, 2008).

### Transfer of Skills and Transformation of Attitude

Competition, pressure and transmutation of life plans come in many forms (complexity of creativity). Apart from evolutionary or gradual change, another recurrent pattern was that all the entrepreneurs (apart from one failed entrepreneur who miscalculated the potential market mainly because of a different cultural upbringing) managed to transfer some of their learned skills from previous professions into the new professions. Such transmission went surprisingly smoothly. What was difficult was the change of attitude. A historian of ideas failed to get a job as a teacher but in contrast to the teacher of foreign languages, the historian of ideas started studying organizational theory and leadership. Together with some of his co-students, he founded a company which offered leadership courses and workshops for public organizations.

After a while, the co-owners of the company disagreed about the future of the company and the historian of ideas set up his own firm, which wanted to take the step from education to practice. He had accumulated experience from working as a consultant to solve leadership conflicts in hospitals, which at the time were going through big changes in leadership philosophy. Doctors were no longer automatically seen as the best quali-fied leaders to run a modern hospital alone but had to share authority with head nurses. Whereas the historian of ideas had little problem transferring the skills he had learned about organization leadership from theory to practice, he had a much harder time judging what his job was worth in monetary terms, a routine practice when a public organization hires services from a private firm. Changing his attitudes towards rewards for work done – a change from the typical attitude of the employee who receives wages in return for hours of contracted work, to the self-employed (entrepreneur) who charges customers by putting a price on products or services, was initially not felt to be right (III.1) for a person coming from teaching and research (problem situation, III.4).

An IT consultant, who had a background in ethnography and sociology, had a similar problem. He had become an IT consultant for firms within the graphic printing industry without having originally planned to pursue this career. The industry was undergoing rapid changes at the time and needed someone to advise them what system to choose but also help them to install and renew the IT system from time to time (keep up with technological change). The self-employed IT consultant had little experi-ence with the IT technology at the start. The way he kept himself informed about the many options and changes of technology was by scanning all the important trade journals and selecting those which seemed relevant for careful reading (Kupferberg, 1996d). This learned skill of discarding irrelevant information (Kupferberg, 1996c) was a general-purpose tool (Rosenberg, 2010) he had learned from his years at university.

Moreover, initiation into the discipline of ethnography, had taught him to stay attuned to the need of others. His difficulties were again a problem of attitude, how to put a price on his services, which he eventually solved by calculating the price of the system installed and adding a certain percentage.

## Pioneers: The Opportunity Factors as Regulative Gene and the Complexity of H-Creativity

### Support Systems and Opportunity

Although opportunities (I.5c) did play some role among the academic entrepreneurs I studied, pressure (I5b) was the overall predominant factor. In contrast opportunities (I.Vc) seem to be crucial in understanding how and why some professionals become pioneers. But opportunities do not grow on trees, they are strongly dependent upon support systems (IV.5). This comes out clearly in studies on scientific pioneers. Without the patronage of the Danish Crown, made possible by belonging to one of the leading aristocratic families in Denmark, Tycho Brahe would never have been provided with the financial means to organize and run an observatory on the isolated island of Hveen, using it basically as his personal fiefdom (Thoren, 1990). The grant from the Danish Crown, which cost around 5% of BNP at the time (Ferguson, 2003, vastly more than the Apollo project), allowed Brahe to recruit both skilled and expert staff, necessary to construct and use the instruments necessary to improve the accuracy of data on the movements of the planets (material cause, V.1). The purpose of these observations which were made during a period of almost 20 years was to falsify (V.4) both the two predominant theoretical models (Ptolemy and Copernicus) a case of a historical and personal-problem situation (III.4) but which would also bring personal prestige to Tycho Brahe and transform him into a scientific pioneer (II.4).

The problem was that the patron (IV.5), the Danish Crown, had been falsely informed. Uranborg (Thoren, 1990) was in reality a kind of "skunk work" (IV.3) similar to Darwin's secret discoveries when traveling on the *Beagle* and Crick and Watson's equally secret work in the office they shared at the Cavendish Laboratory 1951–1953 (Watson, 1968/1996). The Danish Crown had been led to believe that the purpose of Uranborg (V.4) was to produce horoscopes (which according to Aristotle is a kind of productive knowledge, similar to art and rhetoric) but in reality the project was purely theoretical, to falsify both alternative theoretical models trying to explain the errant behavior of the plants (loops).

What can we learn from this? Although Latour assures us that there is no such thing as pure science and that we have never been modern (1987, 1993), this is simply not true. Nor is it true as Kuhn claims that pioneering scholars are not engaged in problem solving (Kuhn, 1959/1977) but merely to produce "taxonomic solutions" (Hacking, 1995). Both models were attempts to solve the same paradox, the strange loops of the planets (Ferguson, 2003). Tycho Brahe believed both models to be wrong and wanted to find proof for his alternative model where the Earth is still in the center of the universe, but where the planets are assumed to go round the Sun as the Sun supposedly goes round the Earth. But if Tycho Brahe could easily switch between the three theoretical models, how could they be "incommensurable" as Kuhn claims (Hacking, 1983)?

But in order to falsify the other theories (Final cause of science, V.4), Brahe needed better data on the exact position of the planets (material case, V.1). How was this to be achieved? This was certainly not by trial and error and not by techniques but by scientific methodology, starting with collecting the correct data. This goal was accomplished by systematic, night after night, observation of the changing position of planets from an observatory (Uranborg), equipped with the most advanced equipment that could be found at the time (state of the art technology, made possible by co-evolution, III.3), the "quadrant" (Wennberg, 2007). Alas the Danish Crown found out the real purpose of Tycho Brahe's Observatory. The wrath of the Danish King (loss of patronage, IV.5) forced Brahe to make a hasty escape and find a new benefactor. He became a geographical migrant (IV.1) in Prague under a new, more tolerant patron (IV.5).

Owing to the hasty escape, Tycho Brahe did not manage to bring with him all the data he had systemically collected during a period of 20 years. He did manage to save the highly accurate March data (V.1). Alas Tycho Brahe (effective cause, V.3 so far) did not master the advanced algebraic methods (V.3) necessary to do the relevant calculations (knowledge constraints, I.3; personal-problem situation, III.4). This is the reason why he hired a Polish monk, Johannes Kepler (intellectual migrant and teamwork, IV.2) to do the necessary calculations (mediated forms of the social which according to Weber, 1904–1905/1958 are completely bereft of meaning) to do the job because Tycho Brahe lacked the necessary skills (but not the right attitude). It so happened that Tycho Brahe's research assistant, having calculated the March data, not only falsified Tycho Brahe's compromise formula (surprise 1) but also managed to falsify Copernicus' model and explain why it was not parsimonious (III.1). Copernicus had in fact used Ptolemy's epicycles (prototype I.2) in order to make his own alternative, Sun-centered model, "save the facts" (Ferguson, 2003).

Both Ptolemy and Copernicus had made the mistake of assuming that the trajectory of planets had to be perfect circles. But this was fiction and not fact (V.4) just as Columbus's belief that Cuba was part of mainland China was fiction and not fact. The indisputable fact was the trajectory of the planets (based upon March data) and was for some obscure reasons, which Kepler could not explain, elliptical and not circular (Koestler, 1964).

The question why the trajectory of planets was elliptical and not circular was only solved by Newton who proved that this could be explained by the assumption that gravity was a universal and not merely a local force (Bohm, 1998; Darling, 2006). This in turn left the outstanding question of how gravity could work over distance. This problem was eventually solved by Einstein's "relativity theory," which is not really a theory of relativity but a theory of how energy forms can be transformed into each other and the role of the speed of light (Isaacson, 1998). The role of the speed of light is absolute and constant and does not change at all, although the role of the observer might marginally influence the measurement of time if a human spaceship one day would be able to travel close to the absolute speed of light (creation of facts, V.4) which is hardly likely.

Returning to Kepler, what is interesting about his discovery of the elliptical shape of planetary trajectories, was that it was unintended (as was the falsification of Tycho Brahe's compromise model). But according to Karl Popper's (1963) theory of falsification, there is no such thing as unintended falsification, only intended falsification. But this cannot be right (III.1). Indeed almost all pioneering work in science originate in unintended forms of falsification. So where did Popper get this idea that falsification had to be intended? Most probably it came from Einstein's *Mein Weltbild*, which seems to have served his prime role model or prototype (I.2).

### Pleasure, Pressure, Opportunity

Support systems (V.5) might be critical not only for providing opportunity (I.5c), they might also put pressure (I.Vb) on potential pioneers to prove themselves (compare the pressure that Matisse and Darwin felt from their fathers). Support systems might also help novices to take pleasure (I.Va) in pursuing a particular type of creative career. Darwin's privileged youth in the countryside, certainly helped him to discover the pleasure he felt as naturalist (he was especially fascinated by collecting beagles at an early age, see Browne, 1995). Early patronage in combination with mentors also helped Chagall both to discover and sustain his feeling of pleasure in the field of painting (Wullschlager, 2008).

Nevertheless, opportunities rather than mere pleasure and pressure turn out to be decisive in order to become a pioneer (II.4). Take the case of Steve Jobs (Isaacson, 2012). The fact that Steve Jobs' family (who had adopted Steve after his mother abandoned him) moved to Silicon Valley and put him in the midst of a creative milieu (Hall, 1999), which was to become the center of the development of the evolving computer industry (Rogers & Larsen, 1984; Saxenian, 1991, 1994; Moon et al., 2000), was a clear opportunity factor (I.5c). His father, who was an electrician, had moved to Silicon Valley because of job opportunities. As a child Steve Jobs watched his father working with electrical equipment (prototype, I.2, novice level, II.2) and then went to the university (which traditionally transforms novices into professionals, II.3) but like Bill Gates he never took an exam.

But whereas Bill Gates' father was a business lawyer and gave his son advice about how to start a very profitable business (mentor, IV.5) when Gates (effective cause,V.3) was still in college, Steve Jobs entered the micro-electric industry as an employee (II.3). Doing skunk work (IV.3) together with another employee, Steve Wozniak, the two soon started designing (V.2) their own primitive versions of the personal computer (Macs). The success (III.1) of this early prototype (I.2) led to improved versions and the idea of starting their own firm (Apple). A firm can best be described as a kind of collective creative mind (effective cause, V.3) but for such a creative mind to function it too needs a support system (patrons, mentors, agents). This seems to be the secret of the success of Silicon Valley as a creative milieu. It provides all the three (in the form of both passive risk capitalists and active business angels). This more or less informal support system (IV.5) provided Steve Jobs and his partner with an immense opportunity to become pioneers within the evolving industry.

Another handy opportunity factor (I.5c) in the creative milieu of Silicon Valley was the presence of Rank Xerox, from which Steve Jobs borrowed or stole the idea of an interface with the help of easily movable icons (prototype, I.2). This idea was later appropriated by Bill Gates and Microsoft. After Steve Jobs was ousted from his own firm, he spent time in Hollywood (intellectual migration, IV.2) working with Pixar, a computer company which had entered the animated films industry. The detailed personal knowledge of how an advanced artistic industry functioned (I.3), prepared Steve Jobs for his triumphant return to Apple and the introduction of a new type of computer which made it possible to access artistic and other types of "content," transforming Apple into the leader of a new type of computer technology company, which crossed the borders between technological and artistic creativity, a form of "hybrid modernity" very similar to Hollywood (Kupferberg, 2003a, 2007).

### The Pressure to Be Original and the Role of the Art Teacher

Marc Chagall was also ousted from what seemed like a successful career when he returned to Russia from Paris to marry the love of his life, Bella. Forced to support a family, he settled down as an art teacher. After the revolution, Chagall became a commissar for the arts and artistic education in his hometown Vitebsk. One of the first things he did was to open an art school providing free education for a large number (300) of young and eager art students. Most of these art students would never become professional artists (II.3), but some of them would probably continue doing art as art teachers. Teaching art is not the same as practicing art. Art teachers are professionals who in contrast to practicing artists (Kupferberg, 2012a) are under no pressure to be original (compare Chagall's, 1922/1965 assessments about his two main art teachers and mentors Pen and Bakst).

How do professional artists who for some reasons accept the role of art teacher (mentor, IV.5), cope with this inherent contradiction between their own professional work as artists, where they are under pressure (I.5b) to be original (Lucie-Smith, 1999) and the professional role of teacher, which is to make learning art feel pleasurable (I.5a)? One strategy could be to lower the ambition of the art teacher to the degree where art students are expected to learn merely the basics of their craft, which they would need if they wanted to become art teachers themselves, without any ambition to practice art as a professional artist (Pen's strategy).

Another strategy could be to provide art students with a broad palette of techniques (V.3) not only traditional but also novel techniques, which provide access to the most advanced art styles (Bakst strategy). A third strategy would be to motivate students to model themselves upon the advanced avant-garde style of the art teacher. This third strategy seems to have been the strategy that Chagall chose when he started his own art school in Vitebsk. Alas this strategy backfired after Chagall hired even more avant-garde artists than himself from St. Petersburg (Lissitsky and Malevich) who, from the point of view of the students, represented an even more advanced, more "modern" and less "traditional" art style than

Chagall's. This experience left Chagall bitter and humiliated and caused him to give up his position as commissar and director of the art school he had founded. He never went back to teaching art again.

### Prototypes and Pioneering Work

All art depends upon learning of prototypes (I.2), but what separates the way pioneers copy prototypes from the way pioneers do it? Current theories of art assume that originality and copying of prototypes contradict each other (Kirton 1989; Krauss, 1986) but this does not take the complexities and paradoxes of creativity seriously (lack of a scientific, methodological approach and ultimately a reflection of a lack of correct First principles). On the contrary to widespread beliefs, it is precisely the eagerness to copy and do it properly and intensely for a period, before moving on to the next prototype (the innovator as voracious imitator) that separates pioneers from mere professionals. Take the case of Matisse. Having been trained in the Renaissance chiaroscuro technique (emphasizing light and shade, "value," see Shiff, 1984 and Aristides, 2016) at the studio of Gustave Moreau (mentor, V.5) and having deepened his knowledge of the techniques of painting (V.2), moved from novice (I.2) to professional (I.3) by close copying and study of Chardin (prototype, I.2), Matisse came under the influence of an Australian painter, John Peter Russell and his admirer Émile Wéry.

> Matisse maintained later, that that the transformation of his palette – the bistre-based palette of the old masters, especially the Dutch – came from watching Wéry squeeze his colors straight from the tube, like Russell, in the order of the prism. "Working beside him I noticed that the was getting more luminous results with his primary colors than I could with my old-fashioned palette." He made a good story of how the two swapped over, Matisse returning to Paris with a passion for all the colors of the rainbow, having bequeathed to Wéry his former love of bistre and bitumen. (Spurling, 2009, p. 48)

Matisse's discovery of the technique (V.3) of color (in particular cobalt blue and crimson red), was a repetition of what had happened in Gustave Moreau's studio and in the Louvres. What changed was the mentor (IV.5 Russell) and the prototype (I.2, Wéry). But change of physical surroundings (physical constraints I.1) also played a role. That summer, July 15 1896,

> Matisse left Paris with the usual Brittany-bound band of painters . . . to Belle Île . . .he and Camille rented a room above the harbor in Le Palais

before settling in Kervilahouen, a scattered hamlet six and a half kilometers away across, flat, furze-covered scrubland on the far side of the island where they stayed in the same house as the Wérys. They had an uninterrupted view out to the sea from the top floor of a stone 'pilot's house' beside the track leading to a great granite lighthouse on the headland, barricaded in by axe-blade-shaped rocks rising from the sea. (Spurling, 2009, p. 46)

A third mediated rather than interpersonal influence was Monet, whose impressionistic painting of the huge rocks visible from Belle Île, Matisse tried to copy that summer (Barr, 1953/1976). Monet was one of the pioneers of the discovery of color as hue (pioneer, II.4; prototype, I.2). It was Russell (mentor, V.5) who

introduced him to the Impressionist's theories of light and color – in particular to the innovations of Claude Monet – and devised exercises to help him assimilate them in practice. Russell had met Monet on Belle Île in 1886 and owned at least one Monet seascape. . . for two summers running Matisse now became Russell's pupil, sending "wildly enthusiastic" letters to fellow art students from Belle Île about the primacy of color and the need to be guided solely by feeling. (Spurling, 2009, p. 49)

The need to be guided by feeling reveals yet another invisible prototype (I.2), van Gogh. Russell had worked closely with van Gogh for many years. "His large collection . . .included twelve drawing made specially by Van Gogh to give his old friend some idea of each of the major canvases painted in the first season at Arles" (Spurling, 2009, p. 49). Combining the prototypes (I.2) of Manet and Gauguin, provided Russell (mentor, IV.5) not only with new skills (techniques of painting) but also an attitude of rebelliousness, which the impressionable and insecure Matisse probably also copied (to great consternation of Camille, his model and mother to his daughter Marguerite). As noted by Spurling. Matisse in one of his letters "catches the authentic Australian's accent of bluntness and subversion: 'We painters should not be gallery slaves. . .Pay no attention to anything except what interests you. . .Work with white, blue, red, paint with your feet if you want to, and if anyone doesn't like it, send him packing'" (Spurling, 2009, p. 49).

## Life Crises and Creativity

Returning from the long summer on Belle Île, Matisse started the painting *Dinner Table* (*La desserte,* Barr, 1953/1976, p. 299). It was presented at the official exhibition of the Salon in 1897 and was to dramatically change his fortune and future prospects, which had seemed so bright only the year before, when he departed for Belle Île. The strongly negative reaction to the paining (Spurling, 2009, p. 52) was repeated ten years later by the strongly negative reactions to Picasso's *Les Demoiselles d'Avignon* (Penrose, 1958/1968; Olivier, 1935/1982; Richardson, 1996/1997).

The negative reactions to *Les demoiselles d'Avignon* led to Cubism and the crises inaugurated by *La deserte,* eventually led to the birth of Fauvism. This pattern appears very frequently among pioneers. Erikson (1968/1982, 1970) has tried to conceptualize or explain this pattern (crises of recognition leading to creativity of the highest sort, the transformation from professional, II.3 to pioneer, II.4) with a theory of life cycles. Youth is the period when individuals are searching for their vocation (life commitment, biographical project). This might take some time and parents, teachers or society should be patient, allowing youth a moratorium for the period of searching. Such a moratorium can be regarded as a kind of prolonged crisis of identity. As an example of how this works, Erikson mentions George Bernard Shaw's several, failed attempts to become a novelist. After four years Shaw gave up and began writing plays instead. Here he experienced immediate success and eventually became one of the great playwrights of the twentieth century (Holroyd, 1988; Bentley, 1968).

The problem with Erikson's theoretical model is that it is essentially based upon Aristotle's "development model" (Nisbet, 1970/1971) rather than Darwin's evolutionary model. The seed of a tree is preprogrammed by nature to grow into a tree and unless unfortunate circumstances block the way (heavy storms, draught, heavy volcanic eruptions, etc.), the seed becomes a full-grown tree. In contrast no one is born to be a great artist, pioneering scientist, technological innovator, etc. Chagall was no doubt highly talented form birth, but without a strong support system which helped him to learn both the basic techniques of painting (V.2) and the types of techniques which were the most advanced at that time and place (III.4), he certainly would neither have become a professional painter nor a pioneer (great artist).

Moreover, there are many types of life crises which influence the transition from professional to pioneer. Sylvia Plath experienced a series of life crises: (1) her father's death when she was a child which led to an interest in poetry as a way of expressing the emotions of mourning (novice, II. 2); (2) a medical history which was triggered by her suicide attempt at the time she was entering collage but eventually led to the transformation as a writer of poetry on a professional level (II.3); (3) the crisis that began with the collapse of her marriage and led to an intensive period of poetry which transformed her from professional to pioneer (II.4; Bain, 2001;

Bredsdorff, 1987), but was abruptly ended when she killed herself (Stevenson, 1989).

Eriksen's model does explain the Swedish playwright Strindberg's choice to become a writer (Kupferberg, 1995b) but not how and why he became a pioneer of modern drama (Sprinchorn, 1982; Bradbury & MacFarlane, 1976). This was probably the result of his many years of exile (IV.1) in France and Denmark. But in order to afford traveling and living abroad with a wife and children to support, Strindberg first had to become a socially recognized, professional writer of fiction (II.3). A closer view of his most popular novels such as *Röda Rummet* and *Hemsöborna* reveals them to be rather conventional. Strindberg's debut novel *Röda Rummet* is modeled upon Balzac. *Hemsöborna* is a Swedish, tragic version of the romantic folktale, which must end with the destruction of the immoral hero. They were both what Sylvia Plath in her letters and diaries called "pot-boilers," aimed at creating an audience of anonymous readers who in practice functioned as "patrons" for a professional writer (IV.5, compare Edström, 2002; Svedjedal, 1999).

Strindberg's writing of popular fiction provided him both with an agent (Bonniers) and patrons (mass audience) which gave him the freedom to live abroad and transform himself to a pioneering playwright (II.4, Lagercrantz, 1979; Brandell, 1983–1989). It is also possible that living abroad gave him access to mentors for how to become a professional playwright in the first place, given his first attempts were not seen as professional enough to be accepted by the Royal Swedish Theater.

From this it does not follow that living abroad (IV.1. Kupferberg, 1998a) is a necessary condition for becoming a great writer. Jane Austen never left England; in fact, she did not even leave her place of birth (although the family resettled in Bath to improve her marriage prospects).

As noted by Shields (2002), the protagonists of all Austen's novels are mostly daughters. The antagonists are, surprisingly mothers, the type of significant others one would expect to be a "helper" of some sort (IV.5). This unusual motif explains the main storyline of Austen's novels: "Daughters ... who win independence by going against the lack of freedom in their own families," a motif which is explained by the role of the mother who is depicted as "lacking motherly warmth," "reserved... passive, indolent," "stupid" or "not present" (Shields, 2002 p. 20).

It would be a mistake though to believe that this was a true psycholog-ical portrait of Jane Austen's real mother (fact). It is a fictive portrait, and the rationale can best be explained by Aristotle's basic rule of "pity and fear." A reader cannot but feel pity for a daughter with such a caricature of what a mother is supposed to be. But the emotions evoked in a work of art are not necessarily the emotions expressed in an artwork (Carroll, 2010). Fiction might be a mirror of society (in this case the social ambitions of young and educated women like Jane Austen in England around 1800, see Johnson, 1991) but they are also masked (Strauss, 1959) partly to protect the intimate sphere of close family, friends and lovers (compare Nabokov) but also to tell a good story.

The need to transform facts into fiction also seems to have an emotional source though. This brings us to the greatest tragedy of her life, the deep disappointment she must have felt when a young and handsome suitor from a "good family," Tom Leroy suddenly left town without informing her of why he had changed his mind (probably pressure from his parents who felt that a marriage with daughter of a simple clergyman was regarded as far beneath the groom's family's social standing). *Pride and Prejudice*, a novel that came out of this life crisis, turned the facts around. In the novel the heroine, Elizabeth Bennet is the one who rejects marriage proposals and attracts an even more handsome and rich suitor than Tom Leroy. Elizabeth Bennet is an invented character and can, from a psychological point of view, perhaps best be seen as an expression of wishful thinking (Elster, 2007). According to Freud (1938) fiction is a kind of "daydreaming" (Kraft, 1984). Writing this novel clearly had therapeutic functions (de Bottom & Armstrong, 2013/2015) for her.

But it was not only therapy (move from pressure, I.5b to pleasure, I.5a). In order to write a novel, some kind of protection is necessary (Dimension IV) and the craft of writing needs to be learned (the move from novice, II.2 to professional, II.3). It seems that the way novelists learn how to write novels is to read the novels of other writers (prototypes, I.2). Shields tells us that the author had read *Pamela* by Samuel Richardson (McKeon, 2000) so closely that she could repeat long passages from memory (compare Matisse in front of Chardin in the Louvre and Monet's painting of the rocks visible from Belle Île hanging in Russell's house). But whereas novels can be studied anywhere in the world, even in the countryside in early nineteenth-century England, great art works have to be seen physically to function as prototypes.

Let us return to Matisse's transformation to pioneer. Such transformations do not arrive out of the blue. They are gradual because they take place step by step. Matisse's transformation from novice to pioneer began when he stopped merely copying copies and began to copy original work in the Louvre. Why did he do this in the Louvre?

This takes us back to the problem that the "original" plays for the aesthetic appreciation of paintings but less so for sculpture (compare Rodin who often worked in clay and had bronze copies made; see Butler, 1993). These distinctive physical aspects (I.1) in the creative process, both from the point of view of creator and the person appreciating (the artist must play both roles and he or she is his/her first critic), is completely absent in writing, where the physical dimension has to do with the time spent writing and reading a novel. In contrast, having physical access to the original is necessary in order to learn the techniques. More generally, painting has a strong physical dimension (studio, model, easel, canvas, brush, palette, colors readily available in tubes to be squeezed out on to the palette or perpahs directly on to the canvas, a technique possibly pioneered by van Gogh and transmitted to the United States by Hans Hofmann who lived in Paris before emigrating there, see Greenberg, 1961/1965).

In Matisse's case, close observation of originals in the Louvre gave rise to a lifelong habit, which best explains how and why Matisse became a pioneer, by close study of many and not just one master (the pioneer as a voracious imitator). According to Spurling (2009):

> The master to whom Matisse returned again and again in these years was J. B. Chardin ... the first painting he ever copied in the Louvre was Chardin's *The Pipe,* which baffled him with an elusive blue on the padded lid of the box in the middle of the canvas; a blue that looked pink one day, green the next. Matisse tried everything he could think of to pin down the secret of this painting, using a magnifying glass, studying the texture of the paint, the grain of the canvas, the glazes, the objects themselves and the transitions form light to shade.

Matisse ended up copying Chardin "four times ... His hardest struggle was with *The Skate,* a majestic painting of a fish and oysters on a kitchen slab, dominated by the great rearing arch of a gutted skate. Matisse's confrontation with this canvas lasted in the end six and a half years, almost exactly the same length of time as his apprenticeship Moureau" (Spurling, 2009, p. 36).

## The Redundancy of Genius

Artists are not free to do what they please, if they want to become professionals and pioneering artists even less so. They are ultimately constrained by the physical constraints (I.1) of their chosen media, by the techniques they learn from the prototypes they chose (I.2), by knowledge constraints ( I.3, compare the role that the psychology of perception played for the Impressionists, see Karmel, 2003), by the rules of art (I.4) to evoke emotions by transforming facts into fiction but also motivational factors (I.5). This is also the reason why intellectual biographies are the best and most parsimonious date to study the entanglements of pioneers (II.3) and creativity regimes (I.4). Pioneers are basically game changers, but from this it does not follow that they change the basic rules (I.4) of creativity regimes. Pioneers transform strategies of problem solving, which in art worlds means the historically imposed professional techniques (V.3) functioning as more or less constraining prototypes (I.2).

But transformation of *techniques* (V.3) only marginally changes the *rules* of art (I.4) or "final cause" (V.4); the rules remain fundamentally the same, evoking and/or expressing senso-motorically mediated emotions. Confusing techniques and rules explain most of the current confusion in studies of artistic creativity, a confusion which in turn has functioned as a major knowledge constraint (I.3) for a creativity science. But for this purpose, we need to look closer at the origins of such artistically mediated emotions. This takes us back to the core role of physical constraints but also how to conceptualize the problem of mediated forms of the social more generally.

Does a theory of genius help us to explain creativity of the highest kind? There are different ways of answering this difficult question. One would be to look closer at the history of the idea of romantic genius (Abrams, 1953; Hegel, 1970). A core claim of the idea of romantic genius is that (great) artists, in contrast to scientists, are the epitome of human freedom (Kant, 1790/1974). The artist as genius is presented as a role model (prototypes, I.2) for the rest of humanity, the humanistic idea (compare Cahn & Meskin, 2008) that to be a human in the full sense requires complete freedom to do as one pleases.

But this ideal at a closer range seems to be fiction rather than fact and science is here to separate facts from fiction, not turn facts into fiction, which is the job of the artist. This does not exclude the possibility that there might be geniuses in some sense, but this is of little help for creativity science. What the theory of genius basically says is that creativity and in particular pioneering work cannot be explained. But is this an indisputable fact or does it instead belong to the category of fiction? How would we go about falsifying such a theory (V.4)? What we want to know is how and why some individuals rather than others become pioneers. But there is no such thing as pioneers in the abstract sense. One can only become a pioneer by renewing an already existing intellectual tradition (Steffensen, 2017). How does this function in practice?

A first principle of postmodernism is that science is a form of art. Science "creates" or "invents" and does not really "discover" (Deleuze,

2004, compare the idea that "culture" provides a privileged understanding of what scientific knowledge is; see McCarthy, 1996). But this cannot be right, the creativity of avant-garde artists such as Picasso and Matisse tells us very little about the creativity of pioneering scientists such as Crick and Watson. This does not exclude that there might be some more general patterns for becoming a pioneer such as the opportunity factor (I.5c) or the need to protect vulnerable versions (Dimension IV). But in order to explain the complexity and paradoxes of pioneering work, we need to take the role of intellectual fields (creativity regimes, see Dimension V) seriously. Matisse's obsession with techniques (V.2) gives us a hint of how he became a pioneer in painting. He took copying art masterpieces seriously; this was the way he related to the tradition. Writers basically do the same. But books are copies and not originals. One might still want to go to Paris to become a professional writer and end up as a pioneer (Putnam, 1947/ 1978), but in this case one does not go there to see the original manuscripts.

The texture of different layers of color painted on the canvas is uninteresting for the reader of novels. The long description of church art at the beginning of Proust's long novel *À la recherche du temps perdu* clearly does not work in this context. What a reader of novels expects, and the professional writer has to learn in order to get it right, is how to make the main characters come alive in the present but also create suspense so that the reader wants to read on, which is best done by a combination of evoking pity and fear (compare Ken Follett's novels) This does not exclude the fact that writers use live models, often people they knew or know intimately to create the types of feelings and emotions (according to Aristotle, emotions are merely reflected feelings) which arose the interest and curiosity of the reader. But such live material (V.1) is not yet fiction or art (Svedjedal, 1999).

Novels are facts transformed into fiction (V.4) and emotions evoked in an artwork are not necessarily even near the private emotions of the writer expressed in the artwork (Carroll, 2005, 2010). Sartre's experience during his year in Berlin was not as pessimistic as the alienated narrator and main character in *Nausea* suggests. For Sartre the year he had spent in Berlin (1933–1934) had been his "Berlin Holiday." It was when he was back to teaching in Le Havre that reality caught up with him. He was approaching 30 and was still a nobody. He would later refer to this period in his life as "the gloomy years." The excitement of Berlin was over, and he was back at his school. In contrast he found his life comrade Simon de Beauvoir "happier than she had been for some time" (Rowley, 2005, p. 55).

Simone de Beauvoir was in the midst of a love affair with a Russian teenager with aristocratic parents, Olga Kosakiewics, whom she later took under her wing both as patron and mentor (IV.5), helping Olga to get an education in Paris, where Simone de Beauvoir had moved after Rouen, the provincial town where she had been teaching at a girls lycée. Olga had a younger sister, Wanda, who was eventually taken up by the older couple as both protégée and shared lover like her older sister before her (Cohen-Solal, 1987). None of this sordid affair is reported accurately in Simone de Beauvoir's first novel, *She Came to Stay*.

First of all, the facts have all changed. Instead of two sisters, there is only one young woman and rather than being seduced by the elderly couple she is the seducer. Moreover, she is mostly interested in the male character who is also a distorted version of Sartre, a successful theater director, with surprisingly little interest in young and beautiful women. The reader is supposed to feel pity for the elderly women alias Simone de Beauvoir who fears losing her male lover to a young and beautiful girl who is only interested in her physical appearance and to further her career, by replacing the older women. Who nevertheless as a gesture of sisterly solidarity takes her young rival under her wings. There is not a shadow of biographical truth here, but the novel does work as fiction. The prototype (I.2) of the model might be a real event though: The friendship between Fernande Olivier, Picasso's first lover and model, and Eva Guël, a young seamstress who secretly had begun a love affair with Picasso while Fernando took the young women under her wings (Richardson, 1996/1997). A possible literary prototype might have been the cynical social climber Becky Sharp in Thackeray's novel *Vanity Fair*.

## Constraints and Creativity: Becoming a Pioneer

An interesting pattern so far is the discovery that physical constraints (I.1) for some reasons seem to be more important for pioneering artists (painters) than for scientists, where knowledge constraints (I.3) seem to be critical. One possible explanation might be that visual art works need to be seen in their physical form ("original," see Sonesson, 1992) in order to have full aesthetic effects upon connoisseurs (patrons, mentors, agents) who in reality decide the careers of artists. But foregrounding physical constraints (I.1) also helps us explain why problem-solving strategies (techniques, V.3) vary with art form. For novel writing, access to the "original" in the physical sense is irrelevant for the senso-emotional (aesthetic) value or appreciation (Levinson, 2006, 2016; Zangwill, 2001), which basically uses words and not color, and hence does not appeal to direct physical experience.

Given that twentieth-century painters are no longer restricted to the physical media of painting (artifacts) but are free to choose (Danto, 1997), any mediated form of the social or cultural tool (text, performance, even art works which require careful mathematical calculations, see the monumental sculptures of Hammond, Tomkins, 2019) will do. Foregrounding the freedom of choice of medium among contemporary avant-garde artists, makes it look as if artistic creativity is contingent rather than constrained or that avant-garde artists are purely driven by pleasure (I.Va). It ignores the possible role of pressure (I.5b) and opportunity (I.5c). I am talking of painters and sculptors (the fine arts) not about imitators such as the avant-garde composer and orchestra director John Cage and experimental novel writers like Susan Sontag at the start of her career (Dollenmayer, 2007/2014). In their cases, avant-garde painting functions as a prototype but also as an "opportunity" (I.5c) legitimizing such creative practices among support systems (IV.5) or the "social forces" of art worlds (White & White, 1965/1993).

But motivational constraints are only one of many constraints influencing creativity and pioneering work. This is the reason why we need a more general constraint theory in order to clarify these issues. Thus, both Picasso and Matisse were obviously constrained by the new art form cinema (Roe, 2015; Spurling, 2009) a case of co-evolution (III.3). In contrast, pioneering filmmakers such as Murnau and Hitchcock were influenced by the visual effects of pictures. But there are also biographical or individual variations that need to be considered. Chaplin's pioneering work as a filmmaker can best be explained by his family and professional background in acting. Ingmar Bergman came from a religious family and originally trained himself to become a writer. He entered the movie industry as a script writer, then became a theater director and made movies in his spare time, all of which certainly constrained the way he made movies and might explain why precisely he became a pioneer of the cinema.

Whereas no one can stop one from learning the techniques of novel writing (the abundance of books functions as both pleasure and opportunity, which raises the critical issue of pressure or personal-problem situations, III.4), to be able to work as a film director is a kind of lifetime opportunity (I.5c), although it, too, brings with it both pleasure (I.5a) and pressure (I.5b). Once given the opportunity, one might advance to pioneer (II.4) or remain a professional (II,3) or even be demoted to novice (II.2). This happened to the Swedish director Moritz Stiller when he arrived in

Hollywood with Greta Garbo (see Idestam-Almquist, 1939). But how does one get such a potentially life-transforming chance? Here Latour's theory of the self-reinforcing credit cycle (Latour & Wolgar, 1986) is too simple.

It is an indisputable fact that reputation alone does not secure continuous success in the movie industry, least so in Hollywood where there are many broken careers. This is yet another reason why we must distinguish distinct creativity regimes (Kupferberg, 2003a) from each other, something contemporary sociology of knowledge is notoriously bad at. But nor can we project the career patterns of pioneering avant-garde artists such as Duchamp and Warhol in the film industry. Duchamp gave up painting as a medium voluntarily. He was not dismissed as, for example von Stroheim, for repeatedly ignoring budget constraints (Koszarski, 1983; Lennig, 2000). Warhol's lifelong dream was to become a celebrity. For some reasons, the avant-garde art milieu in New York provided this commercial artist (Dickey, 2000) with a golden opportunity but also a support system (IV.5) necessary to make this step (Acocella, 2020). In contrast, Griffith, one of the great pioneers of the cinema was gradually marginalized, humiliated and driven out of the industry he had contributed so much to (Schickel, 1996).

In order to understand why social recognition in a popular art form like Hollywood cinema is very different from the pampered careers of successful avant-garde artists in Paris, New York, Copenhagen, Berlin, etc. we need to look closer at the very different forms of support systems (IV.5) for these two art forms. Novel ideas are vulnerable at the start and have to be protected (Dimension IV), and support systems play a critical role here. But to understand why support systems in cinema and painting look very different, we also need to compare the creative practice of these two art forms. In contrast to such "individualistic" art forms as painting and writing, the creative processes necessary to make a movie involve many creative professionals (Monaco, 2000: Gray & Seeber, 1996; Lumet, 1996). The problem of coordinating all these creative professions has become an important aspect of "getting it right" (Dimension III). The other complexity is that not all film directors become pioneers of film art. Most remain solid professionals (compare the discussion of "auteurs" in Hollows et al., 2000 and King, 2002).

A possible way to overcome these methodological difficulties might be to look closer at biographical data (compare Kupferberg, 2018b). It seems as if the way an individual enters the film industry becoming a film director, helps to explain if and how a novice (II.1) and or professional

(II.3) becomes a pioneering film director (II.4). Take the case of Charlie Chaplin (Robinson, 2001; Lynn, 1987;, Chaplin, 1964). He was invited to enter American movies not as a movie director but as an actor. He had been touring in England and was spotted by some talent scouts who persuaded him to try his luck in the new industry.

Charlie Chaplin was a born actor in the sense of having been born into a family of actors and early on learned the two basic techniques of acting (pantomime and empathy) by observing characters from his window (Chaplin, 1964). His mother, a music hall entertainer, encouraged him both to imitate observable behavior (pantomime) and inner thought (empathy). These basic techniques of acting (V.3) can best be explained in turn by the combined effect of (1) rules (I.4) and (2) techniques (V.3) on an open stage where bodies move around and talk to each other before an audience (physical constraints, I.1) to evoke emotions.

In contrast, when actors perform in front of the camera (Naremore, 1988), there is no live action in the sense of live interaction with the audience. This explains why the main technique of film, to compensate for the intensity of live interaction, is editing, a basic technique (V.3) invented by Edwin S. Porter, an engineer working for Edison's studio in New York (Baldwin, 1995) This might also explain why American film had discovered early on one of the possible emotional effects of editing: "action-packed" movies (Jacobs, 1968). Editing is a very powerful technique for evoking emotions among movie audiences (V.4). The point is that editing functions as a "general-purpose tool" (Rosenberg, 2010). It can be used for many different types of emotional effects (Hitchcock seems to have studied the Russian director Pudovkin's editing techniques; see Gottlieb, 1995, 2015).

As noted by Aristotle, the core of drama is "pity and fear." When Chaplin arrived on the West coast, Porter's discovery, that editing could be used for the purpose of action-packed movies or pure spectacle, had colonized film production to the degree that there was hardly any time for a story line which could provide the "unity of action" within which the character is given space to develop morally and allow the audience to identify with the actor (a precondition for pity and fear but also laughter as relief in comedy). This consideration eventually led to the invention of the tragic-comic figure of the "tramp" (Huff, 1972) a poor but proud man who has seen better days but still insists upon some dignity after having fallen from grace. The evolution of this story line is not as straightforward as Chaplin makes it in his autobiography where the character is presumably invented by pure chance (stroke of genius).

But this cannot be right. If one looks at Chaplin's first movies (artifacts), found relatively recently and studied in detail by Robinson (2001), one notices two things. First, Chaplin frequently draws attention to himself (compare "Race in Venice") as a figure apart from the action rather than integrated into the storyline and second, that his character is not recognizable a tramp until later (sometimes he wears a long coat and looks like a real gentleman rather than someone with a proud past). This indicates that the figure of the tramp must have evolved over time. Chaplin, who had learned the techniques of acting at an early age (his mother as mentor) and from vaudeville performances on stage, probably studied the reactions of the film crew, seeing what worked and what did not, using all his skills of pantomime and empathy to evolve pity and fear, in order to get it right (III.4; in contrast to Thalberg, a voracious reader since childhood, who mainly used daily shots for overseeing an ongoing movie production).

The dissonance between Chaplin's own story and his creative practices has important methodological consequences (Chapter 8). Although art is art and not science, this does not exclude a science of art, although the very possibility seems paradoxical (the problem is discussed with great insight by Hegel in the first hundred pages in his *Vorlesungen über die Ästhetik*). Chaplin's own account for the invention of the tramp should be compared with his actual practice (Elster 1983). According to Chaplin, the invention of the tramp came about when the main male star was for some reasons physically absent from the studio and Chaplin was forced to replace him. This is how the distinctive appearance of the tramp (the bowler hat, the too-tight jacket, the baggy trousers and the cane) were invented according to Chaplin himself (1964; Lynn, 1997). But this could only have been a triggering event or "turning point" (Strauss, 1959) and must have evolved over a long period of time (cf. Ebaugh, 1988). But nor does this prove conscious manipulation of the truth (compare Perkins' 1981 comments about the making of the poem *Kublaki Kahn*), but it could also be a case of poor memory (compare Hacomen, 2000 for the example of Karl Popper).

Chaplin's early experience as a professional actor (II.3) was what secured him the opportunity (I.5c) to direct movies, but the same biography transplanted to American cinema at the time Chaplin arrived (III.4) also explains why Chaplin became a pioneering filmmaker (II.4). Techniques (V.4) in art basically constitute what is called "style" (Bordwell, 1997). Studying the techniques pioneered by great film directors provides the key to the origins of "personal voice" (Engdahl, 1994/2005). Chaplin's intellectual biography helps us to explain the origins of Chaplin's peculiar style of filmmaking.

An actor gets much of his or her inspiration from performing (and improvising) in front of a live audience and it seems as if Chaplin transplanted this core technique of the performer to his role as film director. He had neither the skills nor the patience (Orwell, 1946/1968) of a writer to spend time concocting a storyline and filling it out with detailed characters. He never had a written script before starting movie production. In other words, there was no script. The absence of such a script can sometimes enhance the quality of a star actor's movie performance. Compare Ingrid Bergman in *Casablanca* (Sperling & Miller, 1998). Having hired the actress from another studio, Warner Brothers had to start shooting before the script was finished and later had to move the two authors to another production in the making which was in strong need of script doctors (Behlmer, 1986). With the result that neither she nor Humphrey Bogart knew how the movie would end, an uncertainty which might have helped Ingrid Bergman enter the role of a hysterical women at the critical night scene where the morose Humphrey Bogart sits alone with a bottle of whisky in front of him, awaiting the arrival of the great love of his life (a favorite topic of Hollywood movies and preferably with tragic outcome, compare *Gone with the Wind* and *Cast Away* in contrast to romantic comedies such as *It Happened One Night* and *Pretty Woman*).

In this case there was a script though only some details were missing. Chaplin in contrast often started shooting with only a vague idea of story line. A film script is not only helpful for the actors, who can sit at home and prepare their role, it is also necessary for scenographers, dressers and other professionals in this collective art form. These professionals (Sharff, 1982; Katz, 1991; Giannetti, 1999) need to plan the shots of scenes, mostly described in scripts usually translated into visual story boards (Auiler, 1999). But, the storyline comes first, which is the reason why writing them has become a profession in its own right in the functionally divided and constantly nervous art colony (Rosten, 1941; Powdermaker, 1950) called Hollywood (Server, 1987). But as the case of Chaplin shows, so many professionals working closely together (Becker, 1982) also allows for some inter-professional learning and change of roles (Faulkner & Anderson, 1987).

We know there was a lot of drama whenever Chaplin directed a movie. Given that he preferred to improvise the script while on the set, with the staff as vicarious audience, scenography (mise en scène) was improved on the spot as well (compare the first chance meeting with the blind flower girl in *City Lights*). In a Hitchcock or Bergman movie, this problem would never have occurred. Here everything had to be planned in detail before long before the film went into production. But for Chaplin the absence of a script became the core unsolved creative problem because he preferred to improvise in front of a live audience. Sometimes, due to the lack of a clear storyline to start with, the now morose Chaplin had to stop production and send the staff home, to return to the studio only after the storyline had been clarified by the director and star actor.

Having no clear storyline and no scenes or dialogues for the actors to prepare at home, they were often puzzled and did not know what was expected of them. This made Chaplin (effective cause, V.3) irritated and angry until he exploded (evocation of emotion, V.4). In the case of *City Lights,* his inability to control his emotions led to the firing of the main female star, an amateur actor (II.2) specially chosen for the role of the blind flower girl (Virginia Cherrell). Having tried to replace her with another actress (II.3), he ended up rehiring her, so his first instincts had after all been right.

Chaplin's early experience as a child (II.1), novice (II.2) and professional (II.3) actor sometimes also rescued movies from disaster. In *Gold Fever,* none of the technicians present on the set was able to crawl into the skin of the chicken and really play a live chicken, so Chaplin did it himself. Chaplin's unwillingness to hire a skilled scriptwriter also allowed for many inventive solutions such as building up a story from a revolving door at a spa or a staircase in a department store or a false coin found outside a shabby restaurant (Robinson, 2001). This improvised style of making movies helped make Chaplin one of the pioneers (II.4) of film art, but it only worked as long as most movies that came from Hollywood were one-reel (ten-minute) "flicks." As Hollywood gradually switched to 90-minute features, (a new historical and professional problem situation, compare III.4), Chaplin was in big trouble.

Chaplin's improvised techniques of movie making (V.3) became increasingly out of sync with the evolving reality of Hollywood filmmaking during the 1920s. Film production had now become dominated by a new prototype (I.2), interaction of stars rather than the one and lonely star (a reinvention made by the two strongmen at the leading studio at the time, MGM, Mayer and Thalberg (Marx, 1988)). Although Chaplin managed to produce two more films after *City Lights, Modern Times* which can be seen as a protest against this new, tightly planned creativity regime and *The Great Dictator* as a self-critical satire of Chaplin's dictatorial desire to run the show by himself, he was unable to adjust to the classic studio system which had evolved during the 1920s (Schatz, 1988; Bordwell et al., 1988; Staiger, 1995).

Chaplin's movies remained popular for a time among movie audiences. It is difficult to envisage how he was forced out of the industry and why his US residence permit was revoked. Apart from post-war McCarthyism, other possible reasons could have been changing moral attitudes. Chaplin's attraction to under-age women made him the target of moral crusaders (Maland, 1989). But even more important was probably Chaplin's transformation of the long speech in *The Great Dictator* into direct propaganda for the United States to take a more interventionist stance towards Hitler. The scene was not only unartistic, but it also went against popular opinion (the true ruler in the American type of democracy according to de Tocqueville, 1945). Moreover, the film studios in Hollywood were in an especially vulnerable position, given the predominance of Jews in the leading studios (Gabler, 1988; May, 1980; May & May, 1982). Antisemitism was on the rise at the time both among the masses, due to the unwillingness of ordinary Americans to be dragged into war with Germany, and among the Wasp elites due to ethnic competition (Steinberg, 1989; Gerber, 1986). Receiving no help from his previous support system (IV.5) gave Chaplin little choice but to find somewhere other than America where he in turn could hopefully continue making movies.

Hitchcock also had great difficulties working out the storyline (Spoto, 1976/1992). His strength was to visualize the scene in advance. In contrast to Chaplin, Hitchcock accepted the fact that professional techniques for writing have to be learned or at least one needs to have some talent for this type of creativity. This explains why Hitchcock (as Wilder, another European director, see Sikov, 1998) always hired a professional scriptwriter with whom the director worked closely (teamwork, IV.2), both during the pre-production phase and during film production, given that some changes in the script sometimes had to be made to tighten up the storyline and the performance of the actors (see in particular the movie *To Catch a Thief* with Cary Grant and Grace Kelly as the main stars, described in detail in de Rosa, 2001).

But this raises the more general problem of how Hitchcock, who did not know how to construct a tight storyline, nevertheless achieved the status of a pioneering film director (Friedman, 2015). He must have known something, but what? Hitchcock was for a long time looked down upon as a mere Hollywood hack by American film critics and theorists. His status as a major film artist was first established in post-war France (Vest, 2003), where he became the guru (artistic prototype, I.2) for the new wave (Truffaut, 1983/2017). What in particular impressed his French admirers was his ability to combine the popular form of "suspense movies"

(Gottlieb, 1995, 2015) with the interest of European innovative film director in cinematic techniques (V.3).

Hitchcock managed to emulate the strongly symbolic style of evoking emotions typical for both modern literature and art, but at the same time avoided some of the problematic stylistic patterns of twentieth-century avant-garde art (painting) such as Primitivism, incomprehensibility and colonization of other media (homelessness). Rather than trying to alienate lay audiences by naughty jokes of the type pioneered by Picasso and made into a "general-purpose tool" by Duchamp (the pioneer of the homeless mind in painting), this would have been a professionally suicidal strategy in a popular art form (cf. Bergman, 1959, 1989). Hitchcock always insisted upon clarity of storyline (cf. Bordwell, 1997 and Hitchcock O'Connell, & Bouzerau, 2003/2004). His movies were meant mainly for entertainment without having to be interpreted to be enjoyed (compare Sontag, 1966/2013, 1969).

Movies like *Rear Window* and *Vertigo* are clearly suspense movies, but this does not exclude elements of symbolic motifs. Such symbolic motifs influence the formal aspect of art (composition, V.2) and makes art works more emotionally intense and complex, without loss of overall unity, the three main criteria of aesthetic appreciation according to Beardsley (1958). Thus, in *Rear Window* we see a man (played by James Stewart), with a broken leg, confined to his bed and spending his time looking out on the backyard and opposite windows through his binoculars. His beautiful fiancée (played by Grace Kelly) visits him every day to cheer him up, but what cements their relationship is a suspected murder which takes place in an apartment opposite the balcony.

As the suspense tightens (Is the suspected murderer a real murderer and what will happen if the murderer finds out?), the director displays his knowledge of how to make the composition (V.2) more emotionally intense and complex, without loss of unity, such as the technique (V.3) of "doubling." Doubling is based upon the ambivalence of meaning which comes from the use of metaphors (Lakoff & Johnson,1983). A case in point is the "being caught" motif, represented both by a bachelor being tricked into marriage and a murderer who is caught by another person who is in turn caught in the act of prying. This is doubled by the "voyeur" motif, a photographer looking into the windows of other people's homes, referring to movies allowing us to look at a photographer prying into other people's private lives, etc.

*Vertigo* is also full of doubles, but much more complex and for this reason a favorite for interpretative film scholars. The movie is about a male character trying to compensate for his failures both as a policeman and a friend, who, because he is frightened of heights, has watched both a colleague and the wife of a close friend fall and die. What he does not know (suspense technique) is that his so-called friend has trapped him as a false witness, by hiring an actress whom James Stewart is made to believe is the friend's disturbed wife (doubling). Having saved a woman he believes is the real wife from drowning herself in San Francisco Bay (doubling), he is prone to believe that she has killed herself by jumping from a church tower, where he stood paralyzed from fright, passively watching the body of a blond women resembling the actress fall, as seen through a tiny window (doubling). Recognizing the actress one day, he pursues her and forces her to transform herself into the first women (doubling) until the truth is revealed and she too falls to her death, this time for real (doubling).

There are many other techniques which help describe the evolution of Hitchcock's personal style (Ross, 2003). In order to trace these origins, biographical data (Chapter 8) are of value. Hitchcock had trained (Ackroyd, 2015) as a machine engineer (professional role, II.3) but seems to have been bored by the routine of the job. He followed evening classes at an art school, which gave him great pleasure (I.5a). He was promoted to marketing, drawing advertisements for the firm (rhetoric). This opportunity (I.5c) must have raised Hitchcock's professional ambitions, making him look for more artistic work (compare Andy Warhol). It so happened that an American film studio had started production in the London area (physical constraint, I.1). Here he was mainly drawing excerpts of dialogues (this was the time of silent movies, III.4). When the studio closed, he found a job at a British studio where he met Alma, a much more experienced film professional, specializing in continuity problems. They later married, but first after Hitchcock had proven himself (compare Chagall and Bella).

Hitchcock had now become a professional film director (II.3). But how do we explain his transformation to a pioneering film director (II.4)? How did he combine the "suspense" motif with the use of "symbols" techniques (V.3). Spoto in his biography on Hitchcock (1983/1998) has a tendency to "psychologize" Hitchcock's filmmaking to the degree that all his films are ultimately cases of his own repressed longing for beautiful blondes driven by his own self-awareness of physical unattractiveness (Spoto, 2009). This search for the one "deep truth" of a pioneering film director is yet another case of the danger of the one-factor method in science. If Hitchcock was so ashamed of his bodily stature as Spoto assumes, why did he insist upon appearing in so many of his movies (cameo appearance)? Is it not more probable that Hitchcock not only learned to live with his unattractive physical stature but also saw the potential value of his easy recognizable physiognomy (physical constraints, I.1) as a marketing device (compare the profile used for the televised series made in his name at the end of his life)?

Methods matter in science. The best explanation for Hitchcock's transformation from professional to pioneer is a case of "creativity abroad" (Kupferberg, 1998a). Having been promoted to movie director, Hitchcock was given the chance (opportunity, I.5c) to make films in Germany (Gottlieb, 2002), the leading creative milieu in Europe. The combination of "suspense" and "symbols" was the very essence of the German "expressionist" style (Eisner, 1969). The origins of this style deserve a study of their own, but apart from the political chaos of the Weimar Republic, the professional training (II.3) of the predominant filmmakers in Germany at the time (Huaco, 1965) might be a good clue. German film directors entered the film industry mainly from the plastic or visual arts (painting, sculpture, architecture) and hence used the knowledge of physical constraints (I.1) of such art forms for aesthetic effects.

All such art forms are basically static, introducing some kind of dynamic becomes important. Some artists, such as Vermeer use strong light sources, which in film could be replaced by strong electric light. Other artists such as Matisse use such techniques as dancing figures which seems to be removed from the laws of gravity, concentrated energy (Barr, 1953/1976), prolonged long limbs (a typical baroque device, see Gombrich, 1996). Picasso's and Braque's Cubism (Rubin, 1989) foregrounded overlapping planes, collages, flat, paper-like figures, clowns, etc., all of which is clearly visible in German Expressionist movies.

The expressionistic techniques (V.3) of German filmmakers became a prototype (I.2) for Hitchcock, an intellectual migrant (IV.2) who had also become a geographical migrant (IV.1). Both types of social contexts are good for protecting vulnerable versions in the making. As a newcomer to the industry, he was probably also more open to new ideas, but the important thing is that being far away from home (physical constraint) allowed him to work in secret from the organization (skunk works, IV.3), but also confide in Alma (communicational secrecy, IV.4). Finally, he also had the advantage of a support system (IV.5, the studio) which paid the bills (patronage) but also provided access to pioneering German filmmakers such as Murnau whom Hitchcock was allowed to observe at close hand in a German film studio (prototype, I.2). Being in Germany (physical constraint, I.1) also allowed Hitchcock to see a lot of German movies (including those of Fritz Lang, the leading German film director), another prototype (I.2).

Murnau and Lang both, although in different ways, functioned as "mentors" (V.5) for Hitchcock in a critical period of his career. The studio also functioned as an agent (V.5), marketing and distributing his films in England and elsewhere. This is how David Selznick heard of Hitchcock and offered him a film contract and a new career in United States, opportunity (I.5c). Hitchcock made several films with Ingrid Bergman and other leading Hollywood stars and was now regarded as a star director. The mighty support system in Hollywood worked for him as it had done for Chaplin, another expatriate film director.

In his interviews, neither his early professional training and intellectual migration (II.2, II.3, IV.2), nor his apprenticeship in Germany (IV.1, I.1, I.2), nor the role of skunk works and confidants (II.3, II.4), nor the importance of changing support system (IV.5) for his transformation from merely professional to pioneering film director are mentioned. Among the prototypes (I.2), Hitchcock constantly mentions the Russian film director Pudovkin (editing techniques, V.3) but not the expressionistic techniques of Murnau and Lang. Hitchcock's argument that he approached the problem of suspense differently from Agatha Christie, is not convincing either. There are many ways to create suspense. The basic technique of withholding information (Zalewski, 2009) remains the same.

The most important differences between the two are that Agatha Christie wrote novels and plays. In order to function as movies, plays have to be adapted to the big screen (the problem of incommensurability). Moreover, Agatha Christie was a highly successful professional writer (II.3). Hitchcock was a highly successful pioneering filmmaker (II.4).

Like Hitchcock, Bergman never started film production without a script (1989). This is not surprising given that Bergman originally trained himself to become a writer (Koskinen, 2002). This early training and possibly natural talent never left him (compare the creative difficulties he faced when writing the script to his last movie, *Fanny and Alexander*, see Koskinen & Rhodin, 2005). Moreover, in contrast to Hitchcock, Bergman never became a full-time film director; indeed, his main profession was theater director (Sjögren, 2002; Timm 2008). Whereas Hitchcock generally avoided making films which basically registered what could have been seen by a theater audience, many if not most of Bergman's movies are obviously influenced by the theater (Koskinen, 2001), but given the different constraints of a movie setting, this allows Bergman to play with the contrast of a life outdoors, constant change of scene, as on a voyage

(*The Seventh Seal, Wild Strawberries*) and the sense of cramped, narrow quarters and all the tensions and irritations which comes from such a type of physical constraint (I.1, compare *Persona* which takes place on an isolated island as does *The Summer with Monika*).

Another interesting aspect of Bergman's career as a filmmaker was that his films were mostly shot during summer vacations. Although the motif for making these films might have been financial (actors did not earn much money at the time and Bergman's many affairs and growing number of children also played a role, "pressure," I.5b), the most important constraint was the fact that Bergman could constantly juggle between the two roles (intellectual migration, IV.2). This professional juggling was itself highly conducive for creativity and a possible case of the role of skunk works (IV.3). Bergman described his job as movie director as having a "lover" but staying "married" to the same woman (both types of motivation, pleasure, I.5a and pressure, I.5b, are evoked lovingly and ironically in *Smiles of a Summer Night*).

Making these films also provided Bergman with the opportunity (I.5c) to write his own stories, which was not possible as a theater director at the national theater (Sjögren, 2002). Writing for movies and writing novels are not the same thing. How did Bergman learn the craft of writing a viable film script? This motif never appears in his films but is commented upon in his autobiography *Laterna Magica*. Here Bergman reveals that he learned the craft from the wife of Hjalmar Bergman, who had just returned from Hollywood and became his mentor (see IV.5). In *Bilder* (Pictures) published in 1990, a year after the autobiography, Bergman describes in great detail the creative process of writing a film script. Here the core problem is how to integrate the cinematic techniques (V.3) into a film script, given that in film everything is seen by a moving camera (Arnheim, 1957).

Bergman reveals that he got the idea for the title (*Whispers and Cries*) from an opera by Mozart. At the time he was married to a successful concert pianist (Käbi Laritei). They had a son, Daniel Bergman. Bergman fathered many children (nine) with several women, but probably felt that he had not been a good father. As noted above, modern art works do tend to express the emotions of the artist, although this is done in an indirect, evocative rather than a "didactic" manner as in science (Ryle, 1949/2000). This might explain why he chose to project his probably bad conscience in a film on a successful female concert pianist who in contrast to the role model (Käbi Laritei, I.2) has a daughter. The unhappy daughter is played by Liv Ullman with whom he did have a daughter (Linn). Her experiences of her absent father and mother are lovingly retold in Linn Ullmann's autobiographical novel *The worried/De oroliga)*.

As admitted in an article in 1959, Bergman was very well aware of the fact that artists "cannibalize" on intimate secrets shared by family, lovers and friends. All Bergman's films are in this sense masked autobiographies (Long, 1994). Many of them are clearly influenced by the fact that his father was a pastor (religious motifs). Others reflect his personal conflicts and rebellion (father-son relationship) and others again go back to the tensions in his parents' marriage which almost led to their divorce. All the three film directors have become prototypes (I.2) for later filmmakers, although for different reasons and in changing problem situations which involve both historical, professional and personal aspects (III.4). In contrast, Woody Allen (Meade, 2001) never achieved the status of pioneering filmmaker ("great artist") and never will, possibly because he never developed a consistent personal style. Allen's annually produced films in a somewhat too self-conscious and self-ironic way mainly reveal his life as a viewer of old movies.

# CHAPTER 4

# Dimension III: Getting It Right

Disputable and Indisputable Facts

As noted above, disciplines tend to be constrained by their First principles. One of the First principles of twentieth-century philosophy of science has been the assumption that there are no indisputable facts; all facts are disputable. This idea, which originated in the Vienna circle (Hacomen, 2000), was made into a cornerstone of Karl Popper's theory of science. It can be already found in his first book *The Logic of Scientific Discovery* and is repeated in his posthumously published *The World of Parmenides*. But this cannot be right. In order to falsify theories (final cause, V.4), science needs to get the facts right (material cause, V.1). But facts cannot be taken for granted; they have to be discovered. Such discoveries in turn function as knowledge constraints (I.3) for further discoveries (falsifications, the final cause of science, V.4).

Take the case of geology. The belief that the age of the Earth could be calculated in terms of successive generations (historical time, the type of chronology found in the Jewish Bible, prototype, I.2) functioned as a knowledge constraint for thousands of years. Falsifying this belief was the precondition for clarifying one of the First principles of geology, the assumption of geological time. We can all this an *empirical* type of falsification (separation of facts from fiction, V.4). But this in turn led to the problem of how to calculate geological time, using what data. This led to the further discovery that texts cannot be valid as scientific data for this science. In order to get the correct measurement of the age of the Earth, the discipline of geology had to be based upon collection and interpretation of a very different type of data (material cause, V.1), better adapted to the nature of the knowledge object (V.1.), in this case the history of the Earth, namely rocks (with or without fossils). We can call this a *methodological* type of falsification (V.3). A third assumption was that the Earth had no identifiable beginning as it had in the Jewish narrative of creation. The best way to understand the history of the Earth was to describe it as a case of recurrent or repetitive events (the rock cycle). We can call this a *conceptual* type of falsification (V.2). But both the methodological and conceptual type of falsification rested upon an empirical falsification that the idea that the Earth was 6,000 years old was fiction and not fact (data matter, compare Tyco Brahe's March data for astronomy, completely ignored by Kuhn who also ignores the role of instruments and scientific technology; compare Hacking, 1983 and Laudan & Leplin, 1991/2007).

The point is that such indisputable facts have to be discovered; they are not given. Thus, the theory of continental drift was just a theory or working hypothesis before the discovery of the tectonic plates which transformed it from a disputable to an undisputable fact. It is also an undisputable fact (empirical patten) that even pioneering scientists sometimes invent fictive facts in order to explain what they are unable to explain at the moment (Newton's "ether," a pure fiction, but believed to be necessary as a "mechanism" to explain gravity until Einstein found the correct solution). Science advances as a "body of knowledge" (Lloyd, 1991) by the gradual accumulation of such indisputable facts that transform previous working hypotheses or theories into facts (Dawkins, 1996/2006; Mayr, 2002).

Nothing has been so misunderstood as the widely used concept "theory" which can mean anything today, which is the reason we should use it with caution and explain what we mean rather than taking it for granted (the misuse of the concept theory probably originated in Hanson's (1956) concept "theory-laden", which fails to discuss the role of methodology for establishing facts). Interestingly, Popper in *The World of Parmenides* reprimands Aristotle for his presumably incorrect belief in indisputable facts as the ultimate aim of falsification. But if this assumption (First principle) of Popper's theory of science was indeed correct, falsification becomes meaningless. All falsifications are ultimately aiming for the discovery of indisputable facts such as geological time, continental drift, universal gravity, etc. Each step in science (progress) depends upon getting it right, but getting it right is basically an evolutionary process, a gradual, step-by-step overcoming of knowledge constraints (I.3). Interestingly, the overcoming of knowledge constraints is less important for artistic and technological revolutions. Here physical constraints (I.1) are the critical factor. The question is why.

## N-Creativity

In order to understand how technological creativity works, the best way to start is by using Darwin's theory of the creativity of nature as a prototype (I.2) although updated by recent knowledge within evolutionary biology and sociobiology. Sociobiology as discipline is based upon the empirical falsification of the false belief that only humans are able to communicate. But this cannot be true. Ants, who are basically blind, use chemical signals (Hölldobler & Wilson, 1994). Bees use behavioral signals (dance) and other species such as chimpanzees use simple biological (Crystal 1987) sounds or gestures, etc.

What is particularly striking is the inventiveness of non-human species. Beavers invented dams long before humans. Spiders invented glue millions of years ago (Dawkins, 1996/2006) and fruit bats invented highly complicated radar systems 50–100 million years before humans managed to rediscover the same basic principles for a working solution (Dawkins 1986/2006; Tudge 2009). Migrating birds solved the problem of navigating over long distances without landmarks long before England managed to solve the problem in the seventeenth century (Tudge 2008; Boorstin 1985), but the prize probably goes to ants (Keller & Gordon 2010).

This species or genus managed to invent (1) agriculture long before the Neolithic revolution (Pfeiffer, 1977), (2) the use of slaves to do the hard work long before the ancient civilizations (Weber, 1976), (3) hygiene long before the Romans (Cunliffe, 2008 ), (4) kindergartens long before the Scandinavian welfare states (Bok, 1988). But it took human consciousness and communication (talk) to learn how to control fire (Childe, 1951/ 1983). Fire is a precondition for making hardened spears to hunt and kill mammoths (a specialty of the Neanderthals), but it takes more advanced forms of communication, articulate language, to invent replaceable thin spear heads, which can only be found among modern humans (Fagan, 2010; Jensen, 2013). Articulate talk was also a precondition for transforming primitive forms of controlled fire to heating for the purpose of ceramics and metallurgy, two technologies which probably co-evolved (III.3).

## T-Creativity, S-Creativity and A-Creativity

The creativity of nature (N-creativity) is the prototype for all human forms of creativity (H-creativity). But technology is not yet science and nor is art. What artists (effective cause V.3) do is to transform facts into fiction. This is done to evoke and/or express emotions (final cause, V.4). For this purpose, artists need to learn certain techniques (V.3) usually by close study of how artists before them painted (prototype, I.2, compare Matisse's methods of learning and working). Pioneers, being voracious imitators, stand a greater chance of rediscovering (III.2) techniques which have long since been forgotten or ignored.

Such rediscoveries of abandoned artistic techniques might explain why artistic revolutions seem to work in a different way from science. Impressionism was much inspired by the rediscovery of Japanese techniques (Honour & Fleming, 1982/1984). Modern architecture started with the rediscovery of Classical Greek art by Le Corbusier and other young architects. Le Corbusier, when he visited Athens during his first educational journey to the Mediterranean origins and highlights of European architecture, was struck by the structural simplicity of classical architecture (Weber, 2008). For him the physical experience of standing in front of Parthenon told him the elementary lesson of architecture. "The elements of architecture are light and shade, walls and space" (Le Corbusier, 1931/2017, p. 59). As noted by Hegel (1970), such structural elements, which for Le Corbusier allowed architecture to reach parsimonious (economic, elegant solutions) can best be explained by physical constraints (I.1).

Film theorists have found similar structural elements helping them to get it right (find elegant and economic solutions). The basic idea of cinema was the "photoplay" (Gottlieb, 1995, 2015), starting with the written play and theatrical performance as a prototype (I.2). But in film the camera serves as a vicarious audience. It is for the camera that the actors perform, not live audiences (physical constraints, I.1). Film actors (effective cause, V.3) therefore need to develop appropriate techniques (V.3) to perform in front of a camera. Movie directors, another effective cause (V.3), also need to develop appropriate techniques for directing actors but they must also be able (skills and attitudes) to cooperate with and instruct the other creative professionals in a film team (Lumet, 1996), such as the scriptwriter, the camera operator, the editor, etc. Editors are also effective causes (V.3) who in turn have to learn the appropriate techniques of their respective professions.

But movie directors are also, in a sense, specialists. They are known for or have developed a personal style (combination of techniques) which makes them different from other directors. As for painters and writers, this personal style (Engdahl, 1994/2005) tends to be easy recognizable when we are dealing with great (pioneering) artists. As noted by Greenberg (1961/1965) pioneering avant-garde artists are also expected to do precisely that, once they have found the personal style which makes them recognizably different from others ("originality"). But film is a popular art form. It is not aimed at connoisseurs who have the right cultural tools for interpreting avant-garde art in order to enjoy start works. Films are aimed at lay audiences, who expect immediate pleasure, without previous interpretation (entertainment, see Maltby, 1994). This fact creates a tension between the need for clarity of narrative expected by popular media (Bordwell, 1997; Carroll, 1996) and the need for personal style expected by modern artists (Giannetti, 1999, pp. 295–300). The way this tension is solved in practice is what makes the movie director into the most important of the many effective causes (V.3), the role of the "auteur" (Hollows et al., 2000; King, 2002).

## Parsimony As a Criterion of Successful Problem Solving

The fact that S-creativity, A-creativity and T-creativity are all modeled upon N-creativity is the core of constraint theory. It also helps us to identify the core criteria or essence of when problem solving is creative and when it is not. Although it is true that we need to start with retrospective data (recognized creativity) in order to identify successful scientific, artistic and technological revolutions (contributions), it is not social recognition as such that makes a solution successful from a creative science point of view. So, what is it? As always in science it is best to start with the relevant data (material cause, V.1). Take the case of Newton's discovery that gravity is a universal force (Bohm, 1998; Darling, 2006). Newton's theory clearly has "aesthetic qualities" (Morell, 2004) if we with aesthetics mean a solution that looks simple in the sense of being elegant and economic (the core of parsimony). The does not make Newton's theory into art. Parsimony simply means that the theory successfully solved a number of tricky, previously unsolved problems in the history of theoretical physics.

Having identified the criteria for a successful solution (parsimony) the next question becomes the origins of a successful solution (pioneering work). How did Newton arrive at this solution in practice? Was it by combining Galileo's falsification (V.4.) of Aristotle's "biological" theory of the law of fall (Renn, 2001) with Kepler's (Koestler, 1964; Ferguson, 2003) falsification of Aristotle's "geometrical" theory that all celestial objects, including planets, move in perfect circles (modeled upon Plato's theory of ideal forms, prototype, I.2)? The elliptical shape of planetary movements was not known before Kepler. The predominant theory (inherited from Aristotle) had for thousands of years been that celestial phenomena move in perfect circles. This false theory (fiction) had functioned as a knowledge constraint (I.3) for all attempts to explain the erratic behavior of planets (recurrent loops, including Copernicus' model which precisely lacked parsimony for this reason). But how did Kepler manage to falsify Aristotle's wrong theory (V.4)?

## The Importance of Correct Data, Method and Concepts

Neither Kuhn nor Popper put much trust in data although for different reasons. It is a fact though that without correct data (V.1) Kepler would not have been able to falsify (V.4) one of Aristotle's First principles of astronomy, the circular form of how celestial bodies move, proving this principle to be based upon fiction and not facts. The correct data alone did do the job though. The database was collected in a systematic, methodological manner (V.3) by Tyco Brahe and his team at Oranburg, but that was not enough. The data also had to be interpreted by advanced algebra, another scientific method (V.3) in order to falsify the fiction that celestial bodies move in perfect circles (V.4). This led to a change of concept (V.2) which summarized the discovery Kepler arrived at (falsification of one of the First principles of Aristotle's astronomy).

But why could neither Kepler, nor Galileo, combine the two types of falsifications and falsify another of Aristotle's First principles, the assumption that gravity was a local rather than a universal force (change of concept, V.2)? Why could they not do Newton's job? In order to arrive at this even more fundamental falsification, Newton needed an even more advanced mathematical tool, calculus (method, V.3). This is the reason method or rather methodology plays the role of core problem-solving strategy in science. But methodology is not given. It has to be discovered just as the correct data (V.1) and concepts (V.2). All can best be categorized as knowledge constraints (I.3).

## Local and Global Validity

Some remarks can be made here. One is that Latour's argument (First principle) that scientific laboratories only produce locally valid knowledge (Latour & Wolgar, 1979) is clearly modeled upon Aristotle's false theory of how a force like gravity works (prototype I.2). Latour builds this anachronistic theory, the First principle that universal validity of locally produced knowledge (sites) cannot be proven, upon the theory that universal validity is in fact not a result of theoretical but productive knowledge (rhetoric).

The way this works according to Latour is that rhetoric is what in practice propels scientific reputations (Latour, 1983/1994, 1987, 1999). This First principle is based upon anther prototype (I.2), the "symmetry principle," one of the First principles of the Strong program (Bloor, 1976). For Bloor scientific reputation is explained not by successful scientific

discovery (sociocognitve problem-solving capacity) but by scientific reputation (a circular argument; compare Latour's t "credit cycle" and Merton's
"Matthew effect"). Bloor's argument or claim (First principles) is supported by the claim that the advance of mathematical knowledge is
contingent and not constrained. But this cannot be right.

Advanced algebra did not exist at the time Aristotle formulated his
theories of physical and astronomic laws (knowledge constraint, I.3).
This is the main reason why Aristotle got it wrong. He could not have
discovered what Galileo and Kepler discovered (Law of fall, elliptical shape
of planetary movements). But nor could Galileo and Kepler do what
Newton managed to, falsifying the third of Aristotle's three wrong First
principles, the fiction that gravity was a local force. For this calculus was
necessary, which did not exist around 1600 (knowledge constraint, I.3,
historical and professional problem situation, III.4).

Neither Latour nor Bloor therefore managed to get it right. A closer
look at the intellectual source of their mistake, indicates that it derives
from Kuhn's sociological theory of scientific revolutions as recurrent
political or linguistic events (prototype, I.2). But Kuhn's false theory
(fiction) is based upon Copernicus' theoretical model (prototype, I.2)
which turns out not to be parsimonious (unsuccessful problem solving
in science). The lack of parsimony explains why Kuhn's choice of the
"Copernican revolution" led him to the fiction (V.4.) that scientific
revolutions do not solve problems (Kuhn, 1959/1977).

## Intended and Unintended Discovery

Einstein's relativity theory (Isaacson, 2008; Darling, 2006) in contrast to
Copernicus' theoretical model was indeed parsimonious (economic, elegant), but if we look at how Einstein falsified Newton's theory of the
"ether," we find that in contrast to most pioneering work in science,
Einstein's falsification was intentional. He approached the problems of
science in a practical (pragmatic) manner just as engineers tend to do by
asking what the remaining unsolved problems in Newton's physics were,
attempting to solve them one by one (Darling, 2006). Using Einstein's
approach as role model (prototype, I.2) might explain why Popper always
insisted that groundbreaking discoveries (falsification, V.4) in science had
to be of the intended type.

But this much better describes how engineers approach problems. The
Wright Brothers clearly looked for a practical solution for how to make a
motorized airplane maneuverable, so it could lift, land and stay long

enough in the air without coming crashing down with the possible death of the pilot, destruction of costly material and waste of months of efforts. Newcomen did look for a way to help mine owners solve the problem of water-filled mines, which also might have both material and human costs such as miners being drowned and tragedies for the families involved. The engineering firm which got the commission to redesign the Tay railway bridge in Scotland, after the both human and economic catastrophe when the previous design turned out not to be able to resist strong gales (Baxandall, 1985), clearly also approached this practical problem with the intention of avoiding such human costs and economic waste.

In contrast, pioneering work in science as a rule is not intended. Darwin did not set out to falsify the geological explanation of an essentially biological phenomenon ("special creation"), this discovery/falsification only arrived gradually, as Darwin became increasingly skeptical of Lyell's theory of "special creation." Einstein's intended falsification of Newton was an exception to the rule and can best be explained by his background in applied science. Technological innovations are practical solutions to problems of survival and reproduction of species and depend upon the problem-solving strategy of trial and error. But in contrast to nature and science, creativity in technology is clearly intended. How about art?

### Aesthetic Strategies and the Role of Patronage

Art is not in the business of practical problem solving. It does not seek to save life and reduce waste. Art is a kind of unnecessary waste of resources and it often demands human sacrifice for some presumably higher goal or meaning in life. Who decides what that meaning is? Even avant-garde artists often work for commissions. This follows from the strong role of collectors as the main patrons of art. Compare Matisse for whom private commissions for very wealthy collectors played a critical role in his career strategy (Barr,1953/1976; Spurling, 2009). Picasso's career strategy (Barr, 1946) was strikingly different. He relied more upon art gallery owners who functioned as mediators to wealthy but not necessarily extremely wealthy art collectors that Matisse was able to attract such as Shchukin and Barnes (Spurling, 2009).

In Picasso's case, the emphasis was on another type of art collector, the more or less anonymous clients of the art gallery. Where the influence of rich and eccentric art collectors was personal and direct in Matisse's case, it was impersonal and indirect (mediated) in Picasso's case. The aesthetic influence of the indirect type of patronage (IV.5) can be studied by comparing Fitzgerald's (1996) study of Picasso's change of art gallerists during the period when Kahnweiler was no longer a daily presence in his life and Cowling's (2002) study of what happened to Picasso's style during those years (from 1914 to the end of the 1920s). It was most probably Kahnweiler's influence that led Picasso to enter the period of "Cubism" (Richardson, 1996/1997) but also its main aesthetic strategy, never to let the painting become completely abstract, always to leave something, if only a small detail to start from, for the anonymous client to be able gradually to see what or who a Cubist painting represented (Gilot & Lake, 1964/1981).

## Problem-Solving Strategies in Technology, Art and Science

Engineers in contrast to artists tend to use trial and error (V.3) as their main problem-solving strategy. They look at prototypes (I.2) as something to be improved upon. They also look for deficiencies which might explain lack of efficiency, waste, catastrophe, etc. (compare the evolution of cans described in Petrosky, 1996). The core problem-solving strategies of artists are techniques (V.3) and such techniques are very detailed (compare the description of Matisse's observation of pictures). Artists also look at other pictures to learn something about form or composition (V.2) but here close observation is not necessary. A composition can be taken in at one glance; techniques cannot.

Lay audiences are used to looking for compositions (V.2), not how the artist uses color, the core of artistic techniques (V.3).

For the artist, choice of techniques is constrained by the overall rules of art (to evoke emotions in the broad sense) but also physical constraints. How does this work in literature? The foremost physical constraint of novels is their size and this puts the writer under pressure (I.5b) to create suspense. But it also provides opportunities (I.5c) to introduce characters which evoke the emotions of pity and fear. In both cases, the artists need to approach the problem of what is the most parsimonious solution in an intentional manner. The core of such intention is to evoke emotions by turning facts into fiction. Compare how Picasso intentionally painted *Guernica* in a way which made the personal brutality of the civil war in Spain, look insignificant or invisible compared with the impersonal attack from machines in the air with *She Came to Stay*, Simone de Beauvoir's obliterations of any traces of the sordidness of her and her life partners' selfish exploitation of two young exiled Russian aristocratic sisters.

Whereas artists and engineers approach problems in an intentional mode, although for different purposes (V.4) and using different types of problem-solving strategies, trial and error versus techniques (V.3), science is a different game. One can never know in advance what one is going to find, and which theories or assumptions (First principles) will turn out to be false. But nor is this necessary. Approaching problems in a methodological manner makes it possible for pioneering scholars to reduce the uncertainty (Ewers & Nowotny, 1987) enough to discover new facts, empirical patterns and laws which falsify previous theories and assumptions. Popper never managed to solve the problem of what makes science a science, because he believed that falsification in science (V.4) has to be intended, but also because he confused the problem-solving strategy (V.3) of science, methodology, with the problem-solving strategy of technology, which is trial and error (which happens to be the same problem-solving strategy as nature, N-creativity).

### Nature, Technology and Science

What is interesting is that nature, although it uses the same problem-solving strategy as technology, trial and error, in reality (fact) manages to discover elegant and economic solutions (such as the hexagonal shape of honeycombs) unintentionally. Scientists also manage to find successful solutions characterized by parsimony in an unintended manner, although the problem-solving strategy is methodology and not trial and error. I will return to the possible reasons for this paradox later. In this context I merely want to foreground the obvious similarities of both final goal (V.4) (adaption) and effective cause (V.3), problem-solving strategy (trial and error) of both nature and technology, in spite of the fact that technology is intended and the former unintended as in science.

We can now more clearly see Popper's mistake. Generalizing from Einstein's successful revolution, which was both intended and based upon trial and error rather than unintended and based upon methodology or First principles he never managed to clarify how and in what sense Darwin's theory of evolution can help explain Darwin's scientific discovery, apart from one thing, that they both somehow managed to arrive at parsimonious solutions (III.1) and managed to overcome knowledge constraints (I.3).

The problem is Popper's (1) rejection of Aristotle's empirical approach (Kant's "quid juris" rather than "quid facti"), (2) his rejection of "indisputable fact" and (3) his projection of the basic problem-solving technique of nature, trial and error, upon science (compare his claim that there is no essential difference between an amoeba and Einstein). But this does not solve the deeper similarity between N-creativity and S-creativity. Both are essentially unintended. This takes us to another unsolved paradox in Popper's thinking. While on the one hand admitting that nature is capable of highly complex problem solving (N-creativity), which certainly proves that Darwin got it right and arrived at a parsimonious (elegant/economic) solution to the previously unsolved problem of the origins of species, Popper rejects Darwin's evolutionary theory as science (1974). The reasons for this rejection are obscure but can probably be explained by Popper's lack of understanding of the role that methodology (clarification of First principles) plays in science.

Such clarifications are essentially cases of falsification, the final cause of science (V.4). Cases in point are

- Thomsen's falsification of the First principles of archivarian science, replacing texts with artifacts and hermeneutic methods with stylistic comparative analysis as more fitting for the study of preliterate societies (knowledge object).
- Hutton's discovery of geological time, based upon a falsification of the fiction that the Earth is 6,000 years old. This completely false calculation of time was based upon wrong data and wrong method: textual data, hermeneutic interpretation plus simple arithmetic (counting prophets backwards in time).
- Lyell's falsification of text-based methods in science (theories of the flood) and of the assumption that the history of the Earth should be defined as a history of origins rather than a history of repetitions (rock cycle).

This pattern can be compared with three typical cases of technological creativity:

- James Watt's improvement of the steam engine by the idea of an extra chamber for the purpose of saving and using steam energy more effectively.
- The Wright Brothers' solution to the problem of how to maneuver motorized planes in the air and avoid crash landings, by studying how birds do it.
- The solution by Chicago architects of how to build much higher office buildings by replacing masonry with steel frames.

All these solutions were found by the strategy of trial and error, but they were also clearly cases of intended problem solving (creativity).

The final cause (V.4) of these discoveries was the same (adaption) so was the core problem-solving strategy (V.3), trial and error. Now compare these with some cases of N-creativity.

- the lungfish, which has evolved two ways of obtaining oxygen, both from water and air, allowing it to survive in water holes during periods of long drought
- feathered dinosaurs, allowing this species to survive under conditions of colder climate
- fish-shaped feathered king penguins allowing this species both to survive cold periods and catch fish in the cold oceanic waters around Antarctica

All these were unintended forms of problem solving. Now compare the cases above based upon the same problem-solving strategy (V.3) as technology, the strategy of trial and error, with three scientific discoveries, none of which were intended either but nevertheless used the typical problem-solving strategy of science, methodology.

- The falsification of Pauling's model of the DNA by two young new-comers, Crick and Watson, none of whom had set out to solve the "problem of the century" (unintended discovery) but found themselves at the right place at the right time (the Cavendish Laboratory at the beginning of the 1950s shortly after Avery's surprising falsification of DNA; its relative simplicity had made scientists believe that DNA could not be the basics of life, a belief shared by Crick at the start. Both Crick and Watson unintentionally brought with them method-ological (V.3) skills and attitudes which turned out to be crucial for solving the problem, precisely the skills and attitudes lacking among their foremost competitors, Franklin and Pauling.
- The falsification of the belief that only humans use tools by Jane Goodall, a young, single woman, who, in contrast to older, more experienced male researchers with families and academic careers wait-ing at home, had the patience necessary to establish trust between the field researcher and the shy research object. Establishing trust between researcher and research object turned out to be critical for the correct method (V.3) of primatology, field work in the wild, to work properly.
- The falsification of the belief that continental drift is impossible by the combined research methodologies (V.3) of geophysicists and geochem-ists investigating the strange "reversed" magnetic fields of ridges found deep in the bottom of the oceans.

## The Fallacy of Induction

All these cases confirm that Popper was right when he identified falsification as the final cause of science (V.4) but wrong when he assumed (11) that falsification is intended (intended forms of creativity characterize technology and art but not science), (2) that the problem-solving strategy of science is not methodology but trial and error (the problem-solving strategy of both nature and technology, with the important difference that creativity in nature is unintended, just as in science). Paradoxically Popper's false theory of falsification turns out to be (3) a clear case of the fallacy of induction, contrary to his own intention, to solve the problem of the fallacy of induction once and for all (Popper, 1943).

## Independent (Re)discovery and Convergent Evolution

As noted by Dawkins, nature has an uncanny capacity to rediscover the same, parsimonious solution to similar problems again and again (Dawkins, 2005). Merton made a similar, probably independent discovery as well, for science, discussed in the two essays "Singletons and Multiples in Science" (1961/ 1973) and "Multiple Discoveries as Strategic Research Site" (1963/1973a). A closer analysis of these articles though reveals major weaknesses in Merton's theory. Although Merton does raise a number of important issues, among them the observation that pioneers in science, called "scientific genius," tend to be "cosmopolitans" rather than "locals" (see IV.1 and IV.2), Merton's theory of independent (re) discovery does not seem to get it right.

From an empirical point of view (primary data, V.1), there is not one single detailed analysis of independent (re) discoveries. Merton presents a long list of rediscoveries of the phenomenon of independent discoveries. But this quantitative method tends to underestimate the difficulty of getting it right in science (the role of knowledge constraints, I.3). For Merton, independent rediscoveries turn out to be a routine issue. This is the usual way sociologists tend to cope with the problem of creativity (Kupferberg, 1996b) and this bad habit can possibly be explained by the knowledge interest of sociology, which historically have been professionals rather than pioneers (for a critique, see Kupferberg, 2004b). Moreover Merton's claim that "multiples" are more frequent than "singles" is not supported by any empirical proof. As we have seen in Chapter 1, the founding of disciplines tends to be the result of one or possibly two recognizable individuals. It is rarely a mass phenomenon (compare Collins' 1998 apt concept "law of small numbers").

The way Merton arrives at the conclusion that multiples are more frequent than singles is by calculating the distribution of multiple discoveries. Calculating the distribution of multiple discoveries indicates that the only difference between "scientific genius" and less talented scientists is the number of multiple discoveries attributed to them. But if "multiples," far from being the exception actually are the rule, why has this phenomenon never been studied in a systematic manner? This is the third question Merton raises in a follow-up essay, "The Ambivalence of Scientists" (1963/1973b). Resistance to a systematic study of "multiples" is here explained by the contradictory institutionalized values of science, which, on the one hand puts value on originality (pride of original achievement) and on the other calls for the opposite (humility). Given that science is basically a collective and not an individual enterprise (Whitley, 1984), scientific communities tend to resist or remain skeptical towards "too much originality" (compare the last aspect of Merton's 1942/1968 "CUDOS" model, "organized skepticism").

This inherent ambiguity of science (the concept is projected upon society at large in Merton, 1976) leads to the "rule of thumb" that autobiographies by pioneering scientists will first deny any interest in the "struggle for priority," only later to be concerned to establish precisely such priority. This same "ambiguity of science" according to Merton explains what for Merton is seen as a pathological or dysfunctional aspect of science, namely secrecy, such as the tendency to hide data and theories in the making. Secrecy according to Merton violates one of the ethical norms of science, "communism" or free sharing of information. Another potentially pathological aspect from a psychological point of view is the "stress" of scientists, emerging from the fear of being overhauled by an unknown competitor. These presumably dysfunctional elements of science are lamented but strangely not analyzed in depth, which might possibly be explained by the strategy of Merton to ignore the problem of "genius" (in reality how to explain pioneering work in science). Summarizing, Merton's theory of independent (re) discovery, rests on the following arguments, which can conventionally be divided into "manifest" and "latent."

*Manifest Level*

- Discoveries are routine in science; this is what this institution is here for (function).
- In order to motivate scientists to make discoveries, science rewards ambitious (hardworking, talented) scholars by providing them with symbolic capital, priority (function).

- Given that discoveries are routine in science, too many discoveries are made and only a few are in practice rewarded (dysfunction).
- In order to gain an advantage in the struggle for symbolic capital, scientists engaged in the struggle for priority hold their discoveries secret rather than sharing data and results with other (dysfunction).

Behind these "manifest" functions/dysfunction we find some "latent" basic assumptions or First principles.

### Latent Level

Assumption 1: Science is basically a social institution; individuals do not play any important role for the advance of scientific knowledge (iron cage or death of the author).

Assumption 2: Science is mainly a sociological phenomenon. Problem solving is routine and can be discounted. The overproduction of similar solutions makes the struggle for priority (Merton, 1957) the critical issue, not knowledge constraints (I.3) that make the solutions of complex and paradoxical problems possible.

Assumption 3: The discovery of new knowledge in science does not have to be protected by for example geographical or intellectual migration, secrecy or support systems (Dimension IV, the pathology argument).

Assumption 4: The problem of why there are so few pioneers in science (Law of small numbers, Collins, 1998) is a non-issue. The problem is that there are too many scientific discoveries of the routine (professional) type. It is the overproduction of routine solutions which makes the struggle for priority the most important.

Assumption 5: The chance to come out in the struggle for priority among professionals, increases if the scholar is recognized early in his or her career (the concept "Matthew effect," Merton 1968/1973).

### The Evolution of Evolutionary Theory

There is a striking similarity between Merton's theory of science and Darwin's first "Malthus" inspired theory of natural selection (struggles for survival of too many candidates in a narrow ecological niche). It ignores the possibility of geographical (IV.1) and intellectual migration (IV.2) which allows for a different type of adaption (speciation). Here the competition is relatively small. There are not that many candidates (compare Mayr's 2004/2007 concept "competition of the best"). Secrecy might still be necessary (such as "skunk works," IV.3 and the use of confidants, IV.4). Moreover, support systems are also critical to get it right (IV.5).

In Merton's sociology of science, the critical problem of the need to protect vulnerable versions in science is completely ignored. The best explanation is probably the pre-commitment (Elster, 1983) of the sociological discipline to study routinized forms of problem solving, the type we find among professionals (Carter, 2004; Ericson, 1999 ). Not even such an innovative scholar as Giddens, manages to escape this constraint (Kupferberg, 1996b). This can best be explained by the disciplined imagination or type of First principles chosen (V.3) which has come to define the methodology of the sociological tradition and there might also be other explanations why Merton arrived at his theory that multiples in science are more frequent than singletons.

This takes us to the prime role model (I.2) of Merton's theory of science. A core argument of Francis Bacon which Merton cites approvingly is Bacon's claim that discoveries in science are inevitable. It is merely a question of time. "All innovations, social or scientific 'are the births of time... Time is the greatest innovator'." For Merton, this explains why individuals play such a small role for the advance of science that they can, for all practical purposes be discounted (death of the author or absence of "effective causes," V.3). This methodological assumption (First principle) is based upon Bacon's firm belief that "methodological procedures make for greater reliability in the work of science. Once a scientific problem has been defined, profound individual differences among scientists will affect the likelihood of reaching a solution, but the scale of differences in outcome is reduced to the established scientific procedures of scientific work" (Merton, 1961/1973, p. 349). But this takes out the core of scientific discovery which is precisely the clarification of First principles. It reduces science to a routine affair by taking pioneering work in science out of the equation.

### The Sociology of Knowledge

Merton's failure to account for the phenomenon that Dawkins calls "convergent evolution" probably has a deeper cause. Not only are sociologists primarily interested in the routine problem solving of professionals, on a deeper level, sociologists believe that knowledge is basically only a legitimation of the self-interests of professional groups (the rhetoric of scientific disciplines are here to legitimate jurisdiction over contested work areas, see Abbott, 1988, 2004). The prototype (I.2) of this thinking is Max Weber's theory of religion, which is ultimately economic as well. Priests and magicians struggle for jurisdiction about how to deal with matters of life and death, fortunes and misfortunes both in the world and the next, believed to be controlled by the Gods, to which the individuals belonging to these professions claim they have a secret access ("charisma").

## The History of Science

Scientific genius might be interpreted as a special version of the claim to possess charisma and this might explain why the sociology of science is prone to describe science as a purely sociological phenomenon, based upon self-interest and legitimized by charisma or claims of genius. But sociology is not the only discipline that studies scientific creativity. Historians of science, in contrast to sociologists, ignore claims of charisma or genius and seek to retrieve the facts of pioneering work in science (compare Browne's excellent works on Darwin). This takes us to another core assumption which Merton seems to share with Bacon, namely that there is one and only one method of science, the controlled experiments producing accurate data, and discovered by Galileo. If we assume this to be the case, then all future discoveries in science can be regarded as routine applications of that very method. This method was found once, by Galileo. But this belief in the one and only scientific method, result of one and only scientific event, although attractive for historians of science (Cohen, 1994; Lindberg & Westman, 1990) is also a case of the "fallacy of induction" mentioned above.

History as a discipline is mainly interested in explaining unique events. Galileo's discovery of the First principles of physics hence serve as a perfect case for this discipline. This might explain why the birth of science in ancient Greece (Farrington, 1944/1965; Furberg, 1969; Hall, 2015) has been consistently ignored by the history but also philosophy of science (most historians and philosophers of science seem to have been trained in physics, see Jaki, 1984), in spite of the overwhelming empirical proof coming from the discipline studying Greek science (Lloyd 1968, 1970, 1991, 2002), but also the supportive evidence of the critical role of geometry for the birth of Greek science (Rhill, 1999; Kline, 1953/1987).

## The Philosophy of Science

Feyerabend's theory of science as anything goes is also based upon Galileo's discoveries in physics as data (V.1), but in contrast to the historians of science, Feyerabend is not interested in methodological issues (V.3) at all. For Feyerabend, science is not constrained by rules, such as the rules of falsification. Hence Galileo comes out as an example of the anarchic approach to problem solving ("anything goes"). As we know, Feyerabend was a mentor for Kuhn when Kuhn migrated from Harvard to Berkeley. Kuhn had been educated in physics and was not a trained philosopher (compare his awkwardness when invited to present his theory at a symposium of trained philosophers, see Suppe, 1974 ).

But nor had Merton, who served as a referee for Kuhn's book *The Structure of Scientific Revolutions* (Merton & Garton, 1977). This might explain why Merton failed to see the many flaws of Kuhn's book, in particular Kuhn's claim that scientific revolutions are not about problem solving. This is reserved for "normal science." Scientific revolutions are non-cognitive (sociological) phenomena (psychological, political, linguistic) – "taxonomic solution" (Hacking, 1995) or "social constructions" (Hacking, 2000). But this cannot be right. Scientific revolutions are cognitive phenomena but also social phenomena at the same time (socio-cognitive). The two do not have to exclude each other as usually assumed in the literature (cognitive science versus social constructions).

## Convergent Evolution

Richard Dawkins concept "convergent evolution" seems to be a good general concept in order to understand better how the phenomenon of independent (re) discovery works in practice and why such rediscovery can be conceptualized as an aspect of the third dimension (getting it right). The problem is discussed in detail in two of his books (1986/2006, pp. 22–25; 2005, pp. 235–237; pp. 602–610) and I refer the reader to these sections for further concrete evidence. The first case, discussed in *The Blind Watchmaker*, discusses the sonar radar system of bats as an engineering problem, or a problem of "good design" (compare Petrosky 1996). How would an engineer go about solving the core problems of a species which normally moves around and hunts in darkness? Having compared the situation with how blind humans move around, Dawkins arrives at the first solution: such an animal would probably profit from using a system based upon echo or sound. Dawkins returns to the philosophical aspects of whether eyes (seeing) and ears (hearing) (and possibly also noses (smelling)) from a functional point of view comes down to the same thing or not, but this issue will be ignored here.

The constraint of darkness makes the use of echo sounds an economic, parsimonious solution (successful solution/getting it right). Next, he makes the empirical observation that there are many types of bats. Some bats such as fruit bats, Rosettus, use clicking sounds which can be heard by the human ear. Other, smaller bats, mostly living in temperate zones, use ultrasound. These bats seem to have evolved more complex sonar radar systems. The most complex and sophisticated sonar radar system can be found among horseshoe bats. Most of the analysis takes its points of departure from the radar system of horseshoe bats.

Dawkins starts by asking what type of problems a functioning sonic radar system would have to solve (III.4). It turns out that all of these problems are tricky ones that are not that easy to solve (the role of such difficult problems is the black box or dark hole of Merton's sociology of science, in spite of his critique of the sociology of knowledge tradition for making too much of existential issues, see Merton, 1968a, 1968b). Take the problem of developing a sensitive ear to receive weak eco-signals which have been diluted both on the way out and on the way back in a way that can be computed mathematically (expanding circles, radiuses versus diameters, etc.). Ideally the more sensitive the receiving ear the better it is. But for such a sound to be heard in the first place, the outgoing sound has to be very high. All things being equal, this would hurt or possibly distort the sensitive receiving ear. How can such a dilemma be solved?

Radar engineers, using electricity rather than sound confronted a strikingly similar problem situation (III.4):

> When an analogous problem struck the designers of Radar in the Second World War, they hit upon a solution which they called "send-receive" radar. The radar signals were sent out in necessarily very powerful pulses, which might have damaged the highly sensitive aerials (American "antennas") waiting for the faint returning echoes. The "send/receive" circuit temporarily disconnected the receiving aerial just before the outgoing pulse was about to be emitted, then switched the aerial on again in time to receive the echo. (Dawkins, 1986/2006, p. 27)

It tuns out that bats discovered a similar solution to the same basic practical dilemma of survival tens of millions of years ago, long before humans evolved, with the single difference that bats use organic tissue (contracting muscles attached to the stirrup and the hammer) rather than metal. As noted by French (1994) using metal rather than organic material to solve engineering problems seems to be the most important difference between how humans and nature in general solve tricky technological-type

problems. For some reason, "metallurgy" has not been part of the repertoire of problem-solving methods by nature. It is a typical human or
cultural invention. Some animals such as eels use electricity (Dawkins,
2005), but bats for some reason use sound (sonar radar).

Seen as radar systems, the objective problems that human radio engineers and fruit bats have to solve are strikingly similar probably because the
overall problem situation (III.4), to move and hunt in darkness while
flying, is not much different. A second issue that had to be tackled for a
functioning radar system to work was the problem of "noise" (how does a
bat know that the signals received are the sender's own signals and not
signals sent or received by other bats), a problem which is still poorly
understood but can probably best be explained by some kind of "stranger
effect" (signals which are different from the usual ones are ignored by the
computer-brain of the bat). A third problem is whether to use staccato
sounds or long-drawn-out ones. "Ideally, it would seem, bat pulses should
be very brief indeed. But the briefer a sound is, the more difficult it is to
make it energetic enough to produce a decent echo. We seem to have
another unfortunate trade-off imposed by the laws of physics. Two solutions might occur to ingenious engineers, indeed did occur to them when
they encountered the same problem, again in the analogous case of radar.
Which of the two solutions is preferable depends on whether it is more
important to measure range (how far away an object is from the instrument) or velocity (how fast the object is moving relative to the instrument)" (Dawkins, 1988/2006, p. 28).

Radar engineers solved this dilemma by combining two solutions. One
was "chirp radar," which essentially changes the frequency of outgoing
signals, modulating them from high to low. The other was considering the
"Doppler effect," applying the discovery by Christian Doppler that
approaching a target shortens wave distances. In contrast, moving away
from a target increases wave distances (a technique routinely used by police
radar trying to trace cars traveling above the permitted speed limit). Most
bats seem to use the "chirp radar" solution but some bats such as horseshoe
bats seem to use both strategies at the same time (horseshoe bats also seem
to flap their ears to increase their ability to discriminate incoming sounds,
but this advanced device is still poorly understood from the point of view
of engineering science).

Dawkins analysis corroborates Popper's core argument in *All Life is
Problem Solving,* that all creativity is basically a form of problem solving.
In this fundamental sense, there is no essential difference between say an
amoeba or Einstein (or between an engineer or a bat, a painter and an

apple tree, etc.). All life forms are engaged in problem solving of some kind. But it this is indeed correct. Kuhn's argument in *The Essential Tension,* that pioneers in science do not attempt to solve problems but only professionals (normal science) do, cannot be correct. But such problem solving, as Popper notes is constrained by the objective problem situation (see III.4). The Mexican axolotls are neotenic aquatic salamanders, meaning they retain certain larval characteristics in the adult, reproductive state. They possess feathery external gills and finned tails for swimming. They spend their whole lives underwater. Instead of developing lungs and taking to the land, adults remain aquatic and gilled. They exist in the wild in only one place—the lake complex of Xochimilco a network of artificial channels, small lakes, and temporary wetlands that help supply water to nearby Mexico City's 18 million residents. Their eyes are lidless, which means they are in practice blind. Eyes as costly and the axolotl has made a tradeoff (parsimony) between useless eyes and developing other sensitivities better adapted to survival and reproduction under water.

There is the important difference though that nature does not intentionally solve problems like engineers do. To explain how engineers and bats arrive at very similar solutions, we need to look at the role of constraints. Some of these constraints primarily fall under the category of prototypes. As we have seen there is a varying degree of complexity among bats, but all are versions of the most simple solution to the problem of navigating in darkness, the click sounds found in food bats. Click sounds have hence served as the first simple prototypes (I.2). But the invention of this type of simple solution can in turn best be explained by the problem of navigating in darkness, which is a physical constraint (I.1). Indeed, a closer look at the most complex forms of sonic radar invented by bats, indicate that they too are examples of elegant solutions to physical constraints.

This can be illustrated by the evolution of birds (Tudge, 2008). Although all birds have feathers and all, at one time, could fly (this would explain the heavy breast muscles of birds who eventually lost the ability), the ability to use wings for flying requires large wings relative to the rest of the body (physical constraint, I.1). Birds who for some reasons have traded off (parsimony) large wings for other biological advantages (powerful legs to run with or giant claws for defense or fishlike body form and small finlike wings to move around fast in water) have done so basically because of physical constraints (I.1) working in tandem with prototypes (I.2). "Similar problems call for similar solutions ... the materials of life ... allow for only a limited range of solutions to a particular problem. Given any particular evolutionary starting situation, there is only a limited number of ways out of the box … similar selection pressures, developmental constraints, will enhance the tendency to arrive at the same solution" (Dawkins, 2005, p. 610).

### Prototypes and Physical Constraints

As noted above, artists also tend to be constrained both by prototypes and physical constraints. Combining the two in a parsimonious way is often what "getting it right" in art means. Just as in nature, there are probably not that many solutions which serve both purposes at the same time, which might explain why independent (re) discovery can also be found in say modern art:

> The properties of clay and other malleable material restrict modelers. No form that extends far beyond the lump into which it naturally subsides can be held together without a skeleton or armature of wood or metal. Clay figures are impermanent unless baked hard in an oven, the heat of which must be controlled to avoid fragmentation. In the second half of the third millennium BC it was discovered in Mesopotamia that a durable metal version of a clay statue could be made by the lost wax …method of bronze casting. As shells of cast bronze are considerably lighter in weight than equivalent of stone … and also have some resilience, the medium permits a wider range of formal effects. Stone sculptures must be columnar, cubic or pyramidal to stand up upright – the legs of standing figures cannot be placed wide apart unless a third support is provided. Bronze figures, on the other hand, may be delicately, even precariously, balanced. … the comparable technical problems confronting painters is … that of fixing pigments to a ground, by the use of colored stains which are absorbed (as in fresco and water color) or by mixing colored powders with an adhesive binding agent (egg yolk, various oils for oil painting). (Honour & Fleming, 1982/ 1984 p. 11)

But art is not technology. Art is here to evoke emotions (V.4) which is done with the help of techniques and not trial and error (V.3; the "automatism" practiced by surrealists, see Moszynska, 1990, p. 110 is basically also a technique). Art theories have until recently tended to ignore the material aspects of painting techniques (Gage, 1995/2005). Part of the reason might have been that painters and sculptors, during the Renaissance, had a professional interest in being recognized as a distinct group. They were "artists" and not mere "artisans." This gave rise to an ideology of the artist as "romantic genius" (Kant, 1790/1997), a type of professional who is highly knowledgeable about techniques for evoking emotions but at the same time a child or primitive man, who in contrast to civilized man, cannot but follow the natural, basically sound in the sense of honest, authentic instincts of unspoiled human nature (compare Rousseau's pedagogical theory).

Today there seems to be a movement going in a different direction and much of it has to do with the rediscovery of "color" (Gage, 2006). We can see it in Matisse's biography, but it also reflects a general movement among artists since the Impressionists (Shiff, 1984), a revolution which led to the gradual abandonment of the foregrounding of light and darkness invented by the Italian painters (chiaroscuro or "value") for the radiant effects and accompanying feelings associated with bright and "pure" colors ("hue"). The rediscovery of the senso-emotional effects of color was not an effect of the tradition of painting alone though. It can best be seen as an adaption to the new professional problems of the painting profession, starting with the emergence of the new technology of photography. This new technology of mechanical, automatic and much more precise types of naturalistic representation than the central-perspective techniques of Renaissance painting led to a crisis of painting which culminated with the evolution of the cinema.

The cinema could not only represent figures in a much more precise manner, but could also make figures move. It could tell a story in a highly realistic manner (Kracauer, 1965). This crisis of the profession of painting led to two different strategies. One strategy was to abandon the idea that artists were distinct from artisans. This strategy foregrounded the beauty of machine aesthetics and eventually led to the recognition of industrial design as an art form in its own right (with Bauhaus as the most important and influential pioneer). But not all artists working for Bauhaus agreed. Some of them, Klee and Kandinsky, ended up joining the opposite movement, the return to "Primitivism" (Moszynska, 1990). Primitivism in turn split in a "musical" part (imitation of pure emotion by abstraction) and a "theatrical part" (performance art). Both can be seen as cases of imitation or colonization, modeling oneself upon a prototype (I.2) within the traditional fine arts without abandoning the primitivist strategy.

But the two dominant art movements have also influenced each other (co-evolution). "Purism" was invented by two architects (one of which was Le Corbusier) who were inspired by Cubism but wanted to transform the primitivist aesthetics of Cubism into a variety of machine aesthetics. "Conceptual art" was invented by a painter (Duchamp) who wanted to transform machine aesthetics (modern architecture and industrial design) into primitivist art. Conceptual art in turn divided into two main schools, "minimalism" which wanted to translate machine aesthetics into the format of painting and "monumentalism" which wanted to transform paintings and sculpture into physically big and massive works of architecture.

## Co-evolution as Interdependent Discovery

Whereas convergent evolution in the sense of independent (re) discovery is a relatively rare phenomenon among pioneers in science, co-evolution or interdependent discovery seem to be be everywhere it tends to be uninteresting (Latour & Wolgar, 1986), nevertheless there are some interesting patterns here that should be noted. One is that interdependency in nature often takes the form of intra-species physical adaption, a problem that is often left out in the discussion of how evolution works in practice (Jones, 2001). The other is that inter-species physical adaption tends to be both cooperative and conflictual, sometimes both at the same time.

### Intra-Species Physical Adaption

One of Darwin's most important observations was that biological evolution starts within the species itself. Such evolution takes three main forms which are physically adapted to another (Jones, 2001) namely anatomy, physiology and behavior. As noted by Popper (1974, 1999), changes of anatomy and physiology are often triggered by changes of behavior. Whales over time became fishlike in their physical anatomy when they changed their habits from seeking food and reproducing on land to a life in water. But changed diet in turn also influences physiology, the internal mechanisms for digesting food. One of the ways evolutionary processes can be observed among primates is change of teeth (Boyd & Silk, 2003).

Chimpanzees are basically fruit-eaters, but the shape of their teeth and intestines allows them also to eat insects such as termites which they catch by sticking long straws into the nests of termites, after having made them sticky by licking them but also to hunt and eat smaller animals when the opportunity arises. In contrast, the finches that Darwin observed on the Galapagos Islands, over time tended to specialize, which could be seen in the shape of their beaks. Insect-eating finches looked different from grain-eating and fruit-eating finches (Keynes, 2003). Such anatomical changes were a result of finches having been dispersed by the winds from the mainland to the far away islands. But given distinct geological history and plants, a process of speciation set in which transformed visible anatomy.

But in contrast to the chimpanzees who retained a flexibility of behavioral choice, the new behavioral pattern of finches became permanent or rigid, as they were now constrained by anatomical (but also physiological) changes. Elephants have trunks that allow them to reach branches and put them in their mouths. Their intestine system is in turn adapted to digesting this type of food, but the efficiency of drawing out nourishment from trees and branches seems to be very poor, forcing elephants to wander over large areas and eat a huge amount of food to survive and reproduce.

Such intra-species physical adaption can also be seen in the evolution of the human species. Cases in point are (1) the co-evolution of long-distance walking and the restructuring of the inner ear to a kind of Gyro-system (Cela-Conde & Ayala, 2007); (2) the change of teeth retaining the flexible food pattern behavior of chimpanzees but with a clear change of teeth adapted to meat as a regular and not an occasional source of food; (3) anatomical changes related to child-bearing, both among women (broader hips, bigger visible breasts) and children (bigger heads, total helplessness at birth) but also behavioral and physiological changes related to sexual behavior (Ridley, 1994). Exactly how highly complex intra-species physical adaption is interrelated is still very much up for grabs, but the key factor is probably the total helplessness of human children who need a longer period of protection (compare Dimension IV).

But the evolution of scientific disciplines can also be seen as a kind of intra-species evolution. Whatever triggers such evolution, data (V.1), methodology (V.3), concepts (V.2), the final cause, falsification (V.4), forces the three "anatomical" features to adapt to the nature of the knowledge object (V.1), which is the essence of Aristotle's theory of "First principle." This might be the explanations we are looking for, why falsification in science tends to be unintended, a problem I will return to later. But precisely the unintended nature of scientific falsification might explain why science is always belated (Owl of Minerva).

In the beginning, modes of human creativity originated which in contrast to nature was clearly intentional. Such intentional forms of human creativity were enabled by the growth of the human brain and physical changes to the human face and in the throat and mouth regions allowing subtle communication of both emotions and thoughts. Communication of emotions and thoughts was probably a result of the need to protect the totally helpless human child (pressure, I.5b). Although technology uses the basic problem-solving strategy as nature, trial and error, nature has all the time in the world. The total helplessness of the human child puts *Homo sapiens* under pressure to innovate (I.5c), thus the evolution of the human brain, face, throat and mouth regions.

Big brains and sophisticated communication capacity, unintended results of human (biological) evolution, in turn function as opportunity (I.5c) but also pleasure (I.5a) to engage in human creativity. The first important invention, control over fire, had already provided pre-*Homo sapiens* humans with a mighty weapon against dangerous animals. Big-brained *Homo sapiens* and sophisticated communication capacity due to the anatomical changes allowing for articulated language transformed *Homo sapiens* into a formidable inventor of both tools and weapons. Increasingly sophisticated stone tools and later the discovery of metallurgy gave rise to social differentiation and status hierarchies within human societies, increased by long-distance trade. Changes from nomadic to settled forms of life triggered the Neolithic revolution (Gamble, 2007) which in turn led to the invention of writing and arithmetic.

### Co-evolution As Inter-Species Specialization

Dawkins in his many books on biological evolution has very little to say about intra-species physical adaption; indeed, he hardly mentions it at all. A possible reason might be his commitment to a theory of evolution based upon a combination of Crick and Watson's discovery of how life forms evolve on a micro-biological level and mathematical kinship theory. According to the former theory, new species originate from imperfect copying. Small mistakes in copying behavior of the DNA-molecule, leads to small variations of the species, which are in turn selected by natural selection. Kinship theory is an attempt to explain the curious behavior of "altruistic species" such as ants. Why do female ants "sacrifice" themselves in the sense of leaving all biological reproduction to the queen and reduce themselves to house slaves? Such a reproductive strategy will certainly not allow female sisters to transmit their own genes to later generations. The simple answer according to kinship theory is that female ants are all daughters of the same queen, hence they share the same genome on the mother's side. By assisting in the biological reproduction of the queen, they secure the reproduction of their own distinct genome.

The combination of the two theories, is the core of Dawkins' dual theory of "the selfish gene" and "cultural memes" (1976/2006). In contrast to Dawkins' other theories of how evolution works, this theory is not convincing. As we have seen a combination of previous prototypes and physical constraints ultimately explains the intra-species type of physical adaption such as whales being transformed into fishlike creatures in terms of anatomy, physiology, and behavior. The behavioral patterns of the DNA are a minor mechanism which makes this possible, but such mainly spontaneous generation and blind selection (Campbell, 1960) cannot explain the direction of the evolutionary processes. How does nature manage to get it right? Spontaneous variation followed by blind selection is of little help here.

Nevertheless, nature does manage to get it right. How is this possible? This is indirectly admitted by Dawkins when he notes "the set of relationships that have grown up around coral reefs, independently in many parts of the world, between cleaner fish and larger fish. The cleaners belong to several different species, and some are not fish at all but shrimps – a nice case of convergent evolution." But "co-evolution also occurs between species that do not benefit from each other's presence, like predators and prey, or parasites and hosts. These kinds of co-evolution are sometimes called 'arms races'" (Dawkins 2010, pp. 80–81).

But coral reefs, are not only cases of inter-species co-evolution. They are also primarily cases of intra-species physical adaption of prototypes to new ecological niches. Evolution, as Mayr (1982) notes, takes place between life forms. DNA itself is not a life form or species, but bacteria or viruses are, as well as fungi, plants, animals (fishes, birds, mammals, dogs, cats, elephants, whales, primates, humans, etc.). Take the transformation of wasps into ants. The former use wings and poison to hunt. For this purpose they need to be big, have good eyes and keep their wings intact (intra-species selection). Ants only use wings in the rare cases when new queens are impregnated by drones. Most of their life is spent protecting the eggs and finding food and feeding the larva. This is mostly done by crawling on the ground, coordinating attacks on big prey and cooperating carrying big prey to the ant heaps, but also being able to carry material between their beaks. Size is compensated for by number. Eyes are of little use here, as are wings. Problems of recognizing friends from foes are solved by chemical communication.

Spontaneous variation and blind selection have little explanatory value, if at all. Adaption to new ecological niches by processes of speciation, mediated by intra-species physical adaption (physical constraints, I.1) of previous prototypes (I.2) makes much more sense. As already noted by Darwin, such processes of speciation can also be seen as a form of specialization. Each species of the Galapagos finches is specialized in terms of anatomy, physiology and behavior to the natural environment. But such specialization can also have another function; it reduces potential conflict over scarce resources (compare Durkheim's argument in *The Division of Labor in Society* or Wilson's 1991/2001 analysis of the cichlids a several-hundred-thousand-year-old species of fish living in Lake Victoria).

Anatomical adaption is probably slowest of the three types of intra-species physical adaption. Take woodpeckers which are a highly specialized species, adapted by nature to do what they do, hack into the bark of trees for insects. But in those ecological environments where woodpeckers for some reasons are absent, other species, tend to take over this now empty ecological niche. But at the start this has no effect upon anatomy. Woodpeckers have, over time, developed skulls which protect them from brain damage by very rapid hacking. Other birds, taking over an empty niche, hack much more slowly, because their skulls have been adapted to other niches. Over time, if they keep on hacking, they will probably evolve similar skulls to woodpeckers.

## Inter-Species Evolution and Co-evolution in Art

If we want to understand how different forms of human creativity in the sense of problem-solving capacity which makes it possible to get it right (find parsimonious solutions) evolve, Dawkins' theory of "cultural memes" does not take us very far. According to this theory, all species basically function like DNA. They try to survive by coping themselves. But if this is the case why did modern artists end up abandoning naturalistic art, a tradition which is at least 30,000 years old, given that the first naturalistic paintings were made by Paleolithic hunter-gatherers? For this purpose, foregrounding the inter-species competition (arms race) between traditional art forms like paining and new art forms like photography and film seem to be a far more parsimonious explanation.

But the outcome of such competition is fundamentally constrained by physical constraints and not knowledge constraints. If not, how do we explain that the Egyptians abandoned techniques of naturalistic styles of painting which had been discovered tens of thousands of years earlier and evolved gradually with increasing perfection and lifelikeness? As noted by Gombrich (1996) the evolution of naturalistic forms of painting resemble science in the sense that they evolve gradually. Only animals were painted in a naturalistic, life-like style and human figures were indicted by simple symbols. This changed gradually, possibly as a result of a greater concern for how to bury the dead typical of the Neolithic revolution (Jensen, 2013). The transition to food-producing societies eventually gave way to states, governed by kings and priests (Diamond, 1999: Pfeiffer, 1977).

This might explain why previous naturalistic forms of representation were abandoned for highly complex but mainly symbolic forms of representation.

Such abandonment of previous techniques does not support the theory of "cultural memes." But nor does the gradual evolution of increasingly sophisticated techniques (V.3) related to both choice of material (V.1) and composition (V.2) which accompanied the Neolithic revolution. "Unlike paintings from earlier, Paleolithic times, these are on a prepared ground, an evenly colored area of smoothly plastered wall, and not a natural surface. The figures are still depicted as if in a void, without ground lines, let alone a background, but a sense of enclosure within a rectangular field is given by the wall" (Honour & Fleming, 1982, p. 23).

A plausible reason for these changed techniques might have been co-evolution reflecting the fact that hunter-gatherer societies had been nomadic. This changed as the transition to food-producing societies led to permanent settlement which in turn brought about more carefully designed houses in wood or clay which began to replace hastily built huts (Kostof, 1985). This might have led to a greater interest in the physical aspects of architecture, such as walls and roofs which began to function as prototypes (I.2) for a new type of painting which in contrast to earlier attempts were clearly framed, as permanent houses tended to be.

Later evolution of ceramics and metallurgy were probably also cases of cultural co-evolution. Both required knowledge of how to increase temperature (knowledge constraint, I.3). We know that writing originated at about the same time. But the evolution of writing might in tern have co-evolved with another type of innovation, the increasingly complex design of pottery.

> A beaker from Susa 5000–4000 BC is painted boldly and fluently with schematic yet remarkably live animals in pure silhouette: a frieze of very long-necked birds at the top, a band of running dog and, below, and ibex with huge horns.. these animals are distorted expressively, the elongation of the dogs ... suggesting speed of movement (compare Matisse's distorted, elongated figure, which might best be seen as cases of independent rediscovery of these early, symbolized and distorted forms of previously naturalistic painting). What is more, the birds and ibex stand on, and the dogs skim over, firmly marked ground lines, which provide the lower edges of frames enclosing regular "image fields." In this way the image acquires, for the first time, a definite space of its own - in strong contrast to cave painting. This invention preceded that of writing, it should be noted, although its enormous potentials for the arts of representation do not seem to have been recognized until later. (Honour & Fleming, 1982/1984, pp. 27–30)

*Intra-Species and Inter-Species Co-evolution of Science*

Although both artistic and technological forms of evolution are different from biological evolution in the sense that they are clearly intended, the paradox is that the evolutions of scientific revolutions are not. The discovery of geometry, the precondition of science, was unintended. Nevertheless, this crucial unintended discovery turned out to be the knowledge constraint (I.3) that made the birth of science or rather the three scientific disciplines, the philosophy of science, the philosophy of art and the philosophy (First principle) of ethics, possible. The philosophy of ethics regulates the relation between individual and society or moral order, the core knowledge object of sociology (V.1). But geometry is not enough for the discovery or the First principles of physics. The core knowledge constraint (I.3) here was algebra. But whereas Greek science and geometry co-evolved, physics came much later than algebra. The delay, a time span of about 2,000 years, makes it impossible to argue that algebra was intentionally invented to make the birth of physics possible. The birth of physics was clearly an unintended discovery.

Galileo, who admired Aristotle was also very reluctant to admit that he had indeed falsified this important thinker (Renn, 2001). This reluctance might also explain why Galileo rejected Kepler's discovery that planets do not move in perfect circles (Darling, 2006) and why he refused to make a causal connection between the movement of the moon and the tides (Næss, 2007). For a scientist like Galileo, Aristotle had assumed the dimension of God and humans are very much afraid to make our Gods angry. Hence he rationalized the evidence which indicated that all three of Aristotle's First principles of astronomy were indeed fiction rather than fact (V.4). From this it does not follow that science is the same as say religion (or art, myth, magic, etc.) as Bloor claims. But Bloor in turn probably hesitated to go against another God, Max Weber. Although Weber's sociology of religion is brilliant, his concept "rationalization" blurs the core Aristotelian distinctions between practical, productive and theoretical knowledge.

Still, we need to account for the fact that the evolution (creativity) of scientific knowledge, like nature, is unintended, but as nature, manages to get it right. How is this paradox to be explained? The more general answer is that creativity is constrained, but this still does not tell us the mechanism we are looking for. A possible explanation could be that there is something similar to intra-specific physical adaption in science, namely the clarification of First principles. Clarification of first principles is a case of methodology and not trial and error (V.3). Nevertheless, there is a kind of necessary (objective) adaption between the three main aspects of scientific methodology – data, methods of interpretation and knowledge object, strikingly similar to how whales adapt to a life in the seas or king penguins to the ecological environment of the Antarctic.

This does not exclude that scientific disciplines co-evolve according to the inter-species type as does nature. Both mechanisms have to be included in order to account for the complexity of the phenomenon. Evolutionary biology only became possible with the birth of geology, which in turn seems to have learned from archeology. But archeology was clearly constrained by the core discovery of the new discipline geology, the radical change in the concept of time.

Sociology is the discipline of the moral order, but the concept (V.2) seems to have evolved in competition with the economic discipline. Weber probably modeled his core concepts "rationality" and "rationalization" on Marshall's neoclassical economics which is based upon the idea of "rational choice." Owing to Weber's original training in jurisprudence (which is not a science but a kind of rhetoric or "productive knowledge") and later interest in the sociology of religion, the followers of Weber have had great difficulty in understanding the difference between productive and theoretical knowledge.

For Durkheim, the other main founder of sociology, the prototype of the social was schools or pedagogy. A core problem for schools is how to transmit socially accepted norms of behavior which are often in conflict with egoistic self-interests. This might explain why Durkheim's economic sociology became a critique of Adam Smith's moral theory of enlightened self-interest based upon exchange of goods and differentiation of labor (negative prototype, I.2). Durkheim ignored Adam Smith's main point, that division of labor, manual or intellectual, tends to increase the technological (practical) problem-solving capacity of human societies, organizations and individual problem solvers. Moreover, Durkheim focused on something he believed to be missing in Smith's theory, namely the role of trust necessary for regular exchange between seller and buyer. Durkheim was no business economist. He could not imagine that trust might be a result of reputation for delivering goods and services to customers with different preferences and expectations (Kupferberg, 1997, 2001a) in turn constrained by income and social standing in the community ("market segments" see Dickson, 1994/1997).

But there was also a positive prototype (I.2) which might help explain how Durkheim arrived at his First principles about the origins of moral order. Durkheim was a professor of education before he became a professor of sociology (Lukes, 1972). His claim that trust originates in social norms tied to the division of labor in society, is a very good description of how societal norms make a civilized exchange of ideas between teachers and students possible. Without moral order, there can be no teaching and no transmission of knowledge. A teacher can be very stern and punish the whole class for a disobedient act performed by one individual, treating the class as an undifferentiated collective, or the teacher can treat students as individuals, allowing them to pursue their different talents and interests from which everyone will profit. This pedagogical idea seems to have been the prototype (I.2) for Durkheim's main contribution to historical sociology, *The Division of Labor in Society,* where the teacher who punishes the whole class functions as a role model for "mechanical solidarity" and the teacher who treats students as individuals as a role model for "organic solidarity."

The other main founder of sociology, Max Weber, also critiqued Adam Smith for ignoring the embeddedness of economic social action in "moral order" (Parsons, 1937/1968; Etzioni, 1988) but for Weber the role model for a social or moral order (prototype, I.2) was religion and not education. Religion for Weber was described as a value-based type of rationality (Weber, 1922/1964), one of the four main types of social action (the other three were goal-oriented rationality, emotions and traditions, see Weber, 1964). For Weber, modern societies (goal-oriented rationality) had made themselves independent of the religious type of moral order. Modernity was based purely upon mathematical calculations of an economic kind (1904–1905/1958) and hence basically a society without ethics or moral order.

What neither of the two founders of sociology has done is try to explain the origins of science. We have already talked about geometry as a prototype for scientific thinking both in terms of form (concepts, V.1) and procedure (methodology, V3). Both geometry and scientific thinking have a common founding father or prototype, namely writing. But the original forms of writing were pictograms (these traces can still be seen in the Chinese form of writing). But such pictograms in turn seem to have evolved out of increasingly symbolic forms of painting (see page 153).

## Problem Situations and Problem Solvers

### N-Creativity

As noted by Popper (1999) getting it right in nature changes over time. Salamanders who live and reproduce on land need to have functioning lungs and lids to protect eyes and keep them moist. The Mexican axolotl which has adapted to a very different type of life does not need them. In a sense the blocked development of the embryonic features resembles dogs who retain the characteristics of wild wolves when they are still young. Nor can whales crawl on land or climb trees but they can circulate the deep oceans. Penguins can no longer fly, but they can swim and move fast on their big feet and use their feathers to keep warm in cold winds and water. Species over time have adapted to changed problem situations and they have done so by tradeoff (a kind of economy or parsimony) and by refunctionalization (intra-species evolution, another type of parsimony). But similar evolutionary patterns can also be found in cultural (H-creativity). Nevertheless, such creativity is constrained differently.

### Art as imitation

As already noted by Plato (Beardsley, 1966/1967; Cahn & Meskin, 2008) art works imitate. A painting of a bridge cannot be used for transport, Duchamp's "Fountain" was of no use for male visitors to an art museum with a sudden need to urinate. Monsters like King Kong are not real monsters, but machines designed and controlled by engineers for entertaining audiences of Hollywood films. Artists might choose to imitate functional design (the speed and precision of machine aesthetics) but it remains art, nevertheless. Artists might also choose to imitate some of the forms of nature such as "biomorphic forms" (Surrealism) or "geological stratification" (Kirkeby) or "refunctionalization" (rediscovered, III.2 as artistic technique, V.3 by Cubists) but art works remains imitations (facts into fiction, V.4) and not the real thing.

The fact that paintings or sculptures (art works) are "artifacts" or human-made things and objects in their own right (Rothko, 2004) does not devalue them as imitations or "representations" (Eldridge, 2014). But the problem situation of art has changed. Contemporary artists are allowed to imitate (technique, V.3) of any type of media or mediated form of the social (texts, artifact, performances, calculations). They can choose to be figurative or completely abstract. They can choose to make abstract pictures which imitate pure emotion such as music or mixed emotions of the type we find in real life, etc. What a trained painter cannot do is to solve the type of problems that professionals in other art forms are trained to solve. Painting as prototype (I.2) will still shine through one way or another (compare Matisse's last monumental artwork, decorating a chapel outside Nice: "His aim was to give the whole ensemble the fluidity of an oil painting," Spurling, 2009, p. 533).

Ultimately Matisse in his training had become constrained by the physical constraints of paintings (compare Vanessa Beecroft's clearly static installations of live human bodies in art museums, another physical constraint, I.1). Matisse let himself be constrained by church architecture but approached the problem as if it were a painting (compare Chaplin who approached the different specialized tasks of film making as if he was acting in front of a live audience). This element of pretence is, as Walton (1990) noted, a common technique (V.3) for all artists.

That Matisse got the commission, can be explained by his growing reputation as great artist, earned after a long life in painting, but also a support system (IV.5), which not only secured him one commission after another, but protected him in his long and arduous creative process (which in this case took four years, partly because he was physically immobile, was losing his sight and close to dying). But Matisse also functioned as a role model or prototype (I.2) in terms of the special techniques (V.3). He developed a version of "Primitivism" which combined Picasso's (prototype A) idea of painting like a child, simple and distorted figures, with a highly developed skill in symbolic use of color and brushes to express emotions (developed by Gaugin and van Gogh, prototypes B and C) with the bright colors (hue), and geometrical compositions developed by Monet (proto-type D) and Cézanne (prototype E). What Matisse avoided was the idea of transitional forms rediscovered by the Cubists.

All artists use prototypes, great artists (pioneers) paradoxically are more open for learning from prototypes than mediocre artists (professionals) and are more thorough and patient when copying the masters. This indisput-able fact was for a long time a trade secret among painters but has now become a motif of its own (a core idea of postmodernist art). Thus, Sigmar Polke's painting *The Copyist,* "serves as a powerful critique of the notion of unique ownership. The underlying proposition is that the artist, Polke himself, is inevitably one who steals images, from nature and from the rest of the man-made visual world, including the art of the past. The poured, glutinous blob of colored resin occupying the center of the left-hand side of the picture is there to remind us that art's uniqueness – if there is such a thing – lies in its approach to its material and its use of material transfor-mation" (Thompson, 2006, pp. 358–359).

Materials (V.1) are crucial for artistic techniques, but such techniques have to be learned (say by close study of master works as Matisse did in the Louvre). But such materials (the properties or qualities of paint, the size of the canvas or placement on the wall or sometimes rock, the tools used, etc.) function as physical constraints (I.1) as does the fact that the beauty or ugliness of a paintings (bodies in space) can normally be taken in at one glance, whereas one has to sit for 90 minutes to appreciate a film, somewhat longer to enjoy a play and much, much longer to get through a novel however slim or thick. These are indisputable facts. Popper was wrong to deny them and much of the crisis (but also charm) of both twentieth-century philosophy of science and art starts here (Wittgenstein's later work is basically an attempt to deal with works of art).

### Problem Situations as Constraints

Problems constrain problem solvers. Take Chagall, a primitivist painter using symbolic forms of representations although these forms were mainly derived from religious motifs, in particular the clash of Christian and Jewish beliefs (Helfenstein & Osadschty, 2017 ). But to become one of the leading colorists of the twentieth century, Chagall needed to have access to the materials (V.1) necessary to work in color. Matisse at the start of his career to a large degree relied upon family as his primary support system (IV.5). In contrast, Chagall to a large degree relied upon public patronage. Thus, early in his career Chagall pleaded with one of his wealthy patrons in St. Petersburg, Baron Ginzburg for financial assistance in order to be able to pursue his profession: "The main thing. . .is that, with plenty of drawings and sketches, I would now like to move to something bigger, but have no pastels, water colors, oil paints or canvas" (Wullschlager, 2008, pp. 68–69).

Whereas art transforms facts into fiction, technology creates new facts (V.4). Refunctionalization and transitional forms are not imitated; they create new facts or realities. Take the Monadnock Building situated in the center of the business district of Chicago: "Initially planned as four connected buildings, the Monadnock Building, in its unadorned function-alism, embodies Chicago's commercial architecture. It developed on a narrow 400- by 68-foot lot by Bostonians Peter and Shepherd Brooks, with Owen Aldis as their Chicago agent, and is named after Mount Monadnock in New Hampshire" (McBrien, 1996, p. 6). In order to understand in what sense the architects got it right, we need to look at the problem situation that the architect as problem solver was faced with at the time.

Business interests pushed for higher buildings both in Chicago and New York (Condit, 1964), but a big fire in the business district in the center of

Chicago pushed for tighter security and here the choice of steel as the bearing construction could have been one decisive factor (material cause, V.1, see Zukowsky, 1988). But a correct, parsimonious solution (II.4), steel frames, had to be discovered first and it evolved gradually just like the radar system of bats. But large Western-style houses are traditionally built with material such as stone and concrete. This might explain why architects at the beginning mainly used the traditional material and masonry techniques. Steel came later (V.1):

> The northern section, John Root of Burnham & Root... maximized rentable space by stretching the building to the unheard-of sixteen stories and punching put a grid of bay windows that also added light and ventilation. To support this height, exterior masonry walls six feet thick at the base were required ... after Root's death in 1891, the firm of Holabird and Roche was hired to develop the southern half of the block. Here, in the last quadrant, the building is supported by the new steel frame construction, rather than the old-fashioned masonry bearing wall. Thus, in this massive block, constructed over a period of three years, we can see the end of one era in construction and the beginning of another. (McBrien 1996, p. 6)

Inspite of the fact that paintings are imitations they are still artifacts and not texts as novels are. The full aesthetic effects of a painting depend much upon texture (Sonesson, 1992). This explains why owning the "original" or being able to see it at close hand in a museum (two types of physical constraints, I.1) in practice reduces the numbers that can enjoy a famous painting at close hand. The is only one "Mona Lisa" (original in the physical sense). In order just to get a glimpse of it, one needs to (1) go to Paris, (2) stand in line for hours just to be allowed to enter the museum, (3) move slowly through the Louvre following the others and (4) on arrival it is most likely that it can only be seen at distance because of all the people who arrived earlier (physical constraints, I.1).

In contrast novels are easily accessible. The constraint is time, given that a reading of a novel has to be physically interrupted over days and weeks, sometimes months or even years. Physical access to the original manuscript is of no concern for the reader, although it might be of interest for biographers and researchers. Novels can be enjoyed by millions of readers. The cost is relatively small, and it makes it relatively easy for a writer of fiction to reach a mass audience. This very different type of aesthetic appreciation (problem situation) explains why writers of fiction (problem solvers) do not need wealthy patrons (IV.5) to sustain their careers.

Goethe was only a part-time writer, financing his writing through his administrative career (Bruford, 1962). Selma Lagerlöf, although a woman, managed to transform herself from a schoolteacher to a highly successful professional writer with a mass audience of anonymous readers (patrons) supporting her writing (Svedjedahl, 1999; Edström, 2002 ). This is not always the case though. Poets usually only appeal to small audiences and have to support their writing with other types of income (Ackroyd, 1988; Wagner-Martin, 2003), although there seem to be exception to this "law" (Bates, 2015/2016; Pasternak, 2016).

The first full-time professional writer in Sweden was not Selma Lagerlöf but August Strindberg, who managed to make a full-time career as writer of novels, plays and short stories during the last decades of the nineteenth century (Lagercrantz 1979; Brandell 1983–1989). In contrast, painters have always been dependent upon a small group of patrons (V.5) willing to pay for the privilege of supporting an art form which cannot pay for itself on the free market (this pattern can already be found in Italian Renaissance). For some reason, the seventeenth-century Netherlands, seems to be an exception. Although a small country the Netherlands managed to support a relative huge number of painters who basically worked on a commission basis, appealing to the tastes of ordinary citizens. These painters were highly specialized and able to occupy a particular niche (like on Darwin's riverbank or in market economies; compare Adam Smith's theory of the declining costs of learning as a problem-solving advantage of division of labor). This made it possible for the Dutch painters both to be highly skilled in the profession and appeal to the personal preferences of middle-class customers with middle-class tastes (Gronow, 1997; Wright, 1978/1984). Twentieth-century painters as we know have, for some reasons, mostly appealed to very small elite audiences, which requires a very different type of support system (IV.5).

The fact that physical constraints play such a critical role in art, might also help us to better understand what triggers artistic revolutions. We have already discussed why twentieth-century artists abandoned naturalistic techniques (V.3) of representing or imitating the real world. How do we define the problem situation that led to the Impressionist revolution and what if any did physical constraints (I.1) play here? The pioneer here was Manet (J. H. Rubin, 1994; Friedrich, 1992; Wilson-Bareau, 1991/ 1995). Manet's choice of new motifs (V.2) was made possible by the arrival of industrial oil paint in tubes (V.1) which could be placed directly on the palette (historical problem situation, III.4; co-evolution, III.3, see Smith, 1995; Brettell, 2001). But Manet still painted within the naturalistic technique (V.3) of chiaroscuro which foregrounded value (prototype, I.2). The later Impressionists and post-Impressionists (Monet, Cézanne) gradually abandoned the chiaroscuro technique of foregrounding and replaced it with bright colors (hue) as the core technique of painting (V.3) providing paintings with the senso-motorial emotion of a vibrating flat surface (V.4). Another technique was the use of visible brush work which made the picture look "unpolished," but which allowed the painter (effective cause, V.3) to provide the painting with a directly visible personal style (Ross, 2003). This directly visible personal style made it easy to recognize one Impressionist painter from another (Greenberg, 1961/1965; Steffensen, 2017).

Co-evolution (III.3) with technology (T-creativity) is not the only factor that might explain the Impressionist revolution. Thus a critical discovery of the new discipline of perceptual psychology (Karmel, 2003), that the human eye works from memory, based upon the phenomenological theory of perception (it later played an important role in Sartre's transformation from teacher of philosophy to writer of phenomenological novels, see Cohen-Solal, 1987; Iser, 1999), seems to have legitimated the new techniques (V.3) of painting physically separated spots of color. The phenomenological theory of perception told them that that the human eye would do the rest. But the new perceptual psychology also influenced the modern architecture of Le Corbusier (Migayrou, 2015). Le Corbusier learned about these new discoveries from the German school of architecture and design, Werkbund, another case of co-evolution (III.3).

### Historical, Professional and Personal Problem Situations

According to Baxandall (1985), the relation between problem solvers and problem situations can be profitably analyzed by foregrounding the interdependency or co-evolution of three levels – the historical, professional and personal level (compare Kupferberg, 2018a). Take Sylvia Plath. She graduated from Smith College in the 1950s, at a time when women were supposed to support husbands' careers (compare the women who unconditionally supported Matisse, Picasso and Chagall). Sylvia Plath seems to have accepted this historical problem situation (Plath, 2000). It clearly influenced her choice to be a second-rate poet helping her husband to become a great poet (Middlebrook, 2004), a role she accepted until Ted Hughes (Feinstein,/2003) fell madly in love with Assia Wevill (Koren & Negev, 2006). This led to a deep personal crisis (Stevenson, 1989) which had the triple effect of (1) putting pressure on her as sole provider (I.5b), (2) provided her with the opportunity (I.5c) to discover that she was a great poet and (3) reviving her lost pleasure (I.5a) in writing poetry (Plath,

1975). The result was a creative explosion of new, highly original poems (*Ariel*, see Plath, 1992/2008). *Ariel* transformed Sylvia Plath from a mere professional (II.3) to a pioneer of poetry (II.4, see Bredsdorff, 1987; Alexander, 1999; Bain, 2001; Gill, 2006, 2008).

But historical, professional and personal knowledge constraints also influence the creativity of male writers of fiction. Take the two Noble Prize recipients Saul Bellow and Boris Pasternak. Boris Pasternak received the Nobel Prize for Literature mainly for the novel *Dr. Zhivago*, which had to be smuggled abroad (Pasternak, 2016). Combining historical, professional and personal aspects help us conceptualize the complexity and paradoxes of this writer's creativity (see Chapter 8). Boris Pasternak grew up in post-revolutionary Russia, studied music and philosophy, and became a highly estimated poet in his home country, until he met and started an affair with a young female editor and admirer. The real Lara (Olga) was sent to the Gulag as clear warning that the Party did not approve. When Pasternak's secret lover was finally released she was a broken woman, although Pasternak was left alone by the authorities. It was in order to cope with his feelings of guilt, that Pasternak wrote his first and only novel about this tragic love affair. The novel does what all art does, transforms facts into fiction (V.4). It uses surpassingly traditional novelistic techniques of suspense and vraisemblement (V.3).

Like most novels based upon the author's own experiences, the characters and places are disguised (techniques, V.3). In real life the love affair took place in Stalin's Russia. In the novel the historical context is the Russian Revolution. The main character (Dr. Zhivago) is not an old and highly esteemed poet but a young man (II.3) working as a physician (Pasternak allows him though to be an amateur poet II.2). Dr. Zhivago is married like the real author. His young lover is seduced by an older man (Komorovsky) like Pasternak seduced Olga (fact), but in the novel the seducer (older man) is a businessman (fiction), who later becomes a minister in the new revolutionary government. In real life Olga sacrificed herself for Pasternak out of love and admiration of the great poet. In the novel Dr. Zhivago sacrifices himself for his mundane work and great love in life and eventually dies (fiction very far from fact).

Saul Bellow's novel *Herzog*, for which he received the Nobel Prize for Literature, is a tragicomedy. Its main topic is the aftermath of a divorce, where the main character, Herzog, is supposedly a teacher of romantic literature. His academic training and knowledge of world literature is of little help though for the emotional turmoil he is experiencing as he realizes that he has been betrayed by a close friend and colleague who has seduced Herzog's beautiful and much younger wife. Although fiction, the novel is clearly modeled upon real events in his life. This is strengthened by the fact that all the characters come from the same milieu, professionally successful and intellectually curious American Jewry (Leader, 2015). The fiction is a thin surface. What is new is the late-modernist, non-Aristotelian technique (V.3, pioneered by Virginia Woolf in *The Lighthouse*), of breaking up the unity of time and place. This has the effect of making the basic material of fiction, memories, more visible. The physical here and now that penetrates, for example, a novel by Selma Lagerlöf or Leo Tolstoy, is constantly interrupted and replaced by pure memory work, which turns out to be a kind of emotional repair work (Burns, 1992; Kupferberg, 1995b).

CHAPTER 5

# Dimension IV: Protection of Vulnerable Versions

## Contexts and Contents of Discovery

It is general, everyday knowledge that Darwin's voyage on the *Beagle* and in particular the discoveries he made or did not make when visiting the Galapagos Islands had a crucial effect on evolutionary theory. But how are the two events, the voyage and the theory, related to another? Whereas historians of science (Browne, 1995; Keynes, 2003 ) have been particularly interested in (1) what Darwin did or did not discover in the Galapagos Islands (event 1) and how this might have influenced his discovery of evolutionary theory (event 2), sociologists of science have more or less ignored both aspects and asked (1) why Darwin waited so long to publish his book and (2) how he managed to be the one credited with the discovery of evolutionary theory, given that Wallace had independently developed an almost identical theory (Barnes et al., 1996; the problem is also discussed in Browne, 2002). Not a discovery as such, but the "politics" (Shapin & Shaffer, 1985) of social recognition has been in focus.

These two different approaches are very typical for how science works. What might seem to be the same empirical reality (Darwin's discovery of evolutionary theory) is approached in different ways. Even the problem to be solved is not defined in the same way. What this tells us is not that everything in science is contingent or subjective, nor that scientists work like artists. Artists as we have seen are highly constrained in their approach to problem solving. It is not a pure coincidence that they use techniques, nor is it a pure incidence that scientists prefer a methodological approach. But given that the knowledge object of history (how events influence other events) and sociology (the origins of moral order and the role of norms in human life) are clearly different, scholars who have been trained in these two disciplines (the knowledge object of educational psychology), will approach the same empirical reality in different ways. They will ask different questions of relevance or interest for the discipline, but not necessarily for creativity science, which is here to study creativity for its own sake. Scientific creativity from the point of view of creativity science, is only one of several forms of problem solving. In order to arrive at the correct concepts (V.2) we need a different methodology (V.3) but also different data (V.1) although the final cause, falsification, separating facts from fiction (V.4) remains the same.

But sociology is not a homogenous discipline. It has many founders and subdisciplines, some of which have indeed been interested in how moral order might influence creativity (just as the psychology of creativity has been interested in why some individuals turn out to be more creative than other individuals). This is not yet creativity science, but it is a search for a creativity science.

Moreover, disciplines might borrow ideas from each other (Abbott, 2004), a case of intellectual migration (IV.2). Simmel, one of the least known sociologists, invented concepts like "the stranger" and "metropolis and mental life" in order to describe how moral order can influence creativity. Rudwick, a geologist, wrote a seminal work (1996) on Darwin, which is similar to Simmel's sociological theory, but the core idea that the state of "liminality" might have constrained Darwin's discovery of evolutionary theory during his long journey but also after his return to England is based upon another prototype, anthropological theories of initiation rituals (Kupferberg, 1998a).

But before we ask how context might have influenced content, we must clarify what it was that a scientist discovered and how. These are method-ological issues and need to be taken seriously from a creativity science point of view. All science starts with data or observations (V.1). Darwin made many observations, both geological and biological and not the least the relations between the two (Keynes, 2003). These are written down in his diary, notebooks (Chancellor & van Wyhe, 2009) and letters (Burkhardt, 2008) and provide the database for the theory presented in *On the Origin of Species*. A first version of Darwin's observations was published in *Voyage of the Beagle*, 1839. What is interesting is that the book, although written during the years when Darwin had arrived at the core factors of his theory (Gruber, 1981; Sloane, 2009), does not mention evolutionary theory at all.

The first question we must ask ourselves from a creativity science point of view is why *The Voyage of the Beagle*, published in 1938, is dedicated to Admiral FitzRoy, the captain of the *Beagle* who invited Darwin to dinner on board (Darwin slept in a separate cabin with the officers) during the five years (minus the long periods spent on inland expeditions, see Browne & Neve, 1989). FitzRoy in practice functioned as a mentor (IV.5) in the field of geology (just as Ted Hughes had in practice functioned as mentor for Sylvia Plath during their six-year marriage). The arrangement had been made possible through active intervention by Henslow, Darwin's former teacher (mentor) who in practice also functioned as Darwin's agent. The extra expenses were covered by Darwin's father who in practice functioned as Darwin's patron, as well as FitzRoy who as representative of the admiralty did not charge Darwin the full cost of the voyage.

The book is hence part of Darwin's attempt to keep his evolving revolutionary theory secret from the official patron and mentor (IV.5) when Darwin was working secretly on something he had not told FitzRoy (skunk work, IV.3).

The liminality or loosening of social control cannot have been as complete as Rudwick (1996) suggests. Moreover, Darwin still felt grateful to FitzRoy and did not want to hurt his feelings by "coming out" as a full-blown evolutionary theorist. But there were other reasons as well. As noted by Mayr (1982), no scientific community in the world was as hostile to evolutionary theory as England. Darwin had to tread carefully in order not to lose his hard-won scientific reputation. This was the reason that Darwin had chosen another strategy, to work secretly on the book and only invite a small and elect group of "confidants" (V.4). Moreover, Darwin would have to rely upon both Fitzroy and these confidants, among them Lyell, his new confidant (IV.5) and agent (IV.5), for many years, not the least as a way to increase his sources of data (V.1) and clarify both his concepts (V.2) and methodology (V.3) in order to falsify (V.4) the leading theory, the theory of "special creation."

Darwin's did not intend to falsify the theory of special creation at the start, indeed he only heard of it when he read volume Lyell's summery of theories advocating the transmutation of species "in order to reject them all" in November 1832, "just at the time that Darwin was pondering upon his extinct animals" (Chancellor & van Wyhe, 2009, p. 38). Darwin had begun his voyage as a convinced believer in "natural theology" (Eriksen, 1999) which can better be described as a moral theory of creation (compare Darwin's discovery that nature is much more brutal than admitted in natural theology, see Ruse, 1979/1999 and Searle, 1996). In contrast, *On the Origins of Species* is an attempt to falsify a scientific version, the theory of "special creation" presented by Lyell in volume 2 of *Principles of Geology*. The three books by Lyell, in reality served as mediated (Wertsch, 2007) forms of the social (Latour, 2005) and intellectual role model or prototype (I.2) which guided Darwin's observations and thinking about these issues (Wilson, 1972).

FitzRoy was very interested and knowledgeable about geology and Lyell's books and Darwin and FitzRoy must have discussed the three volumes in detail during the five-year, although over time their interpretations became very different. Darwin had become increasingly convinced that the theory of "special creation" was wrong and had to be replaced by a theory of "common descent" as the core of an evolutionary theory and explanation of the origins of species, whereas FitzRoy remained deeply religious in his views on creation.

But Darwin most probably kept these heretical thoughts to himself (skunk works, IV.3). It was only when he had returned home that he began to share his views with a few selected confidants (IV.4). The loosening of social control alone did not do the job. Separation of facts from fiction, based upon new data (V.1), guided by a new methodology (V.3) better adapted to the knowledge object of evolutionary biology (final cause, V.4), allowed Darwin to overcome the knowledge constraints (I.3) that had stopped Carl Linnaeus from discovering what Darwin had found out during the voyage, that the hierarchical nature of the system of classification (taxonomy) that Linnaeus had discovered in nature (systemae naturae) could best be explained (parsimony, III.1) by something that had taken place in nature itself, evolution by "common descent."

Common descent was only one of several factors though that explained how "transmutation" of species took place. Other factors were gradual changes, speciation and natural selection. In order to understand how nature itself arrived at parsimonious solutions of survival and reproduction (III.1), the final cause of the creativity of nature (V.4), both intra-species and intra-species forms of co-evolution should be foregrounded. Having come so far, Darwin to his surprise and consternation (Browne, 2002) found that an unknown rival, Wallace (Smith & Beccaloni, 2009) had independently arrived at an almost identical theory (III.2).

### The Vulnerability of First Versions

Reconstructing the "logic of discovery," as Popper admits in *The Logic of Scientific Discovery*, is not impossible in principle. The problem is that it is very tricky and involves so many aspects that it might be wise to stick to only one aspect ("quid juris" or the logical coherence of the argument as found in the text itself as Kant recommended). But this is the same thing as saying that in order to solve the problem and arrive at an explanation which is able to account for the complexity of such and similar forms of human creativity, we need to consult different disciplines (Gardner, 1988).

This should not be impossible in principle. A core problem for pioneers in whatever intellectual field, is that getting it right takes time (Abbott, 2001a).

This does not prove that the evolution of disciplines, art forms or industries are completely chaotic processes (Abbott, 2001b). They might feel or seem to be so from a subjective point of view (Kupferberg, 1995c, 1996a, 1996b). A deeper understanding of creative processes reveal that they are constrained or structured by factors (Kupferberg, 2003a, 2006a, 2006b, 2007) more or less invisible or rather taken for granted and, if only for this reason, not critically reflected upon (Perkins, 1995). But the fact that problem solving in both nature and culture is constrained (by physical, developmental, knowledge constraints etc.), does not exclude the fact that it takes time to find the best, most parsimonious solution. But what happens in the meantime with those solutions which are very far from being elegant and economic?

As noted by students of technology and entrepreneurship, the first attempts to get it right are often clumsy. The inventor of Nike shoes had to go a very long way before the products envisioned could become competitive on the market. A large number of prototypes (versions) were designed and discarded as not good enough before the company could present a sale able product for the market (Ketteringham & Nayak, 1986). In some cases, the technological solution might be there from the beginning. The problem is to find what the problem the solution is here to solve (What can one to do with a glue which does not glue properly?) (see Peters & Austin, 1985).

The relative clumsiness of the first prototypes is not only a problem for technology but also for nature. Young birds cannot fly because they do not yet know how to use their wings. They must practice before they can make the first attempt to jump off a dangerous cliff or a high tree. Lion cubs have sharp claws and teeth, but they are too inexperienced to hunt and kill prey. They too must practice these skills many times before they can be let loose to kill on their own, without parental protection in the wild. They therefore need to be protected by a strong mother (a lioness) while the young cubs start to train their fighting abilities through play (a similar play instinct can also be found among primates and humans, see Bruner, 2006b). In all these cases, the young and vulnerable have to be protected by strong adults (parents) in order to survive until they can manage on their own.

What Darwin found was that the same basic protection of vulnerable versions also makes evolution of a new species possible. Such species evolve gradually from individual variations, but these variations are held in check by constant interbreeding. This normalizing effect is set out of function in those cases where interbreeding species become separated from each other by geographical barriers (the Galapagos effect). This would explain why geographical barriers tend to trigger processes of "speciation," the separation of the same species into sub-species which over time become separate species. The question is, can a similar process be found say in science (speciation into disciplines, see Hull, 1988)? What about art, what about technology?

## Geographical Isolation

Before we can answer this tricky question we need to know more about how speciation processes in nature (N-creativity) function in practice (prototype, I.2). Take the origins of the unique sweet water fishes, cichlids, that live in Lake Victoria. There are numerous species of various sizes, but the variations have nevertheless been held in check by the fact that they all live within the same geographical area. Wilson (1991/2001) calls this phenomenon "sympatric speciation," or "splitting into two without first having been divided by a physical barrier" (Wilson, 1991/2001, p. 102). The secret behind such evolution is specialization (compare the Dutch painters). The process of speciation is similar to "adaptive radiation" or "the evolution of a single species into many species that occupy diverse ways of life within the same geographical range. Example: the origin of kangaroos, koalas, and other, present-day Australian marsupials from a single distant ancestor" (Wilson, 1991/2001, p. 375).

How does this peculiar form of speciation work and does it falsify the theory of speciation/Galapagos effect? The answer is, not necessarily.

> Recall that only a single trait, such as a change in courtship behavior or a shifting mating seasons, is enough to create a new species. Consider also that Lake Victoria is a large body of water, almost 70,000 square kilometers in area, larger than the combined countries of Rwanda and Burundi nearby, and home for millions of small fishes. It is rimmed by a twisting shoreline over 24,000 kilometers long and occupied by numerous local habitats of a widely varying character, from wave-lapped inlets to deep offshore basins whose bottoms never see sunlight. On many occasions during the hundred or more millennia of their history, cichlid populations must have contracted their ranges along the shoreline, breaking into local, temporarily isolated populations. In theory at least, differences in courtship or habitat preferences could be fixed within tens of hundreds of generations, a process fast enough many times to have generated three hundred cichlid species during the lifespan of Lake Victoria. (Wilson, 1991/2001, pp. 102–103)

Creativity in culture is fundamentally modeled (I.2) upon the constrained and parsimonious problem solving of nature, but the two are not identical, partly because most human creativity is intended. But not all forms of creativity are. Groundbreaking discoveries in science as we have seen are basically unintended just as in nature. This should, paradoxically, make the evolutionary process Darwin describes in *On the Origin of Species* closer to the nature of scientific discovery than pioneering work in both art and technology. The problem of the protection of vulnerable versions is a good way to test one aspect of the complex and paradoxical problem if Darwin can explain himself (Simonton, 1999a, 1999b; Gardner, 1999).

This particular aspect is raised in Rudwick's (1996) seminal article on how the many years Darwin spent far away from England might help to explain how he dared to think his heretical thoughts (Sulloway, 1996). Rudwick's preliminary answer is that geographical distance over long periods of time had a liberating effect upon Darwin's thinking. Geographical liminality relieved him from the strong pressure (I.5b) to conform to what Bacon (Strong & Davies, 2006/2011b) called the "idols of the tribe" had he stayed in Cambridge where creationist thinking was indeed predominant.

This might be so, but as indicated above, support systems (IV.5) are critical for the protection of vulnerable ideas and most of these support systems were waiting for him at home, so he could not have been completely liberated from the pressure (I.5c) to conform. A factor Rudwick does not mention is the sheer pleasure (I.5a) of joining such a voyage around the world. There might have been many reasons why Darwin accepted the opportunity (I.5c) to see the world by traveling the *Beagle* for years to come. One was the pleasure (I.5a) of traveling to unknown continents, which must have felt like an adventure. The personal experience of traveling around the world would be a dream for most of us. Darwin had read Humboldt's personal narratives and clearly saw this as an opportunity (I.5c) to walk in the footsteps of the world-famous pioneer (prototype, I.2). He might also have felt the pressure (I.5b) to prove himself in front of his father but also his fiancée (compare Matisse's similar pressure felt from his main patron, his father and Chagall's pressure to prove himself worthy of marrying Bella). What Darwin did not and could not know was that the voyage would gradually provide a very different type of opportunity (I.5c), to falsify the reigning (geological) theory of the origins of species, the pleasure (I.5.a) of solving such a tricky problem but also the pressure (I.5.b) to provide indisputable proof that he had indeed got it right.

According to Rudwick (1996), what Darwin also discovered during his five years far away from home, was that geographical isolation (IV.1) was very helpful for thinking differently. Rudwick claims that Darwin's move to Downe a few years after his return to England can be seen as a conscious repetition of the same ideal working conditions for a scientific pioneer. The new geographical isolation at Downe helped postpone the moment of truth when he had to reenter society and take credit for the radical, nonconformist ideas he had arrived at (Sulloway, 1996) but which only existed in a highly vulnerable version at the time (Gruber, 1981; Sloan, 2009). But this time around, geographical isolation was intended. His ambition was now to provide proof of his previous discovery and falsification of the theory of "special creation."

There are some problems with this interpretation though. One is that it ignores the problem of skunk works (IV.3) which Darwin must have experienced, sharing a cabin with FitzRoy, a convinced believer in "special creation," precisely the theory that Darwin, unintentionally, had come to falsify by his own discoveries (data, V.1), which he must have kept secret from FitzRoy (skunk works, IV.3). What Darwin needed was a confidant (IV.4) with whom he could share his secret intentions to publish a book which could falsify the theory of "special creation" in an empirically and logically coherent manner (Mokyr, 2002). For this purpose, he did not have to move out of London (compare Freud who lived in the middle of Vienna), as he worked out his heretical theory on dreams, by confiding in Breuer and Fliess (see Gay, 1988).

Rudwick also ignores the fact that Darwin had run into trouble. A core idea of his theory of the origins of species was the process of speciation. But for this purpose, species had in normal cases to migrate, often over long distances. It was possible to imagine how this worked for finches who might be driven by winds, or turtles, who are able to swim, but what about trees, bushes, grass and flowers? How are they transported, and can they survive long journeys, in for example, salt water or in the stomachs of birds (Browne, 1995)? For this particular purpose, his previous method (contrasting comparison) was not enough. He had to make controlled experiments, preferably in a garden-like environment. These methodological (V.3) considerations best explain why Darwin decided to buy and move to a house with a large garden a day's journey from London (although there might also have been other, private reasons as well).

After moving to Downe, Darwin soon ran into other unexpected difficulties. Although this time round he had clearly intended to falsify the theory of "special creation," he had made many new discoveries over the years which were unintended as well. One was the fact that a record of evolution which depended upon fossils as the sole or most important data (V.1) was unreliable as a method (V.3) given the irregularity (contingency) of fossil finds in nature. The best data for biology, fitting the knowledge object, were riverbanks, swarming with life (Darwin, 1859/1985, p. 459). Another important discovery was that one of the basic concepts (V.2) of geology, uniformatism or the "rock cycle" as it is called today, was adapted to the nature of the distinct knowledge object of geology, but it did not fit biology, where the core concept is "common descent." A third important discovery, but for some reasons rarely foregrounded in biological theory was the role of "parsimony" (III.1). A fourth important and unexpected discovery was the answer to the problem of complexity (Who needs half an eye?). Well, half an eye is better than no eye at all. Even small advantages that increase the chances of survival are favored by nature. Thus, we only need to imagine a very simple eye, such as a nerve thread which has become sensitive to light (rediscovered, III.2 by modern engineering, compare photocells). But such early versions are far from perfect and have to be protected from premature death. This is where the problem of protection of vulnerable versions become critical both in nature (N-creativity) and in culture (s-creativity, a- creativity, t-creativity, p-creativity and h-creativity).

The role of geographic isolation for protection of vulnerable versions can take many forms (Kupferberg, 1998a, 2006a, 2006b). Geographically isolated art colonies have played an important role for allowing noncon-formist experiments with new techniques (Shiff, 1984; Sawin, 1995/1997; Svanholm, 2001; Vezin & Vezin, 1992; Richardson, 1996/1997; Spurling, 2009). The move in the 1910s of the American film industry from the East coast to the West coast seems to have led to a creative explosion for similar reasons (French, 1971; Robinson, 1996).

### Artistic Creativity Abroad as Strangers in Paradise

Artistic creativity as we have seen can take many forms, but this does not exclude that it is constrained. The point of a creativity science is to clarify the nature of these constraints. The basic problem-solving strategy of art consists of techniques (II.3) which are neither identical with science (methodology) nor nature (trial and error). Given that art is basically a form of imitation, artists sometimes seek to imitate science (naturalistic forms of representation, machine aesthetics, conceptual art, etc.), some-times what they believe is typical for nature (the Primitivism of children, minimal art, biomorphic forms, automatism and spontaneity, surrealism etc.). Such imitations are always intentional whereas the processes of discovery in both nature and science are basically unintended.

Given that artists are not trained to think like scientists or tend to forget all what they have learned once they become artists (Morell, 2004; Steffensen, 2017), art theories promoted by artists are unreliable. This is the reason why a better strategy is to study artistic practices (Elster, 1983). But from this it does not follow that artistic creativity does not start from intentions (Baxandall, 1985; Carroll,1992/2008). These complexities and paradoxes of artistic creativity might explain why not all cases of geographical isolation turn out to be conducive to creativity. The case of German and Austrian refugee writers and filmmakers who emigrated to Hollywood during the Second World War (Coser, 1984; Kupferberg, 2003b) reveal big problems of adaption due to a simultaneous change of audience and working conditions.

German writers a like Heinrich Mann were used to the solitude and autonomy of the writer (physical constraints, I.1) plus the daily writing in German for German-speaking audiences (Final cause, V.4). After arriving in Hollywood, Heinrich Mann was assigned an office at the Warner Brothers studio and expected to work together with other writers during office hours (physical constraints, I.1). Although standard procedure in Hollywood (Server, 1987; Sikov, 1998; de Rosa, 2001 ), this was certainly very different type of working conditions that this professionally proud German writer had been used to at home (Krüll, 1993). Emotions are important in all forms of creativity although only artists are allowed (I.4) and trained (I.2) to evoke and/or express emotions. What hurt Heinrich Mann's both personal and professional (III.4) pride most was that he was expected to write storylines and scenarios for film scripts and not novels or short stories, which he had trained himself to do mainly by close study of prototypes (I.2).

There were also language difficulties. In order to function as writer ("effective cause," V.3) in the professional context (II.3) of writing film scripts in English, language would need to be mastered, something writers learn when they are children (II.1). Not only was Mann demoted from professional writer of novels to novice writer of film scripts, but he was also even further demoted in the process of learning by his inability to speak the language of the country he was to settle in.

Bertolt Brecht's experiences were somewhat different. He was allowed to work at home and could afford to have his film scripts translated into English if necessary. Brecht's problem was that he had been a highly successful pioneer (II.4) of the modern theater (Bentley, 1968; Schumacher & Schumacher, 1978) before finding himself reduced to a novice (II.2) in the American film industry. In contrast to other pioneering playwrights such as Chekhov, Ibsen, Strindberg and Miller, Brecht also played the role of director and staged his own theatrical plays. Surprisingly Brecht, on his arrival in Hollywood, was very optimistic about his future in the Mecca of global filmmaking (Lyon, 1980).

In contrast to say Heinrich Mann but also other, strongly alienated German academics such as Horkheimer and Adorno (Hughes, 1975), Brecht did not despise Hollywood movies. Brecht did not merely regard them as cheap entertainment for the masses made up of individuals with an authoritarian personality (Adorno, 1969; Horkheimer & Adorno, 1944/ 1979). Brecht believed that those workers who had voted for Hitler had been misled by an ideology which went against their own class interests (Schumacher & Schumacher, 1978). As a convinced Marxist, Brecht also believed that ideologies originate in class interests (Therborn, 1977). Although the ruling ideas of any epoch according to Marx did tend to reflect the interests of the ruling classes, this unfortunate truth could be explained by the fact that the ruling classes had a disproportional degree of soft power (Gramsci's concept "hegemony"; see Gramsci, 1967, 1971) to influence public opinion.

This type of ideological influence (hegemony) was seen as clearly undemocratic and should if for only this reason be resisted. This was the guiding idea behind Brecht's political theater and had always been (Saxtorp, 1982.) Brecht assumed that Hollywood movies, in contrast to his own avant-garde theater in Shiffdammer Platz in the center of Berlin, did reach the masses (proletarians) not only in the United States but all over the world (this calculation was, in contrast to Columbus' geography, not pure fiction but an indisputable fact; see Thompson, 1985; Thompson & Bordwell, 2003). Brecht came to Hollywood with the clear intention to continue where he had left off. If he could not be the director, he could be a scenographer and writer for the Hollywood studios. There were many professionally successful European film artists in Hollywood, "strangers in paradise" (Taylor, 1983). Working in Hollywood, for and with the leading film studios of the world, would provide him with a new world-wide audience. Although the reason he left Nazi Germany was no doubt pressure, fear of persecution (I.5b), he saw his arrival in Hollywood as a great opportunity (I.5c) to reach out with his idea of art as resistance to the ruling interests (Adorno, although far more pessimistic or realistic, shared this basic view of art; see Adorno, 1997).

Moreover, writing for the theater had always given him pleasure (I.5a) and he could see no reason why this should change.

Brecht's naivety might come as a surprise, but part of the reason for his unrealistic expectations of continuing what he had done in Berlin but this time reaching the "world proletariat" (the imagined audience of another political refugee, Karl Marx who ended in London instead, the Metropolis of the leading capitalist nation at the time) might be a pragmatic approach. He must have felt that he had little choice but to adapt to the changed problem situation (historical, professional and personal-problem situation) that he as problem solver had been put in (III.4).

Moreover, Brecht had a surprisingly little faith in humanity. His association with Marxism seems to reflect a more or less cynical world view which expects individuals to act from interests of self-preservation rather than moral concerns (perhaps best expressed in *Mother Courage;* this basic world view also explains his postwar accommodation with the Marxist-Leninist regime when he returned to East Berlin).

Brecht's unrealistic optimism can also be explained by his previous experiences of rough times. He had in his youth felt like a nobody before his sudden breakthrough as a star writer, director and scenographer in the German theater in Berlin. Why should he fail to repeat his success this time? As most great artists Brecht was also essentially apolitical (Reich-Ranicki, 2000). He was interested in what furthered his career most and most of the time his helpers (IV.5) had been on the left (Schumacher & Schumacher, 1978). Among writers and directors in Hollywood, left-leaning (liberal or radical) sympathies were far from unusual at the time. What he probably did not understand was the predominant role of the producers in the American film industry (Dale, 1997) and without a green light from American film producers Brecht's career prospects were slim.

Brecht wrote no fewer than 40 more or less developed film scripts, but with the exception of his early contribution to the Fritz Lang movie, *Fury*, all these scripts were rejected by the film studios. Given his impressive CV, the studios probably saw him as a talent which needed to be encouraged from time to time (compare Ross, 1984; Rosten, 1941; Powdermaker, 1950) and remunerated him handsomely for scripts even when rejected. Brecht had no financial worries (Schumacher & Schumacher, 1978), although the psychological stress of constant and humiliatingly consistent rejections no doubt took its toll over the years. On the other hand, he was far from alone. The idea of the personal rejections that had to be overcome to become a star one day was part of the everyday Hollywood mystique and myth (West, 1939/1986; Williams, 1999).

In the examples of Heinrich Mann and Bertolt Brecht, artistic intentions continued to play an important role. The main reason why they failed was that they had both lost their support systems (IV.5). This was not the case for more successful writers such as Thomas Mann and Lion Feuchtwanger who continued to write successful novels (Schnauber, 1992; Gumrecht, 1998). Strikingly, most of the painters who came as exiles to the United States in the same period were generally professionally successful (Heilbut, 1983). Nor did they have to adapt as Heinrich Mann and Bertolt Brecht were forced to. On the contrary their reputations as successful European artists created curiosity in art circles in New York where most of them settled down, to the degree that local artists, who later became the nucleus of the New York School, felt discriminated by the local support system which did not seem to be interested in American artists at all (Sawin, 1995/1997).

This can partly be explained by the fact that European art and in particular Paris (Hall, 1999) had been seen as the center (Mecca) of the art world (avant-garde art) since the Impressionists. But the very nature of painting as an art form (its physical constraint), explains why prototypes (I.2) enter the learning processes of writer and artists very differently. Physical proximity to both the artworks of the masters (artifacts) and the masters themselves (persons) is crucial for painting. Novels in contrast are texts and do not suffer aesthetically by being distributed and appreciated by the mechanism that Walter Benjamin called "mechanical reproduction." In contrast to novels and films, art works are basically here to be looked at closely as physical objects, which makes the local presence of artists bringing with them or producing works on the spot easily accessible.

This in turn influences the functions of support systems (IV.5). Film and literature aim at mass audiences. They tell a story and in order to attract such audiences, they need to use techniques (V.3) such as suspense, vraisemblement, realism (an illusion as in all art, see Mitchell, 1994), but also and not the least clarity of narrative structure (Bordwell,1997). Although modern novels have long since given up on the Aristotelian principle of unity of time and space, even modernist writers such as Virginia Woolf, need to impose some kind of chronological structure to allow for jumps in time and space (Abbott, 2008; Genette, 1980; Herman & Verwaeck, 2001/2005; Ricoeur, 1981, 1985). This is the reason why novels and films are here for immediate aesthetic appreciation. They do not have to be interpreted first in order to be appreciated aesthetically. But such art forms can only function with a strongly personal type of support system (IV.5). All preliminary versions of artistic creativity have to be protected, but avant-garde art needs a special, both professional and historically unique, form of protection.

## Cultural Impact through Transplantation

Hollywood can from a certain point of view be regarded as one gigantic system of protection ("creative milieu"). Those European actors and film directors who for some reasons fitted into this support system (IV.5) could have very successful careers and if they failed they did so for the same reasons as American failed actors and directors, and regardless of national origins. British actors and movie directors such as, Charles Chaplin (1964), Vivien Leigh (Walker, 1987) and Alfred Hitchcock (Taylor, 1978) had emigrated or worked in Hollywood mainly for professional reasons. Some German actors and directors such as Erich von Stroheim (Lennig, 2000), Marlene Dietrich (Bach, 2000) and Ernst Lubitsch (Eyman, 1993) came for similar reasons (Taylor, 1983; Whittemore & Cecchettini, 1976).

An interesting case of professional migrant was Billy Wilder (Sikov 1998). Opportunity (I.5c) rather than pressure (I.5b) seems to have motivated his decision to try his luck in Hollywood. This can be compared with Fritz Lang, one of the pioneers of the German film industry (II.4) and a well-established (IV.5) film director in the German film industry, when he hastily left Nazi Germany for Hollywood (McGilligan, 1997). Wilder was barely known and had made only one film, *Menschen am Sontag*. From the point of view of filmmaking he was merely a novice (II.2). Wilder liked making films (pleasure, I.5a) as did Fritz Lang, but for Wilder coming to America was a great professional opportunity (I.5c), not a chance to save one's neck and personal integrity as it was for Lang (pressure, I.5b).

Having spent most of his time as an early immigrant learning not only the local language but also the cultural idiom (such as the American fascination with baseball), Billy Wilder began a long and successful career as a co-writer as well as film director of his own movies, mostly financed by Paramount, the most "German" Hollywood Studio in terms of motifs and style (Mordden, 1987). But Paramount's cultural impact might have been short lived. Billy Wilder's typically European combination of comic irony and pessimistic cynicism, which can also be found in Brecht's political theater, fell out with the new more optimistic but also rebellious mood and aesthetic taste of the mainly young movie audiences that became the dominant taste-makers in the 1960s

The new generations of movie-goers, some of whom became successful movie directors in the New Hollywood (King, 2002), present a changing historical problem situations (III.4). This generational change of movie audiences and the real patrons (IV.5) of Hollywood movies for entertainment (V.4), might explain Wilder's increasing professional difficulties to make films in Hollywood. In contrast, Hitchcock's more English type of mordant humor, might explain why he in contrast to Wilder, had fewer difficulties in adapting to changing audiences, taste and fashion in postwar America (Friedman, 2015). This does not exclude a more long-lasting aesthetic impact of German film making such as, "the dark noir" of the German Expressionists film style, which can mostly be found in the typically American gangster genre (Schatz, 1981). Whether this style was transmitted directly by German-speaking film directors such as Fritz Lang and Billy Wilder or by the Englishman Hitchcock whose techniques had also been shaped as an apprentice in Weimar Germany (Gottlieb, 2002) or took another road, would require a more detailed investigation.

The geographical migration of European artists before and during the Second World War did not only have a cultural impact upon American movies. The rise of abstract expressionism in the United States has often been described as a purely home-bred, American phenomenon (Greenberg, 1961/1965) but this belief is probably self-serving. The New York School was influenced by European exiles in many more or less subtle ways (Sawin, 1995/1997). It seems that at least some of the artistic techniques which we associate with the abstract expressionists, such a drip painting, biomorphic forms and more generally the turn to more abstract forms of representation were transmitted to the United States by these exiled painters. With them also came Peggy Guggenheim, who later became the main gallerist for the abstract expressionists, having been persuaded by Clement Greenberg that the future lay in the American school of painters (Rubenfeld, 1997; Dearborn, 2005/2006).

## Intellectual Migration and Teamwork

For new ideas to need being protected, such ideas have first to be discovered. Most of Darwin's ideas came from intellectual borrowing or migration from biology to geology as did Crick and Watson's intellectual migration from physics and zoology to the new and exciting discipline (Schrödinger, 1944/1992 ), molecular biology. Another interesting case is Steve Jobs. He had been ousted from his old firm (Isaacson, 2012). His old firm which he had co-founded was in decline at the time (historical and professional problem situation) when he (problem solver, III.4) was offered the opportunity (I.5c) to return to his own firm to take over his former post as leading innovation manager (Tidd et al., 1997). During the ten years or so that Steve Jobs had been away, he had worked as consultant for Pixar, a firm making animated movies by novel digital techniques. Pixar was a typical "creative industry" (Caves, 2000) combining artistic creativity with commercial considerations (Caves' comparisons with painting are less successful though, comparison with architecture, furniture design and fashion would have been better). What Steve Jobs learned from his years in this industry was how to tell a story. Engineers in principle improve design (V.2), but in order to sell such a design, a good story needs to be told in which suspense is created and fictive facts come alive. It is not enough to create a new fact (a new MacBook, iPhone or iPad) the feeling that facts have entered a dream world and become fiction must also be created (V.4).

But intellectual migration might also have the function of protecting new and vulnerable ideas in the making. A newcomer is not expected to be a serious rival (compare Darwin's lack of suspicion that he indeed had an unknown competitor who had arrived at a similar theory as his by independent discovery, III.2). The competition between the New York School and the Surrealists in exile was probably an exception to the rule or rather foregrounds the teamwork aspect of intellectual migration that enhances creativity. Crick and Watson shared an office during the time they as intellectual migrants and unsuspected newcomers worked on solving the problem of the century (historical and professional problem situation, III.4). Nobody suspected these intellectual migrants to be serious competitors precisely because they were newcomers and not supposed to know anything (personal, III.4, knowledge constraints, I.3).

There is probably a dual effect here. Few would expect a newcomer to come up with groundbreaking ideas. The arrogance of the established workforce towards the newcomer (Kupferberg, 2003c) is of advantage to the newcomer and functions as a kind of protection, giving the newcomer time to clarify the nature of the problem and find a parsimonious solution (III.1). Take the case of Gauguin. Coming from the financial world after a period as common sailor, he was a complete newcomer to the art world (Sweetman, 1995). Gauguin managed to talk himself into this tight and envious world in his capacity as a patron of the arts (IV.5) using Pissarro, his mentor (Thomson, 1987) as his agent (IV.5). Most of the Impressionists saw him as an amateur (II.2) who did not know the first thing about painting (Thomson, 2000). A financial crisis seems to have pushed Gauguin (I. 5b) into seeking a new vocation as artist. An expected large inheritance might have provided Gauguin with the promise of patronage (IV.5) he needed in order to make such an option look realistic (opportunity, I.5c).

Gauguin seems to have deceived his wife about his real intentions of how the money from the expected inheritance should be spent. She naïvely believed that Gauguin had promised to give her the large inheritance for the education of their five children. Mette Gauguin came from a wealthy, cultivated family in Denmark who supported Gauguin (functioned as patron) during his first difficult years. When Gauguin sent his pictures from this first trip to Tahiti, Mette also arranged to exhibit them in Copenhagen (functioned as agent). It was only after he revealed his real intentions and ran away with most of the inheritance, returning to Tahiti for a second time, this time for good, resettling himself permanently in the southern seas (Danielsson, 1965, a case of geographical isolation, IV.1) that he lost his best agent and had to rely completely upon his art dealer in Paris for funding, something Gauguin often complained about (Gauguin, 1983; Thomson, 1993/2004).

During the unhappy years Gauguin spent in Dermark, Mette's relatives got him a job selling tarpaulins, indicating that their view of Gauguin as a successful businessman had not changed and they did not share his dreams of becoming a great artist at all. His return to Paris to pick up his career where he left it, might be seen as a case of pressure (I.5b). The sale of his paintings provided him with the financial means to go to Tahiti the first time (opportunity, I.5c). The inheritance, which he had promised to use for his children's education provided him with the opportunity to settle down in Tahiti indefinitly, although he must have known that this would led to a definite breakdown of the marriage.

Gauguin did engage in teamwork during his career, first in the role of novice (II.2) during his apprenticeship to Pissarro, and then as a professional when he worked in artistic colonies with Bernard and van Gogh (Cachin, 1992). During his first stay in Tahiti, he had intensive communications by letter both with his wife in Copenhagen and his professional art dealer in Paris. During his last and final settlement in the Marquesas Islands, he seems to have been increasingly isolated and probably tried to commit suicide by swallowing large doses of arsenic (Danielsson, 1965). His mood was reflected in his final paintings and sculptures (V.4). Gaugin importance as a pioneer of modern art is strongest in the role he played for the turn to Primitivism (Becker, 1998; Shackleford & Frèche-Thory, 2004; Walther, 2005), but he also pioneered the novel idea at the time of symbolic use of colors (Thomson, 1993/2004; Cachin, 1992) later found in Matisse's and Chagall's paintings.

Gauguin's case illustrates that there is also a heavy emotional price to be paid for not being taken seriously as newcomer. Although the arrogance of the establishment against newcomers helps artists to develop their own personal style, lack of recognition from the art world must create emotional wounds requiring repair work (Kupferberg, 1995b). Such repair work might create its own motive, the pressure to innovate (I.5b) for not being recognized, which is clearly found in van Gogh's work (Stone, 1934/ 1987. Van Gogh's violent brushwork was later imitated by Pollock's action painting. Drip painting can be seen as at transmutation of visible brush work. Given that the brush work can be found already among Dutch seventeenth-century painters (Wright, 1978/1984) it was traditionally seen as the most superficial aspect of painting but precisely for this reason it was a good technique to give the impression of personal originality (Shiff, 1984). But his technique was far from accepted at the time (historical and professional problem situation, III.4) and this might be the reason why van Gogh's role as pioneer (II.4) fell on arid ground.

The problem of the support system (choice of helpers, see IV.5), was probably another reason for van Gogh's failure to be recognized during his lifetime. This aspect comes out clearest by comparing him with Gauguin (Fonsmark & Brettell 2005). Coming from the commercial world, Gauguin was well aware of the need to build personal networks in order to advance careers. Van Gogh's obvious lack of social skills (compare the famous "Arles" episode; see Fonsmark 2014) are also part of the enigma of the delay of van Gogh's social recognition (Walther, 2005). Jackson Pollock did not have the social skills of a Gauguin either, but in his case, he was saved by the social skills of the international art dealer, Peggy Guggenheim, who took the morose Jackson Pollock under her wing (Sawin, 1995/1997; Dearborn, 2005/2006). But Greenberg's role as an art critic or advisor (mentor for Guggenheim, patron and agent for the New York School, IV.5) was also helpful in this case. Art criticism at the time of Impressionism and post-Impressionism, seems not to have been as active and competent as in New York half a century later (change of historical and professional problem situation, III.4).

Problem situations matter (Baxandall, 1985; Hacomen, 2000; Kupferberg, 2018a). At the time Darwin worked on falsifying the theory of "special creation," no country in Europe was as opposed to evolutionary thinking as England (Mayr, 1982). This explains why *On the Origin of Species* was published 20 years after Darwin's return to Britain, and if it had not been for the sudden appearance of a rival who threatened Darwin's scientific priority (role as pioneer, II.4), he might have postponed the completion of his book even longer (Mayr, 2004/2007). In contrast, Crick and Watson spent less than two years (Watson, 1968/1996), working on trying to become the first to solve the "problem of the century" (Ridley, 2006). The historical problem situation (III.4) was very different. The solution this time was "in the air" (Marshall, 1890/1916).

Geographical and intellectual migration often go together with team-work (compare the Skagen painters; see Svanholm, 2001) which might be another way to protect vulnerable versions from premature death. Darwin had intensive geological (but not biological) discussions with Admiral FitzRoy at the dinner table in the captain's cabin on the *Beagle* and Crick and Watson could talk freely because they shared an office. This element of teamwork can also be found in the rise of the New York School (Moszynska, 1990), both amongst the American painters themselves (they often shared the same teacher) (mentor, IV.5) and later also the same art gallerist (patron and agent, IV.5), Parsons (Guggenheim mainly repre-sented Pollock at the start). The Surrealists were also engaged in teamwork both before and after they migrated to the United States (Sawin, 1996/1997). Being in the same place, New York (physical constraints, I.1) made it easier for them to contact each other. Robert Motherwell seems to have played the role of mediator between the two schools who nevertheless continued to work more or less as independent art movements although there was certainly heavy borrowing between them.

The New York School divided into two main movements (Harrison, 1994). One was "action painting," foregrounded by such New York art critics as Meyer Shapiro and Harald Rosenberg (Meecham & Sheldon, 2005). Pollock combined (1) large-scale, monumental canvases, probably influenced by Mexican painters (prototype, I.2); (2) the idea of the painting as a flat surface indicating flat space rather than depth (borrowed from Cubism, prototype, I. 2); (3) automatist practices, including drip painting (borrowed from the Surrealists, prototype, I.2); biomorphic forms (borrowed from the Surrealists, prototype, I.2); (4) mythological motifs and Primitivist art practices imitating Native Americans in North America (prototype I.2). As noted by Honor & Fleming (1982/1984, pp. 607–609), sand painting is a technique found in hunter-gatherer society, but in this case Pollock's imitation is best seen as a translation or intellectual migration between two art forms (music and dance to dancing painting). As noted by Edward Lucie-Smith (1999), the repetitive, circular move-ments on a canvas lying on the ground rather than hanging on the wall clearly resembled the dance of Native American tribes Pollack had seen in the southern parts of the United States (Wyoming, Arizona, Southern

California) where he had grown up (a case of childhood memories, II.1, constraining visual art, see Kuh, 1962/2000).

The other main strand was the color field theory school (Rothko, Newman). Newman also worked with monumental paintings, but their techniques were different from "automatism," the feeling they wanted to evoke was not spontaneity (the Primitivism of the shaman, magician or sorcerer) but deep meaning which provided answers to the theodicy problem (the Primitivism of religious prophets and lawmakers, see Weber, 1922/1964). With their Jewish upbringing, they found resonance in their pictures in the idea of religion as a covenant between God and Man, which gave God the right to punish his people for venerating false Gods. Surrealism probably provided a prototype (I.2) for both directions (process of speciation). Compare Kurt Seligman, one of the leading Surrealist painters who wrote a history of magic while exiled in the United States (Seligman, 1948/1971).

Another interesting case, which in a sense summarizes the complexity and paradoxes of geographic and intellectual migration as an (unintended) condition for protecting vulnerable versions from premature death, are the immigrant entrepreneurs who invented Hollywood (May, 1980; May & May, 1982; Gabler, 1988). These entrepreneurs were usually poorly educated, and as members of a minority, they were under pressure (I.5b) to prove themselves (French, 1971; Lipset, 1979). This group can be compared with the Rothschilds who became rich under very different historical, professional and personal-problem situations (Muhlstein, 1984). Members of a minority often feel socially excluded and might for this reason be more open to spot and grasp risky but potentially highly profitable opportunities (social exclusion due to social class origins might work in a strikingly similar way, see the saga of the Mærsk McKinney Møller family dynasty in Denmark, Benson et al., 2004). This new breed of immigrant entrepreneur in fact transformed the American film industry and made Hollywood the leading center of production of movies for entertainment (Carroll, 1996; Sklar, 1994; Maltby, 1994). But in order to get it right (III.1) this group (team work, IV.2, see Mordden, 1987 and Gabler, 1988) needed to find out what the audience wanted at the time (Irwin, 1928/1970; historical and professional problem situation III.4) which turned out to be morally educative entertainment, fiction based upon communication of the brutal facts of life (Carroll, 1992/2008), mixed with wishful thinking such as "becoming a star" (Duyer, 1987).

The "star system" solved both the financial and organizational aspects of the movie industry (movies as technology-based art aimed at mass audiences and hence an uncertain and expensive industry) and the aesthetic-artistic aspect, the evoking of emotions. But why the Jews? To become a star requires almost superhuman patience, hope against disappointment, dreams against reality. As noted by Johnson (1987) Jews are probably the most stubborn people in the world. They have kept their faith in spite of thousands of years of persecution and discrimination. From an emotional point of view, there is a clear affinity between the historical experience of the Jewish people and the experience of becoming a star.

But if we look at the actors who were the most popular stars at the time, such as Charlie Chaplin or Mary Pickford (Whitfield, 1987 ), few of them were Jews or looked like stereotypical Jews who fitted the racial stereotypes of the Jewish nation. Jewish immigrant entrepreneurs were clearly aware of the strong anti-Semitism which still existed in America at the time (Gerber, 1986) and preferred to engage non-Jews as star material. Take Louis B. Mayer (Marx, 1988). He entered the Hollywood film industry after having been an owner of cinemas in Boston, and then in his next career move, showed up in Hollywood accompanied by a female stage actress whom he helped to become a film star. Although he later became the highest-paid person in the United States, he could not be admitted as member of the exclusive social club opposite the MGM studios (compare the Mærsk family who at least did not suffer from that type of social discrimination).

Stubbornness is only one important personal characteristic to run such a risky business as the film industry (compare the "nobody knows anything" principle, Goldman, 1966) though. A strong degree of realism in the here and now, legitimating why one has to be endlessly patient waiting for the dream or utopia to become reality in an unknown future is also good for such a business. This made Jews excellent star-handlers. They had the right attitude to cope with stars when they had reached their peak, but still had some mileage left to go (Griffith, 1970). The ability to face catastrophes and major disappointments and still not give up might also explain why Jews have often been prominent in radical political movements (Rothman & Lichter, 1982) in particular the communist parties. Strong realism bordering on cynicism and stubborn patience happens to be the basic attitude of Marxism or "scientific socialism" (compare Deutscher's three-volume biography of Trotsky, 1959/1965, 1959, 1963).

## Skunk Works

Whereas both geographical isolation and intellectual migration might function as unconscious strategies for protection of vulnerable ideas, the concept "skunk works" requires consciously devised strategies of secrecy. In this case, the function is probably not only to protect vulnerable versions but also protect the vulnerable inventor or messenger of what might be resented by the establishment ("bad news," see Gouldner, 1973/1979), Both Galileo's and Darwin's discoveries were on a confrontational course with the establishment. This was the reason why both trod carefully and tried to keep their heretical views secret as long as possible (Boorstin, 1985; Browne, 2002). What defines "skunk works" is the special type of secrecy where the pioneer keeps his or her attempts to protect vulnerable versions secret from the organization in which the pioneer is employed (Peters & Austin, 1995; Ketteringhamn & Nayak, 1986). An interesting case is Crick and Watson who kept their work on solving the "problem of the century" secret from their boss, Lawrence Bragg, but also from their closest competitors, Francis Wilkins, Rosalind Franklin and Linus Pauling (Olby, 1974/1994). Franklin and Pauling only heard of Crick and Watson after the discovery had been made and published in a highly respectable scientific journal (Judson, 1996/2013; Goertzel & Goertzel, 1995). Bragg was notified a few weeks before they had solved the problem. At this time Crick and Watson needed his help for scientific reasons, to test which of the theoretical models they were experimenting with worked best, given the data that they had started from, where two-dimensional X-ray photographs of the wet and dry versions of DNA. What they needed was to build three-dimensional models (physical constraints, I.1).

The lack of three-dimensional models therefore functioned as a knowledge constant (I.3) until that problem was solved, with the help of technicians from the organization who helped Crick and Watson to build the models (cultural tools) necessary for three-dimensional representation (compare Latour, 1987, 1990). But these technicians helped Crick and Watson with a practical solution to what was a theoretical problem. Scientific technology (von Hippel, 1988) was a means to an end with a very different final cause (falsification rather than science, V.4). Adaptation (knowledge for its own sake) only arrived with the ancient Greeks (Rihll, 1999) and was made possible by geometry (Kline, 1953/1987). The historical and professional problem situation facing Crick and Watson as problem solvers (III.4) was completely different not only from ancient Greece but also from the hunter-gatherer society, where science (theoretical knowledge) had yet a long way to come into being. Latour's claim that studying modern laboratory practices prove that "we have never been modern" (Latour, 1993), has no basis at all in empirical reality. It is pure fiction.

## Struggle for Priority Versus Becoming a Star

Pioneering scientists do not get rich from their work, but they do get famous (symbolic capital, see Bourdieu 1974a, 1974b). For this particular type of social recognition (a motivation which probably provides both pleasure, I.5a and pressure, I.5b but also further opportunities, I.5c, compare the concept "credit cycle," (Latour & Wolgar, 1986), scientific pioneers need to prove their primacy (Merton, 1957). This was another reason why Crick and Watson kept secret from their competitors the fact that they were trying to solve the problem of the structure of DNA (Wilkins, Franklin, Pauling). But in science, potential pioneers are usually very few. The opposite seems to be the case in the arts (Menger, 1989, 1999; Menger & Gurgang, 1996) in particular the fine arts which have notoriously been overpopulated (White & White, 1965/1993; White, 1993; Kupferberg, 2012a).

Artists in contrast are either highly successful and pampered (achieve star status) or are not noticed at all.

## Lay Audiences and Connoisseurs

The principle of becoming a star, works differently for different art forms. In modern painting (avant-garde art) becoming rich and famous in one's lifetime, is as a rule a good indicator of who is a pioneer and who is merely a successful professional. Matisse after all did become both, although he had to wait longer than Picasso did (Spurling, 2009). Van Gogh was an exception to the rule (or rather "law"). This pattern cannot be found among novelists, where the most commercially successful writers (such as Ken Follett or Agatha Christie) are mere professionals, whereas pioneering writers such as James Joyce, Virginia Woolf, Ernest Hemingway, George Orwell and Saul Bellow had to either find patrons or support themselves from other sources such as journalism, teaching and other occupations. Even when such pioneers became successful, their income was moderate compared with the professionally successful writers (stars). Pioneering film directors represent a third pattern. Some pioneering film directors such as von Stroheim, Griffith, Chaplin and Wilder might experience early professional success only to be ousted from the film industry later in their career, but others like Ingmar Bergman and Alfred Hitchcock managed to hang on right to the end.

The reason that the support system (IV.5) for avant-garde art (painting) is different from the other arts might be that whereas pioneering novelists and film directors primarily try to satisfy the emotional needs and aesthetic tastes of mass audiences, pioneering artists primarily appeal to elites of connoisseurs. Modern artists are basically in the business of inventing new, partly public, partly private forms of language. Thus in order to understand *Les Demoiselles d'Avignon* fully, it is not only necessary to get acquainted with the techniques (V.3) of Cubism, but the biographical details need to be right as well such as (1) the fact that Picasso was a frequent visitor of brothels (material cause, V.1) in order to appreciate the motif of the composition, (V.2) which depicts a scene in a brothel (Steinberg, 1988), (2) that the strange shapes of the two women on the right were not only modeled on African masks (I.2) but also on Picasso's Afghan hound Kazbek; this choice was a private joke, a "comment upon the dog nature of women" (Richardson, 1996/1997), (3) that the crouching women on the right was probably modeled upon Raymonde (material cause, V.1), the teenage stepdaughter, adopted by Fernande Olivier, and returned shortly afterwards to the same children's home in Paris, run by nuns, signifying a crisis between Picasso and his lover (Hobhouse, 1975).

The work of a modern artist requires a large amount of interpretive work and this is the reason they can only be appreciated by connoisseur. Connoisseurs are professionals (II.3) and function as teachers (mentors, IV.5) for lay audiences (novices, II.2). A problem for connoisseurs is that biographical data (material cause, V.1) are not always accessible or might take a long time to dig up. The biographical facts are usually missing and have to be accessed retroactively (compare Steffensen, 2017). Barr's (1946) book on Picasso's art more or less avoids references to Picasso's biography, probably because the intimate relation between Picasso's biography and his art (transformation of facts into fiction, V.4) was not known at the time. The same constraints of access to biographical data (V.1) explains why Barr's intellectual biography of Matisse (1953/1976) is much richer in biographical material and is better able to explain how life constrained creativity.

Picasso's attitude not to reveal the biographical sources of his work is probably more representative for late-modern artists (prototype, I.2) for several reasons: (1) art works must be prevented from being too easily explained. This would take away some of the charm of functioning as connoisseur, the prime audience (V.4) of avant-garde artists; (2) artists tend to take pride not in who they borrowed or stole an idea from, what avant-garde artists do take pride in is the techniques which they have learned to master (V.3) precisely what connoisseurs have been trained to appreciate; (3) avant-garde artists do seek to evoke emotions (V.4) but such emotions should not be felt as merely private emotions (autobiography, self-therapy); thus, modern avant-garde poets since T. S. Eliot (prototype, I.2) have emphasized the need for poets to "objectify" (mask) private emotions (Tafdrup,1991/1997); (4) modern artists need to protect "significant others" (Mead, 1934/1967). Although artists clearly "cannibalize" (Bergman, 1959) intimate, strictly private knowledge of parents, children, lovers, siblings, friends, colleagues, ideological comrades, etc., they should use such knowledge sparingly (this is yet another reason why it is better to turn facts into fiction, V.1); (5) but this is all in vain after a pioneering artist has been recognized as such, then the wolves (the academic industries) come running (unless one does as some avant-garde novelists such as Knausgaard, confess everything from their private worlds, so that there is nothing more to find).

### Dangerous Secrets

A special type of skunk work can best be described as keeping pioneering work secret due to great personal danger. Having the secret revealed might cost a pioneering scholar his or her head. Some pioneers might for obvious reasons be unwilling to pay such a heavy price (compare Giordano Bruno who was burned at the stake for openly criticizing the Catholic church). Brecht once attempted to do both, publicly criticize the communist regime of East Germany for the way it handled the repression of the workers' rebellion in June 1953, but only his statement of loyalty was printed, causing Brecht to fall into a deep depression. He chose not to take matters further as he probably did not want to take the risk of losing his theater, finally rebuilt at Schiffdammer Platz (Jacobsen & Lange, 1972, p. 11).

Ironically Brecht had in his play on Galileo accused this pioneering scientist of the same type of strategic caution (and with an infinitely much greater risk). Brecht had taken Austrian citizenship and could easily have emigrated and continued his career as theater director and playwright abroad. Galileo in contrast did not have the same option, which might explain his choice to repent in public. Using the strategy of artists, Galileo originally tried to mask his agreement with Copernicus' Earth-centered model in an imagined dialogue. The core of Galileo's defense of Copernicus is an argument over the two alternative models of the planetary system (Ptolemy and Copernicus), just as Darwin's *On the Origin of Species* is "one long argument" against Lyell's theory of "special creation" (Darwin, 1892/1958). But art is not here to argue, but merely to suggest or evoke emotional responses (Tolstoy, 1898/1985). This might be the reason why the "masking" technique failed to persuade the inquisitors, who demanded public repentance from Galileo. a demand to which Galileo, understandably agreed (Boorstin, 1985). Nor does he seem to have become deeply depressed after this wise compromise as Brecht did. On the contrary, Galileo continued to undertake significant scientific research as if nothing had happened, although he had officially been placed under house arrest.

There are also other versions of this type of skunk work. Thus, Soviet writers in the 1960s, after the new general secretary Nikita Khrushchev, had revealed Stalin's many crimes during a secret session of the central committee of the Communist party, began to secretly write forbidden books about the same crimes, some of which were smuggled abroad and published by Western publishers. The works of Alexander Solzhenitsyn and Boris Pasternak were both rewarded with the Noble Prize for Literature. Solzhenitsyn was warned not to travel to Stockholm and receive the prize but was later allowed to leave the country after constant harassment (Solzhenitsyn, 1976). In the case of Pasternak, other types of pressures, not in the least the severe punishment of his secret lover disguised in the novel *Dr. Zhivago* (Pasternak, 2016), persuaded him not to travel to Stockholm to accept the prize.

## Moral Resistance and Authentic Lives

Vaclav Havel, another well-known artist and political dissident, did not let himself be cowed by the authorities. He refused to repent publicly and went to prison for upholding his dissident views. Gradually Havel was seen as a symbol of the growing opposition in his country, a "disturber of peace" (Havel, 1990). What is interesting in this case is that Havel's type of skunk work became a role model (I.2) for the political opposition in the form (V.2) of "moral resistance." But why Havel? As a theater professional (II.3) where "everything is pretense, nothing is" (Koskinen, 2001), Havel could easily identify the source of moral collapse, the pressure on ordinary citizens (I.5b) to participate in a public lie. Havel's favorite example (prototype, I.2) is the butcher who, like all butchers displays pieces of raw meet behind the shop window for customers to see. The small difference was that the butcher, as a gesture of loyalty (compare Brecht and Galileo) has put a written sign which praises the leading role of the communist party.

This gesture is theatrical, but in contrast to real theater – an art form intended to help lay audiences to achieve "catharsis," the feeling of relief that they, as audience, in contrast to the tragic outcome of the action, can leave the theater free to get on with their lives – the behavior of the butcher in Prague is inauthentic and insincere. The "theatrical" quality of this imposed behavior is cleansed of aesthetic and emotional artistic functions and has been reduced to naked instruments of power (Kriseova, 1991). Such imposed loyalty with clear theatrical overtones, found in postwar Czechoslovakia, was from a structural point of view strikingly similar (prototype, I.2) to the nightly marches of ordinary Germans during the first years of the Nazi regime (Karlsson & Ruth, 1983). In both cases, the prime function might have been to discourage political resistance based upon moral concerns of common feelings of justice and decency.

## Secrecy and Confidants

As noted above, the secrecy necessary to protect vulnerable versions can take many forms. Hitler's virulent anti-Semitism was unpopular for a long time and the German educated classes were shocked by the radicalism and brutality of the *Kristallnacht*. This forced the Nazi leadership to be more "creative" in finding ways to "solve" the "Jewish question" which revolved around strategic use of secrecy (Fest, 1973/2014a, b). First a clear distinction was established between the Eastern areas, where the cooperation of the local population to take part in the atrocities against the Jews was openly encouraged, and things were done more or less in the open on the one hand and the occupied countries in Western Europe on the other hand. Here the Germans upheld the aesthetics of the sublime. Fear was combined with beauty (personalized in the physical appearance and strict, civilized behavior of German officers, representing the aesthetic aspects of the Third Reich). For this to work, an iron wall had to be erected between what happened in both parts of Europe. Although it is doubtful that no news at all percolated out to the civilian population in Germany about the "dirty work" done in the East by ordinary Germans (Hughes, 1964; Goldhagen, 1996), the strategy of complete secrecy overall seemed to work in the West until the end of the war (Guillou, 2014), giving the Nazi leadership plenty of time to fulfill what it saw as its historic mission (Davidsson, 1966/1997).

Secrecy as Simmel (1964) noted is a critical aspect of social life. Without some form of secrecy, societies would not function. But such secrecy can take many forms. Western democracies take pride in free exchange of information, but this rule too has limits or we would not have the phenomenon of spying and punishing traitors revealing military secrets to the enemy. There is also industrial espionage within the most advanced branches of technology, which might or might not become a political issue. But there are also forms of secrecy in both science and art. The question, from a creativity science point of view, if these are constrained as well, is whether secrecy in science and art is different from secrecy in technology and if so why?

## Functions of Secrecy

In principle, secrecy in pioneering work in technology can have two major functions, either to hide strategic information from an enemy or competitor or to steal such information. During the Cold War, the United States had a considerable technological advantage in most of the strategic fields of military technology compared with the USSR. It was the Soviet Union who tried to steal secret information from the United States. Private firms which do not work for the military industry tend to keep certain types of strategic information secret to preserve or protect a comparative advantage (final cause, V.4). Leonard-Barton (1995) mentions the statistic information assembled by the Ford company of what happens when cars collide. The company has a database which it does not wish to share with anyone outside the company, partly for competitive reasons, and partly because this secret information represents a considerable investment (sunk costs).

Science is not lucrative, but scientific work also represents a considerable personal and professional investment. The way this is paid off is by symbolic capital. Only in rare cases, such as winning a Nobel Prize, does wealth become added to fame, perhaps because the originator of this institutions was a wealthy businessman but with little symbolic capital (Fant, 1991). This prize did not exist during Darwin's lifetime, so we cannot reasonably suspect that he had financial motives to do what he did. Nor did Darwin steal his proof from Wallace. Indeed Wallace had no proof to present, only a raw sketch of a theory which was almost identical with Darwin's. But such a theory clearly belongs to the category of "disputable facts" (V.4). The challenge is how to transform such a theory into an "indisputable fact" (Dawkins, 1996/2006; Mayr, 2002). For this purpose, Darwin needed time in order to work out all the details, in practice discover the proof necessary to make the argument "watertight" (Mokyr, 2002). For this purpose, keeping the fact that he was working on a falsification of the theory of "special creation" only confiding in a few selected confidants, makes sense.

But science is not art. Novelists rarely use confidants. To arrive at the right composition of a novel is far less tricky than to discover the best most parsimonious concepts (V.2). Nevertheless, vulnerable versions have to be protected, which tends to take time (mostly a year or two). Some novels are much longer and might require longer time to write, This might explain the strange behavior of the politically exiled Victor Hugo. Why did he not accept the pardon from the new regime in France (Maurois, 1956/1985) and offer to return to Paris where he had his own house waiting as well as a rich social life to return to?

The best explanation seems to have been that he wanted to avoid resuming his social life, perhaps the most attractive opportunity (I.5c). Hugo made the diagnosis that his inability to finishing the long novel, *Les Misérables*, which he had given up on several times, had been constrained by his popularity as house guest in cheerful Paris. Living on an isolated island, where the local population spoke English and not German, relieved Hugo of such social pastimes. It gave him all the time in the world to do what he had wanted for such a long time, in other words get on with the unfinished novel so that he could put that task behind him.

A similar motive might also have influenced Darwin's decision to move from the center of London to Downe. It gave him an excuse to resign from the prestigious post as Secretary of the Geological society which he had accepted at the start, probably because it gave him the high personal prestige which came with such a position, in particular as this was one of the most prestigious of the many amateur scientific societies that seems to have been unique for England (Merton, 1938/1970; Winchester, 2002). But there was another, more important reason why Darwin chose to move to the countryside.

### Methodology, Calculations and Knowledge Constraints

As noted by Browne (1995), Darwin became increasingly worried about the explanatory power of one of his five factors, geographical isolation or speciation as trigger of change. For this purpose, species had to be able to migrate over long distances, sometimes between continents. How was this possible? Darwin needed to collect the relevant data (material cause, I.1) and for this he needed to make controlled experiments (V.3) as to estimate how long seed could survive in salt water or in the stomach of a bird. But in order to keep such controlled experiments secret, Darwin needed an isolated garden (physical constraints, I.I).

Making controlled experiments is different from the method of comparative observations Darwin did during his five years of traveling. His controlled experiments involved calculations although of a relatively elementary type (arithmetic). Darwin later also did experiments with peas in order to solve the problem of genetic information, but this experiment failed because Darwin lacked competence (I.3) in the necessary mathematics (statistics). But if we are to believe one of the founding fathers of sociology, Max Weber, social action based upon calculations lacks deep meaning. Indeed science, just as technology and bureaucracy are mere "goal-oriented" forms of action, in contrast to religion which is based upon "values" (1904–1905/1958, 1948a, 1964).

But this cannot be right. First of all, Weber's own hermeneutic method (Verstehen, see Friend, 1969) is also a scientific method and aimed at finding the meaning of social action, so how can science lack meaning? Second, calculations do play an important role for the evolution of scientific thinking and the founding of disciplines:

1) The very birth of science as a new type of knowledge of a mainly theoretical type, was ultimately based upon abstract calculations, geometrical thinking which served as both knowledge constraint (I.3) and role model (I.2) for the birth of Greek science (Rihll 1999; Kline, 1953/1987).

2) Further advances in mathematics such as algebra functioned as the main knowledge constraint (I.3) for the discovery of the First principles of physics (Renn, 2001) but also science-based technology, Galileo's discovery of "material science" the core of modern engineering (Petrosky 1996; French 1994).

3) A further mathematical advance, Newton's discovery of calculus (Boorstin 1985) helped him combine Galileo's and Kepler's discoveries and falsify Aristotle's theory of gravity as a merely local cause.

4) Einstein's falsification of Newton's theory of the "ether" as the mechanism which explained how gravity could travel in an empty universe, seems to have been based upon even more advanced mathematics, vector theory. Einstein's knowledge of this mathematical tool was insufficient when he had to formulate a general theory of relativity and for this purpose he had to ask a friend (Darling, 2006).

5) Darwin was not well versed in mathematics. There is only one type of complex calculation indirectly referred to in *On the Origin of Species*, why the hexagonal design of wax cakes seems to be optimal given that this minimizes the amount of labor of the bee colony. But Darwin's lack of mathematical knowledge (personal knowledge constraint, I.3) also seems to be the best explanation why he did not independently discover Mendel's laws (III.3).

Not only is Weber's categorization of quantitative methods in science as bereft of meaning, logically incoherent and empirically false, but also his reduction of qualitative methods to hermeneutic methods (analysis of texts). Such methods are typical for historians, philosophers and literary theorists, but fail as soon as we move on to other types of methods, such as archeology, art history and architectural history which study artifacts; musicology, theater studies, the sociology and psychology of emotions (social psychology) which basically study performance; evolutionary biology, historical sociology and creativity science which rely upon the comparative method of historical cases (see Chapter 8).

### Patents and Tacit Knowledge in Technology

Control over one's primary date (material cause, I.1), until they are published, is necessary for scientists. It is not a pathogenic or pathological feature as Merton (1948/1968; 1963/1973b) claims, but part of the rules of the game. In contrast, stealing data and concepts from another scholar and presenting these as one's own, original ideas is not condoned, but is severely punished. This is the reason why scholars from the very start are socialized into identifying their sources, both within the text and as supplementary notes and references. This practice has become so routine, that scholars who for some reasons ignore referring to stolen or rather "borrowed" (Abbott, 2004) material, are seen as breaking an absolute rule. But why does the same rule not apply to art and technology?

If we start with engineers, they can, in principle, protect their property rights with the help of patent laws provided there are such laws or means to enforce them which is not always the case (national laws and international laws are not enforceable in the same way). This might have been the reason why Edison did not bother about protecting his patents on the film projector. This in turn allowed French engineers to steal the new technology without paying for it, but also using it for other purposes than originally intended. As a trained engineer (Baldwin, 1995), Edison would have preferred to see peephole machines (Robinson, 1996), rather than using the camera as a projector illuminating a large screen. Using a camera as a projector was more artistic. It also transformed looking at movies into a "sociological experience" (Schatz, 1981). The idea was discovered by the Lumière brothers (Ramsey, 1924/1964). It gave European filmmakers a head start in making feature-length movies with artistic content. It was only with the arrival of a new breed of immigrant entrepreneurs, that the artistically more advanced film practices developed in Europe became standard in the United States (Dick, 1997) which in turn explains the fact (V.4) that most of the pioneering American engineering firms had left the industry at the start of the 1920s (Slide, 1970).

An often-heard argument for patent laws is that they are basically here to protect technological inventors (entrepreneurs) from having their ideas stolen before they have their personal and organizational investments repaid (Schumpeter, 1945/1979). Such patents are rarely watertight though. According to Leonard-Barton (1995), companies today use complementary strategies apart from patent laws. One is technological specialization and expertise (esoteric knowledge, skills of the trade, tacit or personal knowledge). Thus, techniques for highly specialized steel are so advanced that only a few possess the necessary knowledge to use them (knowledge constraints, I.3) Another strategy, used by car companies, is to build up a huge database of certain significant properties, such as material resistance during frontal collisions (physical constraints, I.1) which in turn function as knowledge constraints (I.3), which are kept secret from competitors.

Nevertheless, in spite of all preventive measures, stealing ideas seems to be impossible to prevent completely. A case in point is how Steve Jobs got the idea of using icons rather than the usual programming language of the first computers (Isaacson, 2012), during a visit at Rank Xerox Park. Rank Xerox Park was a research facility located in Silicon Valley, far away from the head office in New York, probably as a result of a conscious strategic choice by the top management, taking the Galapagos effect of geographical isolation upon human inventiveness (IV.1) as a possible source of groundbreaking creativity into account, a clear case of how human creativity learns from nature, prototype (I.2), but does not replicate it mechanically (that is without conscious thinking and deliberation). The point is that this specific invention was of no use for the firm, or rather, it did not fit into its main business strategy, photocopying machines, which is why the company (which had invested seed money in Apple, patronage, IV.5) could see no harm in allowing Steve Jobs to steal their own idea (this might also explain why Edison did not bother to protect his invention by patenting the technology in Europe; It did to fit into his business concept which was to sell peephole machines giving individual pleasure). But stealing the idea from Rank Xerox Park only provided Apple with a momentary advantage, as predicted by Schumpeter. Soon Microsoft stole the idea from Apple and introduced basically the same device, the use of icons on the screen to make the interface between user and personal computer easier.

*The Evolution of Style and Conformism of Avant-Garde Art*

In art "stealing" ideas from others has become routine, including pioneers who are perhaps the greatest grave robbers (Krauss, 1986; Cowling, 2002). Creativity in art is essentially accomplished by techniques for how to evoke emotions (V.4). For this purpose, starting with role models (I.2) is usually the most parsimonious strategy (Josephson, 1941/1991; Svedjedal, 1999). Professional painters study paintings made by other artists (Spurling, 2009). Writers of novels, plays and poems read the novels, plays, and poems of other writers not merely for pleasure or delight as audiences do but in order to learn and copy the techniques (V.3) hidden under the surface. Close watching, reading and studying role models, sharpens the skills and attitudes necessary to do creative work in the arts on a professional (II.3) level.

In the popular arts such as film (Hayward, 2000), the tastes and fashions of audiences (patrons, IV.5) are more important than small, elite audiences. In order to enjoy a movie, there is no need to start interpreting it (Sontag, 1969). One just sits down and enjoys the movie (a similar rule applies for reading novels and watching plays). Only other movie directors look at film to learn the craft (Truffaut, 1983/2017) whereas only academics, specializing in film studies are interested in reconstructing the creative practices of say a recognized pioneering film director such as Alfred Hitchcock (Strauss, 2004; Gottlieb, 1995, 2002, 2015; Spoto, 1976/1992, 1983/1998, 2009; Ackroyd, 2015; Freedman, 2015). Some film scholars go even deeper and seek to reconstruct general patterns such as the "auteur principle" (Hollows et al., 2000; King, 2002).

Avant-garde artists hence belong to a different game. Here the guiding rule seems to be to create a feeling of secrecy between the avant-garde artists and the connoisseurs. As noted by Simmel (1964) the feeling of secrecy is one of the strongest sources of sharing and establishing social bonds. Children are the exception to this rule because they have not yet learned the social value of secrecy. They are open books who willingly share whatever they know with everyone else. This might be explained not only as a result of naivety, but also by the fact that the social bond between children and their caretakers (parents, etc.) is natural or biological. It is based upon the instinctive protection of the weak by the strong.

According to Berger and Luckmann (1966), biological instincts among humans are too weak to explain anything, but biological bonds are, as sociobiologists have shown, also a form of social construction, the very concept needs to be rethought. As children grow older and enter schools and professions, they become more cautious of revealing secrets. Some secrets are family secrets and others are of the professional type. A third type is embedded in national, ethnic, religious, erotic cultures, etc.

They become secrets shared by the in-group and create a common identity from which the out-group is excluded (Sumner, 1906/1960). Whatever the type of secrecy, it has the function of creating a social bond. In art this bond is mainly between patrons and artists; thus the type of patronage influences the practices but also stylistic choices of the artist. But whereas the secrets of popular arts such as literature, film and theory are shared by anonymous patrons, in avant-garde art patrons tend to be identifiable persons. Such personal dependence might explain why much of avant-garde art is highly ambivalent (Adams, 1996).

Ambiguity in avant-garde art has different functions: (1) to make it more difficult to understand and enjoy the art work, interpretation as a condition for interpretation (incomprehensibility, Crowther, 1990/1993); (2) to make lay audiences feel excluded and feel angry and resentful (Rauterberg, 2007); (3) to express the resentment of the artists for being so personally dependent upon identifiable patrons (Gilot & Lake, 1964/1981); (4) to prove that the artist is part of the avant garde; (5) to prove that what the artist does is highly relevant to bring the long tradition of painting one step forward, by personal innovation or contribution (Caves, 2000); (6) to avoid competing with other artists by finding one's own ecological niche (Moszynska, 1990; compare the cichlids in Lake Victoria annals by Wilson, 1991/2001).

Paradoxically the feeling of belonging to such an exclusive intellectual aristocracy (perhaps best expressed in the philosophy of Nietzsche), intellectually far above and for this reason consistently misunderstood by the majority (Jørgensen, 2011) creates its own conformism. Avant-garde artists are not as free as the idea of the "romantic genius" still taught in art schools (Elkins, 2001) assumes. Take the abstract expressionist Hans Hofmann. An expatriate German artist well versed in all the early avant-garde are movements in Europe, he is critiqued by Clement Greenberg for not sticking to the same basic personal formula: "The variety of manners and even of styles in which he works, would conspire to deprive even the most sympathetic public a clear idea of his achievement" (Greenberg, 1961/1965, p. 189).

In contrast, Barnett Newman is hailed for doing the right thing, sticking to the same formula in painting after painting once the personal formula or "scheme" (Gombrich, 1996) has been found (Newman chose to destroy almost all of his previous paintings which reveal how he arrived at his singular and easily recognizable but unfathomable style). Newman, according to Greenberg

> displayed both nerve and conviction. I review them at this late date because I feel that the art public should continue to be reminded of anything by which it has been puzzled ... and also because I feel that works of art which genuinely puzzle us are almost always of ultimate consequence...in the presence of these canvases one realizes immediately that he is faced by major art. (Greenberg, 1961/1965,pp. 150–151)

As in science, avant-garde artists are encouraged to be "original but not too original" (Whitley, 1984). The role of the audience (patrons, IV.5) and accompanying final cause (V.4) is still there. This is also the reason why constraint theory is a much better approach to understanding stylistic choices among artists than the idea of romantic genius (I.5). Moreover, a closer view of single artists, reveals that their unique, easily recognizable personal style, if there indeed is such a style (compare the two different interpretations of Picasso's style or styles in O'Brian, 1976/2003 and Cowling, 2002), tends to evolve gradually over time. Artist struggle to achieve what sets them apart (personal style, see Ross, 2003) from other artists (Spurling, 2009; Scholz & Thomsen, 2009).

But group styles tend to evolve as well. As noted by Greenberg (1961/1965), a basic idea of all the abstract expressionists was the idea of "flat" paintings. Their role model (I.2) was the "Cubist" experiments of Picasso and Braque to produce flat geometrical planes. The idea was to destroy the idea of paintings as illusion in a dual sense. Art should (1) not represent anything but itself; (2) the traditional idea of art as naturalistic representation of recognizable figures in everyday life (Lopes, 1996) should be rejected; (3) but so should anything which went beyond the ideas of paintings as representing the "painterly" qualities of a flat surface; (4) such flat pictures can often be found in medieval, Christian, pre-Renaissance (e.g. Giotto) painting and hence represents a form of re-discovery (III.2). The "color field" school of the abstract expressionists also seem to be a rediscovery, in this case, of shimmering effects of bright, natural colors (blue, red, green, yellow, etc.) on the viewer. Shimmering effects of natural colors was discovered by the Venetian Renaissance painters (Berenson, 1930/1960) and rediscovered by Monet and the post-Impressionists such as Cézanne, Matisse and Chagall before they were once again rediscovered by Rothko and Newman.

The idea of the "flat" painting (3) rejected the fundamental discovery of the Florentine painters of how to create the illusion of three-dimensional space with "tactile" qualities (mass, volume and touch, see Berenson, 1930/1960). The first phase of Cubism, solved this self-imposed constraint (Elster, 2000) by replacing the two basic illusionistic techniques invented by the Florentines, shade and central perspective, with overlapping planes but without the use of bright colors. The central perspective technique was only reintroduced in the later "synthetic" version of Cubism (Rubin, 1989; Karmel, 2003).

The Cubist experiment was abandoned mainly because the aesthetic problem Picasso and Braque tried to solve is self-contradictory. Art is by definition imitation and not the real thing and the problem of representation does not disappear (Eldridge, 2014). The only thing that happens is that the outer object of representative art is replaced by the act of painting or the artwork itself as the object for itself (Rothko, 2004). Moreover, art is by its very nature deceptive as Plato discovered (Cahn & Meskin, 2008, cf. Hegel, 1970). The real world is not flat but has indeed volume and space. Picasso transported this idea to sculpture which from now on was treated as if sculpture is basically a painting with painterly and not sculptural qualities. Other artists such as Kandinsky wanted paintings to look like music. Yves Klein transformed painting into performance, etc. (Thompson, 2006; Moszurska, 1990; Gage, 2006; Vezin & Vezin, 1992).

## Patrons, Mentors and Agents

What is problematic both with the theory of art as romantic genius and the counter-theory (death of the author) is that the process of becoming a great artist (moving from child, II.1, to novice, II.2, to professional, II.3, to pioneer, II.4) remains undertheorized. Becoming a pioneer is a long process of struggle, both for social recognition but also aesthetic problem solving. Individuals would never be able to fight this struggle alone. They need "helpers" (Bruner, 1990). But such helpers at a closer view are not identical and they have different functions. Studying these functions leads us to the concept of support systems (Sawin, 1995/1997) which can conveniently be divided into three main categories: patrons, mentors and agents. Artists are very aware of the importance of such support systems, although their memories are not always reliable.

If we are to believe what Picasso told Gilot. Kahnweiler was merely an agent, but this information clearly underestimates Kahnweiler's triple role of patron, mentor and agent during a critical role in Picasso's career, after he had painted *Les Demoiselles d'Avignon* and felt abandoned by everyone (Olivier, 1935/1982; Mailer, 1995/1997). Chagall in his autobiography

(1922/1965), does mention several of his patrons, but clearly underestimates the role of his two most important mentors, Pen and Bakst and is practically silent about the role of agents. Sylvia Plath in practice functioned as both patron (taking jobs to support the family, preparing to write "pot boilers," modeled upon her main patron, the successful novelist Olive Prouty at the time her husband's career was taking off) and agent (promoting her husband's works ), but in exchange Ted Hughes had functioned as her mentor (Middlebrooke, 2004; Feinstein, 2003). Such private support systems are more or less predominant in artistic careers. It played a huge role in Matisse's career (Spurling, 2009)but in the career of Per Kirkeby, it mattered little because public support systems played the predominant role (Steffensen, 2017).

Chagall's original patron was his mother who helped him to become an artist by paying for his enrollment in a local art school (novice, II.2). Chagall's first teacher in Vitebsk (Pen) was also his mentor. This changed as Chagall moved to St. Petersburg. His family could no longer support him financially. Other patrons paid his bills. Chagall also changed teacher (Bakst) who introduced him to the most advanced modernist styles in Paris (mentor). The decisive moment in his life, the opportunity (I.5c) which allowed him to study in Paris for several years and meet new mentors (mainly colleagues rather than teachers this time) and which transformed him from a professional (II.3) into a pioneer (II.4) was the monthly stipend paid by a St. Petersburg patron (Vinaver). While in Paris, Chagall managed to secure his first agent, an art gallerist living in Berlin. Owing to the outbreak of the First World War, Chagall had to return to Russia and lost contact with his German agent who seems to have swindled him. Chagall only managed to find a new agent after returning to Paris in the early 1920s. Although still undertaking art works, Chagall's artistic career was on hold between 1914 and 1922 due to the lack of an honest agent.

### Struggle for Recognition

Darwin only had one main patron during all his intellectual career, his own father (private patron). Darwin's father had to approve and also underwrote his son's travel expenses during the five years on the *Beagle* (including an assistant's wages, see Keynes 2003). The private wealth accumulated by Darwin's father helped Darwin to marry and move into a house in the center of London on his return, and also paid for Darwin's move to Downe a few years later where he spent the rest of his life as an unpaid gentleman scholar doing pioneering research (II.4: Jones, 2001, 2009). Darwin had many mentors, his teachers at school and at Edinburgh and Cambridge. During his voyage on the *Beagle*, FitzRoy served as a mentor initiating Darwin into the new science of geology. But the most important learning came not from a mentor (IV.5) but a prototype (I.2), Lyell's three books (texts, mediated form of the social) on geology together with Darwin's own empirical observations (V.1) plus discussions with FitzRoy (mentor).

During the last part of the trip, Darwin made a significant contribution to geology (the theory of the origins of coral reefs) becoming a minor pioneer or recognized professional ("original but not too original") in the field (Ghiselin, 1984). Lyell also functioned as a mentor to Darwin by serving as one of the secret confidants during most of the 20 years Darwin struggled with the problems of data and methodology that went into the writing of *On the Origin of Species*. Lyell also briefly filled the role of agent for Darwin when Lyell advised Darwin how to secure his primacy after the famous letter from Wallace arrived at Downe (Browne, 2002). Darwin's attempt to function as mentor for Lyell, trying to make his previous mentor understand the First principles of evolutionary biology was less successful though (Rudwick, 1972; Mayr, 2004/2007).

Henslow, Darwin's teacher (mentor) at Cambridge, also functioned as agent, first, when he convinced FitzRoy to accept Darwin as his new "naturalist" sharing dinner conversations with the geology enthusiastic captain, and second, Darwin's return to England. In particular, Henslow's public reading of "extracts from Darwin's letters to him about natural history topics" at

> the Cambridge Philosophical Society meeting on 16 November 1835... brought Darwin's name before some of the most notable natural scientists of the day, serving to generate a great deal of interest in his results, and a general buzz of anticipation about his then impending return ... Henslow acted almost as an agent or business manager for Darwin and completed his task with admirable skill. ... Darwin always believed that Henslow "had made him what he was." (Brown & Neve, 1989, p. 5)

But although agency no doubt played an important role in Darwin's social recognition as a highly competent professional scholar (II.3), it was patronage that ultimately helped transform Darwin into the pioneer of evolutionary theory. In order to become a pioneer in science, sufficient empirical proof and a logically coherent argument necessary to falsify previous theories or explanations need to be provided. This is what

Darwin did, but Wallace could not do, due to lack of sufficient patronage (IV.5). But we also need to take the strong resistance to evolutionary theory in England at the time (historical and professional problem situation, III.4) into account. Crick and Watson only needed to publish two relatively short articles in order to become recognized as pioneers of molecular biology, but the problem situation was very different. Moreover, both Darwin and Crick and Watson achieved their recognition by actually solving the complex problems in a parsimonious manner (III.1). None of them cheated. The "sociology of science" presented in Barnes et al. (1996) misses all the relevant details.

Patronage in science nowadays is usually taken care of by publicly financed research grants or by elite institutions (meritocratic principle), both of which are here to provide the privileged working conditions and research assistance that tend to constrain the opportunities (I.5c) that are necessary for doing pioneering work (Fuchs, 1993). In order to get access to these research grants or elite institutions, a mentor functioning as agent is usually needed. But such agents do not make one a pioneer. For this purpose, pioneering work needs to be done. The problem with pioneering work in science is that it normally has to be protected over a long time in order to get it right (III.1). The length of this protection varies with the historical and professional problem situation (III.4).

In art worlds, patronage systems are still to a large degree run by private gallerists who at the same time function as business agents for their clients. This was historically done on a contract basis, where the artist is provided with a monthly stipend or wage with provisions for delivery of art works in return and according to certain specifications, including commissions held back by the agent if the artwork is sold (if not it becomes the property of the gallerist for later sale). This system of combined patronage and agency was pioneered by Durand-Ruel, the main art dealer of the Impressionists (Roe, 2006/2007) and later copied or independently reinvented by Daniel-Henry Kahnweiler, Picasso's main agent (Richardson, 1996/1997; Gilot & Lake, 1964/1981) and Peggy Guggenheim when she opened her art gallery in New York in the 1940s and became the first patron and agent for the abstract expressionists (Dearborn, 2004/2005) to be followed or emulated by other art gallerists who in turn copied her (Sawin, 1995/1997).

The Hollywood film studies followed a similar model until the 1960s when stars separated from the studios (Davies, 1962; McDougal, 2001). Until then the major studios functioned in the triple role of patrons, mentors and agents (Griffith, 1970; Duyer, 1987). This system fell apart as stars increasingly turned to their own agents and used them to make

more profitable contracts with the studios, until some of the most successful agencies such as MCA begun to produce films of their own. This
led to a transformation of the studio star system to a complex system of
"deal making" which allowed for the growth of independent producers
to enter the filmmaking business, including "stars" who had built a
reputation either as movie directors or actors (Spoto 2009).

Publishing of fiction seen to follow a third pattern. Here the role of
publishers is normally reduced to agents. Publishers usually receive con-
siderably more manuscripts than they are willing to publish (Mizener,
1958; Gedin, 1975/1997). This might explain why publishers essentially
function in the negative role as "gate keeper" (Coser et al., 1982). The best
explanation is probably physical constraints. Learning the techniques for
writing a novel might take even longer then learning the techniques for
painting, but this type of learning can be done anywhere. The novice
writer (II.2) does not need a studio, access to museums, galleries or live
models. Writers learn the techniques for writing by reading the books of
other writers (texts) and physical access to the physical artwork (artifact) is
not necessary. Moreover, most writing is done from memory. Learning to
write can be done part time, in the evening while doing another job and so
can the actual production of a novel.

This explains why writers in principle do not need patrons to pay for all
this. All they need are agents who publish and market their books. A good
case in point for how this works is Hemingway. How did he become a
professional writer? When he returned to Chicago as a war hero, having
been wounded working as voluntary ambulance driver for the Italians on
the border with Austria, he got a job as a professional newspaper journalist
(professional level of creativity, II.3). He was, already at this time dreaming
of becoming a writer of fiction and moved in literary circles (Lynn, 1987).
This was how he was introduced to the accomplished and published
(professional) writer Sherwood Anderson, at a time when Hemingway
was still a novice as writer of fiction (II.2). These meetings took place at
the "beginning of Anderson's period of great success" and the older writer's
support of the young writer, no doubt helped Hemingway launch his
career, but as agent rather than mentor. Anderson "never claimed to have
influenced Hemingway's work as a whole." This does not exclude the fact
that Anderson did in fact function as an agent for the young writer. "It was
'through my efforts' that Hemingway 'first got published'." Anderson was
very explicit about this. "If others said I had shown Hemingway the way,
I myself have never said so. I thought. . . that he had his own gift, which had
nothing particularly to do with me" (Fenton, 1954/1987, pp. 104–195).

It is noteworthy that Hemingway, in contrast to say Matisse, did not learn how to write novels and short stories by going to school (mentors, IV.5). He learned how to write by reading short stories and novels (prototypes, I.2), This learning might have been easier than say for Sartre who had been trained as a philosopher (theoretical knowledge). Writing of fiction is not that different from the writing of journalism. In both cases the "human interest" is in the center. Journalism is not a science. It is also based upon techniques which are very similar to writing, such as how to be concrete or descriptive, avoiding the use of abstract and analytical language (noted by Strindberg, cf. Hegel, 1970). But in his professional role as a journalist Hemingway also learned how to describe events from a neutral, outsider point of view, not revealing the emotions of the narrator. Such skills could be of use for a style of writing where the emotions of the characters in action are also described as neutrally as possible.

Hemingway seems to have developed this personal style or voice (Engdahl, 1994/2005) when he moved to Paris (geographical isolation, IV.1). During the time he learned to write, he was supported partly by his wife (private patron) and partly by the newspaper he was working for, which means that he was doing "skunk work" (III.3). He also confided (IV.4) in Gertrude Stein who became a kind of mentor (IV.5) for him at this stage of his career (transition from professional writer, II.3 to pioneer, II.4). But he also needed an agent (IV.5) a publisher to accept his book for publication and marketing efforts (Bruccoli, 1996).

## The Complexity and Paradoxes of Creativity

All art is based upon the learning of techniques (V.3) and the best, most economical way to learn a new, unknown technique (P-creativity) is by using prototypes (I.2), which in practical terms means imitating pioneer-ing work (II.4, H-creativity) sometimes in the form of a re-discovery (III.2) of a previous, long since forgotten or abandoned tradition (an important aspect of "Primitivism" in the twentieth century, although rediscovering an abandoned tradition is much more complex and para-doxical). But artists whether professional or pioneers are also expected to develop their own personal style ("effective cause," V.3). How is this done in practice?

Painters tend to develop their own style by looking at other paintings, prototype (I.2) as original physical form (I.1). Compare the role that Cézanne's *Three bathers* played as prototype for Matisse's attempts to find a new, personal unique style by close observation of techniques of using color (Spurling, 2009). Writers of fiction learn from reading mechanically reproduced copies of original manuscripts. In both cases, the choice of techniques is constrained by prototypes (I.2), but also physical constraints (I.1). Such physical constraints function on different levels: (1) physical constraints from the point of view of aesthetic appreciation (paintings can be appreciated in one glance; novels require intermittent reading over a long time); (2) physical constraints from the point of view of choice of techniques (naturalistic, symbolic, expressive versus storyline and vraisem-blement; (3) physical constraints from the point of view of means of production. Fiction writers do not need to buy paint, brushes and canvases nor rent for a studio, nor pay a live model. All they need are some relatively cheap writing tools (paper and pen, computer). Live models are taken mostly from real life (participant observation) and sometimes from selec-tive reading ("research"); (4) physical constraints from the point of view of competition both within the field and other art forms (co-evolution, arms race, III.3); (5) physical constraints in the form of historical, professional and personal-problem situations. The arrival of photography and film undermined the tradition of naturalistic but also narrative paintings. But in order to learn to paint in their new manner, and live off painting, artists needed support systems (patrons, mentors, agents, IV.5).

But why did the arrival of photography and film not threaten literature, only painting?

Again, physical constraints (I.1) might be a good start. Photography made the techniques of naturalistic representation anachronistic. Film problematized the literary (narrative) function of art. By abandoning both, painting lost popular appeal overnight and became completely dependent upon a small, audience of wealthy patrons. Wealthy patrons had to be found, which called for the new role of agent (art gallerists). But why should a wealthy patron want to patronize art unless buying such art served as a strategy of distinction (Bourdieu, 1986; Gronow, 1997)? For such a strategy to work, the patron had to be sure that this art did not appeal to mass audiences, which called for a strategy of incomprehensibility (inter-pretation as a precondition of appreciation).

# CHAPTER 6

# The Structure of Creative Processes

## A Darwinian or Aristotelian Model for Analyzing the Structure of Creative Processes

| Creativity Regime | Material Cause V.1 | Formal Cause V.2 | Effective Cause V.3 | Final Cause V.4 |
|---|---|---|---|---|
| Technology | Materials | Design | Trial and error | Creating facts |
| | Physical constraints | Prototypes | Motivation | Adaption |
| | Problem situation | Industrial | Protection | Parsimony |
| | Co-evolution | revolutions | | |
| Art | Materials | Composition | Techniques | Facts to fiction |
| | Physical constraints | Prototypes | Motivation | Evocation |
| | Problem situation | Stylistic | Protection | Parsimony |
| | Convergence | revolutions | | |
| Science | Data | Concepts | Methodology | Fiction to facts |
| | Knowledge constraints | Prototypes | Motivation | Falsification |
| | Intra-species co-evolution | Scientific revolution Knowledge object | Protection | Parsimony |

## Why Is There No Creativity Science?

The theoretical model above is an attempt to summarize the main discoveries of this book. I have called the model a Darwinian or Aristotelian model because it combines traits from both of these thinkers. The ideas of four causes and the tree types of creativity regimes are mainly based upon Aristotle's theories of creativity, knowledge and change. But Aristotle (effective cause, V.3) never solved the problem of evolutionary change. Aristotle's theory is basically a theory of pre-programmed (designed) development. Most of Western history still leans on Aristotle's development theory of change (Nisbet, 1969/1970). The implications of Darwin's theory for understanding pioneering work in science, art and technology has still basically remained unexplored, probably because Darwin's theory has not been contrasted with its Aristotelian roots. The two need to be seen as complementary theoretical sources (prototypes, I.2, V.2) for the purpose of clarifying the First principles of creativity science.

Although Marx wanted to dedicate *Das Kapital* to Darwin, he obviously did not understand the core of Darwin's theory of evolution, that nature itself is creative. For Marx, the decisive difference between nature and humans was consciousness. Although bees can design houses that would make an architect jealous, the difference between the two, according to Marx, was that for bees designing houses is purely instinctive. In contrast the architect already has an image of how the house should look like before the building starts. But this account ignores asking how bee colonies managed to arrive at this particular design. How were vulnerable versions protected (Dimension IV)? And why is it that this solution happens to get it right (Dimension III)?

Popper's solution to this tricky problem was that nature (effective cause, V.3), uses the problem-solving strategy of trial and error. This seems plausible. But if we are to believe Popper, pioneering scientists also basically uses the same problem-solving strategy, trial and error. This cannot be correct. The problem-solving strategy of science as creativity regime or theoretical knowledge according to Aristotle is methodology (the theory of First principles). Indeed the only scientist who used the problem-solving strategy of trial and error mentioned by Popper in *All Life Is Problem Solving* is Einstein. But is Einstein representative of pioneering work in science?

Popper was very critical of Marxism, in particular its theory of history (which he called "historicism," see Popper, 1957/2002). Popper's critique of "historicism" was based upon a critique of the epistemology of Plato

(Popper, 1947/1966). Plato's epistemology fundamentally undermined the idea of democracy and legitimated totalitarian rule (one-party systems). According to Plato, only the educated classes (elites) have access to "ideal forms" (concepts, V.2). Uneducated people (the "masses") are inherently incapable of rational and logical thinking because they are based on the use of precise concepts (compare Hanson, 1956 and the famous cave metaphor, described in Russell, 1957). The point about the planned economy is also basically Platonic. What is important is not to let the market decide, given that this will only cater to the false needs of ordinary citizens who, like the epistemic prisoners in Plato's cave, suffer from false consciousness, alienation or reification (Israel, 1968/1971; Kolakowski, 1980).

In contrast to Plato, Aristotle did not believe in a sharp distinction between the everyday knowledge of ordinary citizens and the educated classes (philosophers). The knowledge of both is based upon observations or experience (material cause, V.1). The main difference between everyday thinking and scientific thinking is that ordinary thinking is mainly of the practical form. Only philosophers (or scientists, scholars), are interested in the theoretical form of knowledge or knowledge for its own sake. This is also the reason why ordinary folks use trial and error (learning by doing) as a core problem-solving strategy. Only scientists approach knowledge in a methodological manner (V.4). The reason is that the final cause (V.4) of science is to separate facts from fiction and, hopefully, arrive at indisputable facts (falsification).

Science foregrounds discovery or curiosity as the highest value in life (Shields, 2007/2014). But in contrast to his teacher Plato (Lloyd, 1968; Collins, 1998), Aristotle did not look down upon practical knowledge which also had its value. Practical knowledge was here not to separate facts from fiction but to create new facts (invention rather than discovery). Although inventions also depend upon discovery but from the point of view of practical problem solving, theoretical knowledge for its own sake lacks value. It can only be a means to the end (a view shared by Marx, compare the last of the Feuerbach theses, "up to now philosophers have only interpreted the world, the point is to change it").

Strangely Popper, although he was very critical of Plato's philosophy of knowledge, was even more critical of Aristotle's epistemology and ontology ("metaphysics"). In particular, Popper rejected Aristotle's concept "indisputable facts" (or fiction to facts, compare Einstein's replacement of Newton's concept "ether" with the dual nature of light waves). According to Popper, the idea that there is such a thing as "indisputable facts" is incompatible with scientific thinking (Popper, 1998). But this cannot be right. The history of scientific disciplines (see Chapter 1) proves Popper to be wrong. Moreover, there are a number of indisputable facts in Popper's theory, such as the presumably indisputable fact that there are no indisputable facts. How did Popper arrive at this logically inherent and empirically false conclusion? For this purpose, looking closer at Popper's theory of falsification is helpful.

According to Popper, there is no such thing as unintended falsification. All scientific falsifications are intended. But this cannot be right. The discovery of tectonic plates (Andreasson, 2006) was unintended as was the discovery that the reason Aristotle had not been able to observe eels breed was the indisputable fact that eels breed in the Sargasso Sea. This was discovered as an indisputable fact by Columbus (Bergreen, 2011/2015), but Columbus was no scientist and moreover had his own agenda. Kepler's groundbreaking discovery that planets move not in perfect circles but in an elliptical shape was also unintended as was Newton's discovery that gravity is a universal force. Darwin did not set out to falsify Lyell's theory of "special creation." Indeed, Darwin did not know that this theory existed until he read about it in volume two of Lyell's *Principles of Geology*. Thomsen certainly did not intend to become the founder of archeology when he accepted what he believed to be a mere practical job to organize the collections sent to the royal palace in Copenhagen. Jane Goodall did not intend to discover that chimpanzees have emotions and can learn to use tools just as humans do, and so on.

Popper's claim in *Conjectures and Verification* that unintended discoveries such as the ones in archeology are an exception to the rule is simply wrong. That Popper stubbornly held on to this false theory, not allowing empirical evidence to falsify it, can possibly be explained by Popper's two main prototypes (I.2, V.2). One prototype was Kant's methodology (V.3) which does not care much about empirical data (V.1, "quid facti") and is only concerned about concepts (V.2, "quid juris"). Another possible prototype was the attempt to test Einstein's relativity theory of gravity by observing light rays close to the surface of the sun (Waller, 2002). But such "critical tests" (Chalmers, 1999) are cases of normal science, scientific creativity on the professional level (II.3). They certainly cannot be categorized as pioneering work in science (II.4). Critical tests are clearly attempted cases of falsification (V.4).

Had Popper compared pioneering work in science (empirical methodology, V.3) based upon representative data (V.1) he would have discovered that falsification in science (V.4) of the pioneering type (II.4) is unintended. But this still does not explain how Popper could arrive at his theory that the problem-solving strategy of scientists is trial and error (V.3). For this purpose, we need to look at a third prototype (I.2, V.2) Einstein's groundbreaking discovery of relativity creativity. Apart from being a case of trial and error, it is also intended. But trial and error are not typical in science. The logic of Einstein's discovery of relativity is a clear exception to the empirical pattern found among most pioneers of science (methodology, unintended discovery). Popper ignores the indisputable fact (V.4) that Einstein was trained in applied science.

This choice of prototype (Einstein) might also explain why Popper (1998) disputes that there is such a thing as indisputable facts. Whether a fact is indisputable or not is of little or no concern for engineers, given that engineers are here to create facts (V.4) and not separate facts from fiction, the core of falsification. There is also a third and final cause (V.4), parsimony or getting it right, but this is not unique for science. This final cause is what science shares with both technology and art (but also with nature).

But Popper also got Einstein wrong. According to Popper (1999) "all life is problem solving," Einstein is just a more sophisticated case of the amoeba. But engineers in contrast with nature, solve problems in an intentional manner. The way Einstein approached the anomalies which had accumulated since Newton was not typical for groundbreaking work in science which is paradoxically homologous to nature in this respect. Both are unintended forms of discovery, probably because getting it right in science is fundamentally based upon intra-species and not inter-species co-evolution (First principles, adapting data and method, see Chapter 8; on the nature of the knowledge object, see Chapter 7).

Popper's fundamental error ironically led to a similar mistake as the one we find in Marx's thinking. Both confused scientific and technological forms of problem solving although in different ways. Marx overvalued the role of consciousness for complex and paradoxical problem solving (creativity) which can be fully explained by the role of constraints (physical constraints, developmental constraints, knowledge constraints etc., see Dimension I). Surprisingly and correctly noted by Popper, natural forms of problem solving or creativity are also constrained by knowledge (I.3).

A case in point is the problem of how to make the stalks of mature apples shrink just in time for the first autumn winds. The correct solution to this problem (parsimony, III.1, V.4) indicates the presence of both chemical and geological knowledge programmed or built into the apple tree (knowledge constraints, I.3). The problem ignored by Popper is that the basic problem-solving strategy of science is methodology and not learning by trial and error (V.3). Trial and error also happen to be the basic problem-solving strategy of technology or engineering. Popper hence ended up confusing the problem-solving strategy of science and technology, although he got one of the final causes of science, falsification (V.4) right. Aristotle does not talk much about falsification as the final cause of science. He is more interested in the operational aspect (demonstration, proof, etc.). Popper has a point here, but he goes too far when he rejects that falsification can lead to "indisputable facts" (compare Barnes, 2003).

### Facts and Fiction

As we know today, the Marxist idea of returning to a presumably sinless, morally pure, state of humanity, "primitive communism" is pure fiction. There never was an original, "classless" society as Engels claimed (Trigger, 2003 ) and all attempts to impose this still surviving myth (Barthes, 1956/2000) upon modern societies inevitably leads to some form of totalitarian society. Social inequality is a constant which is built into human societies, and although it takes endless forms, it cannot be eliminated for good. Social inequality is natural. Too much social inequality is probably not good for political democracies as it tends to lead to plutocracy (rule by the wealthy). The attempt to eliminate social inequality all together ironically leads to terroristic totalitarianism (compare Pol Pot's regime) directed against the elites, the educated classes, precisely the social groups to whom the Platonic idea of the presumably false consciousness of the uneducated classes tends to appeal most strongly.

According to Popper, Marx's and Engels' theories are not science, because they are not falsifiable. But nor is Darwin's theory falsifiable and hence not science either, if we are to believe Popper (1974). But this cannot be right. In contrast to Ptolemy's and Copernicus' deeply flawed attempts to explain the strange loops of the planets, Darwin's theory was parsimonious (III.1, V.4). Moreover, Darwin's theoretical explanation of the origins of species as a combined result of transmutation, common descent, gradual change, speciation and natural selection is the only theory which has stood up to the accumulated "body of knowledge" (Lloyd, 1991) or indisputable facts (V.4) in biology to the degree that the theory has itself achieved the status of fact (Mayr, 2002).

But as Aristotle already noted, there is also a third type of knowledge which is neither theoretical nor practical. Aristotle called this type of knowledge "productive knowledge." Most of Weber's studies on law and religion foreground this type of knowledge, but Weber also studied music, which is an art form (compare Levinson, 2006, 2016). The final cause of art is to evoke emotions or transform facts into fiction (V.4). What is perhaps most surprising is that artistic forms of creativity are also constrained. Feyerbend's (1975) anarchistic theory of science was modeled (I.2) upon fiction and not fact. This mistake probably goes back to Kant's theory of art (prototype, I.2, V.2) as "genius" (II.5) which for Kant is identical with the idea of the artists as free to follow their own inclinations, instincts, wishes, idiosyncrasies, etc. (the "romantic" theory of art).

But this cannot be correct. Artistic creativity is no less constrained than science and technology. Art is here to evoke emotions, but this is usually best achieved by doing the opposite of science, to turn facts into fiction (V.4). For this purpose, the best problem-solving strategy is to rely on techniques (V.3) related both to compositions (V.2) and choice of material (V.1). But art is also a form of imitation or "pretense" (Walton, 1990; Morell, 2004). Thus "conceptual art" is not a science but an attempt to imitate (colonize) science. Conceptual art is not based upon data and knowledge constraints. Its material causes are materials (V.1) and physical constraints (I.1). But physical constraints are not identical for different art forms. For a narrative to motivate intermittent reading it has to have suspense, but suspense in turn makes narratives retrospective (Eo, 2002). The "narrator" in contrast to the characters, has to know in advance what will happen to the characters. This takes us to another technique. Such knowledge should be shared with the readers, who hence tend to be better informed than the characters themselves, a technique (V.3) that seems to provide extra aesthetic pleasure (I.5a, see Kundera, 1987).

Nevertheless, for the sake of suspense, the narrator should only reveal the details gradually by giving away critical information intermittently (as noted by McEwan). This is one of the basic tricks of the novelist (see Zalewski 2009). Different genres use different techniques. Murder mysteries usually start with or expect a murder to take place and spy novels rely on a traitor to be revealed. Fantasy novels anticipate the appearance of the supernatural and adventure stories great adventures to take place. Tragic love stories expect the tragic end of great love, romantic comedies anticipate happy endings. Father-son stories imply a rebellion but also reconciliation to take place, etc. But as noted by Elster (2000), such gradual revealing of strategic information is in reality constrained by the physical form of the novel which only allows for intermittent reading. It does not work for the visual arts such as painting and sculpture, where the aesthetic value (beautiful, repulsive, ugly, powerful, etc.) can be taken in at a glance.

The role that constraints play for different art forms, undermines the whole idea of art as "genius" (II.5). Choices of artistic techniques are not invented out of the blue but structured by materials and physical constraints (V.1, I.1). This explains why visual artists use different artistic techniques (V.3) from writers. More generally, the choice of artistic or aesthetic techniques can best be explained by the materials and physical constraints of different art forms (V.1). Science as vocation (Weber, 1948a) is in a very different game. It aims at falsification and indisputable facts ("disenchantment" rather than charm and magic). Keeping this alive, is something humans seem to need and take pleasure in for some still obscure reasons (compare Dissanayake, 1992/1995 and Carroll, 2010 attempts to open this still black box). Whatever the biological or evolutionary origins of art, its function, to evoke emotions, is difficult to dispute (Elster, 1999). But the fact that art has human value and rests upon a particular type of knowledge (productive knowledge) does not make it a model or prototype for science as postmodernists claim (Schusterman, 2003).Conceptual art is still art. We do not read conceptual art as if it were concepts. We read it as composition (V.2). All compositions are based upon prototypes, but so are concepts. This is the reason why constraint theory is helpful for the purpose of conceptual clarification, the "formal cause" of science (V.2):

Productive knowledge and theoretical knowledge are constrained by (1) different type of material causes (materials and physical constraints, data and knowledge constraints), (2) different types of formal cause (composition and concept), (3) different types of problem-solving strategies (techniques and methodology) and (4) have distinct final causes (evocation and falsification). This might explain why artists normally do not like to talk about or analyze their art works with scholars (Björkman et al., 1971). Avant-garde art seems to be an exception to the rule (Morell, 2004) but this has something to do with the intended strategy of incomprehensibility and the very narrow (elite) type of audience (connoisseurs) of patrons, mentors and agents which function as helpers or support systems for this historically unique type of art (IV.5, V.3).

In spite of the unique historical and professional-problem situation (III.4) of avant-garde art, there are some striking continuities between avant-garde art and art found in premodern societies. The art historian d'Azevedo in a study which seeks to trace the origins of the idea of the artist as genius, notes the prominent idea of "*neme,*" "spiritual forces" (derived from ancestors) which guide all professionals in their work. They are often tied to the idea of art as something "miraculous" (an early version of art as genius). But the belief in art as being able to produce something miraculous is precisely dependent upon the artist's ability not to reveal the "tricks of the trade" (Becker, 1997).

> For the average Gola the processes of artistry, that occurs between the initial inspiration of the artist and the public presentation of the result are only vaguely perceived. Matters of skills and technology are not part of the discourse between the artist and the public and remain mysteries of creation shared only among the producers or held as the cryptic property of an individual. Thus, to the public the product of the archetypical artist is miraculous, and the artist is viewed essentially as a daring entrepreneur in exchanges of gifts between human society and a special supernatural realm. The years of training and arduous application of the artist are seen as tasks imposed upon him by his tutelary for whom he is just a passive instrument. (d'Azevedo 1973/1997, p. 205)

Art is not here to solve practical problems. It is here for other purposes, to gratify human longing for a life beyond facts, both "created facts" (technology) and "fiction into facts" (science). But fictional worlds might be as boring as factual worlds, unless the artist is able to let these worlds sink in and overpower the audience (create a feeling of being in the presence of something miraculous, magic, intensive, scary, wonderful, heartbreaking, etc.; compare Engdahl, 1994/2005). In modern societies this can only be accomplished if the artist is fully acquainted with the many techniques available to solve aesthetic problems in art (Danto, 1997). But this repertoire or toolbox of artistic techniques, has to be learned and this takes a long time. For pioneering artists like Picasso and Matisse (H-creativity) to be an artist means a life-long learning of new techniques, which in practice means abandoning previously learned techniques for newly discovered ones (P-creativity). For pioneers, this in practice means the rediscovery (III.2) of previous solutions in the tradition of what works and what does not (parsimony, III.1, V.4).

But such learning processes have to be protected (Dimension IV, V.3) somehow. One type of protection could be secrecy of some sort (IV.3, IV.4). Another type of protection could come from helpers or support systems (IV). In order to dare to set off on new tracks geographical and/or intellectual migrations might also be helpful (Kirkeby trained as a geologist before he moved to avant-garde art and was always traveling between places). Such opportunities are important for motivation (I.5c, V.3) but they are clearly also privileges.

How does one legitimate such a highly privileged life without awakening feelings of envy and resentment? This is where "neme" comes in handy for the idea of being in a special relationship with the Gods or spirits. Neme is simply an early version of the modern romantic theory of art as genius, the core function of which is to legitimate living the highly privileged "facts into fiction" (V.4) life of a Picasso, Matisse or Per Kirkeby. That these artist were prepared to sacrifice much of what ordinary humans regard as normal (being close to family, not exposing intimate details, hanging dirty linen out for everyone to see, going hungry and suffering from lack of recognition in the hope that such sacrifices will pay off at the end, pioneering work as investment in the future) does not falsify but verifies the privileged nature of a life dedicated to art. Sacrifice as Weber (1922/1964) noted is an integral part of the religious mindset and points to some interesting interfaces between the two which is worth a closer investigation (compare Gauguin and Chagall who both use the crucified Jesus as a symbol, although the meaning of Gauguin's symbol was more narcissistic than Chagall's).

But opportunity is not enough. Artists must also live up to the social expectations and produce great art. The artist is therefore also under pressure (I.5b) to innovate in order to enter or retain a highly privileged lifestyle. The modern idea of art as genius shares this aspect of a privileged life, turning facts into fiction and evoking emotions with "neme." In both cases "neme" or the belief in the "charisma" of the magic of art legitimates "the desired insulation from public scrutiny and control. He encourages the illusion of spontaneous creation and presents his results as the gift of the spirits. The product, therefore, is not perceived by others so much as an embodiment of the intention of the artist but as it is of the intention of a supernatural personality" (d'Azevedo, 1973/1997, p. 205).

## Aristotle's Theory of Change and the Four Causes

The current confusion of the distinct aims of science, art and technology (rules as constraints, I.4) is one of the reasons we need a creativity science. But this is also why Aristotle's empirical, non-Platonic theory of science as (1) a distinct form of knowledge (theoretical knowledge) and (2) the methodological theory of First principles (science in practice as clarification of First principles, disciplines in the making, see Chapter 1) is of great help. Aristotle's theory of the four causes is ultimately based upon his theory of change (Shields, 2007/2014). Greek philosophers were deeply preoccupied with the problem of change (Furberg, 1969). What was change and how was change possible?

Plato, Aristotle's teacher never managed to solve this problem. He was stuck in his theory of "ideal forms," in reality patterned upon geometrical forms, the result of the new abstract mathematics invented by the Greeks (role model, prototype I.2). Aristotle never completely abandoned Plato's theory of forms and there is a continuity (Lloyd, 1968) between Aristotle (effective cause, V.3) and his mentor (IV.5) and prototype (I.2) Plato. But there are also important differences between the two. Aristotle transformed Plato's theory of forms into something much more complex. This was the theory of the "four causes": material, formal, effective and final cause (Hankinson, 1995, 2009).

Aristotle's theory of the four causes is based upon the "techné" or "craft" model of knowledge. All forms of knowledge, whether theoretical, practical or productive, are produced in much the same way a craftsman, say a furniture maker (effective cause, V.3) designs a product, say a kitchen table (Hall 2015). The furniture maker starts with some kind of material, say oak or birch (material cause V.1). He reshapes the material to the form of a table (formal cause, V.2) so it can be used as a kitchen table (V.4, final cause). This very simple model helps us summarize most of what has been said in this book: (1) that creativity is neither determined, nor contingent but constrained; (2) that the creativity of nature (N-creativity) is similar to but not identical with the creativity of humans (H-creativity); (3) that human problem solvers (III.4) are constrained by different type of constraints such as (1) physical constraints (I.1), (2) prototypes (I.2); (3) knowledge constraints (I.3), rules, (I.4) and motivations (I.5); (4) that the level of problem-solving capacity (novice, II.2, professional, II.3, pioneer, II.4) can best be explained by (a) type of motivation (pleasure, I.5a, pressure, I.5b, opportunity, I.5c) but also (b) protection of vulnerable versions (Dimension IV).

In order to account for the great complexity and paradoxes of creativity, combining Aristotle's theory with Darwin's evolutionary theory is helpful. As noted by both French (1994) and Dawkins (1996/2006, 2005), technological creativity (T-creativity) for some reasons is closest to how nature solves problems (N-creativity), by adaption and trial and error. But although adaption (final cause, V.4) and the problem-solving strategy trial and error (V.3) can be found in both nature and technology, the overall creativity of nature is nevertheless unintended, just as pioneering work in science (in particular the founding of disciplines, see Chapter 1). This is one of the many complexities and paradoxes of creativity which a creativity science is here to clarify. Only normal science behaves the way Popper argued it did. There are therefore two forms of falsification, intended (normal science) and unintended (pioneering work in science).

Popper's confusion of the two opened the door for Kuhn's claim, that pioneers in science do not solve tricky scientific problems. Pioneers in science rather than falsifying theories invent new languages, just as pioneering artists do (Goodman, 1976, 1978). This is the core of Kuhn's "taxonomic solution" (Hacking, 1995). But each language invented by an avant-garde artist is unique. They cannot replace each other. Who can claim that Picasso's visual language is better than say Matisse's? All one can say is that they construct meaning in different ways. They are in other words "incommensurable." A Matisse cannot be replaced by a Picasso or the opposite, without both losing and gaining meaning. So, Kuhn's theory of scientific revolutions is therefore ultimately modeled upon twentieth-century art (prototype, I.2, V.3).

Avant-garde art was Kuhn's solution to the problem he set himself (getting it right, Dimension III), to explain that falsification in science does not seem to work the way Popper claimed it worked. But this does not explain how he arrived at his completely false theory that pioneering scientists do not solve problems, only normal science does (Kuhn, 1959/1977) nor that pioneers in science are essentially artists, engaged in inventing new languages. In order to retrospectively reconstruct or trace how Kuhn arrived at this false theory, foregrounding the conspicuous role that Copernicus' theoretical model played for his evolving "body of thought" (Parsons, 1964) is highly revealing. Kuhn's problem was that the prototype (I.2, V.2) he had chosen to generalize his theory of scientific revolutions from, was an unsuccessful revolution, because it clearly lacked parsimony (III.1, V.4). It might be surprising for empirical scientists who are trained in how to avoid the fallacy of induction (Durkheim, 1982) that Kuhn's false theory rests upon such an elementary mistake, but it is nevertheless an indisputable fact.

Let us assume that we have to choose between two alternative models which both conspicuously lack parsimony. What grounds do we have to choose one instead the other? In reality Copernicus' failure to falsify Ptolemy and separate fiction from facts (V.4) can be explained by material cause (V.1): lack of accurate data (Tycho Brahe's much more accurate March data) and knowledge constraints (I.1, V.1, Kepler's discovery that planets move in elliptical forms). This in turn explains why neither Ptolemy, nor Copernicus managed to solve the paradoxical behavior of the planets, why they made these strange loops. Kuhn's theory of scientific revolutions can best be seen as a generalization of this one case, which turns out not to be typical for scientific revolutions either (compare Popper and Einstein). Once again this raises the question of data and method (see Chapter 8).

## Creativity Regimes As Distinct Logics of Discovery

Aristotle's theoretical model of the four causes is first all a constraint theory of creativity. It claims that creativity is not a deterministic phenomenon. It cannot be predicted but it can be explained retrospectively. It is hence essentially a historical theory, a theory of change (Shields, 2007/2014). Philosophers of history consistently confuse the two, in effect reducing the historical theory of change to a cyclical theory, modeled upon (prototype, I.2, V.2) explanation in physics (see Gardiner, 1974). Historians of science (Cohen, 1994), tend to categorize (V.2) the discovery of the First principles of physics – Galileo's discovery of the data (V.1), concepts (V.2) and methods (V.3) of physics – as "*the* scientific revolution" (compare Henry, 1997/2008, for a critique, see Shapin, 1996), ignoring that there are many other disciplines than physics which have managed to clarify their first principles (see Chapter 1).

Artistic or stylistic revolutions from a formal point of view also tend to foreground prototypes (I. 2, V.2), but these have the form of composition and not concepts. From a material point of view (V.1), artists start with material rather than data. The most important constraints are physical constraints (I.1). The importance of these physical constrains explains why the logic of scientific and artistic revolutions are strikingly different. Science advances gradually. The most important constraints are knowledge constraints. Artistic revolutions also evolve gradually within a preferred style (naturalism, symbolism) but suddenly abandons what has been learned and sets off in new directions, often by rediscovery (III.2). Naturalistic styles (V.3) started with the Paleolithic cave paintings, were abandoned by Neolithic artists who opted for a symbolistic style, were rediscovered by Greek artists, abandoned again by early Christian art (return to symbolism), rediscovered again by Renaissance artists, flourished with the Impressionists and abandoned by the post-Impressionists, a transitional form for twentieth-century art's total abandonment and rediscovery of previous symbolic styles, etc.

The prominence of this pattern might explain why stylistic revolutions tend to by cyclical as noted by Martindale (1990). His own explanation foregrounds the role of boredom. Art is supposed to be fresh and look novel, but after a time novelty becomes old hat (routine) and boring.

Hence inevitably boredom sets in and a new cycle of searching for novelty and freshness kicks in. Such inevitable boredom in turn functions as a pressure on professional artists to innovate (I.5b) repeatedly generating pioneering work (cyclical change). What is interesting but not fore-grounded in Martindale's theory of repetitive stylistic revolutions is that the number of basic techniques is not endless (just as parsimonious solutions in nature are not endless, compare Dawkins, 2005). As noted by Hegel (1970), there are in principle only three major styles: symbolic, naturalistic and expressionistic. Artists therefore essentially rediscover the same thing again and again, just as nature does when it reinvents the same limited amounts of basic prototypes for eyes, flying, radar, etc. As noted by Dawkins (1986/2006, 1996/2006, 2010), the basic explanation of such convergence/rediscovery is physical constraints (I.1), which play a match more important role for artistic creativity in general than normally understood.

Interestingly Martindale in his book approvingly quotes Kuhn's cyclical theory of scientific revolutions as verification of his cyclical theory of stylistic revolutions (as does Gould, 2002, a geologist who like Lyell never really understood Darwin's biological theory of evolutionary change). That Kuhn ended up with a cyclical theory of scientific revolutions indicates that his theory of scientific revolutions confuses scientific revolutions with stylistic revolutions, which serve as a prototype (I.2) for the attempts to conceptualize scientific revolutions and falsify Popper's theory of falsifica-tion. Popper's theory of falsification manages to get the final cause of science, falsification (V.4) right, but confuses the intended falsification of normal science (II.3) with the unintended falsification of pioneers in science (II.4). Popper, as we have seen, also confused the basic problem-solving strategy (V.3) of technology and nature (trial and error) with the basic problem-solving strategy of science (methodology). Indeed, the absence of a theory of methodology turns out to be the basic weakness of Popper's theory of science. This would also explain why Popper rejected Aristotle's theory of "indisputable facts" (Popper, 1998).

In order to get out of the current confusion, a good concept to start with is "creativity regimes" (Kupferberg, 2003a, 2006a, 2006b, 2007). The concept might help us describe different logics of discovery. Science is identical with theoretical knowledge; technology is a form of practical knowledge and art is a version of productive knowledge. In order to analyze how this works, Aristotle's theory of the four causes is a good place to start but it has to be complemented by Darwin. How do we explain the paradox that groundbreaking discoveries in science and the creativity of nature are both unintended? For this purpose, we need to foreground the important but under-theorized role of intra-species co-evolution in nature which is homologous (Mayr, 2002; Ruse, 2006) to the role of First principles in science.

The methodological approach of science (V.3) is what helps science arrive at concepts (V.2). They are not givens as (Hanson, 1956) claimed but results of methodological procedures and hence also methods for collection of data, which are constrained by the nature of the knowledge object (V.2). Without Tycho Brahe's systemic observation of March data, Kepler would never have arrived at the concept (V.2) "elliptical course of planetary movements" which in turn falsified one of Aristotle's First principles of astronomy and revealed it to be false (V.4).

In contrast, industrial revolutions or changes of prototypes take the form of change of design (V.2) and not concepts. Such revolutions are driven by physical constraints and the inter-species type of co-evolution (compare the case of human-carrying kites, discussed in Wiener, 1993). But design is basically a practical form of knowledge (R. Laudan, 1984) and the way such design changes is mainly by trial and error (V.3). This is the same problem-solving strategy as nature uses as an effective problem solver. The important difference is time. Nature has all the time in the world to arrive at solutions which are characterized by parsimony (III.1) and time is the great support system of nature, not patrons, mentors and agents (IV.5, V.3) who are less patient. This explains why the creativity of nature is unintended, just as in science. However, support systems are not enough. The critical role of scientific creativity is knowledge constraints which tend to evolve very slowly (compare Hegel's "Owl of Minerva") although not as slowly as in nature. In contrast technological creativity tends to be intended, just like art (Baxandall, 1985). Nevertheless, they are ultimately constrained by material and physical constraints.

## Material Causes

A painter uses paint, canvases and brushes and mostly composes from live models (V.1). A writer uses a pen and paper (or a computer) and mainly composes from memories. Compositions are forms. The way artists learn such forms is by studying the work of other artists, prototypes (V.2). But a painting can be taken in at one glance, a novel cannot. Commitments are subjective (personal-problem situation), but physical constraints of art forms are objective (professional-problem situation) and restrict painters and writers to use different techniques (V.3). Both types of investments of human time, energy, emotions, thinking, skills, attitudes etc., are constrained by some "material" dimension but in very different ways.

## Materials

Transforming facts into fiction in painting (final cause, V.4) involves many types of material causes: first, there are the materials in the direct sense, such as paint, canvas, easel, brush, palette, which can be called the material "tools" of the painter. But tools must be stored somewhere and this is the reason a painter needs a studio. Gamble (2007) calls this type of artifact a "container" (other types of containers could be graves, potteries, houses, boats, carriages, etc.). Once the painter has a studio, he or she can invite live models, arrange still lives, complete pictures started outdoors (landscapes, city life, leisure activities, etc.). Sometimes artists do not work from direct observation but from photographs (a practice started by the Impressionists, see Thomson, 2000). Sometimes they work from memory like Munch, just as writers do (Prideaux, 2005). Some painters such as Matisse and Picasso preferred to remain in the studio and be inspired by live models and/or arranged still lives). Other modern painters preferred to paint outside the studio (landscapes, gardens, city life, leisure palaces and activities, race horses, dancers warming up before a performance starts, etc.).

But canvases and easels are a relatively new invention (Greenberg, 1961/1965). The first paintings were made on rocks and walls (murals). There are also many different types of paint such as water color, oil, tempera, etc. Naturalistic painters who began working outside the studio often discovered other types of physical constrains such as the haze that comes with industrial pollution (one of the sources of Impressionist techniques, see Thompson, 2006) or the erotic effects of naked female bodies covered by water (the Swedish painter Anders Zorn painted sweating female bodies in a saunas or naked females bathing outdoors still wet from getting out of the water, see Brunner, 1965/2000).

## Physical Constraints

The meaning of a painting can usually be grasped instantly, in one single glance, although an experienced, trained, competent observer might easily spend hours, days, weeks, months, etc., to decode the deeper meaning of this or that particular painting (Baxandall, 2003, pp. 109, 129; Thompson, 2006). In contrast, a movie goer has to sit 90 minutes or more to feel fully informed and satisfied from watching a Hitchcock movie. The reader of a very long novel by Tolstoy, Ken Follett or Klaus-Ove Knausgaard may be forced to spend months of intermittent reading in order to get from the beginning to the end. Although most novels are much shorter (200–300 pages), these extreme cases of up to 1,000 pages are clear demonstrations of how art form or choice of medium (Kupferberg, 2013) structures or constrains the creative process. The painter has to evoke emotions in one glance. A movie director or playwright has 90 minutes to accomplish the same "final cause." The novelist and the reader are each other's prisoners for weeks and months ahead.

The fact that the physical constraints of artistic creativity are different for different art forms, helps us better to understand why colors (material constraints, V.I) are so important for painters (compare Matisse). Color has the same function as words has for writers. Hemingway was very careful with his use of words. His basic aesthetic idea was to economize the number of words used to express and evoke emotions (parsimony, III.1, V.4). This choice of technique (V.3) also helps solve a problem of the fiction writer which comes from physical constraints (I.1, V.1), how to create suspense. Take Hemingway's short story "Hills Like White Elephants." A young man and a woman are seated in an outdoor restaurant and talk. We are never told directly what the conversation is about. Gradually, though, the reader begins to make a connection with the magnificent view and the subject of the conversations, the distant white hills that look like elephants and the fact that the woman is pregnant with a child and that the two are talking about how the arrival of the third person (compare Simmel's theory of the role of numbers in Simmel, 1964) will influence the relationship between the two.

### Rediscovery and Co-evolution

Modern art works have for some reasons abandoned naturalistic painting. The stylistic revolutions of the twentieth century (V.2) were all constrained by this negativity or taboo (the absence of a clearly visible figure) but also absence of three-dimensional space (flatness) and the absence of the traditional aesthetic ideal of beauty (disharmony, fragmentation). But modern painters have also abandoned some of the traditional tools of painting such as canvases (body painting), brush and palette (putting the paint directly on the canvas from the tube, drip painting from a can) but also painting as medium. Modern painters can in principle us any kind of medium (texts, artifacts, performances, calculations). Only the museum

setting, another material, defines them as art works. It is this creative
explosion of material in modern art (Danto, 1997) that makes the analysis
of the materials of avant-garde art highly complex but also paradoxical.
This is the reason why it is much simpler to start from the final cause (V.4)
(facts into fiction or evocation of emotions), effective cause (V.3, techniques, motivations, protection) or formal cause (V.2, composition, prototype, stylistic revolutions). Thus, the stylistic revolution in painting
which began with Impressionism can, from a material cause point of view,
best be described as a gradual abandonment of the traditional chiaroscuro
technique (V.3) foregrounding "value" (light and darkness) for the novel
technique of "hue," shimmering or bright colors. But such techniques at a
closer view are far from new. They are rediscoveries or reinventions of
previous techniques (convergence, III.2).

This does not exclude that some stylistic revolutions can be best seen as
co-evolution. A case in point is the invention of oil painting around 1400
(Eastlake, 2001). It led to the abandonment of murals and a transition to
easels (Greenberg, 1961/1965) and canvases (White & White, 1965/1993)
and changed career opportunities (I.5c.) for artists. But it also changed the
techniques of artists (V.3), allowing for much more detailed paintings (the
sfumato technique of Michelangelo, see Gombrich, 1997/2000). But
Renaissance painters had to mix the oil and paint powder themselves.
This was time consuming and might explain why Renaissance painters
spent a very long time painting their pictures. This might in turn explain
why Dutch painters, who also worked within the naturalistic and chiaroscuro, Renaissance style, became highly skilled in painting the smallest
details in the picture, integrating them with the overall composition (one
of the masters here was Vermeer, see Wright, 1984).

Industrially produced oil paints suddenly abolished these cumbersome
practices and made it possible to "paint quickly." But painting quickly is
far from new and has always existed. Face painting is a very old form of
painting using the human skin as canvas. Water colors painting is also
quick painting but it is usually done on paper. It can be undertaken
quickly but the paint tends to float out. Nevertheless, some modern artists
have built successful careers on their ability to use watercolor (Chagall
seems to have been skillful in this field, see Wullschlager, 2008, as was the
Swedish painter Anders Zorn; see Brummer, 1975, 1989, 2000). Other
methods for painting quickly might be to use only a few strokes of the
brush. This is also an old technique (V.3) used by calligraphic painters in
Japan and China. The rediscovery of such paintings clearly influenced
Impressionist painters (Honour & Fleming, 1982). Drip painting using

industrial paint, which dries relatively quickly and rolling-on paint are more modern forms of painting quickly, but the ideas is far from new (the original prototype, I.2, V.2, might possibly be drawing, a tool most painters still use as preparation for large-scale paintings, compare Josephson, 1941/1991 and Jørgensen, 2011).

A much slower technique (V.3) is to use egg yolks (tempera) which can also be made thinner by diluting them with turpentine. This choice of material creates a deeper color than oil painting. But this technique, rediscovered (III.2) by Rothko is also very old. Cubism seems to be based upon the rediscovery of even older art, the "primitive" masks found in African art. Cubism like all semi- abstract forms of art combines naturalistic and symbolic techniques. The reintroduction of symbolic art (Gauguin's use of color for symbolic purposes, Cézanne's use of geometrical symbols for composition, V.2) are also cases of rediscovery.

Most of what can be considered as "modern art" are in fact rediscoveries but co-evolution also plays a role here. Collage, also invented by the Cubists, can be seen as imitating (prototype, I.1) the editing techniques of films which makes it an example of co-evolution (III.3) but also intellectual with migration (IV.2) or (imitation, borrowing, stealing, colonization, etc.). Other painters have colonized or imitated sculptures (installations), film (Duchamp's famous nude descending a staircase), theater (performances), photography ("noncomposed" compositions, see Schiff, 1984), commercial art (Brillo Boxes), aspects of some artistic practice but often in a negated form (absence of background, frame, bright color, dark color), etc. Precisely this strong aspect of negation, can probably best be explained by the rise of photography and film which made naturalistic (narrative) painting look increasingly anachronistic and produced pressure to innovate (I.5b) but also the opportunity (I.5c) to imitate and the pleasure (I.5a) of exploring new materials (V.1), compositions (V.2) and techniques (V.3).

## Formal Causes

Fiction writing transforms facts into fiction (V.4) with words, and for this reason does not seem to be constrained at all as words can be combined endlessly. This might explain why theorists of the novel sometimes talk of the "formlessness" of the novel (Robert, 1980). But this cannot be right. Words have to be composed (V.2) in a way that gives meaning. Interestingly evoking or expressing emotions in a novel might be intensified by breaking grammatical rules (compare the "stream of consciousness" ttechnique probably pioneered by Tolstoy in Anna

Karenina, see Nabokov, 1980). Some avant-garde novelists such as James Joyce in *Finnigan's Wake* seem to bend this technique to the utmost by imitating the incomprehensibility technique typical for avant-garde artists (Ellman, 1959; Symons, 1987). But a book like *Finnegan's Wake* probably only appeals to professional writers, who want to see how far the techniques (V.3) of breaking grammatical rules can be stretched in order to work as fiction. The book becomes a learning tool for would-be writers at the start of their careers (Burgess, 1990), making Joyce a "writer's writer" (Magalaner & Cain, 1955/1990).

According to both Hegel (1970) and Berenson (1933) art from a formal point of view is essentially about how to combine form and content. This "compositional" problem seems to be the core of the formal aspect of art (V.2), sometimes called the "language of art" (Goodman, 1976). But such a language is not contingent as assumed by postmodernist theories of language. It is precisely because different art forms and artistic media present artists with different types of compositional problems, that translation from one art form to another can never be a mere copy of the former. In order to get it right, the compositional constraints of say literature and painting need to be taken into account.

The way this problem is solved is very tricky in orchestral music (Hegel, 1970; Levinson, 2006; Kivy, 2002/2008). It involves at least three types of translations made by three types of effective causes (composer, conductor, musician). This is the reason why the problem is best studied in other areas such as translation from literature to painting. Although it is possible to translate one type of artistic language to another (compare Josephson's 1941/1991 account of Leonardo's early unfinished painting *The Adoration of the Magi*, discussed more in detail in Kupferberg 2013), something is inevitably lost and something is added which was not there before. Baxandall (2003) calls this the combined "divergence" and "incommensurability" of visual and narrative languages:

> A sort of divergence between pictorial rendering of something and verbal rendering of the same thing is inherent in the instruments each employs. One way of thinking about this divergence is as picture and verbal text each being committed to a medium that enforces different systems of discrimination ... painting on the one hand, and theological exegesis on the other are incommensurable and divergent discourses. They are incommensurable in that their required elements and structures cannot conform with each other. They are divergent, because their media force, and had historically and accumulatively enforced different sorts of choice and representational development. (Baxandall, 2003, pp. 122, 126)

Baxandall reaches this conclusion after a close analysis of the relation between depicted objects in Piero della Francesca's painting of 1474, *The Resurrection of Christ,* and its subject or moral meaning (anagogy, Baxandall. 2003, p. 124) which in the narrative version is the mystery or miracle of Christ's resurrection. Both interpretations preserve the ambivalence of the original story as well as some emotional effects (final cause, V.4), but they do it in very different ways, which turn out to be both divergent and incommensurable. In the narrated version, there is a series of events which explain (1) the ambivalence of the biblical narrative (Matthew 27:57–28: 20) and (2) the impact of the miracle. In the Jewish religion there is a sharp separation between God and humans. Jesus, who was himself a pious Jew, presented himself as a Messiah, not a semi-God. As the New Testament is based upon precisely this non-Jewish belief, it has to present the natural explanation of why Jesus' body had disappeared (someone had stolen it while the guards had been asleep), as a miracle (transforming facts into fiction). In the textual version this simple explanation is transformed into a complex narrative of (1) moving the body, closing the tomb with a stone and armed guards watching lest the body should be stolen; (2) the two Marys meeting the angel after a powerful earthquake that had frightened the guards; (3) the angel telling the two Marys not to be frightened because Jesus had risen from the dead, showing them where this had happened and telling them to tell the disciplines of the miracle; (4) the two Marys meeting Jesus alive and well; (5) in the meantime the guards had awakened and hurried to the city, where they told the chief priests, who summoned a council of the elders, what had happened, but were given money to tell a lie, that the disciples had been there during the night and had stolen the body.

This is the textual version. But this is not how the painting depicts (Lopes, 1996) the event. Neither the two Marys, nor the angel are visible in the painting. We see four sleeping soldiers and the resurrected Jesus holding a long staff with a standard bearing the cross. How do we explain the difference? One explanation could be that the biblical narrative is very complex; actors are doing things over time. Painting are basically spatial and something from the complex narrative has to be selected. But what should or should not be included in the painting? The two Marys only met Jesus on the road after having seen the angel at the tomb. In the painting (artifact) we see Jesus with his left foot on top of the tomb, just after the earthquake and the sleeping soldiers below. In the narrative (actors in time) Jesus greets the two Marys who take hold of his feet and worship him. Later on he meets his disciples, telling them to go out in the world and spread the message that he, Jesus has been given all power in Heaven and on Earth, that all people on the Earth will be baptized in the name of the Father, the Son and the Holy Spirit and that he will be with them until the end of the world. We are also told about how the guards were bribed by the chief priests and elders, to tell not what they had seen but what the elders had told them, that the body had been stolen by Jesus' disciples. None of these events are depicted in the painting (bodies in space).

The fact that we are dealing with two different art forms, one which allows for complex narratives over time, the other which only permits the static depiction of bodies in space, the problem of "incommensurability," might explain why we do not see the two Marys, nor the angel, nor the meeting between Jesus and the two Marys and his disciples, nor the soldiers running to the town and being bribed to lie. We can call this the "professional-problem situation" (III.4) of the painter. But this cannot be the full explanation. A closer look at the painting reveals something interesting. In Piero della Francesca's version Jesus' resurrected body dominates the picture. Jesus stands behind his own tomb with his left foot on top of it, holding a pole with a standard bearing the cross on it like a victorious warrior. Why? A possible explanation might have been a change in the historical problem situation. Whereas the original biblical narrative merely wanted to prove that the miracle had indeed happened, rejecting the simple, natural explanation, the visual depiction (painting) has a very different emotional purpose ( V.4). Its function is to help the audience associate the original meaning of resurrection with another meaning, atonement which came to play a critical role in medieval Christianity (compare Dante).

The New Testament was written when the new religion was still young and expanding. For this purpose, those skeptics who would later claim that the disappearance of Jesus' body had a perfectly natural explanation had to be silenced. This was the reason the story told in Matthew 27.57–28:20) was concocted the way it was. This was no longer the problem in medieval times, when Christianity had become the religion of the masses in Europe. The problem when a religion has been institutionalized, as noted by Weber (1922/1964), is how to account for the theodicy paradox. How can a good and mighty God allow evil, suffering, injustice, etc.? The Jewish religion as we know solved this paradox by the idea of the Covenant. Christianity solved it by atonement (Judgment day). But how do we know that the day of reckoning will be just? There is also the further problem that Jesus died to atone for humanity's sins. In order to solve these ambiguities a very complex narrative such as the one presented by Dante in *The Divine Comedy* was required. Since paintings are about bodies in space, a much simpler solution was needed. Piero della Francesca's painting of 1474 might be an attempt to provide a simplified version of what it takes a narrative to tell. But such a version must by its very nature be different from a narrative version. As noticed by Aristotle in *Poetics*, a drama in order to work has to evoke both pity and fear for the main character. Such combined pity and fear provide the pity (harmony, unity) to the drama, demanded by Aristotle's theory of drama. A painting is constrained differently. It can ignore beauty and foreground fear, the "sublime." According to Burke (1959/2014), the sublime is basically built upon a much simpler feeling, fear when facing the overpowering forces of nature, which humans are unable to control (the angry and unforgiving Old Testament attitude Jesus the warrior).

The compositional principles of visual and narrative arts, or how to combine form and content, are hence constrained distinctly in different art forms. This explains why translations between these radically different art forms always leave something out and add something new. This is typical for art forms, although it is indeed possible to translate content from one art from to another but the two artworks will never have identical meaning (Josephson, 1941/1991). They will be "incommensurable." But this is certainly not the case for science as Kuhn's theory of scientific revolutions claims. The problem with Copernicus' model was not because it was incommensurable with Ptolemy's model, but because both theoretical models lacked parsimony (V.4).

This was the reason why Copernicus' model failed to falsify Ptolemy's model. But not only did Copernicus' model lack parsimony. It did not manage to separate fiction from facts either. Both theoretical models based were based on Aristotle's astronomic assumptions (First principle) that all celestial bodies, including planets, move in perfect circles (crystal spheres). But this assumption happens to be wrong. It is fiction and not fact (V.4). The scholar who falsified this fiction was Kepler. How did he managed to do so? As we have seen earlier, the simple explanation, completely ignored by Kuhn and the huge and expanding literature on this deeply flawed theory, was that Kepler had access to correct data, the lack of which functioned as a knowledge constraint (V.1). This data had been systematically collected be Tycho Brahe over a period of 20 years. Kepler managed to use this data and falsify the fiction that the planets move in perfect circles by using the same problem-solving strategy as Tycho Brahe, methodology (V.3). In both cases data and method were adapted to the knowledge object (V.2), measuring the exact position and calculating exact trajectory (form of the movement of planets).

## Effective Cause

What drives artists and makes them want to enter such relative uncertain careers (Menger, 1989, 1999; Menger & Gurgang, 1996)? Deciphering motives for becoming an artist (Stenberg, 2002) is notoriously difficult. According to Orwell there are four main reasons why someone would want to be a fiction writer. Some writers are driven by "political impulse ... desire to push the world in certain directions, to alter other people's idea of the kind of society they should strive after" (compare Brecht). Another prime motive is "historical impulse, the desire to see things as they are, to find out the true facts and store them up for the use of prosperity" (Orwell, 1946/1968, p. 4). The third motive could be "aesthetic enthusiasm" (compare James Joyce and T. S. Eliot), Although "the aesthetic motive is very feeble in a lot of writers" – in contrast to painters, novelists might not be awestruck by the "perception of beauty in the external world" – writers do take "pleasure in the impact of one sound on another" and all writers are attracted by the aesthetic feeling of "the firmness of good prose or the rhythm of a good story." On the more basic level they must have a "desire to share an experience which one feels is valuable and ought not to be missed" (Orwell, 1946/1968, p. 3). This motive can often be found among the less powerful (religious and ethnic or racial minorities, women, sexual minorities, etc., see Kupferberg, 1998a). These groups tend to feel that they have been treated in an unjust manner by the majority or group in power which have previously held a hegemonic position, enforcing its views upon the rest (for the case of women writers, see Thurman, 1984; Lessing, 1994; Weldon, 2002/2011).

Orwell also mentions a psychological or selfish motive: "Desire to seem clever, to be talked about, to be remembered after death, to get your own back on grownups who snubbed you in your childhood, etc." (Orwell, 1946/1968, p. 3). Basically, such psychological motives are very difficult to explain. "All writers are vain, selfish and lazy, and at the very bottom of their motives lies a mystery. Writing a book is a horrible, exhausting struggle, like a long bout of some painful illness. One would never undertake such a thing if one were not driven by some demon whom one can neither resist nor understand. For all one knows, that demon is simply the same instinct that makes a baby squall for attention" (Orwell, 1946/1968, p. 7).

Orwell's description presents a challenge for creativity science, which is indeed here to explain creativity (Sawyer, 2006). But the purpose of the theoretical model presented in this book is not to answer all questions, merely to provide a theoretical framework for more detailed studies of pioneers working in different types of creativity regimes. For a baby to cry for attention there has to be a need (pressure, I.5b) but perhaps the baby also takes pleasure (I.5a) in getting the need to be seen rewarded. In both cases, there has to be a parent or sibling or other significant other around, which provides opportunity (I.5c) to be seen and rewarded by the responsive act of being seen (Asplund, 1987).

Orwell mentions "historical impulse" or getting the facts straight as one of several possible motives for a writer of fiction. But this does not make writers into scholars. The job of the artist is still to evoke emotions, and this is best done by transforming facts into fiction (V.4). The rules of art (I.4) are still in command as are physical constraints (I.1). It is a historical fact that most countries, including the United States, turned a blind eye to what was happening to the Jews in Nazi Germany and later in German occupied Europe (Dawidowicz, 1975/1986). This historical fact has been so well documented that everybody regards it as common knowledge.

But how can people be made to think about that fact and how can they be reminded of the insignificance of Jews during those years? Joyce Carol Oates and Philip Roth have both written novels about this particular experience of how America managed to ignore the known facts at the time of the way humans with a Jewish identity were treated. Both have used fiction for this purpose, but where Oates weaves her suspense story *The Gravedigger Daughter* around a fact, an actual event, the sending back of more than thousand German Jews on a transatlantic ocean liner to certain death in German occupied Europe, Roth in *The Plot Against America*, invents a counterfactual story of the real Nazi sympathizer Charles Lindberg (fact) becoming president of the United States and starting to put Jews there in construction camps (fiction).

In both cases, the writers appeal to the feelings of "pity and fear" at the core of Aristotle's theory of drama (tragedy). Both use suspense, the withholding of information, as well as vraisemblement to extinguish the line between facts and fiction. Why do we as readers ultimately read such books if not because they give us aesthetic pleasure (Lamarque & Olsen, 1994; Carroll, 2005)? This is what remains when the writer of fiction has done his or her job. What this tells us is that the motives for writing and reading fiction (or for creating paintings and looking at them) are not necessarily the same. The writer might be driven by any of the four motives that Orwell typologizes (expression of emotion). But the reader might not have the same motives. Evocation and expression of emotions are not the same. This calls for a deeper knowledge. I guess this is what Popper actually meant when he said that there is no indisputable fact. Science is not satisfied until it has overcome all knowledge constrains but this is sometimes impossible, in particular when science tries to explain art works. Understanding science is not the same though.

Although reading a well written book in science, say a book by Richard Dawkins, might give the reader pleasure, readers of scientific books are usually themselves engaged in some kind of scientific research (collecting data, discovering concepts, etc.). Reading a book by Dawkins makes sense from a scientific point of view if it helps the reader falsify theories of, for example, how the creativity of nature works and helps the reader discover the close similarity between the problem-solving strategy (V.3) of technology (trial and error) with nature which in turn can best be explained by the similarity of the final cause of both, practical problem solving (creating facts) and adaption (survival and reproduction of species).

Trial and error have always been the main problem-solving strategy of technology. This is how the earliest tools such as stone axes developed into tools adapted to a specific purpose (O'Brien et al., 2005) and gradually became more specialized (Rosenberg, 1976, 2010). The earliest form of technological creativity has been the prime knowledge object of archeology (Oppenheimer, 2003; Fagan, 2010; Renfrew & Bahn, 2008; Mithen, 1998; Hodder, 1999) sometimes assisted by anthropology (Boyd & Silk, 2003). Science-based technology only becomes a social force in the first industrial revolution, which for some reason started in Britain and Europe in general. Why these places has been the defining problem (knowledge object, V.1) of the discipline of economic history (Wrigley, 1988; Jacobs, 1997; Mokyr 1990a, 1990b, 2002, 2009; Goldstone, 2008). Medieval historians have looked at the relatively slow but still impressive technological inventions before the industrial revolution (White, 1964). More general theories of technological creativity are relatively rare (for cases in point see Cardwell, 1972; Basalla, 1988; Petrosky, 1996; R. Laudan, 1984).

The fact that technological inventions are the results of trial and error, explains why investments in technology (including movie technology) are risky and according to Schumpeter (1945/1979) require special forms of protection (V.3, Dimension IV) including support systems (IV.5) such as patent laws. The problem pf protection is completely absent in Adam Smith's theory of economics that seems to be based on a very simplified way of learning which identifies learning as a result of specialization and specialization only (Rosenberg, 2000). But as we have seen, novel ideas often come from geographical and intellectual migration (IV.1, IV.2) both of which are also aspects of protection of vulnerable versions (Dimension IV).

## Final Cause

Given that artistic and scientific creativity have almost completely opposite aims, there is something paradoxical in the idea of a science of art (Hegel, 1970). How is such a science possible? One way to solve this paradox, it to make the methodological assumptions that (1) a science of art is here to study artistic practices (Elster, 1983) and (2) that such practices are ultimately constrained in different ways. One constraint could be problem situation (III.4). The rise of the modern novel probably reflects the increasing level of individuation in modern societies, analyzed by Durkheim and Simmel (the problem of individuation and the role the modern novel plays as a mirror of such changes has been a core idea in Giddens' sociological project, see in particular, 1971/1982, 1976, 1984, 1990, 1991).

Giddens seems to ignore the fact that novels and art in general are here to evoke emotion. Tolstoy (1898/1995) argues that for literature to evoke emotions, the writer must have experienced similar emotion at close hand. This raises the ethical problem of revealing family secrets and more generally intimate knowledge (exposing dirty linen) a problem raised by Bergman (1959). This problem situation (III.4) has traditionally been solved by the technique (V.3) of "masks" (Strauss, 1959). But mores about intimacy have changed and this might explain why they are no longer seen as a taboo. Interestingly Sylvia Plath seems to have been a pioneer of this genre, her first novel (*The Bell Jar*) is strongly autobiographical, as was probably her second novel, which her husband, Ted Hughes, managed to destroy as well as making her last diaries written shortly before her death "disappear" (Malcolm, 1993).

The intentional destruction of such data makes it difficult to arrive at the "indisputable facts" about this pioneering poet, but there is no reason to be pessimistic. There is still much to be learned from the data that does exist and which is still far from being uncovered (compare Kirk, 2009). Data, "material cause" is still the best indicator of the "knowledge object," that science is here to study (V.1). Concepts (V.2) are here to clarify these issues, but for this purpose we need the correct methodology (V.3). This is also the reason why the postmodernist First principle that science is a form of art, should be rejected (Kuhn's basic mistake).

But Popper's argument that science imitates the problem-solving strategy of nature, trial and error (V.3), ignores the fact that practical problem solving is a much more urgent than theoretical problem solving. Engineering (or teaching) has an immediate social value both for productive and reproductive purposes (adaption, V.4). Interestingly Bruno Latour arrived at a similar view, although his theory of science is far more radical than Popper's and, like Kuhn, denies that there is such a thing as falsification. For Latour, science is both technology (practical knowledge) and art (or fiction or rhetoric, forms of productive knowledge) at the same time. How did Latour arrive at this utterly confused and confusing theory?

### Science and Mediated Forms of the Social

Science is in principle here to establish indisputable facts. This is the reason why tracing the transformation of facts into fiction should define how creativity science analyzes works of art (V.4). But what about scientific creativity (the science of science)? Let us assume that we regard scientific creativity as postmodernists do, as various examples of artistic creativity in the sense of transforming facts into fiction. This provides us with a clue to what Bloor's the "strong program" in sociology seeks to accomplish. By using the basic operation of artists, the transformation of facts into fiction as role model (I.2, V.2) such First principles assume that what takes place in a late-modern laboratory is the same as what writers do when they produce fictitious facts (Knorr-Certina, 1981, 2005). Strangely, scientists in physics and biology laboratories tend to produce different kinds of fiction (Knorr- Certina, 1999), but on the other hand we also know that there are different genres of fiction (romantic, the spy novel, fantasy, etc.), so why should not the fictive facts produced in scientific laboratories look somewhat different?

But in order to observe such fictive or invented facts, the First principles of the type of science (discipline) need to be understood which constrains the presumed fabrication of facts (knowledge constraints, I.3). This turned out to be a huge methodological (V.3) problem for Bruno Latour when he entered the Salk institute (Latour & Wolgar, 1986). He could hardly know; the offer presented a lifetime opportunity (I.5c) to study pioneering work in science. Latour did discover something important, that laboratory science depends upon scientific instruments which mediate or make possible observations of data which are inaccessible to the human eye

(Latour, 1990). Such instruments (von Hippel, 1988) are indeed artifacts (Latour, 1998), but their prime function in a scientific context is to function as knowledge constraints (I.3).

This role of scientific instruments for some types of scientific discovery might have come as a surprise for a traditionally trained sociologist, but it can best be seen as a rediscovery (III.2). Telescopes have existed since the time of Galileo and Lavoisier's discoveries were made possible by the microscope. Molecular biology (science) was ultimately made possible by the invention of X-ray crystallography (Latour's rediscovery is a case of the belatedness of science, the Owl of Minerva; in the science of art academic industries trying to make sense of pioneers such as Alfred Hitchcock and Sylvia Plath are worth mentioning). What Latour missed was (1) that for scientists (theoretical knowledge) the invention of technologies is only a means. Science is not here to create facts but to separate fiction from facts (V.4) and (2) that science mainly advance by the overcoming of knowledge constraints (I.3), not by overcoming of physical constraints like technology and art.

But in order to arrive at the correct concepts (V.2), scientists must use the correct methodology (V.3). This in practice means that in order to study for example the scientific creativity of molecular biologists, one must begin by studying the First principles of the discipline. If not, one will not get the meaning of what the social agents are doing, talking about or summarizing in scholarly articles. This is precisely what happened in Latour's case (Halldén, 2005). Like Foucault, Latour confused "texts" and "artifacts" (compare the title of Foucault's third book, *The Archeology of Knowledge*); for Latour, everything in principle is an artifact, including texts; compare the concept "inscription," see Latour & Wolgar, 1979; Latour, 1998.

Knowledge constraints (I.3) often originate in narrow disciplined training (compare Franklin's and Pauling's training in physical chemistry). But it also works the other way. Being trained in one discipline, particularly in cases of intellectual migration (IV.2) might help to overcome knowledge constraints (Crick's training in physics explains his positive attitude to the method of critically testing bold conjectures; Watson's training in zoology explains his skill in immediately identifying Pauling's three helixes to be wrong). Taking the role of knowledge constraints completely out of the equation and confusing texts and artifacts helps us identify why and how Latour got it wrong in the "details" (the devil always shows up in the details):

(1) The false argument that Pasteur's falsification of Pouchet's theory of "spontaneous generations" of bacteria in milk cannot be proven,

because Pasteur used different types of technological instruments (Latour, 1999, 2000a); (2) the false argument that the medico-technical application of Pasteur's methodological approach to the study of bacteria (science-based technology) was successful not because the scientist Pasteur had got it right but because Pasteur was good at rhetoric (Latour, 1984/1993); (3) the false argument that success in science and technology are inseparable; the two are two sides of the same coin, techno-science (Latour, 1987); (4) the false argument that, given that there are no such thing as theoretical knowledge ("pure science") there is no such thing as modern societies (Latour. 1993); (5) the false argument that advanced techno-science (Latour, 1987) is basically only a version of the "bricolage" problem-solving strategy (trial and error) of premodern societies (Latour, 1993).

### Personal Reality and Creative Milieus

As noted by Gouldner (1993/1997), great opportunities (I.5c) at the start of an academic career constitute knowledge capital or "personal reality" which often follow a scholar for the rest of his or her career. Gouldner's concept is modeled (I.2) upon Malinowski, whose field work in Polynesia colors all his future work (Malinowski, 1961, 1946; for an overview of Malinowski's life work see Firth, 1957/1970). This is obviously also the case of Latour's works, with very mixed results. Perhaps the weakest part of his theory is his mystical (Collins, 1998) concept, "actants" (1987, 2000b, 2005). Not only does it seem to cover almost everything, from bacteria to train tables (Moll, 2010), The concept makes a mockery of Latour's most important personal discoveries (belated rediscoveries, III.2) of (1) the role of artifacts and (2) mediated forms of the social (compare Latour, 2005, I have retained Latour's use of the concept as a noun). Moreover, the fiction (V.4) of "actants" seems to suggest that physical and biological laws are basically the same, which certainly cannot be right (compare the concluding lines in *On the Origin of Species*).

Latour's valid rediscovery (III.2) of artifacts as a mediated form of the social, can profitably function as an "intellectual tool" (Kupferberg, 2012b) though to clarify another unsolved problem of creativity science, the role of cities as creative milieus (Andersson, 1985; Florida, 2002). Why did Paris (Hall, 1999) become the art center of the world in the second half of the twentieth century? Maybe because it had the art museums (physical constraints, I.1) where one could go and look at the significant works of painters and the art schools and studios where novices (II.2) could make plaster castes and copies of master works before seeing the real thing (compare Matisse). The city also had support systems (patrons, mentors and agents, IV.5, V.3). There were also yearly art exhibitions (salons) where the latest art works (facts into fiction, V.4) could be easily accessed (physical constraints, I.1).

This was still the case when Matisse and Picasso came to Paris (Roe, 2015; Spurling, 1998/2000; Richardson, 1991/1992) although things had changed both because the Impressionists had exhausted the potentialities of the naturalistic tradition (prototype, I.2, V.2; techniques, V.3) and because the support system had changed (IV.5, see Tomkins, 2001). Art gallerists were no longer merely agents. They also functioned as patrons of art by the "monthly stipend" or "buying everything" system (the pioneers here were Durand-Ruel and Vollard, see Rewald, 1983; Richardson, 1991/1992). Most importantly, these art gallerists were there and that physical constraints made it possible for Picasso and Matisse to see each other's avant-garde works exhibited by avant-garde gallerists such as Vollard and avant-garde collectors such as Gertrude and Leo Stein (Hobhouse, 1975).

A complexity of factors explain why Paris was the art world of the twentieth century. Physical constraints (I.1) can work on different levels, such as the time it takes to walk from an artist's studio to a cherished collector's apartment (Picasso walked Gertrude Stain back to her apartment at Rue de Fleuris on the Left Bank almost a hundred times from his studio at Bateaux Lavoir high up in Montmartre). But there is no reason to place a university in a big city (Metropole) in order to profit from short walking distances to, for example, the library or visit the offices of a colleague in the same department. This can just as well be done in a small city. Moreover, walking distances are smaller if the city is relatively small. Moreover a big city might function as a distraction (compare Victor Hugo's decision not to return to Paris from his isolatation in exile). Maybe coming to a big city is too overwhelming for a newcomer and loneliness is not a pleasant feeling. Maybe it is easier to combine the human need for social life and intensive intellectual work in smaller, more isolated environments. Here looking at the role of "artists colonies" (Svanholm, 2001) might explain why most prestigious universities tend to placed in relatively small urban areas outside or on the periphery of larger metropolitan areas (Lund versus Malmö and Uppsala versus Stockholm in Sweden; Cambridge versus London in the UK, Georgetown versus Washington DC, in the USA). In contrast to painting, there has never been "a" center for science. Science in practice is divided into disciplines. But disciplines are based upon methodology (V.3) and methodology in turn requires access to data. If there are physical constraints (I.1) which decide which city becomes the center, this is probably because some cities for some reasons have easy physical access (I.1) to to data (material cause, V.1). According to Dierig et al. (2003) Paris became a research center of anatomical medicine during the nineteenth century mainly because of the regular and cheap supply of cadavers, whereas Leipzig and Berlin become centers of physiological research mainly because the feeding of captive animals could be rationalized and standardized by machines In both cases, physical access to data was decisive. But who said that cities were always the best places to access data? That probably depends upon the discipline. Geologists work all over the world as well as archeologists, sociobiologists, primatologists and anthropologists. This makes financial support for travel and collecting data (the opportunity factor, I.c) important factors that increase the chance of undertaking pioneering work. But as noted above, some pioneers were not even employed by a university at the time (Kepler, Darwin, Wallace, Einstein, Freud, Goodall, etc). Patronage can have many sources. The theory that cities explain creativity are not indisputable facts.

## Social Recognition and Pioneering Work

Pioneering work in science is often undertaken by scholars who for some reasons happen to be employed by or are possibly visiting researchers at elite institutions (Fuchs, 1993). Such privileged access probably reflects the degree of social recognition. But what explains degree of social recognition (Bourdieu, 1974a, 1974b, 1995, 2004; Bloor, 1976; Barnes et al. 1996)? Latour & Wolgar (1986) suggests the theory of "credit cycles" (compare Merton's 1968/1973 concept "Matthew effect"). The idea is that early recognition leads to better working conditions and general buzz, attention or interest for the work of a promising scholar, who has just been "propelled" into a career from early on. In this, model support systems (IV.5) play a critical role.

Again the complexity and paradoxes of creativity have to be foregrounded as a warning signal to avoid premature overgeneralization from limited data. Creativity science is a science and as such is primarily here to falsify theories and separate fiction from facts (V.4). For this purpose multi-factorial explanations are often superior (see Chapter 8). Support systems (IV.5) are only one of may factors which help protect early versions of pioneering work, which are vulnerable for several reasons (Dimension IV). Moreover there is the paradox of latecomers. Not all pioneers have an early kick-off (compare Sartre and Wallace). There is also the fact that social recognition of truly pioneering work takes time. The reason for this is unclear, but a possible explanation could be that pioneering work is itself often characterized by many uncertainties (unsolved issues, mistakes, etc.). This is certainly the case with Darwin's *On the Origin of Species* (Jones, 2001; Hodge & Radick, 2009; Richards & Ruse, 2009). Keynes' attempt to open up a new field of economic theory has also been accused of being very uneven (Skidelsky, 1994).

But the problem might also be that a pioneer is far ahead of his or her time (Popper's (1999) talk about the "thirty years' rule") and that lack or recognition might be a result of great difficulty in understanding what is not currently part of the "idols of the tribe" (Strong & Davies, 2006/ 2011b, 312–314; Wild, 1992). Take Darwin's up and down reputation (Bowler & Morus, 2005; Mayr, 1942/1999). This is probably best explained by the tendency to reduce Darwin's theory of evolution to a "one-factor" theory (natural selection) whereas it is in fact a very complex five-factor theory as recently discovered by the doyen of biological theory, Ernst Mayr (1998, 2004/2007). The complexity of artists such as Shakespeare and Vermeer might also help explain their relatively late social recognition. It is this complexity but also paradoxes of creativity that needs to be foregrounded. What is, for example, the relation between N-creativity and H-creativity? How do we explain the paradox that technology (T-creativity) is closest to N-creativity in terms of aim (adaption) and problem-solving strategy (trial and error) but that science (S-creativity) resembles N-creativity in the sense that both areas are basically unintended and very slow?

## Can Darwin Explain Darwin?

These questions might help us unravel one of the core unsolved problems that creativity science is here to answer, if and in what sense Darwin can explain Darwin (Gardner, 1999). This problem can conveniently be divided into five aspects: (1) Why is technological creativity closest to the creativity of nature in terms of both final cause, adaption (V.4) and effective cause, the problem-solving strategy of trial and error (V.3)? (2) Why are falsifications in normal science (II.3) intended whereas pioneering forms of falsification (II.4) are unintended? (3) Why is pioneering work in science (II.4) similar to the creativity of nature in the sense that both are unintended? (4) Why are biological laws more generally a better prototype (I.2) for explaining scientific revolutions than physical laws, whereas physical laws seem better to explain the pattern of artistic revolutions? (5) Why is Darwin's evolutionary theory of the creative of nature (N-creativity) strikingly similar to Aristotle's theory of the structure of creative process (Dimension V) in both nature and culture?

### N-Creativity as General Prototype of H-Creativity

Although technological creativity is rule based (I.4), technology knowledge is essentially practical. Technology like nature aims at adaption (V.4) to physically and biologically given conditions. This might explain why evolutionary (Darwinian) models of creativity tend to appeal to disciplines studying technology such as economics (Hodgson, 1994), archeology (Lyman & O'Brien, 1998; Hart & Terrell, 2002) and economic history (Basalla, 1988; Mokyr, 1990a, 1990b). But evolutionary models to some degree also function for problem solvers in both science and art (H-creativity).. First, problem solving in both art (A-creativity) and science (S-creativity) is constrained and not contingent. Second, one of the constraints is parsimony (III.1). But A-creativity and S-creativity are not constrained in the same way. In order to get it right (Dimension III), pioneering scientists need to overcome knowledge constraints (I.3) but so does nature (compare the apple-tree argument in Popper, 1999). Getting it right in art is more complex. The historical, professional and personal-problem situation (III.4) has to be foregrounded. Nevertheless, evolutionary models might still be of value. Thus, pioneering artists as a rule start from some prototype (I.2) and add several others along the road. But the choice of techniques (V.3) is not contingent. Compare Greenberg's (1961/1965) argument that abstract expressionism originating in the problem that Cubism tried to solve, how to avoid the illusion of three dimensionality of paintings and foreground the physical flatness of paintings instead (physical constraints, I.1).

### N-Creativity and Protection

Darwin's evolutionary model also helps us explain a core aspect of effective cause (V.3). Vulnerable versions must be protected (Dimesion IV) regardless of whether we are dealing with science, art or technology. The difference is that nature mainly uses geographical migration (IV.1) with accompanying isolation to protect vulnerable versions. Humans (culture) also use intellectual migration (IV.5), different versions of secrecy (IV.3, IV.4) and institutionalized support systems (IV.5). But such support systems can also be found in biological nature, with the important reason that they are instinctive and not intended. This also influences motivations.

## N-Creativity, Motivations and Prototypes

A comparison between humans and mammals reveals very similar types of motivations. Lion cubs take great pleasure (I.5a) in imitating adult lions and testing what it means to have the types of potentials that lions must subdue and kill predators. Lions whether young or old get hungry and this puts pressure (I.5b) on them to find food (hunt down prey). But to find food, there have to be opportunities (I.5c) such as prey strolling around unaware of imminent danger to be killed and eaten. Similar motives as we have seen can also be found among pioneers in science, art and technology, although the way this works in practice tuns out to be ultimately constrained by the creativity regime.

Artists are here to evoke emotions (V.4). For this purpose they need to learn the proper techniques (V.3). This puts pressure on artists (I.5b) to learn the relevant techniques. This is best done by imitating or copying prototypes (V.2, I.2). But such prototypes will vary with different art forms due to different physical constraints from the audience's point of view (I.1) and material causes (V.1) from the artist's point of view. The existence of such prototypes provides opportunities (I.5c) to learn the craft of say writing or painting. Artists, both writers and patients are in the game of transforming facts to fiction for the purpose of evoking emotions (V.4). As lion cubs, the experience of growing mastery probably produces the feeling of pleasure as well (I.5a).

### Darwin and Aristotle

There is no fundamental difference between Aristotle's basic theory of the structure of creative processes and Darwin's theory of the creativity of nature. Both are essentially constraint theories. One of Aristotle's two theories is more parsimonious, it allows us to include Darwin's theory as an aspect, mainly when trying to clarify the structure of effective cause (V.3). Aristotle's model is also helpful to clarify the nature of artistic forms of creativity. Most attempts to describe how artistic creativity works, tend to be either too descriptive or too judgmental, instead of being analytical and systematic (Carroll, 1992/2008, 2010). This is probably a result of trying to stay close to (reflect) the final cause of art which is evocation rather than falsification (V.4). But this ignores the fact that the rules (I.4) of art and science are completely different. For a work of, for example, fiction to work, the writer has to leave out important details, or the suspense necessary for intermittent reading (physical constraints, I.1) will disappear. This leaves holes in information which engages the reader in imagining different types of outcome (Eco, 1984). In contrast, a scholar is expected from the very start to provide a summary of what type of theory will be falsified and how.

The intended beauty or ugliness of a painting can be taken in at one glance, but modern artists intentionally seek to delay aesthetic apparition of art works, say by refusing to easily categorize it as either painting or sculpture. The pioneer here was Picasso, the prototype, of numerous imitators (compare the debate between Greenberg and Judd, cited in Thompson, 2006). Such ambivalence (Adams, 1996) has become a common, generalized technique (V.3) in all avant-garde art. A closer look at Cubist paintings reveals that such ambivalence can be built into paintings themselves (Greenberg was right), by (1) intentionally making it difficult to see what a figure represents, by (2) letting details of the painting fill several functions, by (3) intentional flatness (extinguishing the distinction between background and foreground) but also as in most contemporary art, by (4) the strategy to condense paintings or sculptures (installations) to mere perceptual effects to be appreciated by the connoisseur but leaving the lay audience cold, angry or merely puzzled (Rauterberg, 2007).

This type of problem-solving strategy does not work in movies which are aimed at mass audiences looking for entertainment (V.4). Here techniques (V.3) aiming at clarifying the structure of the visual narrative (who does what to whom and in what order) becomes important, at least in the early years of film making when film audiences were unused to the way the film communicates messages (Bordwell, 1997). Physical constraints (I.1) hence matter in artistic creativity, but so do other forms of material constraints. (V.1). But physical constraints (I.3) are also critical for technology. In contrast the critical factor for science seems to be knowledge constraints (I.1).

### S-Creativity, A-Creativity, T-Creativity

The question if Darwin can explain Darwin, might be misleading. For a creativity science to be possible, we should combine Aristotle's general theory of the structure of creative processes with Darwin's theory of N-creativity. If we want to clarify why science aims at falsification, art as evocation and technology as adaption (V.4), Aristotle's theories of change, knowledge forms and the four causes (structure of creative processes) seem to be a better start. If we want to understand why groundbreaking scientific discoveries tend to be unintentional, just like the creativity of nature, we need to foreground the homology between Darwin's theory of inter-species co-evolution (V.11 and Aristotle's methodological theory of First principles (V.3). If we want to understand how protection of vulnerable versions work (Dimension IV) and how and why some problem solvers manage to get it right (Dimension III), a close reading of Darwin's *On the Origin of Species,* combined with the latest literature in sociobiology (Wilson) and evolutionary theory (Dawkins) is probably the best strategy. It is also via a close reading of Darwin that we can clarify why artistic revolutions seem to be patterned upon the cyclical model foregrounded in Martindale's (1990) seminal study on stylistic revolutions but also why the attempt to project this type of revolution upon scientific revolutions is bound to fail (Kuhn's mistake). Science is not here to produce new languages (techniques, styles, V.3). Science works by First principles (methodology). Science aims at falsification of theories, and not evocation of emotion (V.4). Although a very simple discovery, it should work as one of the First principles for a creativity science.

## Science and Rhetoric

This book is about science, art and technology and not rhetoric, but rhetoric is nevertheless the other form of productive knowledge and some preliminary clarification of what this is might be of value. Rhetoric is a strange bedfellow. It imitates science in so far as it presents an argument, but this argument is basically of a moral nature which in reality means it sets out to evoke emotion just as art does (V.4). For this purpose, such moral arguments use materials (V.1), forms of composition (V.2) and techniques (V.3). Most rhetoric uses literary techniques such as suspense, vraisemblement, tragic destiny, the reader being better informed than the characters, etc.

A core technique of all rhetoric according to Aristotle is to evoke the emotions of empathy or sympathy with the main character. It could be a recently deceased person (say Churchill), a person accused of some monstrous crime (say Hitler) or a role model (say Moses, Jesus, Mohammed or the Buddha). It could also be a work about a well-known scientist such as Bertolt Brecht's famous play based on the life of Galileo Galilei. Let us see how this works.

## Reading Art Works

Bertolt Brecht's play *Life of Galileo* like all works of art, can be read in many ways. One reading would foreground art as "mirror" of society. The other possible strategy is to read Brecht's *Galileo* as a "masked" version of Brecht's own life as pioneering avant-garde director, writer and scenographer (historical and professional-problem situation and personal-problem solver, III.4). But these two types of reading complement each other. This is one of the advantages of creativity science, allowing us to retain the complexity of reality as part of scientific methodology (see Chapter 8).

## Facts into Fiction

During the nineteenth century, science was generally identified with both moral and epistemic progress. In particular, the case of Galileo seemed to be the prototype (I.2) of how the two historical roles could be combined in one and the same person. This no longer seems to be the case. The image of the scientist has changed dramatically because scientists have (somewhat rashly) been made as scapegoats or at least co-responsible both for the dropping of atomic bombs over Hiroshima and Nagasaki and the hideous crimes against humanity in Nazi Germany. This claim arises from the fact that both events relied upon advanced, science-based technology (Horkheimer & Adorno, 1944/1979; Bauman, 1989).

The problem with this interpretation is that science-based technology is neither a sufficient nor a necessary condition of say genocide (compare the chapter on Rwanda and Burundi in Diamond 2005/2011 which foregrounds ethnic competition and effective propaganda, factors which certainly can also be found in Nazi Germany). Relativity theory, which did open the way for the atomic bomb, was intentionally discovered by a trained engineer. But this type of discovery is not typical for pioneering work in science which tends to be unintended. So how can pioneering scientists be blamed for intentionally discovering what they tend to discover unintentionally? In order to explain how this works, you need to look at the role of constraints (First principle of creativity science) but for this purpose the core technique of artists needs to be avoided, to transform facts into fiction (V.4).

Fiction (Brecht's Galileo): Galileo turns out to be against the idea of knowledge for its own sake.

> Ich halte dafür, das einzige Ziel der Wissenschaft, darin besteht, die Mühseligkeit der menschlichen Existenz zu erleichtern. Wenn Wissenschaftler, eingeschüchtert durch selbst-süchtige Machthaber, sich damit begnügen, Wissen um des Wissens willen aufzuhäufen, kann die Wissenschaft zum Krüppel gemacht werden, und eure neuen Maschinen mögen nur Drangsale bedeuten. Ihr mögt mit der Zeit alles entdecken, was es zu entdecken gibt, und eurer Fortschritt wird doch nur ein Fortschreiten von der Menschheit weg sein. (Brecht 1955/1972, p. 141 )
> [My opinion is that the only goal of science must be to make the tiresome lives of humans easier. When scientists, subdued be self-serving rulers, let themselves become satisfied with building heaps of knowledge for the sake of knowledge, science might shrink to a cripple and your instruments can only bring distress. You scientists might over time discover everything there is to be discovered, but your progress will only be a development away from humanity.]

Fact: in reality Galileo rejected the idea that science only has value if it has a practical goal. Galileo would not have been the founder of both physics (theoretical knowledge, science) and materials science (practical knowledge, science-based technology) if he had not understood that the two forms of knowledge are completely different and should not be confused with each other. Brecht projects his own personal world view – compare Marx's well known last Feuerbach thesis (philosophers have so far only interpreted the world, the point is to change it) but also the negative view of the theoretical achievements of Greek science frequent among Marxist historians of science (Farrington, 1944/1965) upon a scientist who happened to be knowledgeable in both type of knowledge but basically remained a scientist committed to theoretical knowledge.

Fiction: Galileo was a coward who tried to save his own life by publicly repudiating his support for Copernicus theoretical model and he knew it. Had he not bowed to the demands of the Church wonderful things would have happened and history would have been very different.

> Ich hatte als Wissenschaftler eine einzigartige Möglichkeit. In meiner Zeit erreichte die Astronomie die Marktplätze. Unter diesen gang besonderen Umständen, hätte die Stand- Haftigkeit eines Mannes grosse Erschütterungen herforrufen können. Hätte ich wieder- standen hätten die Wissenschaftler etwas wie den hippokratischen Eid der Ärzte entwickeln können, das Gelöbnis ihr Wissen einzig zum Wohle der Menschheit anzuwenden. Wie es nur steht, ist das Höchste was man erhoffen kann, ein Geschlecht erfinderische Zwerge, die für alles gemietet werden

können ... ich überlieferte mein Wissen den Machthabern, es zu gebrauchen es nicht zu gebrauchen, es zu missbrauchen, ganz wie es ihre Zwecken diente ... ich habe meinen Beruf Verraten. Ein Mensch, der dass tut was ich getan habe, kann in der Reihen der Wissenchaftler nicht geduldet werden. (Brecht 1955/1972,p. 142)

[As a scientist I had a unique opportunity. In my times, astronomy reached the marketplaces. In such special circumstances, the courage of one man could have had great repercussions. If I had only resisted, scientists could have developed something similar to the Hippocratic oath of the medical professions, the oath only to use their knowledge for the welfare of humanity. As it stands, the best you can hope for, is a species of inventive dwarfs, who can be hired for anything ... I gave my knowledge away to the rulers, to use it or not to use it, to abuse it, whatever their choice were. ... I have betrayed my profession. A man who acts like I have done, should not be permitted into the rows of science.]

## Facts

Counterfactual arguments in historical science are notoriously difficult and are often speculative. There is a point in "Whig history," which starts from facts and does not engage in wishful thinking. In this particular case, it seems highly unlikely that Galileo's refusal would have created miracles. Moreover, the words put into Galileo's mouth seem contrived. Why should Galileo not take pride in his scientific achievements? From the point of view of hindsight, his personal discoveries were among the greatest in the history of both science and science-based technology (P-creativity as H-creativity). Both removed important knowledge constraints (I.3). The method of controlled experiments became a prototype (I.2) for many disciplines (both for good and for bad). Galileo's discovery of material science came very late in life, after his public repentance. Had he been as brave (or rather foolish) as Brecht's fictitious version makes him regret that the was not, he would certainly not have been the effective cause (V.3) of this new, practical science.

## Intellectual Migration and Rules of the Game

The fact that science is a distinct form of knowledge does not mean that pioneering scientists do not sometimes move between different forms of knowledge. Einstein certainly did and so did Galileo. Although the Pope and Catholic clergy were constrained by the rhetorical type of thinking (rules of the game. I.4) Galileo, a scientist, was (in principle) not. For an empirical scientist, data or proof (material cause, V.1) always beats religious rhetoric (compare Galileo's comments after having made the discovery that the sun has spots, see Shapin, 1996). But in order to observe these spots, Galileo needed a telescope. He seems to have been the only scholar at the time who could build such a telescope (co-evolution III.3). Galileo's knowledge of practical engineering (knowledge constraints, I.3, rules of the game, I.4) allowed him to improve the telescope (prototype, I.2) originally invented by Dutch engineers (Boorstin, 1985).

This move by a scientist into technological creativity (intellectual migration, IV.2) in turn made it possible for Galileo to make a number of groundbreaking scientific discoveries in astronomy such as the discovery that Jupiter had moons of its own (Biagioli, 2001). The improved telescope Galileo used when he observed the moon though, was too clumsy to allow him to discover the presence of craters on the moon. Here Galileo's complementary knowledge (Rosenberg, 1976, 2010) of Renaissance art (intellectual migration, IV.2), in particular techniques to produce the illusion (Gombrich, 1960/2000) of three-dimensional depth (the "tactical" quality of Renaissance art, see Berenson, 1930/1960), made it possible for Galileo to use shadows to produce the illusion of volume (Shapin, 1996).

## Science as Rhetoric and Fiction

Pioneering work in science can be explained, but for a scientific explanation to be possible we must make a clear distinction between theoretical, practical and productive knowledge. Postmodernists rarely uphold the distinction though; all concepts tend to float into each other as in a Color Field painting by Rothko. Take the example of Bruno Latour's works on science. In *We Have Never Been Modern* we are told that there is no such thing as "pure science" in the sense of theoretical thinking or knowledge for its own sake. Greek philosophy of science never happened; from a knowledge point of view, we are still living in a hunter-gatherers society dominated by the bricolage technique attributed to the "primitive mind" by Claude Lévi-Strauss.

In *The Pasteurization of France*, Latour argues that the greatness of Pasteur lies not in his scientific work, that he was the first to falsify the theories of "spontaneous generation" of dangerous microbes (bacteria) in milk (Latour, 1999, 2000a). The reason France was "pasteurized" if we are to believe Latour was due to Pasteur's rhetorical skills. Pasteur managed to convince the scientific community that his theory was correct (a case of rhetoric and not scientific demonstration) and this together with support from the strong social hygiene movement in France (another case of rhetoric), explains why Pasteur conquered medical science in France.

But this conclusion completely contradicts the First principle mentioned at the start of his book on Pasteur. Here Latour tells us that the best method to explain the rhetorical power of Pasteur might be Tolstoy's novel *War and Peace*. We are then told that the brilliance of Tolstoy's novel is to show that generals who commanded great battles in reality have no idea or control over their troops. Hence they cannot possibly control the outcome and are completely irrelevant for history. But if this is indeed the case, Pasteur could not have been the major mover. The hygiene movement in France (troops) fought the battle alone and won. Pasteur was merely a symbol, a herald on their shields. So how can Pasteur be both a "genius" who with his superior rhetorical skills conquered not only France but also its colonies, and at the same time a mere symbol or sign for a battle won by groups (actants)? Which battle, one might ask as a follow-up question, the battle for scientific reputation or the battle against bacteria? In order to win the first battle, theoretical knowledge is needed. In order to win the real battle against the bacteria (life and death), technological knowledge is also required. By letting all his concepts float, all Latour accomplishes is to make his own ideas incomprehensible. In other words, he has modeled himself upon avant-garde art (prototype, I.2), a form of "primitivism" but projected upon science.

### Rhetoric and the Complexity of Late Modernity

One way to describe late modernity is the epistemic democratization foregrounded in Giddens' theories. Whereas theories inspired by Marx but also Nietzsche (Boundas, & Olkowski, 1994; Foucault, 1971/1994), have continued to use the Platonic model of "false consciousness" in order to describe the epistemic relation between the educated classes (elites) and the less educated (masses), Giddens has in a number of works moved closer to an Aristotelian point of view (Giddens, 1976, 1977, 1979b, 1981). Concepts like "reflexivity" and "double hermeneutics" (Giddens, 1984, 1990, 1991) are clear signs of this intellectual rethinking.

How do we account for this epistemic democratization? One possible explanation could be that one of the two predictions of Schumpeter's *Capitalism, Socialism and Democracy* from 1946, that science-based technology would radically democratize access to consumer goods, has turned out to be correct. What was previously only accessible for a small elite (aristocrats) such as good food, travel, vacations, fashionable clothes, beautiful furniture, higher education, etc., has now become accessible for the majority (middle classes). These societal changes have dramatically eroded the cultural barriers between the educated classes and elites who only hundred or so years ago lived totally different lives from the masses (compare the Bloomsbury Group, Edel, 1979; Lee, 1996).

The other prediction made by Schumpeter, that science-based technology would work best in a socialist, planned economy, has not materialized though. Instead, the "false consciousness" of the mass consumer, presumably alienated at work and with a reified view of commodities has prevailed. Epistemic democratization has instead been driven by expanding access to goods and services to ordinary citizens in liberal democratic, capitalist societies of the Western type (Aron, 1965). This has in turn led to a rapid growth of new forms of knowledge of a partly artistic, partly rhetorical type (productive knowledge). Examples are the increasing role of mass media technology for democratic politics (McQuail, 2002), new and less exclusive ways of shopping (mostly appealing to women, see Woodhead, 2012), the transformation of marketing into a science-based technology (Dickson, 1997), the rise of the "experience economy" (Pine & Gilmore, 1998, 1999) and the growing economic importance of the cultural industries and cultural economy (Caves, 2000; Du Gay & Prike, 2002; Hesmondalgh, 2002).

This expansion of productive forms of knowledge is unproblematic from the point of view of creativity science, as long as the analytical distinction between different forms of knowledge (theoretical, practical, productive) is upheld. The problem is when all these forms of knowledge are allowed to float into each other as in a watercolor painting and science itself is transformed into a kind of rhetoric. It is interesting that one of the institutions which has so far been able to withstand the epistemic democratization driven by late-capitalist consumer culture has been avant-garde art. Here the Platonic, elitist theory of epistemology, seems to work undisturbed (Crowther, 1993/1996; Adorno, 1997). This might possibly help to explain the attractiveness of avant-garde art, within academia, the training ground of the educated classes and with material cause (IV.1) of the constant rediscovery (III.2) of Platonic epistemology.

But avant-garde art is after all art, not science. In order to hold up avant-garde art as the last stand or prototype (I.2, V.2) outside academia against epistemic democratization, academics studying avant-garde art, might be tempted to evade the core issue of facts and fiction (V.4). This motif, to save Plato from the return of Aristotle, might be the basic project of postmodernist thought (Lamarque & Olsen, 1994; Schusterman, 2003).

Postmodern rhetoric rejects the epistemological democratization that has been the result of late modernity, but it is, paradoxically also a reflection of the increasing role of rhetoric as knowledge form and creativity in late-modern societies. As such, postmodern rhetoric far from being rebellious is a strongly conformist intellectual movement. It is both a child of our times and a strongly reactionary (epistemically elitist) intellectual movement.

# PART III

# Conclusions: First Principles of Creativity Science

# CHAPTER 7

# Concepts and Knowledge Object

## The Nature and Culture Divide

Scientific concepts in the social sciences and humanities in modern, science-based societies, have a strangely dual or even triple quality. On the one hand they are re-descriptions of phenomena which have already been categorized by other humans. Compare the core distinction between "in vivo" and "in vitro" in the Grounded Theory tradition (Glaser & Strauss, 1967). On the other hand, the former also tends to reflect or incorporate scientific theories or concepts. Compare Giddens' concepts "double hermeneutics," "discursive practices" and "reflexivity" (Giddens, 1976, 1984, 1990). Schön's (1983) concept "the reflexive practitioner" tries to capture the same type of insight or discovery (compare Schön's attempt to conceptualize what takes place in an architect's office as the professional tries to solve a problem for a client with Le Corbusier's practices described in Cinqualabre & Migayrou, 2015).

These methodological considerations in the social sciences, might help to clarify what it is that scholars working within the social sciences and humanities try to do, but they have also, paradoxically, functioned as an epistemic barrier for creativity science. A core assumption (First principle) of creativity science, which goes back to Aristotle, is that both nature and humans are creative. Aristotle, was a student of Plato (Lloyd, 1968) who had in his theory of art (Cahn & Meskin, 2008; Beardsley, 1966/1967) developed a craft model of artistic creativity (imitation of imitation)

which Aristotle reformulated as his theory of the four causes (Hankinson, 1995, 2009). The idea of this reformulation came from Aristotle's intimate knowledge of biology (according to Mayr, 1982, Aristotle was the founder of the discipline of biology).

For Aristotle, nature in principle functions like a craftsman, for example a carpenter producing kitchen tables does. (Hall, 2015). A carpenter (effective cause, V.3) gets a commission to design something and produces a kitchen table (final cause,V.4). For this purpose, the carpenter needs some material to start with, oak for example (material cause, V.1). He starts with material, planks from an oak tree and reshapes those pieces of wood into a desired form (formal cause, V.2) such as round, square or rectangular and attaches legs to the surface.

Aristotle was convinced that nature works in a similar manner. A tiny seed falling from a tree (effective cause) already contains the design (formal cause) of its majestic shape (final cause), provided it is protected long enough during its life cycle, say by becomes buried in soil (earth) and receiving the necessary water, sun and air (material cause, the natural elements) to grow until old age. Aristotle never managed to solve the problem of where trees and seeds came from (origins of species). This problem remained unsolved until Darwin rediscovered Aristotle's theory of the creativity of nature (n-creativity). Darwin's novelty or creativity was that he in contrast to Aristotle studied the natural history of trees (compare Tudge, 2005). The difference between the two thinkers was therefore the concept of "natural history" which is absent in Aristotle's thinking (compare the distinction between ontogeny and phylogeny).

The discovery of a new continent, "natural history" served as a proto-type (I.2) or intellectual tool for Darwin's rethinking of the unsolved problem of the origins of species (evolutionary type of N-creativity). But from where did Darwin get this concept? This leads us to the role that Lyell's *Principles of Geology* (prototype, I. 2) played for Darwin's (effective cause, V.3) transmutation from a convinced believer in natural theology (novice, II.2) to the discoverer of the previously unknown continent of the evolutionary type of N-creativity (pioneer, II.4). In order to get from II.2 to II.4, Darwin had first to become a professional (II.3) in a discipline other than biology (intellectual migration, IV.2).

But why could Lyell, who was after all the pioneer (II.4) of geology and Darwin's intellectual role model (I.2) not discover this previously unknown continent (N-creativity as evolution)? It tuns out that Lyell not only did not discover what Darwin discovered, he strongly disagreed with Darwin's theory; he was not convinced (Lyell, 1863/1970). According to Rudwick (1972) Lyell after many years finally sided with Darwin, but according to Mayr (2004/2007) Lyell's reservations or intel-lectual resistance was terminal. Lyell never understood what it was that Darwin was trying to say. Something in Lyell's training as a geologist, stopped him from fully grasping Darwin's theory. But how is this possible? Lyell one of Darwin's confidant during the 20 or so years that Darwin worked on *On the Origin of Species*. Lyell wrote a book, *The Ancestry of*

*Man,* published a few years *after On the Origin of Species* (1863). How could Lyell not understand Darwin despite the fact that Lyell's geological concept "natural history" was what allowed Darwin to solve a problem which Aristotle could not solve?

This is the type of complex and paradoxical question that creativity science is here to answer. Actually, such puzzles are also good ways to disentangle a number of core problems of creativity science, such as the problem of what makes a science a science and why groundbreaking discoveries in science tend to be unintended (falsifying, V4 both Kuhn's and Popper's theories of science). The concept (V.2) "natural history" did not exist in ancient Greece (Nisbet, 1969/1970). It evolved around 1800 and can probably best be seen as a case of both intra-species and inter-species co-evolution (III.3). The concept (V.2) "natural history" arose out of Hutton's discovery of geological time, the natural history of minerals (Repcheck, 2003/2009) and was soon followed by Thomsen's discovery of another type of natural history, the history of preliterate societies (inter-species co-evolution, III.3). Using natural (geologically time-constrained) history as a prototype (I.2, V.2) helped Thomsen to arrive at his natural history of culture which made a division between Stone Age, Bronze Age and Iron Age societies. Thomsen arrived at his chronology by assuming that these technologies (stone, bronze, iron) represented different types of complexity, which all things being equal, should also be reflected in ornaments or aesthetics. In this way he achieved a powerful alternative methodology to hermeneutics (stylistic analysis) which could be used as intellectual tool to analyze the time and place of the origins of artifacts, without recourse to historical texts, which, per definition, had to be much younger than the artifacts themselves, and therefore invalid as data (V.1) for a discipline focusing on preliterate societies.

This methodological insight can be seen as an independent rediscovery (III.2) of Aristotle's theory of First principles (that choice of data and methods should be adapted to the nature of the knowledge object). It is also a case of intra-species co-evolution (III.3) very similar to Darwin's neglected theory of this aspect of co-evolution (anatomy, physiology, behavior). Although Lyell's reference to the same type of methodological problems in the first chapter of volume one of *Principles of Geology,* shows that Lyell was very much aware of how Thomsen had managed to clarify the First principles of archeology (prototype, I.2), his clarification of the First disciplines of geology can also be seen as an example of intra-species co-evolution (III.3). In order to arrive at a simple, elegant, economic solution (parsimony, III.1), the data and methods, but also guiding concepts, had to adapted to the nature of the knowledge object (V.2).

Lyell, in practice, combined Hutton's discovery of the knowledge object of geology, natural history of minerals (called "uniformatism" at the time, see Fortey, 2005 and Laudan, 1987; it was later replaced by the concept "rock cycle," see Rotary, 2008) with the methodological discoveries of Thomsen, the crucial role of data and methods. Without these previous discoveries, it is doubtful that Darwin would have managed to solve the problem of the origin of species. This problem is built upon a third version of natural history, different from both, but at the same time confirming Aristotle's First principle of creativity science, that nature and humans are creative in much the same way (although for Aristotle N-creativity imitates H-creativity, prototype, I.2 and not the opposite as in Darwin's case, the core of Darwin's scientific revolution and theory of "natural selection"; compare Ruse, 2006, 2008).

What this tells us is that concepts (V.2) such as "natural history" can be very complex. But this complexity, from a creativity science point of view has first to be discovered, which is what makes these tasks of creativity science even more complex. Who (Dimension II) makes such discoveries, what makes them right (Dimension III), how (Dimension IV) and why (Dimensions I and V)? But this also raises more fundamental philosophical issues that a creativity science has to deal with (clarify). Given that groundbreaking discoveries in science are cases of human creativity (H-creativity), there has to be individuals to make this type of discovery (P-creativity). But the natural history of mineralogy goes on in the real world (ontology). According to Kant, only "words" count and "things" belong to the unknowable ("das Ding an sich"). It is interesting that Weber's method of Verstehen ultimately rests upon Kant's attempt to keep words and things, epistemology and ontology, apart (Freund, 1969) like Foucault and Kuhn, for example. Moreover, just as Kant, Weber (as Foucault) basically used texts as primary data (V.1), Popper did as well which might explain why he never understood the importance of the revolution that transformed archivarian science into archeology, nor did he integrate it into his thinking on these issues.

So, we have not one concept of "natural history" but three: (1) the natural history of minerals, (2) the natural history of preliterate societies and (3) the new continent Darwin discovered, the natural history of species. But if we compare the three types of natural history we discover something strange. Archeological history is a natural history of human creativity (H-creativity, see Mithen, 1998) and evolutionary theory is a natural history of the transmutation of species (N-creativity). But the natural history of minerals is not creative. It is destructive. It reshuffles minerals, heaves them up from under the thin crust of the Earth (igneous rock), lets them erode by the weather (sedimentary rock formations) or sink back into the deep and reappear again in re-crystallized forms (metamorphic rock). The dynamics of the three alternating types of minerals repeats itself in eternally returning cycles. This perpetual ("uniformatism") recurrent "rock cycle" (Rothery, 2008) is the core of the knowledge object of the type of natural history of interest for geology (V.2).

But if the natural history of minerals or rocks cannot be creative, theories of scientific revolutions (S-creativity) which assume that human creativity (H-creativity) works like geology (cyclical, receptive laws, compare Kuhn) cannot be right. Such laws have the advantage of being predictive in the strict sense. But the point about creativity is not that it can be predicted. It is constrained, just like biological laws. A theory of science exclusively based upon physical laws creates the artificial problem of "under-determination" (Laudan, 1990) making the problem of what makes a science into a science impossible to solve in principle (Laudan, 1996). Kuhn's theory of scientific revolutions models itself precisely upon the physical type of laws. Scientific revolutions according to Kuhn are paradigm shifts which happen regularly and which can therefore be predicted but not explained (taxonomic solution, compare Foucault's very similar solution). Paradoxically such regularly occurring paradigm shifts fit artistic revolutions much better than scientific revolutions (V.2).

## Choice of Prototype

According to Thomsen, stylistic changes (art) in premodern societies, evolved simultaneously with technology. This was the reason why such changes could be used for the purpose of chronology of technological change. The increasing complexity of ornamentation (A-creativity) reflected the increasing complexity of technological change (T-creativity, see Lyell, 1863/1970). But Thomsen was basically talking of technological creativity. Artistic creativity is something else and does not necessarily follow the same laws. Artistic revolutions have their own logic closer to Kuhn's theory of cyclical, repetitive events than Popper's evolutionary logic. It is also interesting, from a creativity science point of view, that Kuhn started with an evolutionary approach to science but later converted to the cyclical view. Why did he do so?

One obvious reason is change of support system (IV.5) as Kuhn moved from Cambridge and Harvard to Berkeley, where he had intensive discussions with Feyerabend (confidant, IV.4) aiding Kuhn's secret transmutation to a cyclical view of scientific revolutions. But there are already problems in Kuhn's monograph *The Copernican Revolution*. As I have tried to show in this book, this revolution was unsuccessful because it lacks parsimony (III.1). This might explain why Kuhn in his Foreword to the book, is somewhat hesitant about his commitment to an evolutionary approach to scientific change. In science, as Einstein said, the problem is not to find the right answer but to find the right way to formulate the problem.

Kuhn's completely false way of approaching the problem of what makes a science a science, would not have survived so long if Popper had managed to clarify the issues properly. Popper's failure to solve the "demarcation problem" opened the way for all kinds of obscure theories and in practice returned the issue to the time of Linnaeus and Kant. This is the reason why we need to take empirical data (V.1) seriously and ask whether Popper might also have used the wrong prototype (I.2) when generalizing his theory of scientific revolutions. What would happen if we replaced Copernicus and Einstein with Thomsen?

The core problem-solving strategy of science is methodology (V.3), not concepts (V.2). Concepts are result of methodology and not the opposite (this comes out most clearly when we study the history of chemistry), but Thomsen is a good start for clarifying the problem because it is simpler and tells us why methodology is critical (the theory of First principles). In his case, the methodological problem was relatively easy to clarify because the relation between epistemology and ontology (words and things) was so obvious. Although latter discoveries have partly replaced the need for stylistic comparison (Libby's atomic clock, see Stringer & Andrews, 2005; bristle cones Ross, 2020 etc.), Thomsen's intuition was right. In the case of chemistry, the very nature of the knowledge object took much longer to clarify, but this made the issue of methodology (what type of data to collect and how to analyze them) much more complicated. Nevertheless, it is relatively easy retrospectively to identify when, how and why chemistry became a science and also who the pioneer was (Pauling). But as I have tried to show in the book, the problem of who and the problem of what, how and why are closely entangled. This is yet another reason why we need to regard creativity as a highly complex phenomenon. The problem is not always to find the correct answer but to formulate the problem correctly.

## Patterns of Creativity

In spite of the complexity and paradoxes of artistic creativity, Aristotle's model of the structure of creative processes helps us clarify the type of problems which are interesting from an educational psychology point of view such as the role of personal discovery (P-creativity) in human creativity (H-creativity). A major finding of the book is that P-creativity as H-creativity is a very complex problem, but in order to account for the exact nature of this complexity, we need to clarify the concept of creativity regimes. There is not one but several logics of discovery: S-creativity, A-creativity and T-creativity.

Take the problem of becoming a pioneer (P-creativity as H-creativity) in art (A-creativity). In order to evoke emotions or " move" audiences (V.4, Engdahl 1994/2005), the artist needs to learn the techniques of the art form (V.3) thoroughly. In reality, levels of problem-solving capacity (Dimension II) depend upon learning such techniques in great detail. The role of techniques is in turn constrained by physical constraints (I.1) and the material causes of art (V.1), the function of which are to transform facts to fiction (V.4). But in order to become an effective cause (V.3), artists also need support systems consisting of patrons, mentors and agents (IV.5) such as Peggy Guggenheim and Clement Greenberg for the abstract expressionists. Yuri Pen, Leon Bakst, Maxim Vinaver and the German art dealer Herwarth Walden played a similar role for Marc Chagall's and Per Kirkeby's artistic careers. Sherwood Anderson merely served as an agent for Hemingway at an early stage of Hemingway's career while he still lived in Chicago. Moving to Paris, Hemingway found his mentor Gertrude Stein, the writer who helped and encouraged Hemingway to find his own personal style (Putnam, 1947/1987).

Stein played a mentoring role (IV.5) for Hemingway. She was herself a pioneer (II.4) in literature, an avant-garde writer (Brinnon, 1959/1987; Will, 2000). But she played a very different role for Picasso and Matisse. For them she was mainly a patron. The main reason seems to be that she understood little about painting (problem situation and problem solver, III.4). Her brother Leo Stein did because he had studied with Berenson. Both of them became early patrons (IV.5) for Matisse and Picasso (Hobhouse, 1975) although Leo Stein preferred Matisse. Hemingway's prime agent was Maxwell Perkins at Scribner's (Bruccoli, 1991). His patrons before he became a famous writer were his parents, his two first wives and the newspaper in Chicago for which he worked (a case of skunk works, IV.3). These personal patrons were later replaced by impersonal patrons, Hemingway's millions of anonymous readers (fans).

All avant-garde modernists, such as Virginia Woolf, James Joyce, T. S. Eliot and Sylvia Plath, had support systems to sustain them during their search for personal style (Ross, 2003) as had such great writers as George Orwell, Céline and Jean-Paul Sartre. The support system for avant-garde writers and popular writers are not identical though (compare the case of Susan Sontag; see Dollenmayer, 2007/2014 with Ernest Hemingway, see Griffin, 1990). Sylvia Plath's talent was discovered very early in her career. She wrote poems which were published when she was still a child (II.1, Kirk, 2009). By the time she entered Smith College she was a promising novice (II.2) on the way to becoming a professional poet (II.3, Bain, 2001). Most poets seem to live from teaching poetry, and this seems to have been Sylvia Plath's original "biographical project" or life plan (Kupferberg, 1995b). She had already attracted attention from the literary world and was generously supported (IV.5) by a female writer of bestselling novels, Olivia Prout (Wagner-Martin, 2003). This patron (not mentor) later also paid for the huge medical bills for Sylvia Plath's long recuperation after her first attempt to commit suicide (Butscher, 1976/2003) and continued to provide financial support or patronage right up until Sylvia Plath's suicide (Stevenson, 1999; Malcolm, 1993; Hayman, 1991/2003).

Sylvia Plath's life plans changed dramatically during her first year as a Fulbright scholar at Cambridge (geographical isolation, V.1), where she met, fell in love with and soon married another promising poet, Ted Hughes. The marriage lasted six years (Middlebrook, 2004; Feinstein, 2003), during which Plath functioned as private patron and agent (IV.5) for her husband, whereas he functioned as private mentor for her. It was the breakup of the marriage, that led to the creative explosion manifested in *Ariel* (*Ariel* was named after a beloved horse), for which she later (posthumously) became famous. A combination of pressure, pleasure and opportunity (V.3, I.5a, I.5b, I.5c) probably explains how Plath during the last half of her short (plus 30 years) life managed to transform herself (Bredsdorff, 1987) from a mere professional poet (II.3) to a pioneer (II.4).

The cause of her suicide has been widely debated in the literature, but one possible explanation could be problems with her support system (IV.5). She had hoped that her first novel, *The Bell Jar*, would become a best seller ("pot boiler"), providing her with financial security (patronage), but bad reviews in January 1963, a few weeks before she killed herself, probably depressed her (Stevensen, 1989). Another possible reason might have been the fact that in the autumn of 1961, Al Alvarez, the literary critic at *The Observer*, had complimented her, calling her a new Emily Dickinson (Plath, 1975), indicating that he might be willing to take up the role of agent himself (IV.5). This encouragement (opportunity, I.5c) probably explains why she signed a contract for a flat in London to which she moved with her two small children in the autumn of 1962.

Al Alvarez came to visit her. Exactly what happened between the two is difficult to conclude with certainty (disputable fact, V.4), but given (1) her "non-female" mating behavior at the start of breakup of her marriage, (2) her consistently active pursuit of men she liked since her college years (Plath, 2000), plus (3) her poem "Lazarus" where she complains of feeling physically unattractive in her present state as a mother surrounded by small children who smell of soiled nappies, Plath probably made a pass at Alvarez after which he fled not to return again. She might also (4) have misunderstood the relationship between agent and poet and probably had her own intimate type of relationship (prototype. I.2) in mind. The feeling of embarrassment after this failed courtship closely tied to her career plans, might have been the "last straw" (Ebaugh, 1988; Strauss, 1959), which led her to kill herself (to Alvarez's great regret, see Alvarez, 1971/1990).

In contrast to Plath, the three male novelists Orwell (Shelden, 1991), Céline (Vitoux, 1992) and Sartre (Hayman, 1985) were all latecomers. All became professionals (II.3) in other types of creativity regimes (I.4) before they switched to literature (imperial police, medic, teacher of philosophy). A similar latecomer pattern can also be found in the careers of Paul Gauguin (Sweetman, 1995) and van Gogh (Stone, 1934/1987). Gauguin had been a stockbroker, van Gogh an art dealer. But whereas both van Gogh and Gauguin experienced great difficulties of social recognition when they changed profession, Orwell, Céline and Sartre did not seem to have the same problem, once their first novel had been accepted for publication (publishers as agents, IV.5).

The question is why. The best answer might be that in contrast to panting, there does not seem be a strongly institutionalized (Strauss & Glaser, 1971) support system for becoming a professional writer (II.3). There are no patrons, no mentors, only agents (publishers). This absence of institutionalized support might delay the debut of writers, who need to learn the techniques (V.3) of writing not with the help of mentors (IV.5) but mainly from prototypes (II.2). This has the advantage though of relieving the budding writer from the pressure (I.5b) to demonstrate previous educational credentials (compare the problems experienced by Matisse).

It is enough if the writer is able to produce a publishable manuscript which an agent (IV.5) can accept (Gedin, 1975/1997). The relatively low entrance barriers in terms of formal education or "credentialism" (Collins 1998) for becoming a writer, explains say the phenomenon of "proletarian writers" in Sweden (Hägg, 1996), but also the fact that most renowned Swedish writers, until August Strindberg (Lagercrantz, 1979) and Selma Lagerlöf (Edström, 2002) were part time writers (skunk works, IV.3), supporting themselves by regular work, mostly as state employees (Strindberg worked as a librarian and later as journalist; Lagerlöf was a schoolteacher). Knausgaard's long description of how he became a professional writer is highly illustrative of the role that "skunk works" play for becoming a writer (this pattern can also be found in the case of Hemingway who had his first novel published at his early twenties).

Support systems (IV.5) in science are different form both painting and literature. Apart from book publishers and editors of scholarly journals, there are basically no agents in science. This follows from the fact that scholars need to provide proof for their original contribution (falsify some theory, separate fiction into facts V.4). The patronage (IV.5) necessary to accomplish original work is mainly public rather than private, and usually takes the form of employment as an academic teacher at a university. Mentors (previous teachers) usually serve as referees providing references for professional positions, but they do not serve as agents for pioneering work in science, given that the scholar has to solve the core problem of scientific recognition, proven priority, which makes the scientific pioneer the prime agent.

This pattern is confirmed by Karl Popper's case. It was the publication of the original, German version of *The Logic of Scientific Discovery* (published in 1934, see Hacomen, 2000) that triggered his career and made him into one of the pioneers of twentieth-century philosophy of science. Popper seems to have developed his theory of falsification during the years he worked as teacher of mathematics and physics in a secondary school in Vienna. But secondary schoolteachers do not have time for empirical research. This lack of training in empirical research methods might explain why Popper was attracted to Kant, a philosopher for whom empirical research is much less important than logical analysis (methodology, V.3). Once Popper began his career as a university teacher of philosophy, first at the university of Auckland, New Zealand and at the London School of Economics after the Second World War, this rejection of empirical methods became legitimized by the discipline and profession in which he found himself (for personal reality, see Gouldner, 1973/1979).

Popper's last book *The World of Parmenides*, published posthumously, is probably based upon his lecture notes from his first academic position (data, V.1). He freely admits that he is no specialist on this early period of Greek philosophy. He mainly relies upon textbook types of literature, which describe the essentials and avoid the many details in which only specialists can participate in a competent, professional (II.3) manner. This foregrounding of the essential is typical for how a philosopher but also a teacher (pedagogy) works The two type of professions are surprisingly similar (compare empirical science, where methodological training is critical and which explains why teaching methods are constrained by disciplines).

Teachers are professionals (II.3). They are here to save time and energy (parsimony, III.1) for students (novices, II.2) by not forcing (I.5b) the students to rediscover the wheel (Säljö, 2000) but on the contrary by being highly selective in the choice of relatively easy reading materials (Sartre, a teacher of philosophy in his first novel *Nausea*, evokes the wastefulness of the unprofessional learning method of the autodidact who acquires knowledge by reading all the books in the library in alphabetical order). The criteria for selecting such texts is that they should economize the intellectual energy necessary for learning (Collins 2000a, 2000b) by focusing the attention of the reader/student on the essentials, the most fundamental ideas and concepts (First principles) of any given knowledge or field (educational parsimony). This is best accomplished by starting with introductory textbooks (prototypes, I.2). These use simple language and simple examples to illuminate or elaborate upon the concepts presented (as I have tried in this book, but with somewhat closer attention to methodological issues than Popper ever did).

Such illustrative, clarifying examples might be either visual or narrative or both at the same time (Kress et al., 2001; Kress & van Leeuwen, 2001, 2006). In contrast to scientific (empirical) research, there is no rule or routinized expectation guiding the choice of such examples to be representative (Durkheim 1982), only that they illuminate the idea or concept. From this, it does not follow that the thinking of educational theorists and philosophers are identical. Philosophers are basically knowledgeable about pioneers (H-creativity, II.4), in particular in philosophy. Modeling themselves upon these prototypes (I.2), philosophers in contrast to educational theorists, become trained to look for paradoxes and work from there.

Educational theorists in contrast are knowledgeable about how novices (P-creativity, II.2), usually called "learners," think. Their knowledge object is the problem situation (III.4) of the schoolteacher, how to motivate (I.5) students or pupils (novices) and become sensitive to the core paradox of pedagogy. Why is it that the natural curiosity of children tends to die at the moment they enter school (Dewey, 1917/1997)? Given that pedagogy is mainly a practical science (Durkheim, 1922/1956) – a kind of science-based technology or engineering in modern societies with "adaption" as final cause (V.4) – the core problem is not to ask *why* but *how* to find ways to solve the problem in practice (Bruner 2006a, 2006b; compare Einstein's approach to the accumulated problems in Newton's physics).

In both cases though the reading and selection of texts is critical. The prime "data" (V.1) and "method" (V.3) of philosophy is the reading of texts (Popper, 1934/1959).One of the reasons that curiosity in schools is killed systematically by the school system, might be that teacher education of primary school teachers ignore the lessons of archeology. Artifacts are natural, texts are unnatural. Children have a natural curiosity for investigating artifacts, the curiosity for investigating texts has to be cultivated (compare the lesson on "the eye" in Frost, 1997; see Kupferberg, 2009b, c). Reading and writing appear relatively late in the human record (Donald, 1990). The human mind, having been shaped in hunter-gatherer societies is programmed to learn to talk quickly, solve practical problems and communicate emotions by performances (already found among chimpanzees) but has to be introduced to reading and writing gradually (the same goes for learning mathematics, this cannot be done quickly either, as Bruner's 1960/1977 theory postulated, with catastrophic results for the educational systems in Western societies and misdirected goals of teacher education).

The fact that reading and writing is unnatural and has to be learned (techniques, V.3) explains why this problem can be found also among older students, entering universities (Säljö, 1984/1986;, Marton & Booth, 1997). That something is difficult does not imply that the problem cannot be solved, but at least we have to acknowledge the problem before we attempt to solve it. Let us assume that talking comes natural for humans (Wilson, 2012; Donald, 2001) and is rapidly learned during the first years of life (Pinker, 1995; Crystal, 1987). This might explain why the pedagogical tool of talking might be a good way to learn how to read texts (Säljö, 2000). But learning to read a text always has a purpose (final cause). Scientific tests are not identical with say literature which requires different types of reading. Moreover, we must ask for what purpose we read a text. Writers read literature in a very different way from a scholar. The former reads a text for the purpose of copying the techniques for writing (just as a painter looks at paintings in order to decipher the more or less hidden techniques, V.3; compare how Matisse looked at paintings). A scholar reads novels for the purpose of understanding the knowledge object better, which is most economically done by trying to clarify the guiding concepts (V.2, compare Proust's *À la recherche de temps perdu* with Genette's 1980 analytical categorizations of Proust's main techniques in the form of concepts; for an attempt to use these concepts for descriptive interpretation of biographical data, see Kupferberg, 2012b).

## Physical Constraints and Inter-Species Co-evolution

Whereas the problem of the logic of scientific discovery is relatively easy to solve, once we have clarified the different logics of discovery (science, art and technology) the problem of stylistic revolutions (V.2) is much more complex. In order to understand why, we need to make a clear distinction between rules (I.4) and techniques (V.3) of art. Feyerabend's (1975) "anarchistic" theory of science fails because he fails to make these important distinctions, but also because he makes the even more important mistake to assume that artistic creativity is completely free (Kant's First principle in *Kritik der Urteilskraft*, repeated by Picasso's gallerist, see Kahnweiler, 1980). But this cannot be right. On the contrary artistic creativity is also constrained (Elster, 1983, 2000, 2007) but in a different way. One of the tasks of creativity science is to explain how this works and why. This is where constraint theory is of great help.

As noted by Hegel, the human eye is not perfect (physical constraint, I.1). This imperfection was taken into account by Greek architects, who designed slightly bulging columns to make them look straight (Hegel, 1970) But for such physical constraints to effect choice of techniques (V.3), artists need to learn the imperfection of the human eye. This is only one of many examples of the critical role that physical constraints (I.1) play for all forms of artistic creativity. This might explain why (1) rediscovery (III.2) is much more frequent in art than in science and (2) why parsimonious solutions in art tend to be constrained more by physical constraints (I.1) than by knowledge constraints (I.3). Picasso and Matisse did not abandon naturalistic forms of representation because they could not master them (this would explain Kirkeby's strategy more clearly, see Steffensen, 2009), but because painting cannot compete with photography and film. This does not exclude the fact that knowledge constraints do play a role in art as well. The birth of classical art in ancient Greece, depended upon the technique of the Golden Mean (Dondis, 1973). But this required a type of scientific (mathematical) knowledge, geometry, which the Egyptians did not have. Advanced mathematics hence functioned as a knowledge constraint (I.3) for this art form.

Although knowledge constraints do influence artistic forms of creativity, such knowledge constraints seem to be more important for science. Greek painters, in contrast to Egyptian painters, used naturalistic forms of representation (they painted what they "saw" rather than what they "knew," see Gombrich,1960/2000). But the Greeks did not invent naturalistic forms of representations. They rediscovered them (III.2).The pioneers of naturalist paintings were Paleolithic hunter-gatherer societies (Honour & Fleming, 1982/1984). Egyptian painters must have intentionally abandoned previous knowledge (I.3) of how to use naturalistic forms of representation (prototypes, I.2), because it did not suit their purposes (changed problem situation, III.4). The emotions that Paleolithic hunter gatherers and Neolithic farmers sought to evoke (rules, I.4) were probably not identical.

Why? Egypt as a country revered the dead. As in Northern Europe, the Neolithic revolution gave rise to monumental graveyards (Romer, 2012/2013; Jensen, 2013). These were mainly symbolic and the choice of the strongly symbolic forms of painting by Egyptian artists (Gombrich, 1960/2000, 1997) might have reflected these new types of emotions of a settled society of previous nomads (Gamble, 2007). Such strongly symbolic monuments might have had the intended function to claim the eternal right to land (Jensen, 2013). What could be a better proof than monumental tombs revering dead ancestors? The gigantic moments were physically visible signs of the great sacrifices made to win the right of this particular land (compare some books of the Old Testament, written by an elite driven into exile; instead of graveyards as physical proof of their sacrifice to claim the right for a piece of land, the exiled elite produced the first piece of great literature expressing the emotion of the "right to return" to one's sacred land).

## Knowledge Constraints and Correct Data

Archeology only becoming a science when Hegel wrote his book on aesthetics, based upon his lectures at the Humboldt University (attended by the young Marx). But, at this time the magnificent cave paintings of the Paleolithic hunter-gatherer had not yet been discovered. This might explain why Hegel (1970) made the mistake of claiming that symbolic art is the earliest of all art forms and that this was the reason why Egyptians preferred symbolic forms of representations This reflects the fact that scientific knowledge works by slow, gradual falsification of beliefs which later turn out to be fiction and not facts (V.4). But in order to separate facts from fiction, the facts have to be known or rather discovered (Pfeiffer, 1982; Lewis-William, 2002). This confirms that knowledge constraints and not physical constraints are critical in S-creativity. Gombrich (1996) makes a similar mistake but probably for other reasons. Having chosen to specialize in the problem of naturalistic art, the problem of meaning raised by students of symbolic art and symbols in general (Langer, 1948/1958; Aachen, 1986) was a niche already occupied by Gombrich's main rival Panofsky (Eribon, 1991/1993; Fausing & Larsen, 1980). Gombrich simply chose to ignore the aesthetic and historical problems of symbols and meaning. Science is probably the type of creativity regime which is closest to Adam Smith's theory of the advantages of functional differentiation (specialization). But as noted by Durkheim (1893/1974), specialization might also be a strategy to reduce the level of competition, making it less "murderous" (giving everyone a chance by cultivating his or her own garden or ecological niche). Such a pattern can also be found in the history of painting (Dutch painters, the contemporary New York school of painting) but these are probably exceptions to the rule. Thus, most European painters tend to choose the opposite strategy of generalization or colonization rather than specialization (compare such cases as Yves Klein and Per Kirkeby). This might also explain why most contemporary American art (Thompson, 2006) seems bereft of feelings ("cool"). As noted by Dewey, 1934/2005, expressing and evoking strong feelings is best done by some kind of holistic approach.

## First Principles of Creativity Science

In order to understand why the psychology of creativity failed to clarify the First principles of creativity "niche"-thinking (Abbott, 2004) is probably the best, most parsimonious explanation. Although some psychologists such as Koestler (1964) and Gruber (1981, 1989) did make detailed studies of how Darwin's theory of evolution evolved, most psychologists of creativity have not dared to enter the field of "the science of science" (Mayr, 1982, 1998) feeling that this is outside their professional (II.3) competence and that they should stick to what they know. This is no way to arrive at "bold conjectures" which is what we have pioneers (II.4) in science for. Niche thinking can take many forms though. Although Simonton has certain written a lot of books and articles on Darwin, he has chosen to foreground only a very small part of the theory, the theory of "natural selection." But natural selection is only a "mechanism" (Elster, 2007). In order to understand how N-creativity works in practice, we need to take into account the fact that Darwin's theory of evolution is a complex, five-factor theory (Mayr 2004/2007).

As Mayr has shown, the core discovery that set Darwin on the track was not "natural selection" – this mechanism can already be found in volume two of Lyell's *Principles of Geology* (which might explain why Lyell failed to understand what Darwin was trying to say, the concept plays very different functions in the two theories) – but "common descent." Common descent was in turn the result of the core distinction between "homology" and "analogy" (Ruse, 2006; Mayr, 2002). What Darwin discovered was that the bone structure of mammals such as apes, whales and bats was structurally similar (homology), although their surface anatomy had clearly adapted to different environments in ways that were very similar (analogy) to animals living in the same type of natural element (water, land, air). This observation was at the heart of all "creationist" theories. Evolutionary theory started with a much deeper understanding of "origins." Later adaption of species never starts from point zero. It always starts from something (common descent, prototype).

The way this works can be illustrated by the history of the psychology of creativity which was launched in the 1950s (Cropley, 2001) and based on the idea that creativity was a kind of "non-conformist" thinking (dissent). This led to the idea that creative minds must have a different personality, the "creative personality" approach (Barron, 1955; Barron & Harrington, 1981). But where do creative personalities come from and how are they to be explained? And how do we define a creative personality in the first place? This led to a rethinking of creativity which looked closer into the role of context (Amabile, 1996). Amabile's most important insight was that what separates highly creative individuals from less creative ones, is that the former avoid the easiest ways to solve problems (cross a labyrinth). They prefer or enjoy the longer, more tricky way. Why, because they obviously take pleasure in such tricky problem solving. This led to the theory of "intrinsic motivation" (pleasure, I.5a) as the dominating factor but also to a rethinking of creativity as a type of motivated problem solving. What was important from the point of view of context, was not to disturb those problem solvers who took their time. "Extrinsic motivation" (pressure, I.5b) should be avoided. Amabile elaborated the model further, admitting that some kind of extrinsic motivation might fare just as well (1997, 1998, but never managed to show how this worked).

These difficulties led to a rethinking of the whole issue and brought about a number of competing paradigms starting in the late 1980s such as Csikszentmihalyi's (1994, 1999) "system's approach," the "family order" approach (Sulloway, 1996), Sternberg's career-oriented "investment" theory approach, Torrance's pedagogical "elaboration" theory approach, etc. What none of these "niche"-driven attempts to clarify the issue managed to solve was the methodological problems of a creative science (First principles). What is the knowledge object of such science? What type of data should we collect? How should these data be analyzed and by what methods etc.?

First of all, there is the problem of what level of creativity should be explained by creativity science. According to Boden (1990), the core knowledge object of creativity science should be the everyday type or normal imaginative problem solving that can be found among all human beings, starting with children and novices (II.1, II.2). For Gardner (1993) the core knowledge object of creativity science should be the extraordinary creativity of advanced thinkers or creative minds (pioneers, II.4). For Csikszentmihalyi (1996), creativity science should focus upon the group in between, professionals (II.3) in different intellectual fields such as science, art and technology, an opinion shared by Sawyer (2006).

Another, more fundamental problem, is what separates a creativity science from other sciences or disciplines which also study creativity but in different ways. In what ways is a psychological approach different from these other approaches? And how do we know that the psychological approach is up to the task in the first place (compare the problem of niche thinking). Perhaps a broad, interdisciplinary approach is necessary (compare Gardner, 1988). But interdisciplinarity as such does not answer the problem, given that each science is defined by its own knowledge object, data and methodology (First principles).

This suddenly makes the methodological problems the key issue. A creativity science is a general science. It cannot only study one form of creativity but needs to compare different forms of creativity such as art and technology (Weisberg, 1993; Sawyer, 2006) with each other. But what about science, should it not be included in our sample as well (Gardner, 1993; Simonton, 1999a, 1999b)? But this raises the unanswered issue of what makes scientific creativity different from technological and artistic creativity (I.4, Dimension V), which certainly goes against niche thinking (let the experts decide). And is it meaningful to make such clear distinctions in the first place (Latour, 1987, 1993)? This problem should be separated from the fact that distinct intellectual fields such as science, art and technology tend to be entangled with each other (co-evolution, III.3), but the even more intriguing paradox that nature and technology, independently of each other (III.2), tend to arrive at almost identical solutions to highly complex problems (Dawkins, 1986/2006; French, 1994). This in turn raises the unsolved problem of the relation between conscious and unconscious or intended and unintended forms of problem solving. These are the type of problems we need a creativity science to ponder upon. But this presupposes a break with niche thinking. From this it does not follow that creativity science must start from scratch ("project Zero"). Nothing in nature starts from scratch (compare the theory of common descent). The point is what prototype to start from and here N-creativity might provide the best answer and why we need to be more critical of how scientists studying this or that form of creativity tend to go about choosing prototypes (I.2) when they seek to answer these types of questions, which again is a methodological issue (everything in science is methodology, V.3).

## Main Discoveries

### 1) Complexity and Paradoxes

A surprising discovery of this book (unintended falsification, V.4,) is that the core of creativity cannot be novelty or originality as usually assumed. Originality only describes pioneering work (II.4). But the fact of independent discovery (rediscovery, convergent evolution) indicates that the core of creativity must be getting it right or arriving at the most parsimonious solution (III.1). This would explain why professionals (II.3) also manage to get it right. They model themselves upon pioneers (prototype, I.2). Novices (II.2) model themselves upon professionals and manage to get it right as well. They are all creative but in different ways.

That creativity is essentially the process of getting it right (Dimension III, "what") is a paradox. But in order to understand how this works, we need to take into account the complexity of creativity. Getting it right means very different things (creativity regimes) and moreover has to be discovered or rediscovered. In technology getting it right (Dimension III) is ultimately constrained by the rule (I.4) or principles of creating facts and adaption (V.4) or survival and reproduction of species. In science, getting it right means falsifying theories and separate facts from fiction (V.4). In art, getting it right means to transform facts into fiction and evoke emotions (V.4).

But in order to explain the complexity of creativity, merely foregrounding the rules (I.4) is not enough. Science, art and technology use different types of problem-solving strategies (V.3). Engineers basically use the strategy of trial and error; artists use techniques and scientists use methodologies. But in order to become a pioneer (II.4) within any given creativity regime, problem-solving strategies are not enough. Pioneers need to be motivated and the most important motivational factor, the one that separates pioneers from both professionals and novices, is opportunity (I.Vc). Moreover, novel ideas are vulnerable. They need to be protected. For this purpose, geographical and intellectual migration (IV.1, IV.2), skunk works and confidants (IV.3, IV.4) and last but not least support systems or helpers (patrons, mentors, agents) are of utmost importance (IV.5). But support systems seem to function very differently in different creative regimes. Moreover, they also function differently within such creativity regimes. In the book I have mainly foregrounded the differences between disciplines and art forms, but a similar analysis can in principle also be made within technology (industries).

### 2) The Disciplined Imagination

As noted above, psychological creativity research tends to divide its attention among different levels of problem-solving capacity. Some creativity researchers are mainly interested in the problem-solving capacity of children or novices (II.1, II.2). Others foreground professional creativity (II.3) and yet more others are interested in explaining the problem-solving capacity of pioneers (II.4, sometimes incorrectly categorized as "geniuses," II.5). A creativity science should be able to explain all three levels of problem-solving capacity. The lack of consensus among psychological creative researchers might perhaps best be explained by the unconscious modeling of creativity science upon some intellectual prototype (discipline) specializing in one of the three levels of creativity.

There is a huge literature on the creativity of children and novices. Indeed what we call educational theory or pedagogy (Bruner, 2006a, 2006b) is basically a science of the creativity of children and novices (II.1, II.2) guided by teachers as professionals (II.3, see Frost, 1997; Starko, 2001; Craft, 2003, 2005, 2007; Tan, 2007). Philosophers are mainly interested in and tend to define P-creativity as H-creativity (pioneering work, II.4). Sociologists are mainly interested in professional levels of creativity (II.3). Economists are mainly interested in technological forms of creativity as are archeologists. The important difference is that economists are mainly interested in the knowledge object of science-based technology, which only began around 1600 with Galileo's discovery of materials science, in turn based upon the falsification of Aristotle's First principles of physics (incorrectly generalized as "the scientific revolution" by historians of science), whereas archeologists have traditionally studied technological tools and inventions in prehistorical, preliterate societies up until the Neolithic revolution. This has left a niche for historians of medieval technology (White, 1964). Such technology was not science based but still existed in societies where science or theoretical thinking has played an important role since 600 BC starting in ancient Greece.

### 3) The Poverty of Social Constructionism

The knowledge object (V.2) of the humanities are two main types of human creativity, artistic forms of creativity and linguistic creativity. Some disciplines such as art history, architecture, literary theory and criticism, theater studies and film studies foreground one or another art form as its knowledge object. Languages are studied by many disciplines divided into departments such as English, Spanish, French, German, Slavonic and other languages. Language has also been studied by philosophers (*la langue, le parole*). The idea that art is a kind of language therefore comes natural for the humanistic disciplines, but this combination of art and language does not necessarily provide the proper methodology (V.3) to study say scientific and technological forms of creativity (for a critique, see Popper, 1994a) nor is it helpful to study the creativity of nature. Indeed, the lack of a theory of N-creativity is the black hole of both the humanities and the social sciences. But if Lyell could not understand how N-creativity works, how can we expect a Weber, Foucault, Lyotard and Deleuze to understand how this works?

Humanities Scholars are not the only ones who have been unable to absorb the lessons of evolutionary biology and sociobiology. The concept of "social construction" launched by Berger and Luckmann (1966) also tends to shun naturalistic explanations. But the rejection of naturalistic explanations of cultural phenomena is not convincing for several reasons:

1) Biological instincts are not "weak" as Berger & Luckmann assume (First principle), biological instincts are very strong and can most probably be explained by the total helplessness of the human child. The human child needs to be protected as it grows up to become a biologically nature individual, which means that much of what we call

"society" (families, education, morals, law) are fundamentally structured by the need to protect vulnerable versions of the human species (later extended to adults and the elderly, the "welfare state"). This physical constraint (I.1) of the human child to a large extent constrains the core of societies, what sociologists call "moral order" (Parsons, 1937/1968; Gouldner, 1973/1979; Therborn, 1977; Etzioni, 1988).

2) The moral dimensions of societies are essentially conservative. In contrast science, art and technology tend to be innovative. Sociologists are trained to look with suspicion at anything that smacks of modernity (compare Tönnies's distinction between "community" and "society" and Durkheim's famous analysis of the reasons why individuals commit suicide; egoism and anomie beats altruism). This conservative streak might ultimately explain why there is no sociology of creativity and why sociologists studying science, art and technology are notoriously uninterested in the cognitive (problem-solving) aspects of knowledge and in a self-defensive mode tend to foreground issues related to the struggle for social recognition (Honneth, 1992) such as "presentations of self" (Goffman, 1959), "symbolic capital" (Bourdieu, 1974a, 1974b), "strong program (Bloor, 1976; Barnes et al., 1996), "actor-networks" (Latour, 2005), etc.

3) A special version of the moral conservatism of sociology is the "social forces" model introduced by Durkheim (Lukes, 1972; Giddens, 1972, 1979a). Thus, White in *Careers and Creativity. Social Forces in the Arts,* argues that stylistic revolutions (V.2) can best be explained as an effect of social forces in society. In his study *Suicide,* Durkheim mentions a special form of moral order or rather disorder, namely anomie. This sociological theory serves as prototype (I.2) for White's theory of "social forces." White's theory essentially reduces or seeks to account for the stylistic revolution of the Impressionists by foregrounding the particular type of anomie (prototype, I.2) that comes from the overcrowding of artistic labor markets (White & White, 1965/1993). This anomie or overcrowding presumably puts pressure (I.5b) on artists to innovate, hence Impressionism can be explained by this particular "social force."

The problem with this explanation is that it does not fit the facts at all. Only very few (less than 10) artists constituted the group of Impressionists. Pioneering work, as Collins (1998) noted, is better described by the apt phrase "law of small numbers." But in order to explain this law, we would need a method (V.3) which is better adapted to the knowledge object (V.2), in this case stylistic innovations (V.2). But for such methods to work we need the correct data (I.1). Perhaps a better sample than studying the many novices (II.2) trying to become mere professionals (II.3) would be to select a few pioneers (II.4) for a close comparative study, based upon mainly biographical data (compare Chapter 8).

4)   Class interests, social status and parties, the core aspects of social stratification in modern societies foregrounded by Max Weber (1948b) are ultimately also rooted in biology. The long period necessary to transform totally helpless children into individuals who can take responsibility for their own life in modern or late-modern societies, has not weakened but on the contrary tended to strengthen the strong social ties between parents and children. Families are far from dead (compare Bertaux & Delcroiz, 2000). Globalization processes have made each and every one more aware of the indisputable fact that filial ties play a far stronger role in the moral order than social constructionist theories allow us to admit (the rhetoric of political correctness).

### 4)   The Ambiguity of the "System's Model" of Creativity

As noted by Ericsson (1999) the "system's model" of creativity (Csikszentmihalyi, 1988, 1994, 1999) is basically adapted to the problem situation of professionals (II.3). The model evolved from Amabile's (1982) model for measuring creativity, but since Amabile's research program (Lakatos, 1978) was mainly interested in children (II.1) or novices (II.2), it foregrounded "intrinsic motivation" (pleasure. I.5a) as the critical dimension (Amabile, 1989). Csikszentmihalyi needed a model which also included the role of extrinsic motivation (struggle for social recognition, pressure, I.5b) and this is how he arrived at his system's theory (Csikszentmihalyi, 1999; Sawyer, 2006). In contrast, Amabile never managed to solve the ambiguity between these two types of motives, pleasure (I.5a) and pressure (I.5b, see Amabile, 1996, 1997).

   The problem with both models is that the role of opportunity (I.5c) as a constraining motivational factor tends to disappear. But the opportunity factor as we have seen is what separates mere professionals (II.3) from pioneers (II.4). Opportunities provided a new type of motivation which made the pioneering work of Thomsen, Darwin, Einstein, Freud, Crick and Watson, Goodall but also Gauguin, Matisse, Picasso, Chagall, Kirkby possible. In contrast, Csikszentmihalyi's model evolved out of the need to understand what motivates professionals and here Flow (pleasure) is only one of the motivational factors. Pressure to innovate is another (compare the female writer who felt a need to write about the problems of career women mentioned in Csikszentmihalyi, 1996).

But there is also another problem with the system's model, the one developed by Howard Gardner and Mihalyi Csikszentmihalyi together (Gardner, 1987). But the core interest of Gardner is how to explain the creativity of pioneers (II.4), mainly in avant-garde art and not professionals (II.3). Czikszentmihalyi's model was developed in order to study the motivational issues (intrinsic and extrinsic) that drive professionals. Gardner's model of the "seven intelligences" (1983, 1993) was developed in order to study how and why some creative minds manage to solve the types of tricky problems that call for pioneering work. But for pioneering work to be possible, opportunity (I.5c) and not merely pleasure (I.5a) and pressure (I.5b) have to be taken into consideration.

But opportunities do not derive from nothing. They tend to take the form of protection of vulnerable ideas (Dimension V) and in praxis depend upon support systems (V.5) such as the Fulbright program that made it possible for Sylvia Plath to study in Cambridge where she met a new mentor, Ted Hughes, helping her to become a better poet, or the private wealth of Darwin's father which made it possible for Darwin both to spend five years traveling around the earth and 20 years trying to prove what he had discovered.

Gardner and Csikszentmihalyi basically studied two different things. Scientific explanations need to be watertight (Mokyr, 2002). In contrast, the combined Csikszentmihalyi/Gardner model "leaks." One of the reasons why it leaks is that recognition of the creativity of pioneers tends to be more irregular and drawn out than routine recognition of the creativity of professionals (compare the delayed social recognition of the Impressionists, which seems to follow the "thirty years rule" mentioned by Popper 1999). The other is that the role of opportunities (I.5c) as well as helpers (V.5) in the case of pioneers need to be theorized to understand pioneering work.

But leaving out these factors also creates difficulties in describing the process of social recognition of the two levels of creativity. The rules of science, art and technology (I.4) are constrained differently. Science is here to separate facts from fiction and falsify theories (V.4). Its problem-solving strategy is methodology (V.3). In contrast, artists use techniques (V.3) in order to evoke emotions and transform facts into fiction (V.4). None of these aspects is conceptualized or clarified in the combined

Csikszentmihalyi/ Gardner model. The model talks about "individual contributions" made to "intellectual domains." The value of these contributions (social recognition) is supposedly decided by "social fields." But in the model, "social fields" live in a completely different world from intellectual domains. The former represents the "extra personal" (sociology) and the latter the "sub-personal" (biology). Gardner also mentions two more dimensions, the "personal" and the "multi-personal." But strangely these two have no place in the model. This is because Gardner ends up reducing both the personal (biographies) and multi-personal (traditions, disciplines, fields) into the sub-personal (death of the author and culture) but also because Csikszentmihalyi ends up reducing social fields to symbolic capital, ignoring Bourdieu's more complex theory: economic, educational, social and symbolic capital. Bourdieu's theory in practice is very similar to the concept support system. Symbolic capital is a result of economic (patrons), educational (mentors) and social (agents) capital (type of helpers).

But as we have seen, support systems function very differently not only between science, art and technology. They also function differently within art forms themselves. Thus, the support systems for painting are very different from the support system for literature which in turn is very different from the support system of filmmaking, etc.

But in order to see how this works, we need a representative sample (data V.1). In order to construct a representative sample, we need to define the knowledge object properly (V.2). But if we look at the artists chosen by Gardner in *Creating Minds*, they all happen to be avant-garde artists and all basically follow the prototype (I.2) of Picasso. But pioneers in art outside painting are rarely avant-garde artists. They are pioneers within their respective art form, but this does not make them avant-garde artists.

A defining criterion of avant-garde artists (painters) is incomprehensibility. But the leading pioneers of twentieth-century filmmaking such as Chaplin, Hitchcock and Bergman did not try to be incomprehensible. Their visual narratives strived for clarity, which made it easy to follow for mass audiences. Most pioneering novelists (Austen, Hemingway, Sartre, Orwell) and playwrights (Chekhov, Ibsen, Strindberg, Miller) follow this pattern. They are not avant-garde artists but great popular artists. But why has not one great popular artist been found worthy of being included in Gardner's sample?

For this purpose, we need to look closer at the theoretical framework from which Gardner has collected his sample, the theory of "multiple intelligences" (1983). The theory is basically an application of cognitive science which has functioned as a prototype (I.2) for Gardner's theory of how intelligences are rooted in the human mind. But this cannot be right. Novelists and playwrights read and write texts but reading and writing is a relatively recent invention in human history. Filmmaking is even more recent. It is based upon a scientific discovery made possible but the invention of photography (knowledge constraint, I.3), of the perceptual limits of the human eye which cannot distinguish images if their speed of presentation exceeds 16 per second.

A First principle of the cognitive-science approach to creativity is that all the intellectual facilities humans need to be creative, are already instilled or "hardwired" (Donald, 2001,) into the human mind (Donald, 2001) by evolution (nature). But as Dawkins (2005) notes, nature is basically opportunistic. It cannot foresee the future. Nature could not foresee the Neolithic revolution which led to the discovery of metallurgy (Killick, 2000), a type of creativity nature never uses (French, 1994), nor cold nature foresee the birth of science, aiming for theoretical knowledge or knowledge for its own sake.

There is also the problem of selecting only avant-garde artists in order to clarify how art works. Art is here to evoke emotions, but avant-garde art is intentionally incomprehensible, in order to appreciate such art works, they have first to be interpreted (Sontag, 1969). It is highly doubtful that say the Paleolithic cave painters expected such a distanced, "academic" or "pedagogical" approach to art. All art probably derives from the need to express emotions by simple gestural language (performances) which can already be found among our closest relatives, the chimpanzees (Mead, 1934/1967: van Lawick-Goodall, 1971). But there is nothing in the human brain itself which preprograms it to master the techniques of naturalistic paintings, invented some 25,000 years ago. Why is it that children even today find such techniques difficult to master? Why do they tend to lose interest in art when this type of artistic technique (V.3) is required of them (Vygotsky, 1995)?

## What is Avant-Garde Art?

Perhaps the trickiest part of creativity science is making sense of art, in particular avant-garde art, which is both very different from previous art (paintings) and nevertheless the same (the problem of "continuity," see Weisberg, 1993). I do not want to pretend that I have come very far in this venture, only that I have learned something such as the fact that most late-modern paintings tend to be about painting (flat surface, colors, lines, shapes, shadow, pattern, figures, painterly space, the use of frames, background, what is visible from the front and not visible when one looks at the painting from the back, what a painting represents if it represents something other than itself, etc.). Both the act of painting (process, see Pollock's action paintings) and the result (product, see Rothko's Color Field paintings) have increasingly become the "content" of painting, to which the chosen form has to be adapted.

Combining form with content is the core formal constraint of art and helps us explain why artists are preoccupied with "composition" (V.2) which is precisely the problem of combining the two (Barr, 1943/1974) For this purpose painters tend to use prototypes (I.2). They never start from scratch (see Josephson, 1941/1991 for a systematic study of this problem based upon historical cases). But such choices are themselves controlled by the problem situation (III.4). Changing historical and professional constraints but also personal constraints help us to better understand how this works in practice. The idea of paintings on painting is far from new (most motifs rarely are). Velásquez's *Las Meninas* is an early case, but it was untypical for the time. Nevertheless, it was typical in the sense that the painting illustrates the strongly personal relationship between patron and artist in painting, which is manifested in the support system (IV.5, V.3) which has, at least since the Renaissance, always been in the form of an elite of connoisseurs (Baxandall, 1972) rather than mass audiences appreciating and supporting the painter. But why this is indeed the case, has rarely been investigated in detail. For this purpose, a constraint theory might be of value.

### Avant-garde Art and Scientific Revolutions

Painting is based upon certain material constraints and physical constraints (V.1, I.1) typical for this art form. The personal relationship between patron and artist, comes out strongly in Françoise Gilot's co-written (Gilot & Lake, 1964/1981) autobiography on her 10 years spent with Picasso, Barr's (1953/1976) study of Matisse and Steffensen's (2017) biography of Kirkeby. Strangely, this aspect and the problem of patronage of painters as a constraint of artistic creativity is completely absent in Foucault's chapter on Velásquez's painting in his book *The Order of Things* (translation of *Les Mots et les Choses*) as if the ambiguity of the painting (sign, word) did not somehow reflect the ambiguous feelings (Merton, 1976) of the artist towards his patron (real world, thing).

One might ask what the analysis of a painting from 1656 has to do with a book on scientific revolutions from the same period, given that the professional problem situation of scholars is different from painters, unless the book intends to discuss this problem (III.4), which is certainly not the case. Foucault's book does mention the problem of disciplines in the making (compare Chapter 1) but these are completely impersonalized as well. This might reflect differences in the support systems in science and art but given that the nature of these support systems (IV.5) are not discussed, Foucault's method (V.3) makes it difficult to say whether this is indeed the case or not. Why is it that the support system in science tends to be even more impersonal as say the relationship between the publisher and writer in fiction? Foucault's widely talked about but rarely read (Eribon, 1991), intentionally unreadable book *Les Mots et Les Choses,* is based upon the rediscovery (III.2) of Saussure's printed lectures from the First World War on the contingency of words and things. For the author of *Les Mots et Les Choses,* Saussure's theory of the presumably contingent relations between "words" and "things" is treated as a revelation or insight, helping us to explain what happened in a few selected disciplines in the same historical (classical period) in which Velásquez's picture was painted. But Saussure's theory is not strictly about words and things. The word "chien" in France, does not refer to any single concrete living or dead dog. It refers to the abstract meaning or concept "dog" (Sholes, 1981).

Where did Saussure get this idea from? Probably from Plato's theory of forms. In contrast to Aristotle, for whom forms or abstract categories (concepts, V.2) were merely convenient summaries of living and dead individual members of the same species, for Plato it was the opposite. Individual members of the same species, such as "dogs," were merely imperfect imitations of the ideal form of what a dog should look like. Such ideal forms were perfect and unchanging, and the job of science (or philosophy) was to discover these ideal or perfect forms which were inaccessible to ordinary humans. Ideal forms were essentially divine (just as celestial phenomena); hence they must have been created by Godlike creatures (it is difficult not to see the parallel between this Platonic idea of ideal forms and Kant's theory of art as genius or divine).

But Plato had been dead a long time when Saussure held his lectures on "La Langue." It is hence more probable that he relied upon Kant's updated version of Platonic epistemology. This can best be seen as an abstract version of Linnaeus' eighteenth-century biology, still within the "classical period" in which Foucault was an expert, having written a doctoral dissertation on the history of psychiatry during this period during the years he worked at the French Institute in Uppsala, the town where Linnaeus is everywhere to be seen. But Kant's "taxonomic" philosophy in turn clearly leans upon Linnaeus (prototype, I.2). A core idea of Kant was that ontological issues, the nature of material things (V.1) is inaccessible for the human mind ("das Ding an Sich"). The human mind is basically a categorizing machine, but the operative principles for categorization rest solely in the human mind (this "Kantian" principle as we know is also the First principle of cognitive science).

Where did Kant get his idea from? The best possible candidate (prototype, I.2) is the Swedish taxonomic botanist Carl Linnaeus. For Linnaeus the question of how plants or species in general had come to this earth (the problem of the origins of species) was not a problem of concern for the scientist. Species had been created by an omniscient God, and it was not the business of scientists to ask how and why. The job of the scientist or botanist was to walk around in "God's garden" and merely categorize and classify what he saw. Categorizing and classifying was a pure epistemic operation. It had nothing to do with ontological issues. In principle, any kind of system of categorization was possible. The relation between taxonomy (words) and reality (things) was purely contingent. Systems of categorizations ware hence merely languages just as national languages (French, German, English), etc. For a French speaker "chien" (signifier) refers to the abstract meaning or category (signified) that English speakers call "dog" and German speakers call "hund." Together they constitute a "sign" which is not of this world but completely a prisoner of language (a "word" and not a "thing" which, standing outside language, remains inaccessible, das "Ding and sich").

But this is clearly a pre-Darwinian understanding of science. Nowhere in *Les Mots and Les Choses* does Foucault refer to this fact, nor that it was Darwin who proved that Linnaeus's *Systema Naturae* was not as contingent as it looked. The hierarchy of levels discovered by Linnaeus in reality reflects the evolution of species, the hierarchy of species was the role model (I.2) for Darwin's principle of "common descent." Darwin's evolutionary theory and methodology does not support a contingency theory of creativity; it is a constraint theory of creativity. Nature, in contrast to the imagined Creator ("God," in reality a kind of super engineer of the type that designed the Egyptian pyramids; the Jews who were slaves under Pharaoh probably got the idea of Yahweh from this prototype, I.2) is able to solve the most complex problems given enough time.

Another curious assumption in Linnaeus' methodology, uncritically copied by Foucault, is that science is here not to explain empirical data, but merely to categorize them (compare Kuhn's "taxonomic solution"). But this cannot be right. The first empirical scientists Thales (Furberg, 1969; Lloyd, 1970), did not only note the phenomenon of regularly occurring tides but wanted to explain their causes. The problem remained unsolved though until Newton managed to falsify Aristotle's false assumption that that gravity is a mere local force (III.4). The long history of physics falsifies not only Linnaeus and Foucault's claim that science is only here to categorize (it cannot and should not try to explain empirical patterns). It also falsifies a number of Kuhn's assumptions: (1) that scientific revolutions are not a cognitive but a linguistic phenomenon; (2) that science revolutions do not explain anything; they merely categorize things; (3) that the problem of demarcation is a political phenomenon, the fact that Aristotle's false theory dominated for almost 2,000 years is proof enough that physics was already a science 300 BC; (4) that falsification does not play any important role in science; (5) that the logics of scientific revolutions are similar to artistic revolutions (cyclical, repetitive); (6) pioneering scientists do not attempt to solve problems, only professionals (normal science) do.

## Ontology and Epistemology

Most attempts to cope with Kuhn's false theories of scientific revolutions have ignored not only Kuhn's intellectual biography, prototype and confusion of artistic and scientific revolutions but also the clear parallels between him and Foucault. But as Darwin showed, the theory of evolution was not a mere "word" imprisoned in language. In evolutionary theory, concept and knowledge object are two aspects of the same thing (V.2). The great advantage of this prototype (I.2) is that it allows us to falsify Kant's, Saussure's and Foucault's contrived distinction between words and things, epistemology and ontology. Take language. Physical constants are not merely linguistic phenomena (forms of human communication). Such communication is itself contained by physical constraints (local dialects). When analyzing art works, we also need to take into account their physical form (Stecker, 2003; Davies, 2003). Not only are the "means of production" costly and raise the entrance barrier for becoming an artist. The work of art (aimed at evoking emotions, final cause, V.4) has to be an "original" in the physical sense and not a mere copy or it will automatically lose value.

Language and the world are intimately connected. It is only when we spend most of our time in archives and give lectures to the Collège de France based upon such close studies of texts, including the lecture manuscript we hold in our hand, that we can come to believe the illusion that only texts (words) matter. When so much time is spent reading texts, it tends to be forgotten who wrote what. This might be the simple explanation of the popularity of the theory of the "death of the author" among humanistic academics and teachers in general. In order to wake up from this dream world, comparing paintings (artifacts) with books (texts) might be a good start.

Why is it that "signature" and "originals" play such an important role in painting but not in literature? Signature becomes a problem to be settled in those cases where there is strong doubt or a suspicion that the artwork or artifact is not made by the artist This problem does not exist in literature. Owing to the length of the novel, it is impossible to copy it without anyone noticing it. That is easy to understand. But what about the problem of originals? The pleasure of reading a novel does not suffer the least from being copied from the original manuscript sent to the publisher. Such books are routinely mass produced and reprinted over and over again without losing value as aesthetic experience (such as novels by Jane Austen, Ernest Hemingway and George Orwell). The do not lose their "aura" by "mechanical reproduction." Art works do, why?

A copy of Mona Lisa is just a copy and almost worthless. The real excitement and pleasure ("aura") derives from being in the presence of the real thing, the physical original (even the physical reality of being close to Leonardo's most famous painting is enough to create aesthetic pleasure and excitement). For the anonymous reader of fiction, the pleasure comes from intermittent reading. Any copy will do, even a cheap paperback or borrowing it from a friend or a library. Lack of physical presence to the original has no effect at all on the aesthetic pleasure of reading the novel. Original manuscripts by famous writers are usually sold to or donated to university libraries, where researchers might access them. But anyone can afford to buy a novel (or just go into a public library and wait until it is your turn). Only wealthy people or established professionals dream of entering a gallery and ask to see and possibly buy an original painting.

Nevertheless, something has changed in the art world, and this has something to do with the fact that most paintings today resemble Velásquez' *Las Meninas*. They are paintings about paintings. Why this is indeed the case is still a problem that has been poorly understood. Some art theories argue that modern art reflects modern societies. Thus the "speed" of modern means of transportation such as cars and airplanes and more generally machine aesthetics have been foregrounded both by the "futurists" and the "purists" (Le Corbusier's critique of Cubism). But then how do we explain the opposite tendency, the turn to "Primitivism," which seems to celebrate primitive societies or rather which is imagined to be associated with primitivism, properties such as being fresh, raw, brutal, instinctive, natural, childish, etc.?

## Problem Situations

Support systems (IV.5, V.3) might be a possible explanation, but they have changed. What changed them? Already Renaissance artists worked for wealthy and powerful patrons who commissioned art works, mostly of the religious type (Welch, 1984; Murray & Murray, 1963). Twentieth-century artists are also ultimately supported by wealthy and powerful patrons (Rauterberg, 2007) including public or private commissions. So, what has changed? How do we explain the appearance of new professions such as art gallerists, art critics and art curators (the "art world")? The evolution of art curators seems to have something to do with the fact that the new techniques (V.3) aim at a type of connoisseurship which has to be educated or trained. Art works can no longer be taken in at one glance. They have to be interpreted in order to give rise to aesthetic appreciation. The new discipline "semiotics" (Eco, 1979) might have co-evolved (III.3) precisely for this purpose. Just as Newton's universal theory of gravity became the common language of the ruling classes in England that inaugurated the industrial revolution, semiotics has become the language of the cultural elite which has arisen to interpret avant-garde art (art gallerists, art critics, art theorists, art historians, art curators, etc.).

But this change in the support system (IV.5) is closely related to the need to interpret the techniques of avant-garde artists (V.3). It does not come out of nothing but has to be explained as well. For the purpose looking at another factor, the co-evolution (III.3) of painting with two new, typically modern art forms (photography and cinema) provides additional data (V.1) which can clarify the nature of the changed problem situation (III.4). The appearance of these new, late-modern art forms, for some reason fundamentally changed not only the historical but also the professional problem situation of art (compare Roe's, 2015 remark that 1906, the year Picasso began on the painting that would become *Les Demoiselles d'Avignon*, the city of Paris "exploded with cinemas").

But if this is indeed that case, if painting as art form has basically been under pressure to innovate (I.5b) due to the appearance of new and threatening modern art forms unknown in the previous evolution of art, one might ask how the turn to "Primitivism" might help. Is this not a self-defeating strategy? Not necessarily, for this purpose we need to look at the close relations between (1) material and physical constraints (V.1, I.1) and

(2) paintings as the predominant motif of painting which constrains compositional choice (V.2). These aspects in turn seem to come together in (3) the close relationship between the choice of techniques (V.3) and support systems (IV.5).

First, Primitivism alienates lay audiences but not necessary connoisseurs. It provides rich patrons with a new strategy of distinction (Platonic epistemology, appeal to the refined taste of a cultural aristocracy, which is both refined and brutal at the same time, compare Nietzsche's distinction between slave morality and the morality of heroes or supermen). Second, in order for these rich patrons to feel like supermen, they have to be educated in order to be able to aesthetically appreciate modern paintings. Third, this in turn calls for new mediating professions like art gallerists, art critics and art curators who are expert on techniques (V.3) of both traditional and modern forms of art, given that modern art is so often based upon the rediscovery (III.2) of previous styles in art history (the role of the tradition increases rather than diminishes, compare Steffensen, 2017). Fourth, this new support system, as it becomes institutionalized, evolves its own strategy of distinction which is precisely "painting on painting," as the dominating motif and accompanying problem of composition (V.2), adapting form to content.

The problem situation for fiction writers looks very different. The distinct physical (I.1) or material (V.1) constraints of distinct art forms, explains why novelists (unless they choose to become avant-garde novelist like Gertrude Stein, Virginia Woolf and Susan Sontag) can in principle replace the normal support system for becoming a professional artist by learning to write part time, using skunk works (IV.3) to solve the problem of patronage. Popular writers in contrast accept the constraints of the media and work from here. Take the case of George Orwell. Having been educated at Eton (Orwell, 1947/1968) (Shelden, 1991), Eric Blair spent some years working as a police officer for the British Empire in Burma (Orwell, 1931/1968a). Both these two early life experiences influenced Orwell's choice of artistic medium (literature). Once he had decided to become a professional writer (II.3), he spent some years learning the craft of writing, mainly in Paris (Crick, 1980) and in London (Orwell, 1931/1968b).

The result of the early experiences as a novice (II.2) are documented in Orwell's first novel *Down and out in Paris and London*. Given that he had quit his job, he needed to support himself, which he did partly be working as a dishwasher in different restaurants in Paris. But he also had an aunt with literary interests who probably functioned as both patron, mentor and agent (IV.5). Back in London, having finished his first novel, *Down and out in Paris and London,* Orwell (who was still known as Eric Blair at the time) contacted a literary agent who in turn helped him to find the right publisher, another type of agent (IV.5). Although Orwell was now a published writer, he had not yet created the mass audience of anonymous readers necessary to sustain a professional career as a writer (Edström, 2002). In contrast to Scandinavian writers, who might be offered stipends after publishing their first novel (historical and professional problem situation, III.4), Orwell had to continue doing skunk work in order to finance his writing career.

For some years he worked as schoolteacher and shop assistant until his literary reputation got him jobs as a journalist and reviewer of books. This is the usual sign of having become a professional writer (Burgess, 1990). Orwell published a number of novels and essays during these years as a professional writer (II.3). His transformation to a great writer (pioneer, II.4) only came with his two post-Second World War novels *Animal Farm* and *1984,* both of which relate previous experiences (fact into fiction, V.4). One was his previous disillusion with communism after his experiences as a volunteer in the Spanish Civil War, previously told in a naturalistic fashion in *Homage to Catalonia* (but this time around as a fable or in a symbolic manner). The other was his years as a reader of propaganda for the BBC during the Second World War (fact, Orwell, 1985), which Orwell transformed into emotionally evoking fiction (V.4) in his futuristic novel *Nineteen Eighty-Four.*

Whereas it is in practice impossible to pursue a career as artist (painter) and support oneself with other jobs, one has to choose one or the other (Kupferberg, 2012a), the case of Orwell proves beyond doubt that writers of fiction are more flexible in their choice of profession. Philip Roth, a highly successful writer, eventually chose to become a full-time writer as did Norman Mailer (Mills, 1982/1983). Joyce Carol Oates has continued to teach literature and Saul Bellow never stopped teaching either, although he began writing and publishing novels relatively early in his career (Leader 2015). Céline also continued to work as a doctor (Vitoux, 1992) in spite of his great success with his first stylistically groundbreaking novel, *Journey to the End of the Night.* In contrast, both Sartre and Simone de Beauvoir left teaching after a few years. Why did they do so? Most interpretations of the two writers see them as representatives of a new type of "engaged litera-ture" where moral or ethical questions about the responsibility of the individual is foregrounded. Such problems reflected the historical problem situation after the Second World War, when many French intellectuals had collaborated with the Nazis. Recent studies (Rowley, 2005; Seymour-Jones, 2008) reveal that the two writers were basically apolitical both when they became writers and during the war. The language of literature was changing in the 1930s. Publishers (agents) were on the look-out for new "voices" (Engdahl, 1994/2005). They were both bored with teaching (professional personal reality) and wanted to experiment with new types of romantic relationships (private-problem situation). For both these personal purposes, being a writer seemed to be perfect which in turn corroborates that facts matter in science, whereas fiction is here to transform facts into anything we would like the world to be or look like.

But none of them would have become writers without support systems. The Sorbonne and the École Normale Superieure, two elite French educational institutions, provided them with mentors and agents to help them pursue a literary career. The teaching jobs permitted them to do skunk works (secrecy protected by unknowing patrons). But having been educated in philosophy not literature, caused them considerable difficulties at the beginning and explains why the two literary figures had such difficulties in getting it right (Dimension III). Biographical data matter, not death of the author.

Sartre's and Simone de Beauvoir's case also illustrates the complexity and paradoxes of creativity. For this purpose, the method of contrasting comparisons across intellectual fields is helpful. Sartre and Simone de Beauvoir covered three fields: philosophy (theoretical knowledge), teaching (practical knowledge), literature (productive knowledge). But there are many ways to become a writer. In contrast there is only one way to become a painter. Artists who have not attended art school are exceptional cases. Why this is the case is yet another reason why we need a creativity science.

The role that educational credentials (symbolic capital) played in Sartre's and Simone de Beauvoir's case is exceptional for writers' careers, but it is normal for artistic careers In order to become an artist, educational credentials are necessary. Having had the right "mentors" (compare Picasso, Chagall and Kirkeby) seems to be the decisive criterion for accumulating the necessary "symbolic capital" (Bourdieu, 1974a, 1974b) to become a professional artist in the sense of being able to live off and not only for art (Kupferberg, 2012a). Mentoring is what creates the feeling of being in the same "in-group" (Sumner, 1906/1960). The lack of such educational credentials might have put pressure (I.5b) on Matisse, Gauguin, van Gogh, all latecomers in painting to "innovate" (Lipset, 1979; Coser, 1967) in order to prove themselves worthy (such pressure can also be found among immigrant and female entrepreneurs, see Kupferberg, 2003c, 2004).

Pioneering scholars might also sometimes be put under pressure (I.5b) to prove themselves by innovation. Compare the case of Crick and Watson. The former was a latecomer in his scientific career. He mainly worked at the Cavendish Laboratory to finish his Ph.D. at an age when people normally started a family (Olby, 2009). Watson, who had a Ph.D. in zoology (he had also studied genetics) also felt under pressure to prove himself. In his case though he needed something more to show, given that his fiancé was the daughter of Ernst Mayr, the doyen of biology at Harvard University (Watson, 2001). Darwin probably felt under similar pressure (I.5b) during his five years traveling on the *Beagle* and this might very well have contributed to his discovery of evolutionary theory. Nevertheless, the decisive factor in both cases was probably opportunity (I.5c). Compare the case of Jane Goodall who had no immediate plans to marry, but only later and mostly for practical reasons.

Matisse and Picasso probably also felt under pressure to prove themselves. Matisse needed to convince his father (main private patron) that he had chosen the right career. Picasso's father had been not only his patron but also his prime mentor and agent (Cowling, 2002), which might explain why his pressure to innovate might have been stronger than Matisse's. Matisse ended up as a "decorative painter," a role emphatically rejected by the abstract expressionists following in the footsteps of the Cubists for whom formal problems of composition (V.2) and innovative material techniques of painting (V.3) were seen as more important than evoking emotions (V.4; see Greenberg, 1961/1965; Rothko, 2004; cf. Barr, 1953/1976). The pressure to innovate (I.5b) might also come from other sources such as not being able to speak the language properly (Coser, 1984; Cowling, 2002), but also ethnic, religious, racial minority status (Gay, 1988; Ostow, 1982; Kupferberg, 1998a). Moreover, the awareness of being a latecomer can itself function as pressure to innovate (compare Orwell and Gauguin); in this case the basic feeling or motive is the need to "catch-up," Veblen, 1962, 1968). In all these cases a constraint theory approach to creativity might be helpful.

CHAPTER 8

# Data, Methods and Constraints

## Retrospective Analysis

Creativity science is basically a historical science and the cases to be selected should be analyzed retrospectively. This might cause problems in border cases. Was Steven Spielberg a pioneer or merely a good and successful professional (Schickel, 2012)? In order to avoid these difficulties, we might start by identifying artists who have achieved the status of great film artists such as Ingmar Bergman, Charlie Chaplin and Alfred Hitchcock. Using such data, we find that all the three seemed to have been able to protect vulnerable versions by one or several of the factors mentioned in Chapter 5 (geographical isolation, intellectual migration, secrecy and confidants, support systems).

An interesting case is Albert Hirschman. He began his career as a student of underdevelopment in particular in Latin American countries (Mendelosi, 1995; Adelman, 2013). Why could the countries in this particular continent not catch up fast as Germany did and as well as some countries in South East Asia (Corbridge, 1995)? Hirschman's investigations led him to develop the theory of "complementary competencies" – a concept later borrowed, prototype (I.2) or possibly independently rediscovered (III.2) by Nathan Rosenberg, a pioneer (II.4) of the economics of technology – as one explanation for the lack of catch-up capacity in Latin America (Hirschman, 1956, 1963, 1967). The other was lack of political and economic attention (degree of responding, Asplund, 1987) to the needs of voters or customers, seen as having similar functions (Hirschman, 1970).

Hirschman later went on to make a number of pioneering studies about the origins of economics as a discipline (Why and how did the warm concept "passion" disappear from of economics and be replaced by the cold concept "interest"?, see Hirschman, 1977). Here his early literary training in a Berlin Gymnasium (novice II.2) was of importance for him becoming a pioneer (II. 4) in the general discipline of economics. But his comparative knowledge of how Western and development economies work probably also helped him to take up other difficult issues which economics has tended to marginalize such as the entanglements of economic and political aspects of welfare states. How can welfare states strike a balance between the problem of social justice to which the government is committed and economic efficiency, to which economics as discipline has been committed ever since its founder, Adam Smith (1982, 1986). In the last part of his career, Hirschman became interested in more general issues of scientific creativity such as the difficulties but also the potential rewards of interdisciplinary thinking (1995, 2001). Again, the complexity should be foregrounded. This highly innovative social scientist was both a geographical (IV.1) and intellectual migrant (IV.2), trained in several disciplines (literature, economics, politics). As such, he was constantly engaged in "skunk works" (IV.3) but he was also assisted by support system (IV.5), which helped him solve the core problem of pioneers to protect vulnerable versions from premature death (he does not seem to have used confidants (IV.4) like Darwin, Freud, and Einstein but resembled Karl Popper and Victor Hugo more).

## Biographies and Autobiographies

Dismissed by standard methods in the social sciences (Bourdieu 2000; Kuhn 1962/1970), such biographical details are of great value for creativity science. Interestingly the use of biographical data is also routinely dismissed in the humanities although humanties in practice studies different forms of artistic creativity (art, film, literature, etc.). How do we explain this methodological (IV.3) behavioral pattern? Part of the dismissal of biographical data (V.1) might be explained by the confusion of facts and fiction (V.4) typical for postmodernist thinking (Lamarque & Olsen, 1994). Thus Bain (2001) claims that there are no such things as biographical facts, given that all such facts are in principle disputable and hence a kind of fiction.

But this ignores two things: (1) there is a special genre of (Bakhtin, 1986b) artistic and literary biographies, which try to separate fiction from fact (Edel 1973). (2) The main reason that most literary theorists and art historians (compare Gombrich, 1996) tend to look down upon this genre might be a case of what Elster (1983) called "sour grapes." Take the genre of literary biography. This genre is in practice inaccessible for most academics because it requires a support system (IV.5) of its own, which comes from the publishing industry rather than academia. In contrast, the support system in academia makes it almost impossible to engage in such very long projects with dubious social recognition as an anticipated reward. The more books and articles that an academic publishes the more it increases their chances of promotion and it is therefore important for academic CVs. But what about the booming academic industry on Sylvia Plath? A possible explanation for this exception might be a combination of the marketing concerns of publishers and career concerns of academics. Moreover most of the relevant biographical details were published early (Butcher, 1976/2003) and there is also a lot of other materials (diaries, letters, literary works) that have been made easily accessible and well known, allowing Sylvia Plath scholars to do what they do best, select a special niche and work from there.

It so happens that literary and artistic biographers also sometimes quote autobiographical sources (compare Wullschlager, 2008) that are not always reliable (compare Kupferberg, 2012a, 2016). Such data have to be checked with the help of other types of independent data (Elster, 1983; Carroll, 1992/2008). Thus Chagall in his autobiography has a clear tendency to underestimate the role that his two main mentors (Pen and Bakst) played for his career, although he is more generous about his patrons and probably realistic about the behavior of his first agent. But there is probably more to be learned about the emotional reality of his childhood memories in Vitebsk in his art works (artifacts) than in his autobiography (words). Visual language is a very concentrated language and it resembles poetry more than the novel (Lynton, 1980/1989). Poetry is in itself very visual (compare Plath's poem *Daddy* and in particular the emotionally strong detail of the "black shoe") and could, as an art form, perhaps best be seen as a transitional form between painting and fiction. This would explain why Sylvia Plath, who expressed herself fluently in drawing and painting as a child (Kirk, 2009) found herself most at home in poetry.

There is also something strongly poetic about Chagall's paintings in the sense that they condense very complex feeling with the help of strong, easily recognized visual symbols such as flying couples (love as floating in happiness), rabbis with a parcel on their back flying over the roofs in a city where the churches are golden globes (symbolizing constant persecution of the Jewish religion in a Orthodox-Christian nation-state), cows and goats (symbolizing the premodernity of life in Vitebsk), wrinkled rabbis (symbolizing the general hardship of Jewish life in pre-revolutionary Russia), a naked Jesus wrapped in a white cloth with a blue Star of David (a reminder of the fact that Jesus was a Jew and that his suffering is also Jewish suffering), etc.

It is difficult to see how biographical facts do not help to explain Chagall's art. Biographies are very complex entities because they reflect not only the personal or private level of the lives of artists, but also certainly include professional learning experiences (II.2 to II.3 to II.4) as well as historical circumstances (III.4). Creativity science is here to decode or reconstruct such complexities. For this purpose, biographical data in the broad sense, which might or might not include autobiographical accounts (the least reliable of data, but valuable if checked with other biographical data), are good to start with. Biographical data in this sense also help us better to understand why creativity regimes have different logics of discovery but also why becoming a pioneer in whatever scientific discipline, art form or technological industry nevertheless has some common traits.

Take Per Kirkeby and Ingmar Bergman. There are strong religious motives in many (but not all) of Kirkeby's paintings and Bergman's movies. Both reflect childhood experience (II.1), but in the case of Kirkeby these experiences originated when visiting his paternal grandparents. In contrast, Bergman's religious influence came from his own father. The father-son syndrome is emotionally (V.4) much more powerful than the grandfather-grandson relationship. Kirkeby's relationship with his father seems to have been unproblematic. His relationship to his mother was much more tense and unpredictable. In particular, her repeated disloyalty towards her son seems to have impregnated his relations with women later in life, making him the unsecure, dominated part. On the contrary, Bergman's relationships with women showed the opposite trait.

These early memories from primary socialization (II.1 to II.2) are not only visible in the private biographies of these two artists. They also influence their transformations from novice to professionals (II.2 to II.3) but also their transformations from professionals to pioneers (II.3 to II.4). From a professional point of view it is interesting that Kirkeby trained as a geologist but became an avant-garde artist, whereas Bergman trained to become a writer, but ended up becoming a professional theater director and a pioneering filmmaker. Their professional background are clearly visible in their art works (as they are in Céline's, Sartre's, Hemingway's, Orwell's, Plath's, Bellow's and Pasternak's novels), But when we compare the two, we need to take into consideration that their pioneering work took place in two different art forms, painting and film, the creativity of which are both strongly constrained by physical constraints (I.1). There is also the historical and professional-problem situation to take into account.

Kirkeby became a painter at the time of "pop art" (historical- and professional-problem situation, III.4) and with Asger Jorn's "primitivism" as prime prototype (I.2). Bergman became a movie director at a time when Chaplin's "lyrical" form of filmmaking (tragi-comedy) was being replaced by Hitchcock's clearly "cinematic" form of filmmaking (combining visual poetry with a strong narrative thread based upon suspense) and learned the craft of scriptwriting from a mentor who had just returned from Hollywood.

Biographical methods in the social sciences, usually avoid analyzing only one case in detail because it is interested is in general patterns (Kupferberg, 2018b). This might help us avoid misinterpretations based upon too small a sample. Spoto in his attempt to explain the relationship between life and work in Hitchcock's art, seems to put all his cards on two types of biographical data (V.1). One is the indisputable fact of Hitchcock's physical unattractiveness (which might explains his preference for beautiful blonde stars), the other a more disputable piece of information, an often retold story (Taylor, 1978) for which we only have one unreliable source, personal memory of early childhood. According to this "just so" story, Hitchcock sometime in his early childhood, was arrested by the local police and held prisoner for a few hours. This event should presumably explains the "innocently suspected" motif found in most of his films plus possibly the horror motif in some of his last films such as *Psycho* and *The Birds*.

Although there might be some emotional truth in both motives, they do not explain Hitchcock's transformation from a professional to a pioneer (II.4) of film art. For this purpose, other types of biographical data about Hitchcock's early training as an engineer (profession I.3), attendance at art classes (novice, I. 2, intellectual migration, IV.2, skunk works, IV.3) and his apprenticeship in Germany (geographical isolation, IV.1, support system, V.5) might be more relevant for the evolution of Hitchcock's "cinematic" type of movies so admired by the French "New wave" of filmmakers. His English background (obsession with spectacular crime stories) in combination with living and working in Weimar Germany at the height of the Expressionist style, closely observing German directors such as Murnau at work but also seeing a lot of German movies, in particular those of Fritz Lang (physical constraints) helped Hitchcock develop a unique but also easily recognizable style.

Geographical mobility (IV.1) only influenced Bergman's later films (he left Sweden after having been arrested for tax reasons and worked in Munich as a theater director for many years before returning to Sweden and Dramaten in Stockholm). His transformation to a pioneering film maker can best be explained by his professional juggling between the two very different professional roles (II.3) of theater director and film director but also his early experience (novice, II.2) of trying to become a writer. Paradoxically these early experiences never left him. During his first job as a theater director at Malmö Stadsteater, Bergman faced the problem of how to create intimacy in a physically large scene. The techniques (V.3) he discovered to solve this special problem, later became a prototype (I.2) for the technique of choosing and filming scenes in his films. His long years in the theater might explain the traits of "theatrality" in all his movies (Koskinen, 2001). His early training as a writer who never managed to get a novel published (Koskinen, 2002) nevertheless induced a habit of following several characters in action, a technique for composition (V.2) which fits the format of the novel but not film (compare the problems that Bergman experienced when writing the script to Fanny and Alexander; see Koskinen & Rhodin, 2005). Biographical data is helpful in unlocking the creativity of the artist, but from a creativity science point of view, contrasting comparative cases work even better.

## Why Data and Methods Matter

Comparing biographical data across domains are also valuable when we try to understand the creativity of pioneering scientists. Science is not here to evoke emotions, although it certainly can be used to explain what emotions are and how they come about (compare Elster, 1999, 2007; Frijda, 2007). Again, choice of method (V.3) is important to note. Whereas Frijda models himself upon the First principle of physics (Galileo's idea of the controlled experiment), Elster believes that literature is much better for this purpose of describing how emotions work. His main prototype (I.2) seems to be Aristotle's close analysis of how to evoke emotions in *Poetics* and how to categorize and manipulate emotions in *Rhetoric*. Darwin also spends a whole book trying to explain emotions (1972/2009) but his method (V.3) is contrasting comparison, in this case between chimpanzees and humans. Darwin discovers (V.4) the interesting fact that the human face is covered with an incredible amount of small, very fintuned muscles, which have no other reasonable function than to express emotions (Barthes' comment on Greta Garbo in *Queen Christina* ignores how much professional training it takes not to reveal any emotions at all, which we as humans have been biologically preprogrammed for by nature). This physical constraint (I.1) provides humans with a far greater range of expressing emotions than any other animal or life form in general.

Why this is the case is another problem that Darwin does not comment upon, probably because film technology was still the music of the future (knowledge constraint, historical-problem situation). Given the role that emotions play in the social life of the human animal, the problem is highly relevant for the social sciences. So why have emotions so far played such a small role in the methodology of the social sciences? A possible explanation could be the role model (I.2) for most social scientists, Max Weber's method of interpretative explanation. For Weber there are four major types of social action: (1) goal-oriented rationality, (2) value-based ratio-nality, (3) emotional action and (4) traditional action. Only the first two are, according to Weber, open for scientific (rational) analysis. The latter two are to obscure or distract the methodologically trained eye of the social scientist to penetrate according to Weber (compare Wittgenstein's similar attitude).

It is easy to prove Weber wrong. Thus value-based rationality is mod-eled upon religion, but what would religion be without traditions and emotions? This raises the next question, why does Weber insist that religion can after all be analyzed as if it was a pure rational form of action, although of the value-based type (Wert rationalität)? A closer view reveals that this can be best explained by his choice of data (V.1). World religion are all based upon reading of texts (Weber studied theology in his youth but never became a priest), rather than observing and participating in religious ceremonies. Moreover, Weber in his sociology of religion (1922/1964) constantly confuses such concepts as rationality and rationalization which are two very different things (Elster, 2007). Rationality in the scientific sense means to explain the logic of things. But calculations based upon quantitive data is only one of many scientific methods. Moreover, many art forms describe exactly how rationalization works, and are hence good intellectual tools for social science to penetrate into the world of emotions.

### Beyond Rationalism and Empiricism

Educational psychologists have lately undertaken much research about the structural similarity of novels and the pedagogics of classrooms (Dysthe, 1995;,Dysthe et al., 2002). In particular, the concept " dialogue" has been foregrounded as a good intellectual tool (Bakhtin, 1986a, 1986b; Dysthe, 1995; Holquist, 2002). Philosophy as a discipline also started from the idea of thinking as a kind of dialogue (Kroksmark, 2003). For some reasons, the "question and answers" method seems to be good for logical thinking. But logical thinking is not enough to constitute a science because scientific explanations ultimately aim at falsification (V.4) and for this purpose methodological issues are critical (V.3). But methodology is meaningless unless we have a knowledge object (V.2) and data (V.1) to constrain logical thinking.

The problem with both the rationalistic and empiricist answer to how knowledge advances (metaphysics) is that they both tend to ignore the basic lesson of Aristotle, that choice of data (V.1) is ultimately constrained by the nature of the knowledge object (V.2). The nature of the knowledge object also constrains choice of concepts (V.2) and methodology (V.3). Where did Aristotle get this idea from? It was not Plato who was basically a teacher. Indeed, what Popper called "rationalism" and Kant called "quid juris" rather them "quid facti" reflects the dialogical, "question and answers" method of the teacher in the classroom (compare Deutsch's 2012 description of Popper's teaching practices). But Aristotle, during the years he spent in exile doing empirical research, closely observed and compared in detail animal life forms and this is how he began to understand that research is very different from teaching. Researchers observe data, but such observations are not merely empirical. They are methodological (V.3) and involve concepts (V.2) as well. But choice of methods for both choice of data (V.1) and methods for interpreting data with the help of concepts (V.2) are not contingent as both the rationalistic and empiricist tradition assume. They are constrained by the nature of the knowledge object (V.2), given the basic rule of science (I.4) is falsification and separation of facts from fiction (V.4).

Data (V.1) have to be collected, but they have also to be interpreted. Both are usually described or categorized as methods but as we have seen the choice of what data to collect (data-collecting methods) and how to interpret collected data (interpretative methods, mediated by concepts, V.2) are not contingent but constrained. The problem with the two major schools of the philosophy of science, rationalism and empiricism, is that they lack a theory of how epistemological issues (knowledge) are constrained by ontological issues (reality). None of the two schools has been able to solve this problem, which is why they describe it as a problem of metaphysics and not a problem of methodology in the Aristotelian sense. Rationalists and empiricists lack a theory of methodology. There is nothing like the theory of First principles in either of the schools.

Aristotle's theory of First principles is very simple. Methods for both collection of data (V.1) and interpretation of data with the help of concepts (V.2) are ultimately constrained by the nature of the knowledge object (V.2). This is the same thing as saying that epistemology is constrained by ontology. What does that mean in the real world? In order to think like a scientist, say categorize and explain natural phenomena, there has first of all be human beings or minds (Gardner, 1993). But human creative minds cannot be taken for given (Kant's mistake, mindlessly repeated prototype I.2, by most humanities scholars trained in reading texts, with the exception of archeology which has been consistently misunderstood; compare Foucault's fiction "archeology of knowledge").

Humans are a relatively recent phenomenon. They evolved from the big apes, which evolved out of the mammals which evolved out of reptiles, which evolved out of the transitional forms between fish and land animals etc. Nature itself is creative and what we call human creativity can best be understood by studying closely how such creativity works (Darwin). But this is not enough. We also need to take Aristotle's theory of the structure of the creative process into account (but turn it upside down).

How did Darwin arrive at his discovery? What methods of data collection did he use and what methods of interpretation? Methodological considerations are critical not only when collecting but also for the purpose of interpreting data (compare Thomsen). But how do we know that the methods Darwin used in both cases were right (dimension III)? Again the nature of the knowledge object (V.2) is decisive. But this, although given from an ontological point of view, has first to be discovered or clarified from an epistemological point of view. This is what Aristotle's theory of methodology, First principles has understood and why his methodological approach is superior to the two alternative "metaphysics" of rationalism and empiricism.

The methodological problem, from the point of view of creativity science, is that the knowledge object of this science, creativity science, is extremely complex and often paradoxical. This is the reason why studying only one very narrow type of creativity (avant-garde art, Einstein's theory of relativity, Copernicus' theoretical model, etc.) tends to give us a very skewed picture of what creativity is and how it works. Foregrounding avant-garde art as the prototype (I.2) of art in general ignores that there are many other art forms in late-modern societies, and that we need a broader, more representative sample, if we want to arrive at a science of artistic creativity. For this purpose, comparing avant-garde art with say popular arts such as fiction (novels, poetry, plays) and film might be a good start, although a more detailed analysis also has to include other art forms such as architecture, sculpture, music, dance, etc.

But choice of data is always constrained by the knowledge object. Say that we want to understand what scientific creativity is and how it works. In order to avoid the fallacy of induction, we first of all have to be critical of the indiscriminate use of exceptional cases. Copernicus' theoretical model lacked parsimony which might explain why generalizing a theory of scientific revolutions from this one, unsuccessful revolution, led the science of science (Mayr, 1982, 1998) astray. But say that our knowledge object is more complex than that, that we want to move from a "science of science" to a creativity science. For this purpose we need to compare different logics of discovery (creativity regimes) with each other. Here foregrounding the role of rules (I.3) of final causes (V.4) might be a good start. But the difference between the three also concerns constraints related to other types of constraints.

This makes the model relatively complex. What should such a complex model look like and what is the best prototype (I.2) to start with? Although science generally seeks to simplify our understanding of the world (compare the analysis of the history of science of electricity mentioned in Suppe, 1974), the history of theoretical physics (which ended with two alternative simplifications, relativity theory and Heisenberg's uncertainty theorem) might not be the best choice for the simple reason that theoretical physics as a discipline is not representative for the other scientific disciplines (Hesse, 1974). As noted by Lloyd (1991) a core problem of theoretical physics is that the First principles of physics (controlled experiment) do not apply to astronomy (cosmology) and subatomic physics.

The method of the controlled experiment discovered by Galileo is both a method to collect data which are measurable and accurate in a mathematical sense and a method to interpret such data in an accurate, mathematical manner (in his case with the help of algebra). But in order to make a controlled experiment, objects need to manipulated or there has to be "intervention" (Hacking, 1983). But humans cannot move planets and stars around at will. Celestial phenomena can only be observed (measured) as accurately as our current state of scientific instruments (telescopes, radiometrics, etc.) allow. The particles of subatomic physics on the other hand are so small and move so quickly that it is impossible to measure the speed and position accurately at the same time. The observer has to make a choice between the two (this is the core idea of the Heisenberg uncertainty principle which is basically a methodological principle). But what reasons do we have to generalize the methodological dilemma of this particular discipline (theoretical physics) to the science of science or creativity science more generally? The dilemma does not exist for say archeology, geology, biology and primatology.

There is also another reason why theoretical physics might be a bad choice as a prototype (I.2) for creativity science, namely the complexity and paradoxes of creativity. Physics is a physical science, but physical phenomena tend to be cyclical or repetitive. Creativity, both n-creatvity and h-creativity in contrast tend to evolve over time. The two types of creativity tend to resemble each other (compare Kuhn's basically cyclical theory of scientific revolutions). For this purpose Darwin's biological theory of evolution might be a much better role model (I.2) to start with. Darwin's five-factor theory of evolution (1) fits the criteria of complexity; (2) helps us solve one of the paradoxes of the creativity of nature (N-creativity), that getting it right in the sense of arriving at parsimonious solutions (III.1) does not require a conscious problem solver (a super engineer, harboring in the sky); (3) solves the riddle of why groundbreaking discoveries in science tend to be unintended as well (intra-and inter-species coevolution, III.3); (4) explains why the basic constraints of science are knowledge constraints (I.3) and not physical constraints (I.1) as in say art; (5) clarifies why the core problem-solving strategy of science (V.3), is methodology, not trial and error (the problem-solving strategy of technology) as Popper claimed, nor techniques (the problem-solving strategy of artists) like the postmodernist school (Feyerabend, Kuhn, Foucault, Deleuze, Bloor) claimed, nor a combination of techniques and trial and error (Latour).

### Natural Experiments and the Method of Contrasting Cases

One of the reasons we do not have a creativity science is that we have until lately lacked a good description of the type of data (V.1) which creativity science is here to collect. Such data have to be adapted to the nature of the knowledge object (V.2) but what does that mean in practice? Here I have found Diamond's methodology (V.3) of contrasting cases, based upon the collection of natural experiments (V.1) a good intellectual tool ( parsimonious, III.1). From the point of view of physics, the controlled experiment is the method which fits the knowledge object of physics (natural forces) best (although this creates its own problems as we have seen). From the point of view of creativity science though, Galileo's discovery of the First principles of physics was a natural experiment.

Creative science cannot control what Galileo did or did not do as demanded by the method of controlled experiments (First principles).

Creativity scientists can only observe and compare such cases, using historical and biographical data. But such comparisons tend to be very complex. Like Darwin, we need a multi-factor rather than a one-factor explanatory model (Gardner, 1988). Diamond has used the "Anna Karenina" principle the to describe the multi-factor explanatory model. At the start of Tolstoy's novel, the narrator or "implied author" asks: "Why are all happy marriages similar, whereas all unhappy marriages are different?" A reasonable explanation we are told, could be that there are many different factors which influence whether a marriage will become happy or not such as psychological temperament, physical appearance, religious and ethnic background, social ambitions, financial expectations, hobbies, views on having or not having children but also how to raise them, political ideology, sexual needs and preferences, tolerance and intolerance towards infidelity, etc. All happy marriages are similar in the sense that all these factors have to fit together. But given that only one of them has to fail for the marriage to become unhappy, all unhappy marriages tend to be different.

From a creativity science point of view, it might be interesting to ask how Tolstoy arrived at this insight but also what function it plays in the novel. A novel is not a work of social science as Latour (1984/1993) seems to suggest. It is science. This does not exclude that fiction might have some valid experience which the writer has arrived at by living and writing novels, but exactly how the two are related is still up for grabs (Carroll, 1992/2008). For this purpose, creativity scientists need to know something about how they might be entangled. The techniques (V.3) of fiction writing are best described in literary theory which becomes one type of data for creative science (V.1). The life aspect comes out clearest in intellectual biographies which represent a second type of data (V.1). But the creativity scientist also needs to see how these go together in the actual composition (V.2) of the art work (novel, etc.). For this purpose, the creativity scientist needs to study the the techniques visible in the artwork, which becomes a third type of important data (V.3).

Let us see how this works in this case. The comment upon marriages comes at the very start of the Tolstoy's novel which is about the destiny of an invented character (fiction), but, it turns out, is based upon reading a news item in a Moscow morning paper ( Nabokov, 1980) about a women who had thrown herself in front of a train (fact).Transformations of fact into fiction is what fiction writers do in order to evoke emotions (V.4), but this is only one of many factors which allows the writer to get it right (Dimension III). In order to understand Tolstoy's artistic practices, we also need to include other factors such as the physical constraints (I.1) of novel writing, prototypes (I.2) necessary for the purpose of the composition of a novel (V.2), Tolstoy's motivations to write the novel (I.5) but also how he protected vulnerable versions of the (Dimension IV) of his evolving manuscript.

Narrators are fictive characters, just as other characters and events. Such fictive facts are never completely identical with the actual facts or live models (see Lamarque & Olsen, 1994). This fictionality (pretence, see Walton, 1990) is assumed or agreed upon. It is a convention in the sense of shared knowledge of this particular technique of fiction (V.3) by writers and anonymous patrons or readers (IV.5). Another convention is that the narrator knows how the story ends (most stories are told retrospectively, just like the stories that creativity science is interested in). In this case, we can assume that the real author (Tolstoy) does not merely hide behind the implied (fictive) narrator, but that the Anna Karenina principle is a discovery of the author. The role of the narrator becomes more tricky in *Lolita*, but this is because here it is much closer to the life of the author. Reading a news item in a newspaper about an anonymous person's suicide is from an emotional point of view very different from trying to make sense of traumatic events in the author's own life. The problem situation (III.4) is very different.

How did Tolstoy arrive at this principle and what is it actually about? Does he talk about his one marriage or does he perhaps talk about his life as writer of fiction? We will probably never know. It could be both. Interpretations of art works are notoriously open ended, mainly because "doubling" is one of the routine techniques of art (V.3). In order to test whether Tolstoy might have possibly written a novel not only about marriage but also about the life of a fiction writer, we need to compare or contrast the core idea of the Anna Karenina principle with how other writers of fiction have described what the life of the fiction writer means.

All art works with some degree of complexity and intensity (Beardsley, 1958) require concentrated efforts (compare Orwell, 1946/1968 with Spurling's 2009 biography of Matisse; the reason Picasso at the end of his life could paint several paintings each day was that he simply repeated himself). But even if a painter has spent several years on one painting (as Matisse and Chagall often did) it is nevertheless a fact that the beauty of a painting can be taken in at one glance (Lessing, 2008). A novel can only be enjoyed by intermittent reading (Elster, 2000). This physical constraint (I.1) explains why one of the basic techniques (V.3) of fiction is suspense.

There are also other techniques of fiction. The writer needs to present some characters whose destiny we care about (Eco, 2002). It could also be an exotic milieu of some sort and this technique has become standard in Hollywood movies (Maltby, 1994). But nothing can stop a fiction writer from borrowing ideas from other media (prototypes, I.2) provided they can be incorporated into the techniques of fiction writing (this technique might be another reason behind the theory of the "formlessness of the novel"). What is most important from a compositional (V.2) point of view is the frequent (routine) use of anticipatory techniques (Barthes, 1966/2000). Anticipatory techniques are meant to awaken curiosity and postpone the answer to the many questions raised by the act of reading. This aspect of anticipation and curiosity can also be called postponing information or creating suspense, the core technique of the novelist (Zalewski, 2009).

But characters depicted in novels are only one of the many techniques of fiction writing. The choice of this particular particular technique (V.3), suspense or withholding of information after having raised curiosity by anticipation with the help of clues can best be explained by the physical constraints (I.1, V.1) of fiction from the point of view of the patron/reader (IV.5). Other techniques such as vraisemblement (Culler, 1975/2002) can best be explained by one of the final causes, to transform facts into fiction (V.4). Characters and events have to be believable. A third technique is that the narrator shares information with the reader/patron (IV.5), which the character does not possess yet (Kundera, 1987). This can be doe in many ways. One is to create a certain mood at the start of the novel which provides the reader with information (if only of a suggestive type) and what will happen in the novel, the "destiny" of the main character (Eco, 2002; Oates, 2005).

Hence, what Diamond as a social scientist, read as methodology for how to do science, was for Tolstoy mainly a technique of fiction, to create the type of mood (a feeling of doom) which makes the reader prepared to read this almost thousand-page-long novel. So far we have looked at the creativity of the fiction writer from the point of view of the patron (reader). This perspective is probably shared by the "agents" of the support systems as well as perhaps the book publisher. But we can also look upon the creativity of fiction writing from the point of view of the writer. For the writer, the core problem of "material cause" is not so much the physical constraints of interrupted reading, but the fact that the writer has to have something interesting to write about (material in the sense of motifs or lived experiences).

As noted by Tolstoy, such experiences, for example the experience of a women in an unhappy marriage, do not have to be literal but nevertheless close to what the writer has experienced in real life. A man who has been married to a women for a long time might, if he is sensitive enough, must have made certain observations about what makes a married woman happy and what makes her unhappy. In this sense the writer does not have to invent from scratch, but actually starts from certain prototypes (I.2) which are taken from real life (live models as "material," V.1, compare Cohen-Solal, 1987). Any such close observations of signifiant others, all things being equal, increase the ability of the writer to express the emotions of the characters (V.4) and make such descriptions feel more authentic or sincere (Tolstoy, 1898/1995). To be able to express the emotions of a character in a sincere/authentic manner is not identical with the emotions evoked in the mind of the reader (Hjort & Laver, 1997). The former emotions tend to be very complex. What is expected by the reader (IV. 5) is merely the emotional response of "pity and fear."

Tolstoy's point is rather that such relatively simple emotional responses cannot be accomplished merely by knowing the rules of art (I.4, V.4), nor by knowledge of techniques (V.3) and imitation of prototypes (V.2). The fiction writer also needs to know something about real emotions (V.1; "Das Ding and Sich," ontology). The writer, must have lived and closely observed (experience, compare Dewey, 1934/2005) emotions similar to the depicted fictive character in order to get it right (Dimension III), in this case evoking the emotions of "pity and fear" (V.4). Tolstoy here addresses the problems of fiction writing not from the point of the patron (reader), or agent (publisher) but from the point of view of the real author (Dimension II, V.3).

Live models (material, V.1) do influence fiction writer but in a different way from painters. Writers mainly write from memory. Compare Kausgaard's six-volume autobiographical novel. The live models (material, V.1) included the main character and narrator and we can presume that most characters in the novel are based on such live models. Some are drawn form the time before the writer became a writer or even imagined becoming a writer, some from the period of struggling to become a writer, some from the ethical dilemmas of writing and publishing a series of strongly autobiographical novels. But in contrast to Matisse, Knausgård did not have to pay live models to sit for him, nor did he need a studio to host the live model, store art canvases, easels, palettes, paint, turpentine, brushes, etc. (physical constraints, I.1).

Fiction writing can be done anywhere, in a hotel room, at home, sitting on a train, etc. Contrast this with the life of the painter. Matisse needed live models as factual "material" (V.1) to start the process which transformed facts into fiction (V.4). Such models had to be hired and paid, but he also needed a studio in order to protect vulnerable versions (Dimension IV). Apart from paid models and rent for a studio, Matisse also needed to buy paint, canvases, easels and brushes besides supporting a family. Tolstoy was an aristocrat. The many peasants working on his lands explain why he could spend many years writing very long novels and at the same time afford to support a large family (Hansson, 2015/2016). Published writers in Scandinavia today live on stipends, granted by public funding for this purpose (which explains Klau-Ove Knausgaard's series of long novels).

In both cases some support system (IV.5) is necessary to protect vulnerable versions. The situation for unpublished fiction writers is somewhat different, but nevertheless helped by the low material costs of writing fiction which can be done in one's spare time, as a kind of hobby. Such writing has to be protected as well, but here "skunk works" (IV.3) can pay for fiction writing as a secret form of patronage. A budding writer might say be gainfully employed as a teacher, doctor or journalist, while secretly (skunk works, IV.3) working on becoming a great writer (compare the cases of Sartre, Céline and Hemingway). Such protection can also be assisted by the confidants reading the unpublished novel written in great secret and commenting upon it (compare Hemingway's case described in IV.4).

### Contrasting Comparison of Natural Experiments

The two interpretations, that the Anna Karenina principle might be modeled (I.2) upon an unhappy marriage or, alternatively upon the creative lives of fiction writers (Arana, 2003), do not necessarily exclude each other. The problem is rather the complexity of the problem explaining how fiction writing constrains the life of fiction writers, once an individual had committed himself or herself to this occupation (for the concept of commitment, see Elster, 1979, 1983; Kupferberg, 1999b). This is the rational core of the idea of the "death of the author." The lives of fiction writers are constrained like all human or biological life forms. The problem from a scientific point of view (creativity science) is how to conceptualize (V.2) these constraints. But creativity science is not here merely to describe and explain the creative lives of fiction writers. Its knowledge object (V.2, see Chapter 7) is to study all forms of creativity, or creativity in general. But such a more general model has to start somewhere and here the method of contrasting cases, seen as natural experiments works as well as a general methodology (V.3).

As we broaden our sources of data (V.1) we discover that things are more complex than the "death of the author" (the intuition that the constraints of writing do influence the lives and work of fiction writers) assumes. Although it is true that a French writer is influenced by and contributes to the living organism we call "French literary language" (Barthes, 1968/1977), the creativity of the fiction writer, as Barthes himself has discovered and noted elsewhere, is more complex. Certain techniques (V.3) have to be learned, such as the technique of "anticipation" (Barthes, 1966/2000). But what is the point of the technique and how is it to be explained? What for example is the role of the physical constraints of reading a novel (V.1)? And how does one learn it and how does one become a writer (novice, II.2 to professional, II.3)?

Why do some writers but not others become "great writers" (pioneers, II.4)? What role do support systems (IV.5) and more generally protection of vulnerable ideas (Dimension IV) play here? How does the problem situation of the writer (III.4) influence getting it right in the sense of arriving at parsimonious solutions (III.1)? Not all writers are French writers. Some are Germans and some are Swedes; some are old and some are young, etc. Some wrote their books around 1800 and others wrote books in the post Second War years. How can such changed problem situations not matter for the problem solver (III.4)? Barthes avoids and never really answers these critical questions, as if the important discovery that fiction writing is constrained by its own distinctive techniques (V.3, the core discovery of literary theory) must exclude the fact that there might be many other constraints which makes an explanation of why writers write or why they write as they do much more complex. In reality the "death of the author" is a one-factor theory which leaves out the complexity of writing fiction and artistic creative practices in genre. It might be a theory of appreciating literature but it is not a theory of literary creativity. Barthes does make some interesting observations though of relevance for the problem of how and why someone becomes a writer though.

Thus in "Writers, Intellectuals, Teachers" Barthes (1971/1977) notes that the life of a teacher is constrained (physical constraints, I.1) by the watchful eyes and ears of the students. Given that the professional tool of the teacher is talking (Säljö, 2000) and the fact that words said in the classroom context cannot be taken back, teaching from the point of view of the teacher is a kind of interrogation with the students playing the role of interrogator: "Anything you say can be held against you, so watch your tongue!" From this comparative point of view (profession as teacher, profession as writer, II.3) the profession of writing comes as a form of relief. Writing takes place on paper, but the "utterances" (Bakhtin, 1986b) of the writer remain unseen until someone is allowed to see it. The evolving versions are hence protected (Dimension IV). But eventually someone has to see it and who is that person? And what are the possible consequences of this type of "coming out" (Goffman, 1963)?

The reason that Barthes has very little to say about these questions is that his method is basically semiotic (Ette, 1998). Barthes has written about and compared many art forms and most of his analyses are very informed and highly intelligent, but they all tend to treat art works as "texts." The question what makes a "text" into an "art work" is never raised (Olsen, 1987). But art works are essentially about expressing and evoking emotions (final cause, V.4). The way this works is for several reasons hidden or masked but this does not make the problem of emotions less relevant. The point is that we do not know what the emotions expressed (not only evoked) in the art work, are unless we gather biographical data. But precisely this type of data is what the "semiotic method" (death of the author) forbids to be used as a methodological tool (V.3). The "death of the author" therefore becomes a First principle for this particular methodology (semiotics), which ignores the fact that modern art works intend both to evoke and express emotions at the same time and that the two are not necessarily identical (Carroll, 2002,2005, 2010).

Why is it that becoming a published writer, from the point of view of protection of vulnerable versions (Dimension IV), tends to take place in secret rather than in the full glare of publicity which is the case of exhibiting painters? How do writers cope with the ethical dilemmas of writing novels that feel sincere (V.4) without revealing their life models (materials, V.1)? Why do novels tend to foreground moral dilemmas and how do the predominant role of such moral dilemmas influence choice of techniques (V.3) such as timeframe, first person or third person narrator, mode or genre (tragedy, comedy, etc.)? What if any role does the peculiar type of support system for becoming a writer and writing novels have upon the mode of writing, etc.?

It is rarely told; indeed it is mostly kept as a trade secret, that there are infinitely many more unpublished manuscripts than published ones (Gedin, 1975/1997). Even highly accomplished writers such as F. Scott Fitzgerald, can tell eye-opening tales about the astonishing number of accumulatively depressing (and most probably possibly discouraging) rejection slips they received early on in a successful writing career (enough to decorate the wall of a room, see Mizener, 1958). In contrast, becoming an artist (painter) is very different (Stenberg, 2002). The selection process starts very early and in full glare. This has something to do with the distinct way that support systems (IV.5) function for artists compared with writers. All these questions can best be answered by collecting biographical data (no death of the author).

For artists, mentors (teachers) are very much present in the process of selecting talents, so are private patrons paying for the cost of education. Later private patrons might have to be asked to support travels to centers of artistic learning at home or abroad to become acquainted with the most advanced forms of art (compare the careers of Anders Zorn and Marc Chagall). There is no way one can become an artist (painter) merely by skunk works and use of confidants alone (compare the cases of George Orwell and Ernest Hemingway). Emerging empirical patterns like this, based upon analytically representative data, is what creativity science is here to collect, categorize and explain, if possible.

For this purpose, a theoretical model or framework of some kind might be of help. But such a model has first to be discovered and clarified, before it can be of use The overall method to (1) discover this framework and (2) analyzing concrete cases seems to be the same, namely collecting and contrasting cases of creativity seen as natural experiments. The best description of this need can be found in books by Jarred Diamond (1999, 2005/2011), Diamond & Robinson, (2010). How did Diamond discover this particular method? Interestingly Diamond trained as an evolutionary biologist. One of his early books compares the genome of big apes (chimpanzees and gorillas) with humans (Diamond, 1993/2006). Diamond is also an environmentalist and a keen observer of birds (ornithology, see Diamond, 2012) and this personal knowledge (III.4), might explain Daimond's discovery of the method of comparing contrasting cases (biology, environmental concerns and prototypes, I.2 of a fitting methodology (V.3) based not upon the idea of controlled experiments (Galileo's method) but natural experiments (Aristotle's and Darwin's basic method)

### Mediated Forms of the Social (Cultural Tools)

I have never met Diamond in person but I have read all of his published books, and this is probably also how writers of fiction learn to write. They do not have to meet their teacher (mentor) in person and reading the works of other novelists (prototypes, I.2) is enough. Artists also spend a lot of time learning from observing and copying other art works, but this copying is closely observed by the teacher (mentor), who comments upon works in progress (critique sessions, see Elkins, 2001). This difference in "pedagogy" explains why becoming an artists is a public affair and why "skunk works" (IV.3) are the exception for becoming an artist whereas they seem to be a rule in fiction writing.

But how do we explain the relative lack of secrecy in the process of becoming an artist? Here material constraints (V.1) probably provide the best explanation. Painting is a much more visible activity, given that the materials of painting such as canvases, easels, paint, brush, palette are physical objects which are very difficult to hide. Moreover painters use turpentine to clean their brushes (and sometimes as painting technique as well) which emits a distinct smell. Paint might be dropped on the floor. After a while the number of canvases expand and they have to stored but be easily available at the same time (a constant problem for Chagall who had to move his paintings with him, in contrast with Picasso who had studios all over France).

These material constraints (materials, V.1) necessary for painting, probably explain why the support systems (IV.5) of the two types of careers seem to be completely different. Both artistic professions have to learn the proper techniques adapted to physical constraints (V.1, glance versus intermittent reading) and both use prototypes (I.2) for the purpose of solving formal problems relate to composition (V.2) but the heavy role of visible material (V.1) for painting, sets the artists off from the start. Budding writers can become their own patrons because writing is cheap and can be done in one's spare time. They can also become their own mentors by reading books (prototypes). They only need agents to publish their books, but this is where it becomes tricky. Precisely because entrance barriers are so low, publishers are overburdened with manuscripts from hopeful writers, waiting for the chance to be published. From a comparative perspective, getting once first novel accepted for publication, has the same function as the offer Darwin received to travel on the *Beagle*, a once-in-a-lifetime opportunity (I.5c).

Non-published writers do not need patrons. They can support their attempt to learn the techniques of writing (V.3) by entering a profession, any profession (police officer, doctor, teacher, secretary, etc.) or engage in skunk works (IV.3) until they finally manage to get their first novel published (see the cases of Simone de Beauvoir and Jean Paul Sartre).

In contrast to art gallerists, who function both as patrons and agent and sometimes as mentors as well (see the case of Kahnweiler), publishers are mainly agents. As such, they function as (mainly negative) gatekeepers for writers to break out of secrecy and become published writers. Given that the real patrons from now on are anonymous mass audiences (Edström, 2002), the relation between writers and their patrons tends to be impersonal. In contrast the relationship between the patrons of art (art gallerists, private collectors) and artists tends to be strongly personal (compare the careers of Picasso, Matisse and Kirkeby).

Reading novels and comparing them for the purpose of studying the techniques of fiction writing (Death of the author) is not enough from a creativity science point of view. It tells us very little about the meaning of a work of art nor how art works come about, which turn out to be more complicated than we might expect. Given the critical role that support systems play for artists, how do we know that the emotions related to these support systems are not part of the emotions expressed or evoked? But in order to understand how support systems influence art works, we must be aware of the fact that support systems function differently in different art forms. In order to understand the type of emotions Chaplin expressed or evoked in *Modern Times*, we must know something about Chaplin's life and the history of American movies. But in order to understand how support systems influenced *Guernica* and *Les Demoiselles d'Avignon* we certainly also need to know the role that techniques play in artistic practices. Such techniques do not exist in a vacuum, but are constrained further. The point of creativity science is to search for these constraints and systematize them critically.

## Concepts and Knowledge Object

Data (I.1) and methods (V.3) alone do not make a creativity science. We also need to clarify our leading concepts (V.2) which are constrained not only by the general rules of science (V.4, falsification, separating facts from fiction), but also by the nature of the knowledge object (V.2). What is the knowledge object of creativity science? Psychologists often foreground motivations, in particular pleasure and pressure (I.5a, I.5b) but tend to forget opportunity (I.5.c) which is what makes pioneering work possible. But pioneering work in the making (vulnerable versions) has to be protected (Dimension IV). One of the most important but often neglected factors of protection turns out to be support systems (IV.5). The closest to a support system in science of the type we find in art (V.3) is what Merton

(1968/1973) called the "Matthew effect" in science, the idea that promising scholars are provided with better working conditions. This increases their chances to do pioneering work (II.4). Compare the concept "credit cycle" (Latour & Wolgar, 1986 ) and Bloor's (1976) argument about the role of early social recognition for careers in science.

But although early professional recognition might influence the chances of doing pioneering work in science, it does not explain it for two reasons. First of all, the "credit cycle" or "Matthew effect" theory ignores the fact (V.4) that the most important barrier to pioneering work in science is not social recognition. The main reason Darwin became a recognized pioneer of science was the patronage (IV.5) he received from his father, not the social recognition as a promising scholar he received from his mentor, Henslow, temporarily working as his agent. Moreover, in order to be recognized as a scientific pioneer, the scholar needs to prove his or her ability to provide proof. This takes a lot of cognitive work (completely ignored by Bloor and Latour, misconstrued by Kuhn, understood but not fully clarified by Popper). This is also what Darwin did and why he managed to get it right (III.1). But for this purpose, his father's role as patron (IV.5) was critical.

Why Wallace failed to provide the necessary proof is very simple. He lacked the financial resources to spend 20 years doing what Darwin did. Wallace's letter proved that he had in principle discovered the same thing that Darwin had discovered during his five years traveling around the world, but whereas Wallace had to keep on traveling to finance his scientific work (the scientist as entrepreneur, obeying other rules, I.4) Darwin retired to a life of a scholar exclusively dedicated to theoretical knowledge, knowledge for its own sake. This was the reason why the support system (IV.5) mattered in Darwin's case. His father's wealth secured access to the best university (Cambridge) where the leading literary lights lived and worked and whom he had to convince. He secured support from Henslow as an agent for getting the opportunity to travel broad and collect the necessary data (V.2) as well as acquiring a suitable method of interpreting data (V.3). But most of all it provided Darwin with the biographical time necessary to falsify the leading theory of the origins of species (V.4). This turned out to be decisive for "getting it right" (Dimension III) and for this reason to secure that Darwin was being credited as the founder of evolutionary biology.

## The Owl of Minerva

In order to understand how scientific creativity works, comparing it with other forms of creativity such as art and technology (method of contrasting comparison) seems to be a good approach (V.3). One of the striking patterns that emerges from such a comparison is the belatedness of sciences (already noticed by Hegel). Not only does science appear surprisingly late in the human record (2600–2300 BC). The discovery of the First principles for a number of sciences, such as physics, economics, archeology, geology, evolutionary biology, sociobiology, primatology, etc., have been belated as well. A similar phenomenon of the belatedness of science appears when studying art (compare Hegel's lectures on aesthetics and Barnett Newman's quip that artists need aesthetic theories just as birds need ornithology).

Thus, it is striking that what we call "academic industries" always evolve after some artist has managed to take the step from professional to pioneer. Take the burgeoning academic industry on Sylvia Plath (summarized in Kendall, 2001; Gill, 2006, 2008). All academic books written on this pioneering female poet were written well after her death, so at least this bird had no need for ornithology. Other artists such as Picasso, Sartre and Bergman had books written about them while they were still alive, but this does not prove that these academic books had any significant influence upon their art, given that academics tend to address different audiences from artists (Kupferberg, 2010).

The same pattern, the belatedness of science, also fits the birth of cognitive science. American psychology for a long time believed that human brains were like "black boxes" (knowledge constraint, I.3) This First principle was only abandoned (found false, V.4) as a leading psychologist (Jerome Bruner, one of the pioneers of cognitive science) became aware of the core discovery of computer science (intellectual migration, IV.2), that computers can "think" in the sense of solving complex problems. This led to a basic rethinking of the knowledge object (V.2) of psychology. If computers which are man-made machines can think, then certainly human brains can also think in the sense of solving problems. The only difference is that computers are man-made, human brains have been designed by nature.

The fact that cognitive science was late in discovering its own First principle (if machines can think, so can humans) confirms one of the main discoveries of this book, that the critical constraint for the evolution of scientific thinking are knowledge constraints (I.3). There is a strange inconsistency though between this fact and another First principle of cognitive science. If scientific understanding (theoretical thinking) tends to be belated, then the skills and attitudes necessary to think like a scientist, cannot have been built into the human brain. The many indicators of the historical belatedness of science prove that the other main First principles of cognitive science – the belief that the capacity for scientific thinking (Carruthers, 2002) must be "hardwired" (Donald 2001) or preprogrammed into the human brain – must be wrong. Theoretical thinking is unnatural because it is a result of culture and not nature.

This does not exclude that studying the creativity of nature, in particular the many constraints of creativity in nature, allows us to explain two paradoxes, one detected and one undetected. (1) The detected paradox: How can nature, which lacks language and consciousness in the human sense, nevertheless solves highly complex problems (getting it right, Dimension III)? (2) The undetected paradox: How do we explain that pioneering work in science (groundbreaking creativity) tends to be unintended, just as in nature? This is the type of problem we need a creativity science for. Creativity as a phenomenon is highly complex and paradoxical at the same time, but in order to study this knowledge object (V.2) in a scientific way, we need to clarify our data (V.I.), concepts (V.2) and proper methods (V.3). We also need to reject the argument that science is not here to falsify theories and separate facts from fiction (V.4). For this purpose, the method of collecting and comparing natural experiments, pioneering work in the three intellectual fields (creativity regimes) science, art and technology seems to be the way forward. The logics of discovery of these three creativity regimes are radically different and the best way to approach this issue is to regard creativity as a strongly constrained cognitive but at the same time also a social (historical, psychological, cultural) phenomenon.

# References

Abbott, A. (1988). *The system of professions*. Chicago, IL: University of Chicago Press.
(1995). Things of boundaries. *Social Research, 62*(4), 858–882.
(2001a). *Time matters*. Chicago, IL: University of Chicago Press.
(2001b). *Chaos of disciplines*. Chicago, IL: University of Chicago Press.
(2004). *Methods of discovery: Heuristics for the social sciences*. New York: W. W. Norton.
Abbott, H. P. (2008). *The Cambridge introduction to narrative* (2nd ed). Cambridge: Cambridge University Press.
Abrams, M. H. (1953). *The mirror and the lamp: Romantic theory and the critical tradition*. New York: Oxford University Press.
Achen, S. T. (1986). *Symboler- hvad er det?* Copenhagen: Gad.
Ackroyd, P. (1988). *T. S. Eliot*. London: Cardinal.
(2005/2006). *Shakespeare. The biography*. London: Vintage.
(2015). *Alfred Hitchcock*. London: Vintage.
Acocella, J. (2020). Bigger things to hide behind: Andy Warhol and the reign of pop. *The New Yorker*, June 8 & 15, 62–68.
Adams, L. S. (1996). *The methodologies of art. An introduction*. Boulder, CO: Westview Press.
Adelman, J. (2013). *Wordly philosopher. The odyssey of Albert O. Hirschman*. Oxford: Oxford University Press.
Adorno, T. W. (1969). *The authoritarian personality*. New York: Norton.
(1997). *Aesthetic theory* (G. Adorno & R. Tiedemann ed.). London: Athlone Press.
Agassi, J. (2002). Kuhn's way. *The Philosophy of Science, 32*(3), 391–430.
Alexander, P. (1999). *Rough magic. A biography of Sylvia Plath*. New York: Da Capo Press.
Alexander, V. D. (2003). *Sociology of the arts*. Oxford: Blackwell.
Alperson, P. (2003). Creativity in art. In J. Levinson (Ed.), *The Oxford handbook of aesthetics* (pp. 225–244). Oxford: Oxford University Press.
Alvarez, A. (1971/1990). *The savage god. A study of suicide*. New York: W. W. Norton.
Amabile, T. M. (1982). Social psychology of creativity: A consensual assessment technique. *Journal of Personality and Social Psychology, 43* (5), 997–1013.

(1989). *Growing up creative. Nurturing a lifetime of creativity.* New York: Crown.

(1998). How to kill creativity. *Harvard Business Review*, September–October, 77–87.

(1996). *Creativity in context.* Boulder, CO: Westview Press.

(1997). Entrepreneurial creativity through motivational synergy. *Journal of Creative Behavior, 31*(1), 18–26.

Anagnostopolous, G. (Ed.). (2009). *A Companion to Aristotle.* Malden, MA: Wiley-Blackwell.

Andersen, H. & Faye, J. (Eds.). (2006). *Arven efter Kuhn.* Frederiksberg: Forlaget Samfundslitteratur.

Anderson, P. (1975). *Lineages of the absolute state.* London: New Left Books.

Andersson, Å. E. (1985). *Kreativitet. Storstadens framtid.* Stockholm: Prisma.

Andersson, Å. E. & Sahlin, N.-E. (1997). *The complexity of creativity.* Dordrecht: Kluwer Academic.

Andersson, D. E., Andersson Å. E. & Melander, C. (Eds.). (2011) *Handbook of creative cities.* Northampton, MA: Edward Elgar.

Andréasson,P.- G. (Ed.). (2006). *Geobiosfären – en introduktion.* Lund: Studentlitteratur.

Anzhi, Z. (2006). *A history of Chinese painting.* Bejing: Foreign Languages Press.

Arana, M. (2003). *The writing life. Writers on how they think and work.* New York: Public Affairs.

Aristides, J. (2016) *Lessons in classical painting.* Berkeley, CA: Watson-Guptill.

Aristotle. (1967). *Den Nikomakiska Etiken.* Stockholm: Natur & Kultur.

(1984a). Poetics. In J. Barnes (Ed.), *The complete works of Aristotle* (Vol. 2) (pp. 2316–2340). Princeton, NJ: Princeton University Press.

(1984b). Rhetoric. In J. Barnes (Ed.), *The complete works of Aristotle* (Vol. 2) (pp. 2152–2269). Princeton, NJ: Princeton University Press.

Arnheim, R. (1957). *Film as art (ch. 1).* Berkeley, CA: University of California Press.

(1962). *The genesis of a painting: Picasso's Guernica.* Berkeley, CA: University of California Press.

(1966). *Toward a psychology of art.* Berkeley, CA: University of California Press.

Aron, R. (1965). *Democracy and totalitarianism.* London: Weidenfeld & Nicolson.

(1967/1980). *Main currents in sociological thought* (Vols. 1 & 2). Harmondsworth: Penguin Books.

Aronson, R. (1980). *Sartre. Philosophy in the World.* London: Verso.

Asplund, J. (1987) *Det sociala livets elementära former.* Gothernburg: Korpen.

Auiler, D. (1999). *Hitchcock's notebooks.* New York: Avon Books.

Austin, J. L. (1975). *How to do things with words* (2nd ed.). Cambridge, MA: Harvard University Press.

Azevedo, W. d' (1973/1997). Sources of Gola Artistru. In S. Feagin & P. Maynard (Eds.), *Aesthetics* (pp. 197–206). Oxford: Oxford University Press.

Bach, S. (1992). *Marlene Dietrich. Life and legend.* New York: Da Capo Press.

Bain, T. (2001). *The other Sylvia Plath.* Harlow: Pearson Education.

Baker, C. (1969). *Ernest Hemingway. A life story.* Harmondsworth: Penguin Books.

Bakhtin, M. (1986a). *The dialogical imagination* (M. Holquist ed.). Austin, TX: University of Texas Press.

    (1986b) *Speech genres and other late essays* (C. Emerson & M. Holquist ed.). Austin, TX: University of Texas Press.

Baldwin, N. (1995). *Edison: Inventing the century.* New York: Hyperion.

Barnes, B. (1982). *T. S. Kuhn and social science.* Basingstoke: Macmillan.

    (2003). Thomas Kuhn and the problem of social order in science. In T. Nickles (Ed.), *Thomas Kuhn* (pp. 122–144). Cambridge: Cambridge University Press.

Barnes, B., Bloor, D. & Henry, J. (1996). *Scientific knowledge. A sociological analysis.* Chicago, IL: University of Chicago Press.

Barr, A. H. Jr. (1943/1974). *What is a modern painting* (1st ed.). New York: Museum of Modern Art.

    (1946). *Picasso. Fifty years of his art.* New York: Museum of Modern Art.

    (1953/1976). *Matisse. His art and his public.* London: Secker & Warburg.

Barron, F. (1955). The disposition towards originality. *Journal of Abnormal and Social Psychology, 51*, 476–485.

Barron, F. & Harrington, D. M. (1981). Creativity, intelligence, and personality. *Annual Reviews of Psychology, 32*, 439–476.

Barthes, R. (1956/2000). Myth today. In S. Sontag (Ed.), *A Roland Barthes Reader* (pp. 93–149). New York: Vintage.

    (1960/2000). Authors and writers. In S. Sontag (Ed.), *A Roland Barthes Reader* (pp. 185–193, v. 251–295). New York: Vintage.

    (1964/1977). Rhetoric of the image. In *Music, image, text.* (pp. 52–91). London: Fontana.

    (1966/2000). Introduction to the structural analysis of narratives. In S. Sontag (Ed.), *A Roland Barthes reader* (pp. 251–295). New York: Vintage.

    (1968/1977). The death of the author. In *Music, image, text* (pp. 142–198). London: Fontana.

    (1971/1977). Writers, intellectuals, teachers. In *Image, music, text* (pp. 190–215). London: Fontana.

    (2000). In S. Sontag (Ed.), *A Roland Barthes reader* (S. Sontag Intoduction). New York: Vintage.

Basalla, G. (1988). *The evolution of technology.* Cambridge: Cambridge University Press.

Bate, J. (1997/2008). *The genius of Shakespeare.* London: Picador.

    (2015/2016). *Ted Hughes. The unauthorized life.* London: William Collins.

Bauer, H. H. (1990). Barriers against interdisciplinarity: Implications for studies of science, technology and society (STS). *Science, Technology & Human Values, 15*(1), 105–119.

Bauman, Z. (1989). *Modernity and the holocaust.* Ithaca, NY: Cornell University Press.

Baxandall, M. (1972). *Painting and experience in fifteenth century Italy*. London: Oxford University Press.

(1985). *Patterns of intention. On the historical explanation of pictures*. New Haven, CT: Yale University Press.

(2003). *Words for pictures*. New Haven, CT: Yale University Press.

Bazerman, C. (1988). *Shaping written knowledge*. Madison, WI: University of Wisconsin Press.

Beardsley, M. C. (1958). *Aesthetics. problems in the philosophy of criticism*. New York: Harcourt, Brace & World.

(1966/1967). *Aesthetics. From classical Greece to the present*. Tuscaloosa AL: University of Alabama Press.

Becker, C. (Ed.). (1998). *Paul Gauguin. Tahiti*. Ostfildern-Ruit: Verlag Gerd Hatje.

Becker, H. S. (1951). *Role and career problems of the Chicago public school teacher*. Chicago, IL: University of Chicago Press.

(1960). Notes on the concept of commitment. *American Journal of Sociology, 66* (1), 32–40.

(1966). *Outsiders. Studies in the sociology of deviance*. New York: Free Press.

(1982). *Art worlds*. Berkeley, CA. University of California Press.

(1997). *Tricks of the trade*. Chicago, IL: University of Chicago Press.

Beevor, A. (1982/1999). *The Spanish civil war*. London: Cassel.

Behlmer, R. (1986). *Inside Warner Brothers*. London: Weidenfeld and Nicolson.

Bendix, R. (1962). *Max Weber – An intellectual portrait*. Garden City, NY: Anchor Books.

(1982/1999). *The Spanush civil war*. London: Cassel.

Benjamin, W. (2008). The work of art in the age of mechanical reproduction. In S. M. Cahn & A. Meskin (Eds.), *Aesthetics. A comprehensive anthology* (pp. 327–343). Malden, MA: Blackwell.

Benson, P. S., Lambek, B. & Ørskov, S. (2004). *Mærsk manden og magten*. Copenhagen: Politiken Bøger.

Bentley, E. (1968). *The theory of the modern stage*. Harmondsworth: Penguin Books.

Berenson, B. (1933). *Seeing and knowing*. Greenwich, CT: New York Graphic Society.

(1930/1960). *The Italian painters of the Renaissance*. London: Collins.

Berger, P., Berger, B. & Kellner, H. (1973). *The homeless mind: Modernization and consciousness*. New York: Vintage.

Berger, P. & Luckmann, T. (1966). *The social construction of reality*. Garden City, NY: Doubleday & Anchor.

Berglund, K. (2007). *Jag tänker på Linné. Han som såg allt*. Stockholm: Albert Bonniers.

Bergman, I. (1959). Varje film är min sista film. *Filmnyheter, 14*(9–10), 1–8.

(1989). *Laterna magica*. Stockholm: Månpocket.

(1990). *Bilder*. Stockholm: Norstedts

Bergreen, L. (2011/2015). *Columbus. De Fyra Resorna*. Stockholm: Leopard fåorlag.

Bertaux, D. & Delcroiz, C. (2000). Case histories of families and social processes enriching sockologi. In P. Chamberlayne, J. Bornat & T. Wengraf (Eds.), *The turn to biographical Methods in social science* (pp. 71–89). London: Routledge.

Biagioli, M. (2001). Replication or monopoly? The economies of invention and discovery in Galileo's Observations of 1610. In J. Renn (Ed.), *Galileo in Context* (pp. 277–322). Cambridge: Cambridge University Press.

Bierstedt, R. (1981). *American Sociological Theory. A Critical History.* New York: Academic Press.

Björkman, S., Manns, T. & Sima, J. (1971). *Bergman om Bergman.* Copenhagen: Rhodos.

Bloch, M. (1953). *The historian's craft.* New York: Vintage.

Bloor, D. (1976). *Knowledge and social imagery.* London: Routledge and Kegan Paul.

(1999). *Anti-Latour History and Philosphy of Sci.ence,* 30(1), 81–112.

Blunt, W. (1971/2001). *Carl von Linné.* Stockholm: Bonniers.

Boden, M. A. (1990). *The creative mind. Myths and mechanisms.* New York: Basic Books.

Boden, M. A. (Ed.). (1994). *Dimensions of creativity.* Cambridge, MA: MIT Press.

Bohm, D. (1998). *On creativity.* London: Routledge.

Bok, S. (1988). *Alva. Ett kninnoliv.* Stockholm: Bonniers.

Bono, E. de (1994). *Verklig kreativitet.* Jönköping: Brain Books.

(2009). Contribution to ambassadors meeting: Manifesto for creativity and innovation. *Brussels,* March 25.

Boorstin, D. L. (1985). *The discoverers.* New York: Vintage.

Booth, W. C. (1961/1983). *The rhetoric of fiction.* Chicago, IL: University of Chicago Press.

Bordwell, D. (1997). *On the history of film style.* Cambridge, MA: Harvard University Press.

Bordwell, D. & Carroll, N. (Eds.). (1996). *Post-theory. Reconstructing film studies.* Madison, WI: University of Wisconsin Press.

Bordwell, D, Staiger, J. & Thompson, K. (1988). *The classical Hollywood cinema. Film style & mode of production to 1960.* London: Routledge.

Botton. A. de & Armstrong, J. (2013/2015). *Art as therapy.* London: Phaidon. Beauvoir,

Bottomore, T. & Nisbet, R. (Eds.). (1978) *A history of sociological analysis.* New York: Basic Books.

Boundas, C. V. & Olkowski, D. (1994). *Gilles Deleuze and the theatre of philosophy.* London: Routledge.

Bourdieu, P. (1974a). The specifity of the scientific field and the social conditions of the progress of reason. *Social Science Information,* 14(6), pp. 19–47.

(1974b). *Zur Soziologie der symbolischen Formen.* Frankfurt am Main: Suhrkamp.

(1986). *Distinction. A social critique of the judgement of taste.* New York: Routledge.

(1984/1996). *Homo academicus*. Stockholm: Symposion.

(1990a). *The logic of practice*. Stanford, CA: Stanford University Press.

(1990b). *In other words*. Stanford, CA: Stanford University Press.

(1995). *The rules of art. Genesis and structure of the literary field*. Stanford: Stanford University Press.

(2000). Die biographische Illusion. In E. M. Hoerning (Ed.), *Biographische Sozialisation* (pp. 51–60). Stuttgart: Lucius & Lucius

(2004). *Science of science and reflexivity*, Chicago. University of Chicago Press.

Boyd, B. (1990). *Vladimir Nabokov. The Russian years*. Princeton, NJ: Princeton University Press.

(1991). *Vladimir Nabokov. The American years*. Princeton, NJ: Princeton University Press.

Boyd, R. & Silk, J. B. (2003). *How humans evolved* (3rd.). New York: W. W. Norton.

Bradbury, M. & McFarlane, J. (Eds.). (1976). *Modernism 1890–1930*. London: Penguin.

Brandell, G. (1983–1989). *Strindberg – ett författarliv I–IV*. Stockholm: Alba.

Brante, T. (1984). *Vetenskapens sociala grunder – en studie av konflikter i forskarvärlden*. Stockholm: Prisma.

Brecht, B. (1955/1972). *Leben des Galilei*. Copenhagen: Gyldendal.

Bredsdorff, T. (1987). *Den bratte forvandling. Om digteren Sylvia Plath med digtene ved Uffe Haarder*. Copenhagen: Gad.

Brettell, R. R. (2001). *Impressionism. Painting quickly in France, 1860–1890*. New Haven, CT: Yale University Press

Brinnin, J. M. (1959/1987). *The third rose. Gertrude Stein and her world*. Reading, MA: Addison Wesley.

Brothwell, D. R. & Pollard, A. M. (Eds.). (2000). *Handbook of archeological sciences*. Chichester: Wiley.

Browne, J. (1995). *Darwin. Voyaging*. London: Jonathan Cape.

(2002). *Charles Darwin. The power of place*. New York: Knopf.

Browne, J. & Neve, M. (1989). Introduction. In C. Darwin (1839/1989). *Voyage on the Beagle* (pp. 1–28). London: Penguin.

Brownlow, K. (1968). *The parade's gone by*. London: Abacus.

(1979). *The pioneers*. London: Collins.

Bruccoli, M. J. (1991). *The only thing that counts. The Ernest Hemingway- Maxwell Perkins correspondence*. Columbia, SC: University of South Carolina Press.

Bruford, W. H. (1962). *Culture and society in classical Weimar. 1775–1806*. London: Cambridge University Press.

Bruner, J. (1960/1977). *The process of education*. Cambridge, MA: Harvard University Press.

(1986). *Actual minds, possible worlds*. Cambridge, MA: Harvard University Press.

(1990). *Acts of meaning*. Cambridge, MA: Harvard University Press.

(1990). *Acts of Meaning*. Cambridge, MA: Harvard University Press.

(2004). *Kulturens väv. Utbildning i kulturpsykologisk belysning*. Gothenburg: Daidalos.

(2006a). *In search of pedagogy. Volume I. The selected works of Jerome S. Bruner.* London: Routledge.

(2006b). *In search of pedagogy. Volume II. The selected works of Jerome S. Bruner.* London: Routledge.

Brummer, H. H. (1975). *Zorn Svensk målare i världen.* Stockholm: Bonniers.

(1989). *ZORNMCMLXXXIX.* Mora: Zornsamlingrna

(2000). *Till ögats fröjd och nationens förgyllning – Ander Zorn.* Stockholm: Norstedts.

Burgess, A. (1990). *You had your time.* New York: Grove Weidenfeld.

Burke, E. (1759/2014). *A philosophical enquiry into the origins of our ideas of the sublime and the beautiful.* Cambridge: Cambridge University Press.

Burkhardt. F. (Ed.). (2008). *Charles Darwin. The Beagle letters.* Cambridge: Cambridge University Press.

Burns, T. (1992). *Erving Goffman.* London: Routledge.

Butler, R. (1993). *Rodin. The shape of genius.* New Haven, CT: Yale University Press.

Butscher, E. (1976/2003). *Sylvia Plath. Method and madness.* Tucson, AZ: Schaffner Press.

Butterfield, H. (1957/1965). *Origins of modern science.* New York: Free Press.

Cachin, F. (1992). *Gauguin. The quest for paradise.* London: Thames & Hudson.

Cahn, S. M. & Meskin, A. (Eds.). (2008). *Aesthetics. A comprehensive antholoogy.* Malden: MA. Blackwell.

Campbell, D. T. (1960). Blind variation and selective retention in creative thought as in other knowledge processes. *Psychological Review, 67*(6), 380–400.

Cardwell, D. S. L. (1972). *Turning points in western technology.* New York: Neale Watson.

Carrol, N. (1992/2008). Art, intention and conversation. In S. M. Cahn & A. Meskin (Eds.), *Aesthetics. A comparative anthology* (pp. 568–588). Malden, MA: Blackwell.

(1996). *Theorizing the moving image.* Cambridge: Cambridge University Press.

(Ed). (2000). *Theories of art today.* Madison, WI: University of Wisconsin Press.

(2002). Why horror? In A. Neill & A. Ridley (Eds.), *Arguing about art. Contemporary philosophical debates* (2nd ed.). (pp. 275–294). London: Routledge

(2005). Aesthetic experience. A question of contents. In M. Kieran (Ed.), *Aesthetics and the philosophy of art* (pp. 69–97). Malden, MA: Blackwell.

(2010). *Art in three dimensions.* Oxford: Oxford University Press.

Carruthers, P. (2002). The roots of scientific reasoning: infancy, modularity and the art of tracking. In P. Carruthers, S. Stich & M. Siegal (Eds.), *The cognitive basis of science* (pp. 73–95). Cambridge: Cambridge University Press.

Carter, R. (2004). *Language and creativity. The art of common talk.* London: Routledge.

Caves, R. E. (2000). *Creative industries. Contracts between art and commerce.* Cambridge, MA: Harvard University Press.

Cela-Conde, C. J. & Ayala, F. J. (2007). *Human evolution. Trails from the past.* Oxford: Oxford University Press.

Chagall, M. (1922/1965). *My life.* London: Penguin.

Chalmers, A. H. (1999). *What is this thing called science?* Maidenhead: Open University Press.

Chancellor, G. & van Wyhe, J. (Eds.). (2009). *Charles Darwin's notebooks from the voyage of the Beagle.* Cambridge: Cambridge University Press.

Chaplin, C. (1964). *My autobiography.* New York: Simon & Schuster.

Chaplin, E. (1994) *Sociology and visual representation.* London: Routledge.

Chekhov, M. (1953/2002). *To the actor.* London: Routledge.

Childe, V. G. (195/1983) *Man Makes Himself.* New York: New American Library.

Cinqualabre, O. & Migayrou, F. (Eds.). (2015). *Le Corbusier. The measures of man.* Zurich: Scheidegger & Spiess.

Cohen, H. F. (1994). *The scientific revolution.* Chicago, IL: University of Chicago Press.

Cohen-Solal, A. (1987). *Sartre. A life.* New York: Pantheon Books.

Collingwood, R. G. (1925/1997). *Outlines of a philosophy of art.* Bristol: Thammes.

(1945). *The principles of art.* Oxford: Clarendon Press.

Collins, R. (1998). *The sociology of philosophies: A global theory of intellectual change.* Cambridge, MA: Harvard University Press

(2000a). The sociology of philosophies. A présis. *Philosophy of Social Sciences, 30* (2): 157–201.

(2000b). Reply to reviewers and symposium commentators. *Philosophy of Social Sciences, 30*(2), 299–325.

Condit, C. W. (1964). *The Chicago school of architecture.* Chicago, IL: University of Chicago Press.

Corbridge, S. (1995). *Development studies. A reader.* London: Arnold.

Cornwall, I. W. (1966). *The world of ancient man.* New York: New American Library.

Corrigan, P. (1997). *The sociology of consumption.* London: Sage.

Coser, L. A. (1967). *Continuities in the study of social conflict.* New York: Free Press.

(1971). *Masters of sociological thought.* New York: Harcourt Brace Jovanovich.

(1970). *Men of ideas.* New York: Free Press.

(1984). *Refugee scholars in America. Their impact and their experiences.* New Haven, CT: Yale University Press.

Coser, L. A, Kadushin, C. & Powell, W. W. (1982). *Books. The culture and commerce of publishing.* New York: Basic Books.

Cowling, E. (2002). *Picasso. Style and meaning.* London: Phaidon.

Craft, A. (2003). The limits to creativity in education: Dilemmas for educator. *British Journal of Educational Studies, 1*(2), 113–127.

(2005). *Creativity in schools. Tensions and dilemmas.* London: Routledge.

(2007). Possibility thinking in the early years and primary classroom education. In A.-G. Tan, (Ed.), *Creativity. A handbook for teachers* (pp. 231–249). Singapore: World Scientific.

Crick, B. (1980). *George Orwell. A life.* Harmondsworth: Penguin.

Crick, F. (1988). *What mad pursuit. A personal view of scientific discovery.* New York: Basic Books.

Cropley, A. J. (2001). *Creativity in education and learning.* London: Kogan Page.

Crowther, P. (1993/1996). *Critical aesthetics and postmodernism.* Oxford: Clarendon Press.

Crystal, D. (1987). *The Cambridge encyclopedia of language.* Cambridge: Cambridge University Press.

Culler, J. (1975/2002). *Structuralist poetics.* London: Routledge.

Cunliffe, B. (2008). *Europe between the oceans.* New Haven, CT: Yale University Press.

Curran, J. (2016). *Agatha Christie's complete secret notebooks.* New York: HarperCollins.

Csiksmenthalyi, M. (1988). Society, culture, person: A systems view of creativity. In R. J. Sternberg (Ed.), *The nature of creativity* (pp. 325–339). New York: Cambridge University Press.

Csikszentmihalyi, M. (1994). Creativity. In R. J. Sternberg (Ed.), *Encyclopedia of human intelligence. Volume 1* (pp. 298–306). New York: Macmillan.

(1996). *Creativity. Flow and the psychology of discovery and invention.* New York: HarperCollins.

(1999). Implications of a systems perspective for the study of creativity. In R. J. Sternberg (Ed.), *Handbook of creativity* (pp. 313–335). Cambridge: Cambridge University Press.

Dahn D. (1999). *Vertreibung ins Paradies.* Hamburg: Rowohlt.

Daiches, D., Jones, J. & Jones, P. (Eds.). (1986). *A hotbed of genius. The Scottish enlightenment 1730–1790.* Edinburgh: Edinburgh University Press.

Dale, M. (1997). *The movie game. The film business in Britain. Europe and America.* London: Cassell.

Danielsson, B. (1965). *Gauguins sydhavsår.* Copenhagen: Nyt Nordisk Forlag Arnold Busck.

Danto, A. C. (1964/2008). Art worlds. In M. Cahn & A. Meskin (Eds.), *Aesthetics. A comprehensive anthology* (pp. 416–425). Malden, MA: Blackwell.

(1997). *After the end of art. Contemporary art and the pale of History.* Princeton, NJ: Princeton University Press.

(2000). Art and meaning. In N. Carroll (Ed.), *Theories of art today* (pp. 130–140). Madison: University of Wisconsin Press.

Dardis, T. (1989). *The thirsty muse. Alcohol and the American writer.* New York: Ticknor & Fields.

Darling, D. (2006). *Gravity's arc.* Hoboken, NJ: Wiley.

Darwin, C. (1839/1989). *Voyage on the Beagle.* London: Penguin.

(1859/1985). *The origin of species.* London: Penguin.

(1872/2009). *The expression of emotions in man and animals*. London: Penguin.

(1879/2004). *The descent of man*. London: Penguin.

(1892/1958). *The autobiography of Charles Darwin and selected letters* (F. Darwin ed.). New York: Dover.

(1881). *The formation of vegetable mould through the action of worms with observations of their habits*. Gloucester: Dodo Press.

Dawidowicz. L. (1975/1986). *The war against the Jews 1933–1945*. Toronto: Bantam Books.

Davidson, E. (1996/1997). *The trial of the Germans*. Columbia, MO: The University of Missouri Press.

Davies, S. (2003) Ontology of art. In J. Levinson (Ed.), *The Oxford handbook of aesthetics* (pp. 155– 180). Oxford: Oxford University Press.

Davis, B. (1962). *The lonely life*. New York: Putnam.

Dawkins, R. (1976/2006). *The selfish gene* (30th anniversary ed.). Oxford: Oxford University Press.

(1986/2006). *The blind watchmaker*. London: Penguin.

(1996/2006). *Climbing mount improbable*. London: Penguin.

(2005). *The ancestor's tale. A pilgrimage to the dawn of life*. London: Phoenix.

(2010). *The greatest show on earth*. London: Transworld.

Dearborn, M. (2005/2006). *Peggy Guggenheim. Mistress of modernism* London: Voirago Press.

Deleuze, G. (2004). Att ha en bra idé i film. In T. Lundemo (Eds.), *Konst och film–texter efter 1970* (pp. 85, - 96). Lund: Raster.

Dennet, D. C. (1995). *Darwin's dangerous idea. Evolution and the meaning of life*. New York: Simon & Schuster.

Desmond, A. & Moore, J. (1992). *Darwin*. London: Penguin.

Deutsch, D. (2012). *The beginning of infinity*. London: Penguin.

Deutscher, I. (1954/1965). *The prophet armed. Trotsky 1879–1921*. New York: Vintage.

(1959). *The prophet unarmed. Trotsky: 1921–1929*. New York: Vintage.

(1963).*The prophet outcast. Trotsky 1929–1940*. New York: Vintage.

Dewey, J. (1902/2000). Skolan og læreplanen. In K. Illeris (Ed.), *Tekster om læring* (pp. 120–133). Frederiksberg: Roskilde Universitetsforlag.

(1917/1997). *How we think*. Mineola, NY: Dover Publications.

(1934/2005). *Art as experience*. New York: Capricorn Books.

Diamond, J. (1993/2006). *The third chimpanzee. The evolution and future of the human animal*. New York: HarperPerennial.

(1999). *Guns, germs and steel. The fates of human societies*. New York: W. W. Norton.

(2005/2011). *Collapse. How societies choose to fail or succeed*. London: Penguin.

Diamond, J. & Robinson, J. A. (2010). *Natural experiments of history*. Cambridge, MA: Belknap.

(2012). *The world until yesterday*. London: Allen Lane.

Dick, B. F. (1997). *City of dreams.The making and remaking of Universal Pictures*. Lexington: University Press of Kentucky.

Dickie, G. (1964/2008). The myth of the aesthetic attitude. In M. Cahn & A. Meskin (Eds.), *Aesthetics. A comprehensive anthology* (pp. 455–465). Malden, MA: Blackwell.

(1974/2008). What is art? An institutional analysis. In M. Cahn & A. Meskin (Eds.), *Aesthetics. A comprehensive anthology* (pp. 426–437). Malden, MA: Blackwell.

(1997). *Introduction to aesthetics. An analytical approach.* New York: Oxford University Press.

(2000). The institutional theory of art. In N. Carroll (Ed.), *Theories of art today* (pp. 93–108). Madison: University of Wisconsin Press.

Dickson, P. R. (1994/1997). *Marketing management* (2nd ed.). Fort Worth, TX: The Dryden Press.

Dierig, S., Lachmund, J. & Mendelsohn, J. A. (2003). *Science and the city.* Osiris 18 (special volume).

Dissanyake, E. (1992/1995). *Homo aestheticus.* Seattle, WA: University of Washington Press.

Dobres, M.-A. & Robb, J. (Eds.). (2000). *Agency in archeology.* London: Routledge.

Dollenmayter, D. (2007/2014). *Susan Sontag. A biography.* Evanston, IL. Northwestern University Press.

Donald, M. (1990). *The origins of the modern mind.* Cambridge, MA: Harvard University Press.

(2001). *A mind so rare. The evolution of human consciousness.* New York: W. W. Norton.

Dondis, A. (1973). *A primar of visual literacy.* Cambridge, MA: MIT Press.

Donner, J. (2009). *Ingmar Bergman: PM.* Stockholm: Ekerlids förlag.

Dudek, P. & Tenort, H.-E. (1994). *Transformationen der deuschen Bildungslandshaft. Lernprozess mit ungewissen Ausgang.* Weinheim: Beltz Verlag.

Due, R. (2007). *Deleuze.* Cambridge: Polity Press.

Durkheim, É. (1893/1964). *The division of labor in society.* New York: Free Press.

(1897/1966). *Suicide.* New York: Free Press.

(1912/1964). *The elementary forms of religious life.* New York: Free Press.

(1982). *The rules of the sociological method and selected texts on sociology and its method.* New York: Free Press.

(1922/1956). *Education and sociology.* New York: Free Press.

Durkheim, É. & Mauss, M. (1903/1963). *Primitive classification.* Chicago, IL: University of Chicago Press.

Duyer, R. (1987). *Heavenly bodies: Film stars and society.* London: Macmillan.

Dysthe, O. (1995). *Det flerstämmiga klassrummet.* Lund: Studentlitteratur.

Dysthe, O., Hertzberg, F. & Hoel, T. L. (2002). *Skriva för att lära.* Lund: Studentlitteratur.

Eastlake, C. L. (2001). *Methods and materials of painting of the great schools and masters.* Mineola, NY: Dover Publications.

Ebaugh, F. R. M. (1988). *Becoming an ex*. Chicago, IL: University of Chicago Press.

Eco, U. (1979). *A theory of semiotics*. Bloomington, IN: Indiana University Press.

(1984). *The role of the reader. Explorations in the semiotics of texts*. Bloomington, IN: Indiana University Press.

(2002). *Tankar om litteratur*. Stockholm: Brombergs.

Edström, V. (2002). *Selma Lagerlöf. Livets vågspel*. Stockholm: Natur & Kultur.

Edel, L. (1979). *Bloomsbury. A house of lions*. Harmondsworth: Penguin.

Edwards, S. (2006). *Photography – a very short introduction*. Oxford: Oxford University Press.

Eisner, L. (1969). *The haunted screen: Expressionism and the German cinema*. London: Thames & Hudson.

Eldridge, R. (2014). *An introduction to the philosophy of art*. Cambridge: Cambridge University Press.

Elkins, J. (2001). *Why art cannot be taught*. Urbana, IL: University of Illinois Press.

Ellman, R. (1959). *James Joyce*. Oxford: Oxford University Press.

Elster, J. (1979). *Ulysses and the sirens*. Cambridge: Cambridge University Press.

(1983). *Sour grapes. Studies in the subversion of rationality*. Cambridge: Cambridge University Press.

(1999). *Alchemies of the mind. Rationality and the emotions*. Cambridge: Cambridge University Press.

(2000). *Ulysses unbound. Studies in rationality, precommitment, and constraints*. Cambridge: Cambridge University Press.

(2007). *Explaining social behavior*. Cambridge: Cambridge University Press.

Engdahl, H. (1994/2005). *Beröringens ABC*. Stockholm: Bonniers.

Engholm, I. & Michelsen, A. (1999/2000). *Designmaskinen*. Copenhagen: Gyldendalske Boghandel.

Engler, W. (1999). *Die Ostdeutschen. Kunde von einem verlorenen Land*. Berlin: Aufbau Verlag.

Epstein, I. (1959/1982). *Judaism*. Harmondsworth: Penguin.

Eribon, D. (1991). *Michel Foucault*. Kungshult: Symposion.

(1991/1993). *E. H. Gombrich. A life-long interest. Conversations on art and science*. London: Thames and Hudson.

Ericson, K. A. (1999). Creative expertise as superior reproducible performance: Innovative and flexible aspects of expert performanc. *Psychological Inquiry*, *10*(4), 329–338.

Eriksen, T. H. (1999). *Charles Darwin*. Stockholm: Nya Doxa.

Erikson, E. H. (1968/1982). *Identitet – ungdom och kriser*. Köpenhamn: Hans Reitzel.

(1970). Autobiographical notes on the identity crises, *Daedalus*, *99*(4), 730–759.

Ette, O. (1998). *Roland Barthes. Eine intellektuelle Biographie*. Frankfurt am Main: Suhrkamp.

Etzioni, A. (1969). *The semi-professions and their organizations: Teachers, nurses, social workers.* New York: Free Press.

(1988). *The moral dimension. Toward a new economics.* New York: Free Press.

Eyman, S. (1993). *Laughter in paradise.* New York: Simon & Schuster.

Ewers, S. & Nowotny, H. (1987). *Über den Umgang mit Unsicherheit. Die Elndeckung der Gestaltlbarkeit von Gesellschaft.* Frankfurt am Main: Suhrkamp.

Fagan, B. (2010). *Cro-Magnon. How the Ice Age gave birth to the first modern humans.* New York: Bloomsbury.

Fant, K. (1991). *Alfred Bernhard Nobel.* Stockholm: Norstedts.

Farrington, B. (1944/1965). *Grekisk vetenskap.* Stockholm: Prisma.

Faulkner, R. R. & Anderson, A. B. (1987). Short-term projects and emergent careers: Evidence from Hollywood. *American Journal of Sociology, 92*(4), 879–909.

Fausing, B. & Larsen, P. (Ed.). (1980). *Visuel komunikation Volume 1 & 2.* Copenhagen: Medusa.

Feinstein, E. (2003). *Ted Hughes. The life of a poet.* New York: W. W. Norton.

Felt, U., Nowotny, H. & Taschwer, K. (1995). *Wissenschaftsforschung. Eine Einführung.* Frankfurt am Main: Campus.

Fenton, C. A. (1954/1987). *The apprenticeship of Ernest Hemingway.* London: Plantin.

Ferejohn, M. (2009). Empiricism and the first principles of Aristotelian science. In G. Anagnostopoulos (Ed.), *A companion to Aristotle* (pp. 66–80). Malden, MA: Wiley-Blackwell.

Ferguson, K. (2003). *Tycho Brahe och Johannes Kepler.* Stockholm: Prisma.

Fest, J. (1973/2014a). *Hitler. En Biografi. Del I: Från ett liv udan mål till kampens tid.* Stockholm: Fischer.

(1973/2014b). *Hitler. En biografi. Del II. Från maktövertagndet till undergången.* Scockholm: Discher.

Feuer, L. S. (1969). *The conflict of generations: The character and significance of student movements.* New York: Basic Books.

Feyerabend, P. (1974). Review of Popper's objective knowledge. In A. O'Hear (Ed.), *Karl Popper. Critical assessment of leading philosophers. Volume III: Philosophy of science 2* (pp. 533–537). London: Routledge.

(1975). *Against method. Outline of an anarchistic theory of science.* London: Verso.

Firth, R. (Ed.). (1957/1970). *Man and culture. An evaluation of the work of Bronislaw Malinowski.* London: Routledge & Kegan Paul.

Fitzgerald, M. C. (1996). *Making modernism. Picasso and the creation of the art market for twentieth century art.* Berkeley, CA: University of California Press.

Fleming, D. (1969). Émigré physicists and the biological revolution. In D. Fleming & B. Bailyn (Eds.), *The intellectual migration* (pp. 152–189). Cambridge: Cambridge University Press.

Florida, R. (2002). *The rise of the creative class.* New York: Basic Books.

Flyvbjerg, B. (2001). *Making social science matter: why social inquiry fails and how it can succeed again.* Cambridge: Cambridge University Press.

Fosnmark. A.-B. (2014). *Van Gogh, Bernard, Gauguin. Dramaet i Arles*. Copenhagen: Ordrupgaard.

Fonsmark, A.-B. & Brettell, R. (2005). *Gauguin og Impressionismen. Maleri, skulptur og keramik*. Copenhagen: Ordrupgaard museum.

Fortey, R. (2001). *Trilobites. Eyewitness to evolution*. London: Flamingo.

(2005). *Earth. An intimate history*. London: Harper Perennial.

Foucault, M. (1966/1970). *The order of things*. New York: Random House.

(1969/2002). *Vetandets arkeologi*. Lund: Archiv.

(1969/1994). What is an author? In P. Rabinow (Eds.), *Aesthetics, method, and methodology. Essential works of Foucault 1954–1982:* Volume 2 (pp. 205–224). New York: New Press.

(1971/1972). The discourse on language. In *The Archeology of Knowledge* (pp. 215–237. London: Routledge.

(1971/1994). Nietzsche, genealogy, history. In P. Rabinow (Ed.), *Aesthetics, method, and methodology. Essential works of Foucault 1954–1982. Volume 2* (pp. 369–382). New York: New Press.

Frankel. H. (1987). The continental drift debate. In H. T. Engelhardt Jr. & A. L. Caplan (Eds.), *Scientific controversies. Case studies in the resolution and closure of disputes in science and technology* (pp. 243–248). Cambridge: Cambridge University Press.

(2009). Plate tectonics. In P. J. Bowler & J. V. Pickstone (Eds.), *The Cambridge history of science. Volume 6: The modern biological and earth sciences* (pp. 385–394). Cambridge: Cambridge University Press.

Frängsmyr, T. (Ed.). (1983). *Linnaeus. The man and his work Frängsmyr*. Berkeley, CA: University of California Press.

French, P. (1971). *The movie moguls. An informal history of the Hollywood tycoons*. Harmondsworth: Penguin Books.

French, M. (1994). *Invention and evolution. Design in nature and engineering* (2nd ed.). Cambridge: Cambridge University Press.

Freud, S. (1938). *The basic writings of Sigmund Freud* (A. A. Brill ed and *Introduction*. New York: The Modern Library.

(1968). *Drömtydning*. Stockholm: Aldus/Bonniers.

(1977). *Introductory lectures on psychoanalysis*. New York: W. W. Norton.

Freund, J. (1969). *The Sociology of Max Weber*. New York: Vintage.

Friedman, J. (Ed.). (2015). *The Cambridge companion to Alfred Hitchcock*. Cambridge: Cambridge University Press.

Friedrich, O. (1992). *Olympia. Paris in the age of Manet*. New York: HarperCollins.

Frijda, N. H. (2007). *The laws of emotions*. Mahwah, NJ: Erlbaum.

Frisby, D. (1981). *Sociological impressionism. A reassessment of Georg Simmel's social theory*. London: Heinemann.

Frost, J. (1997). *Creativity in primary science*. Buckingham: Open University Press.

Frye, N. (1971). *Anatomy of criticism*. Princeton, NJ: Princeton University Press.

Fuchs, S. (1993). A sociological theory of scientific change. *Social Forces, 71*(4), 933–953.

Fuery, P. (2000). *New developments in film theory*. Basingstoke: Palgrave.

Furberg, M. (1969). *Vision och skepsis. Från Thales till skeptikerna.* Stockholm: Aldus/Bonniers.

Gabler, N. (1988). *An empire of their own. How the Jews invented Hollywood.* New York: Crown.

Gabora, L. (2005). Creative thought as a non-Darwinian evolutionary process. *Journal of Creative Behavior, 39*(4), 262–283.

Gage, J. (1995/2005). *Colour and culture. Practice and meaning from antiquity to abstraction.* London: Thames & Hudson.

(2006). *Colour in art.* London: Thames and Hudson.

Gale. M. (1997). *Dada and Surrealism.* London: Phaidon.

Gamble, C. (2004). *Archaeology: The basics.* London: Routledge.

(2007). *Origins and revolutions. Human identity in early prehistory.* Cambridge: Cambridge University Press.

Gamble, C. & Porr, M. (Eds.). (2005). *The hominid individual in context.* London: Routledge.

Gardner, H. (1983). *Frames of mind: The theory of multiple intelligences.* New York: Basic Books.

(1987). *The mind's new sciennce. A history of the cognitive revolution.* New York: Basic Books.

(1988). Creative lives and creative works: A synthetic scientific approach. In R. J.Sternberg (Ed.), *The nature of creativity* (pp. 298–321). New York: Cambridge University Press.

(1993). *Creating minds.* New York: Basic Books.

(1999). Was Darwin's Creativity Darwinian? *Psychological Inquiry, 10*(4), 338–340.

Gardiner, P. (Ed.). (1974). *The philosophy of history.* Oxford: Oxford University Press.

Gauguin, P. (1983). *För og efter.* Copenhagen: Carit Andesens Forlag.

(1956). *Mette och Paul Gauguin.* Copenhagen: Gyldendel.

Gay, P. (1988). *Freud. A Life for our time.* New York: W. W. Norton.

Gay, P. du & Pryke, M. (2002).*Cultural economy.* London: Sage.

Gedin, P. (1975/1997). *Litteraturen i verkligheten.* Stockholm: Rabém.

Genette, G. (1980). *Narrative discource.* Ithaca, NY: Cornell University Press.

Gerber, D. A. (1986). *Antisemitism in American history.* Urbana, IL: University of Illinois Press.

Ghiselin, M. T. (1984). *The triumph of the Darwinian method.* Chicago, IL: University of Chicago Press.

Giannetti, L. (1999). *Understanding movies.* Upper Saddle River, NJ: Prentice Hall.

Gimpel, J. (1983). *The cathedral builders.* New York: Grove Press.

Giddens. A. (1971/1982).*Capitalism and modern social theory. An analysis of the writings of Marx, Durkheim and Max Weber.* Cambridge: Cambridge University Press.

(Ed.). (1972). *Durkheim's writings in sociology and social philosophy. Introduction to Émile Durkheim selected writings* (pp. 1–50). Cambridge: Cambridge University Press.

(1976). *New rules of sociological method*. London: Hutchinson.

(1977). *Studies in social and political theory*. New York: Basic Books.

(1979a). *Émile Durkheim*. New York: Viking.

(1979b). *Central problems in social theory. Action, structure and contradiction in social analysis*. Berkeley, CA: University of California Press.

(1981). *A contemporary critique of historical materialism*. Basingstoke: Macmillan.

(1984). *The constitution of society*. Berkeley, CA: University of California Press.

(1990). *The consequences of modernity*. Cambridge: Polity Press.

(1991). *Modernity and self-identity*. Cambridge: Polity Press.

(1993). *Sociology* (2nd ed.). Cambridge: Polity Press.

Gilfillan, S. C. (1935/1963). *The sociology of invention*. Cambridge, MA: MIT Press.

Gill, J. (2006). *The Cambridge companion to Sylvia Plath*. Cambridge: Cambridge University Press.

(2008). *The Cambridge introduction to Sylvia Plath*. Cambridge: Cambridge University Press.

Gilot, F. & Lake, C. (1964/1981). *Leben mit Picasso*. Zurich: Diogenes.

(1983). *The cathedral builders*. New York: Grove Press.

Glaser, B. & Strauss, A. (1967). *The discovery of grounded theory. Strategies for qualitative research*. Chicago, IL: Aldine & Atherton.

Gleick, J. (1993). *Genius. The life and science of Richard Feynman*. New York: Vintage.

Goertzel. T. & Goertzel, B. (1995). *Linus Pauling. A life in science and politics*. New York: Basic Books.

Goffman. E. (1959). *The presentation of self in everyday life*. New York: Anchor Books.

Goffman, E. (1963). *Stigma: Notes on the management of spoiled identity*. Englewood Cliffs, NJ: Prentice Hall.

Gohr, S. (2008). *Per Kirkeby. Reisen in der Malerei und anderswo*. Ostfildern: Hatje.

Goldberg, R. (2004). *Performance. Live art since the 60s*. London: Thames & Hudson.

Goldhagen, D. J. (1996). *Hitler's willing executioners. Ordinary Germans and the holocaust*. New York: Knopf.

Goldman, W. (1966). *Adventures in the film trade*. London: Abacus.

Goldstone, J. (2008). *Why Europe? The rise of the West in world history, 1500–1850*. Boston: McGraw Hill.

Goldwyn, S. (1923). *Behind the screen*. New York: George H. Doran.

Golinski, Jan (1998). *Making natural knowledge*. Cambridge: Cambridge University Press.

Golinski, J. (2003). Chemistry. In R. Porter (Ed.), *The history of science. Volume 4: Eighteenth century science* (pp. 375–396). Cambridge: Cambridge University Press.

Gombrich, E. H. (1996). In R. Woodfield (Ed.), *The essential Gombrich*. London: Phaidon Press.

(1997). *Kunstens historie*. Copenhagen: Gyldendal.

(1960/2000). *Art and illusion*. Princeton, NJ: Princeton University Press.

Goodman, D. & Russell, C. (Eds.). (1991). *The rise of scientific Europe 1500–1800*. London: Indianapolis, IN: Hacket Publishing Company.

Goodman, N. (1976). *Languages of art*. Indianapolis, IN: Hackett.

(1978). *Ways of worldmaking*. Indianapolis, IN: Hackett.

Gottfried, M. (2003). *Arthur Miller. His life and work*. New York: DaCapo.

Gottlieb, S. (Ed.). (1995). *Hitchcock on Hitchcock. Selected writings and Interviews*. Berkeley, CA: University of California Press.

(2002). Early Hitchcock: The German influence. In S. C. (Eds.), Framing Hitchcock (). Detroit, MI: Wayne State University Press.

(Ed.). (2015). *Hitchcock on Hitchcock. Selected writings and interviews (Vol. 2)*. Berkeley, CA: University of California Press.

Gould, S. J. (1996). Why Darwin? *The New York Review of Books*, XLIII, 10–14.

(2002). *The structure of evolutionary theory*. Cambridge, MA: Belknap.

Gouldner, A. W. (1971). *Enter Plato. Classical Greece and the origins of social theory*. New York: Basic Books.

(1973/1979). *The coming crisis of western sociology*. London: Heinemann.

(1976) *The dialectic of ideology and technology*. Basingstoke: Macmillan.

(1979). *The future of intellectuals and the rise of the new class*. Basingstoke: Macmillan.

(1985). *Against fragmentation. The origins of Marxism and the sociology of intellectuals*. Oxford: Oxford University Press.

Graham, G. (2003). Architecture. In J. Levinson (Ed.), *The Oxford handbook of aesthetics* (pp. 555–571). Oxford: Oxford University Press.

Gramsci, A. (1967). *En kollektiv intellektuell*. Lund: Bo Cavefors Bokförlag.

(1971). *Selections from prison notebooks*. London: Lawrence & Wishart.

Gray, L. S. & Seeber, R. S. (1996). *Under the Stars*. Ithaca, NY: Cornell University Press.

Green, C. (Ed.). (2001). *Picasso's Les Demoiselles d'Avignon*. Cambridge: Cambridge University Press.

Greenberg, C. (1961/1965). *Art and culture. Critical essays*. Boston, MA: Beacon Press.

Greene, M. (2009). Geology. In P. J. Bowler & J. V. Pickstone (Eds.), *The Cambridge history of science. Volume 6: The modern biological and earth Sciences* (pp. 167–184). Cambridge: Cambridge University Press.

Griffin, P. (1990). *Less then a treason. Hemingway in Paris*. Oxford: Oxford University Press.

Griffith, R. (1970). *The movie stars*. Garden City, NY: Doubleday.

Gronow, J. (1997). *The sociology of taste*. London: Routledge.

Grosskurth, P. (1991). *The secret ring. Freud's inner circle and the politics of psychoanalysis*. Reading, MA: Addison-Wesley.

Gruber, H. E. (1981). *Darwin on man: A psychological study of scientific creativity.* Chicago, IL: University of Chicago Press.

(1989). *Creative people at work.* New York: Oxford University Press.

Guilford, J. P, (1950). Creativity. *American Psychologist, 5,* 444–454.

Guillou, J. (2014). *Att inte vilja se.* Stockholm. Piratförlaget.

Gustafsson, B. (Ed.). (1965). *Karl Marx and Friedrich Engels.* Stockholm: Wahlström & Widstrand.

Guttman, B., Griffiths, A. Suzuki, D. & Cullis, T. (2002/2011). *Genetics: A beginners guide.* Oxford: Oneworld.

Gumprecht, H. (1998). *"New Weimar unter Palmen." Deutsche Schriftsteller im Exil in Los Angeles.* Berlin: Afbau Taschenbuch Verlag.

Habermas, J. (1968a). *Erkenntniss und Interesse.* Frankfurt am Main: Suhrkamp.

(1968b). *Technik und Wissenschaft als Ideologie.* Frankfurt am Main: Suhrkamp.

Hacking, I. (1983). *Representing and intervening.* Cambridge: Cambridge University Press.

(1995). Working in a new world: The taxonomic solution. In P. Harnich (Ed.), *World changes. Thomas Kuhn and the nature of science* (pp. 259–274). Cambridge MA: MIT Press.

(2000). *Social konstruktion av vad?* Stockholm: Thales.

Hackstaff, K., Kupferberg, F. & Negroni, C. (Eds.). (2012). *Biography and turning points in Europe and America.* Bristol: Policy Press.

Hacomen, M. H. (2000). *Karl Popper. The formative years.* Cambridge: Cambridge University Press.

Hall, E. (2015). *The Ancient Greeks.* London: Vintage.

Hall, P. (1999). *Cities in civilization. Innovation and urban order.* London: Phoenix.

Halldén, S. (2005). *Hur går det till inom vetenskapen?* Stockholm: Thales.

Hägg, G. (1996). *Den svenska litteraturhistorien.* Stockholm: Wahlström & Widstrand.

Hankinson R. J. (1995). Philosophy of science. In J. Barnes (Ed.), *The Cambridge Companion to Aristotle* (pp. 109–139). Cambridge: Cambridge University Press.

Hankinson, R. J. (2009). Causes. In G. Anagnostopoulos (Ed.), *A Companion to Aristotle* (pp. 213–229). Malden, MA: Wiley-Blackwell.

Hanson, R. N. (1956). *Patterns of Discovery.* Cambridge: Cambridge University Press.

Hansson, C. (2015/2016). *Masja.* Stockholm: Bonnier Pocket.

Harrigan, C. & Capon, R. (2007/2013). *Abstract and colour. Techniques in painting.* London: Batsford.

Harris, N. (1982). *The art of Cézanne.* Twickenham: Optimum Books.

Harrison, C. (1994). Abstract expressionism. In G. Stangos (Eds.), *Concepts of modern art* (3rd enlarged and updated ed.) (pp. 169–211). London: Thames & Hudson.

Hart, J. P. & Terrell, E. (Ed.). (2002). *Darwin and archaeology. A handbook of key concepts* (pp. 69–87). Westport, CT: Bergin & Garvey.

Hastrup, K. (1999). *Viljen til Viden*. Copenhagen: Gyldendal.

Hauser, A. (1979). *Kunstens og litteraturens socialhistoria 1 & 2*. Copenhagen: Rhodos.

Hayman, R. (1985). *Writing against. A biography of Sartre*. London: Weidenfeld & Nicolson.

(1991/2003). *The death and life of Sylvia Plath*.Phoenix Mill: Sutton.

Hayward, S. (2000). *Cinema studies*. London: Routledge.

Havel, V. (1990). *En dåre i Prag. Brev, tal, texter 1975–1989*. Stockholm: Symposion.

Helfenstein, J. & Osadtschy, O. (Eds.) (2017).*Chagall. The breakthrough years 1911–1917*. Cologne: Kunstmuseum Basel/Verlag der Buchhandlung Walter König.

Hegel, G. W. F. (1970). *Vorlesungen übet die Ästhetik I–III*. Frankfurt am Main: Suhrkamp.

Heilbut, A. (1983). *Exiled in paradise. German refugee artists and intellectuals in America from the 1930s to the present*. New York: Viking.

Helgeson, S. & Nyberg, K. (2002). *Swedish design. The best in Swedish design today*. Stockholm: Prisma.

Heller, N. (2020). Big spenders.Venture capital shaped the past decade. Will it destroy the next? *The New Yorker*, Jan. 27, 26–31.

Henrikson, A. (1963/1988). *Svensk historia*. Stockholm: BonnierPocket.

Henry J. (1997/2008). *The scientific revolution and the origins of modern science* (3rd ed.). London:Palgrave Macmillan.

Herbert, R. L. (1988). *Impressionism. art, leisure and Parisian society*. New Haven, CT: Yale University Press.

Herbert, S. & Norman, D. (2009). Darwin's geology and perspective on the fossil record. In M. Ruse & R. J. Richards (Eds.), *The Cambridge companion to the "Origins of species"* (pp. 129–152). Cambridge: Cambridge University Press.

Herf, J. (1997). *Divided memory. The Nazi past in the two Germanys*. Cambridge, MA: Harvard University Press.

Herman, A. (2001). *The Scottish enlightenment*. London: Fourth Estate.

Herman, L. & Vervaeck, B. (2001/2005). *Handbook of narrative analysis*. Lincoln, NE: University of Nebraska Press.

Hermann, A. (1996). *Einstein. Der Weltweise und sein Jahrhundert. Eine Biographie*. Munich: Piper.

Hesmondalgh, D. (2002). *The cultural industries*. London: Sage.

Hess, D. J. (1997). *Science studies*. New York: New York University Press.

Hesse, M. (1974). *The structure of scientific inference*. Basingstoke: Macmillan.

Hippel, E. von (1988). *The sources of innovation*. Oxford: Oxford University Press

Hirschman, A. O. (1956). *The strategy of economic development*. New Haven, CT: Yale University Press.

(1963). *Journeys towards progress. Studies of economic policymaking in America*. Westport, CT: Greenwood Press.

(1967). *Development projects observed*. Washington, DC: Brookings Institution.

(1970). *Exit, voice, and loyality. Responses to decline in firms, organizations and states*. Cambridge, MA: Harvard University Press.

(1977). *The passions and the interests.* Princeton, NJ: Princeton University Press.

(1982). *Shifting involvements. Private interest and public action.* Oxford: Martin Robertson.

(1986). *Rival views of market society and other recent essays.* New York: Viking.

(1995). *A propensity to self-subversion.* Cambridge, MA: Harvard University Press.

(2001). *Crossing boundaries. Selected writings.* New York: Zone Books.

Hitchcock O'Connel, P. & Bouzerau. L (2003/2004). *Alma Hitchcock. The woman behind the man.* New York: Berkeley Books.

Hjort, M. & Laver, S. (Eds.). (1997). *Emotion and the arts.* New York: Oxford University Press.

Hobhouse, J. (1975). *Everybody who was anybody. A biography of Gertrude Stein.* New York: Anchor Books.

Hodder, I. (1999). *The archeological process. An introduction.* Oxford: Blackwell.

Hodge, A. (Ed.). (2000). *Twentieth century acting.* London: Routledge.

Hodge, J. & Radick, G. (Eds.). (2009). *The Cambridge companion to Darwin.* Cambridge: Cambridge University Press.

Hodgson, G. (1994). *Economics and evolution. Bringing life back into economics.* Cambridge: Polity Press.

Hof Hoyningen- Huene, P. (1993). *Reconstructing scientific revolutions: Thomas S. Kuhn's philosophy of science.* Chicago, IL: University of Chicago Press.

Højsgaard, M. (2001). *Robert Jacobsen and Paris.* Copenhagen: Bjerggaard Publishers.

Hollander, P. (1981). *Political pilgrims: Travels of western intellectuals to the Soviet Union, China, and Cuba 1928–1979.* New York: Harper Colophon Editions.

Holm, M. H. & Tøjner, P. E. (2008). *Per Kirkeby Louisiana.* Humlebæk: Louisiana Museum of Modern Art.

Holquist, M. (2002). *Dialogism. Bakhtin and his world.* London: Routledge.

Hölldobler B. & Wilson, E. O. (1994). *Journey to the Ants.* Cambridge, MA: Belknap.

Hollows, J., Hutchins, P. & Jancovick, M. (2000). *The film studies reader.* London: Arnold.

Holroyd, M. (1988). *George Bernard Shaw 1. The search for love.* New York: Random House.

Holton, G. (1988). *Thematic origins in scientific thought.* Cambridge, MA: Harvard University Press.

Honneth, A. (1992). *Kampf um Anerkennung. Zur moralischen Grammatik sozialer Konflikte.* Frankfurt am Main: Suhrkamp.

Honour, H. & Fleming, J. (1982/1984). *The visual arts. A history.* Englewood Cliffs, NJ: Prentice-Hall.

Horkheimer, M. & Adorno, T. W. (1944/1979). *Dialektik der Aufklärung.* Frankfurt am Main: Fischer Taschenbuch Verlag.

Hornung, P. M. (2005). *Peter Severin Krøyer.* Copenhagen: Forlaget Palle Fogtdal.

Huaco, G. A. (1965). *The sociology of film art.* New York: Basic Books.

Huff, T. (1972). *Charlie Chaplin.* New York: Arno Press.

Huffington, A. S. (1988). *Picasso. Creator and destroyer.* New York: Simon and Schuster.

Hughes, E. C. (1964). *Men and their work.* Glencoe, IL: Free Press.

Hughes, H. S. (1975). *The sea change. The migration of social thought, 1930–1965.* New York: Harper & Row.

Hull, D. L. (1988) *Science as process.* Chicago, IL: University of Chicago Press.

Idestam-Almquist, B. (1939). *Den svenska filmens drama.* Stockholm: Wahlström & Widstrand.

Illeris, K. (2007). *Lärande.* Lund: Studentlitteratur.

Irwin, W. H. (1928/1970). *The house the shadows built.* New York: Arno Press & The New York Times.

Isaacson, W. (2008). *Einstein. His life and universe.* New York: Simon & Schuster Paperbacks.

(2012). *Steve Jobs – en biografi.* Stockholm: Bonnier Pocket.

(2014/2015). *Innovatörerna.* Stockholm: Bonniers.

Iser, W. (1974). *The implied reader: Patterns of communication in prose fiction from Bunyan to Becket.* Baltimore, MD: Johns Hopkins University Press.

(1989). *Prospecting. From reader response to literary anthropology.* Baltimore, MD: Johns Hopkins University Press.

(1999). The Imaginary. In J. Wolfreys (Ed.), *Literary theories* (pp. 178– 196). Edinburgh: Edinburgh University Press.

Israel, J. (1968/1971). *Alienation. Från Marx till modern sociologi* (2nd rev. ed.). Stockholm: Rabén & Sjögren.

Jacob, M. C. (1997). *Scientific culture and the making of the industrial west.* New York: Oxford University Press.

Jacobs, L. (1968). *The rise of American film.* New York: Teachers College Press.

Jaki, S. L. (1984). *Uneasy genius: The life and work of Pierre Duhem.* The Hague: Nijhoff.

Jakobsen, H. & Lange. H. (1972). *Bertold Brecht. Leben des Galileo.* Copenhagen: Gyldendal.

Jalving, C. (2011). *Vaerk som handling.* Copenhagen: Museum Tusculanums Förlag.

Jensen, J. (1992). *Thomsens Museum.* Copenhagen: Gyldendal.

(2013). *Danmarks oldtid.* Copenhagen: Gyldendal.

Johnson, P. (1987). *A history of the Jews.* New York: Harper & Row.

(1991). *The birth of the modern. World society 1815–1830.* New York: Harper Collins.

Jones, S. (1994/2000). *The language of genes. Biology, history and the evolutionary future.* London: Flamingo.

(2001). *Almost like a whale. The origins of species updated.* London: Transworld Publishers.

(2009). *Darwin's island. The Galapagos and the garden of England.* London: Little Brown.

Jørgensen, J.-E. (2011). *Jorn international.* Aarhus: AROS.

Josephson, R. (1940/1991). *Konstverkets födelse.* Stockholm: Natur & Kultur.

Judson, H. F. (1996/2013). *The eighth day of creation. Makers of the revolution in biology*. Cold Spring Harbor, NY: Cold Spring Harbor Laboratory Press.

Kahnweiler, D. H. (1980). Introduction: A free man. In R. Penrose & J. Golding (Eds.), *Picasso in retrospect* (pp. 1–3). New York: Harper & Row.

Kant, I. (1790/1997). Art and genius. In S. Feagin & P. Patrick Maynard (Eds.), *Aesthetics* (pp. 180–191). Oxford: Oxford University Press.

(1790/1974). *Kritik der Urteilskraft*. Frankfurt am Main: Suhrkamp.

Karlsson, I. & Ruth, A. (1983). *Samhället som teater. Estetik och politik i Tredje Riket*. Stockholm: Liberförlag.

Karmel, P. (2003). *Picasso and the invention of Cubism*, New Haven, CT: Yale University Press.

Katz, S. D. (1991). *Film directing, shot by shot*. Studio City, CA: Michael Wiese Productions.

Keller, L. & Gordon, É. (2010). *The lives of ants*. Oxford: Oxford University Press.

Kendall, T. (2001). *Sylvia Plath: A critical study*. London: Faber and Faber.

Kennedy, J. (1927). *The story of films*. Chicago, IL: A. W. Shaw.

Ketteringham, J. & Nayak, R. (1986). *Breakthroughs!* New York: Rawson Associates.

Keynes, R. (2003). *Fossils, finches and fuegians. Charles Darwin's adventures and discoveries on the Beagle. 1832–1836*. London: HarperCollins.

Killick, D. (2000). Science, speculation and the origins of extractive metallurgy. In D. R. Brothwell & A. M. Pollard (Eds.), *Handbook of archeological sciences* (pp. 483–492). Chichester: Wiley.

King, G. (2002). *New Hollywood cinema. An introduction*. New York: Columbia University Press.

Kirk, M. A (2009). *Sylvia Plath. A biography*. Amherst, MA: Pormetheus Books.

Kirton, M. (1989). *Adaptors and innovators. Styles of creativity and problem solving*. London: Routledge.

Kitcher, P. (1993). *The advancement of science*. New York: Oxford University Press.

Kivy, P. (2002/2008). Emotions in the music. In S. M. Can & A. Meskin (Eds.), *Aesthetics. A comprehensive anthology* (pp. 628–636). Malden, MA: Blackwell.

Kjørup, S. (1971). *Aestiske problemer. En indfoering i kunstens filosofi*. Copenhagen: Munksgaard.

(1995). *Hvorfor smiler Mona Lisa? En bog om billeder og billedbrug*. Frederiksberg: Roskilde Universitetsforlag.

Kline, M. (1953/1987). *Mathematics in western culture*. London: Penguin.

Knausgård, K.-O. (2010/2015). *Min kamp 5*. Stockholm: Ppocketfåorlaget.

Knorr-Cetina, K. (1981). *The manufacture of knowledge: An essay on the constructivist and contextual nature of science*. Oxford: Pergamon.

(1999). *Epistemic cultures. How the sciences Make knowledge*. Cambridge, MA: Harvard University Press.

(2005). The fabrication of facts: Toward a microsociology of scientific knowledge. In N. Stehr & V. Meja (Eds.), *Society and knowledge. Contemporary perspectives in the sociology of knowledge and Ssience* (pp. 175–195). New Brunswick: Transaction Publisher.

Koestler, A. (1964). *The act of creation.* New York: Macmillan.

Kolakowski, L. (1980). *Leben trotz Geschichte.* Munich: Deutscher Tachenbuch Verlag.

Koren, Y. & Negev, E. (2006). *Lover of unreason. Assia Wevill, Sylvia Plath's rival and Ted Hughes' doomed love.* New York: Da Capo Press.

Koskinen, M. (2001). *Ingmar Bergman: "Allting föreställer, ingenting är."* Nora: Ny Doxa.

(2002). *I begynnelsen var ordet: Ingmar Bergman och hans tidiga författarskap.* Stockholm: Wahlström & Widstrand.

Koskinen, M. & Rhodin, M. (2005). *Fanny och Alexander.* Stockholm: Walsttröm & Widstrand.

Kostof, S. (1985). *A history of architecture. Settings and rituals.* New York: Oxford University Press.

Koszarski, R. (1983). *The man you love to hate. Erich von Stroheim and Hollywood.* Oxford: Oxford University Press.

Kracauer, S. (1965).*Theory of Film. The Redemption of Physical Reality.* London: Oxford University Press.

Kraft, H. (Ed.). (1984). *Psychoanalyse, Kunst und Kreativität heute. Die Entwicklung der analytischen Kunstpsychologie seit Freud.* Cologne: DuMont Buchverlag.

Krauss, R. E. (1986). *The originality of the avant-garde and other modernist myths.* Cambridge, MA: MIT Press.

Kress, G. (2000). Repraesentation, laering og subjektivitet: Et socialsemiotisk perspektiv. In J. Bjerg (Eds.), *Paedagogik – en grundbog til et fag* (pp. 210–244). Copenhagen: Hans Reitzel.

Kress, G., Jewitt, C., Ogburn, J. & Tsaratelis, C. (2001). *Multimodal teaching and learning. The rethorics of the science class room.* London: Continuum.

Kress, G. & van Leeuwen, T. (2001). *Multimodal discourse.* London: Hodder.

(2006). *Reading images: The grammar of visual design.* London: Routledge.

Kriseovà, E. (1991). *Václav Havel. Dichter und Präsident.* Berlin: Rowohlt.

Kristeller, P.-O. (1978/2008). The modern system of the arts. In S. M. Can & A. Meskin (Eds.), *Aesthetics. A comprehensive anthology* (pp. 3–15). Malden, MA: Blackwell.

Kroksmark, T. (Ed.). (2003). *Den tidlösa pedagogiken.* Lund: Studentlitteratur.

Kroll, J. (1976/2007). *Chapters in a mythology. The poetry of Sylvia Plath.* Chalford: Sutton Publishing.

Krüll, M. (1993). *Im Netz der Zauberer.* Frankfurt am Main: Fischer Taschenbuch.

Kuh, K. (1962/2000). *The artist's voice.* New York: Da Capo Press.

Kuhn, T. (1957/1959). *The Copernican revolution.* New York: Vintage.

(1959/1977). The essential tension: Tradition and innovation in scientific research. In *The Essential tension* (pp. 225–239). Chicago, IL: University of Chicago Press.

(1962/1970). *The structure of scientific revolutions.* Chicago and London: University of Chicago Press.

(1969/1977). Comment on the relation of science and art. In *The Essential Tension* (pp. 340–352). Chicago, IL: University of Chicago Press.

(1974). Second thoughts on paradigm. In F. Suppe (Ed.), *The structure of scientific theories* (pp. 459–482). Urbana, IL: University of Illinois Press.

(2000). *The road since structure.* Chicago, IL: University of Chicago Press.

Kundera, M. (1987). *Romankunsten.* Copenhagen: Gyldendal.

Kupferberg, F. (1991). *Outline to a theory of creativity.* Aalborg: Institute of Development and Planning, Aalborg University.

(1995a). Bevidsthedens elementære former. *Dansk Sociologi, 2,* 26–45.

(1995b). Biografisk Självgestaltning. *Sociologisk Forskning, 32*(4), 32–57.

(1995c). *Nabo til kaos.* Unnpublished doctoral dissertation. Aalborg University, Aalborg.

(1996a). *Kreativt kaos i projektarbejdet.* Aalborg: Aalborg Universitetsforlag.

(1996b). The reality of teaching: Bringing disorder back into social theory and the sociology of education. *British Journal of Sociology of Education, 17*(2), 227–247.

(1996c). From "information control" to "creative chaos." In H. Best, U. Becker & A. Marks (Eds.), *Social science in transition. Social science information needs and provisions in a changing Europe* (pp. 219–247). Bonn: Informationszentrum Sozialwissenschaften.

(1996d). *Humanistiske iværksættere.* Institut for Udvikling og Planlægning, Aalborg Universitet.

(1996e). The passing of socialism: Transformation, modernity and the East German Sonderweg. In P. Karasz, J. Plichtova & V. Krivy (Eds.), *Economics and politics. Fifth Bratislava Symposium and East Central Roundtable Conference 17th–20th November, 1994. Proceedings* (pp. 41–52). Bratislava: European Cultural Foundation.

(1997). Soziologie des berufligen Neuanfangs: Von akademischer Lehrtätigkeit zu beruflicher Selbständigkeit. In M. Thomas (Ed.), *Selbständige, Gründer, Unternehmer. Passagen und Passformen im Umbruch* (pp. 188–207). Berlin: Berliner Debatte Wissenschaft Verlag.

(1998a). Models of creativity abroad. Migrants, strangers and travellers. *European Archive of Sociology, 39,* 179–206.

(1998b). Transformation as biographical experience. Personal destinies of East Berlin graduates before and after unification. *Acta Sociologica, 41*(3), 243–267.

(1998c). Humanistic entrepreneurship and entrepreneurial career commitment. *Entrepreneurship and Regional Development, 10,* 171–187.

(1999a). *The break-up of communism in East Germany and Eastern Europe.* London: Macmillan.

(1999b). *Kald eller profession. At indtræde i sygeplejeprofessionen.* Copenhagen: Nyt Nordisk Forlag Arnold Busck.

(1999c). Projektarbejde og kreativitetsteori In S. V. Kunudsen (Ed.), *Projektarbejdets fortid og fremtid* (pp. 187–304). Copenhagen: Denmark.

336   *References*

(2000). Nationale Identität als existentielle Entscheidung. Frauen in der DDR. In E. M. Hoerning (Ed.), *Biographische Sozialisation* (pp. 325–341). Stuttgart: Lucius & Lucius.

(2001a). Passagen in die Selbständigkeit – Typische Verlaufsmuster von Hochschulabsolventen. In D. Bögenhold, B. Hodenius, F. Kupferberg & R. Woderich (Eds.), *Gründerfernstudium.P assagen in die Selbständigkeit* (pp. 83–124). Fernuniversität-Gesamthochschule in Hagen/Fachbereich Wirtschaftswissenschaft.

(2001b). Talcott Parsons. Moralske handlinger og social orden. In M. H. Jakobsen, M. Carleheden & S. Kristiansen (Eds.), *Tradition og fornyelse. En problemorientert teorihistorie for sociologien* (pp. 361–328). Aalborg: Aalborg Universitetsforlag.

(2002a). *The rise and fall of the German Democratic Republic.* Piscataway, NJ: Transaction.

(2002b). Entreprenörskap som existentiell handling. *Sociologisk Forskning, 39* (2), 68–103.

(2003a). Kritik, tilpassning, autenticitet og kommunikation. Kreativitetsregimer i moderniteten. *Dansk Sociologi, 14*(3), 43–62.

(2003b). From Berlin to Hollywood: German-speaking refugees in the American film industry. In E. Timms & J. Hughes (Eds.), *Intellectual Migration and Cultural Transformation* (pp. 139–154). New York: Springer.

(2003c). The established and the newcomers: What makes immigrant and women entrepreneurs so special? *International Review of Sociology, 13*(1), 89–104.

(2004a). Ethnic entrepreneurship as innovation. Theoretical considerations and policy implications. In P. Chamberlayne, J. Bornat & U. Apitzsch (Eds.), *Biographical methods and professional practice* (pp. 73–90). Bristol: Policy.

(2004b). Læring eller kreativitet. Pædagogisk professionalitet i den kreative økonomi. In K. Hjort (Ed.), *Professionsforskning* (pp. 43–56). Frederiksberg: Samfundslitteratur.

(2006a). *Kreative Tider.* Copenhagen: Hans Reitzel.

(2006b). Creativity regimes. Innovation norms and struggles for recognition in the early U.S. car and film industries. *International Studies of Management & Organization, 36*(1), 81–103.

(2006c). Pædagogik, læring og kreativitet. *Kvan, 76,* 13–37.

(2007).Läraruppdragets egenart och rollmodeller: Kreativitetsregimer i hybrid-moderniteten. *Educare, 1,* 53–75.

(2008a). Pedagogisk iscensättande av kreativt lärande. In C. Ali and U. Blossing (Eds.), *Lärares liv och arbete.* Stockholm: Pedagogiska magasinet.

(2008b). Konstnärligt skapande och konstpedagogik i hybridmoderniteten. In F. Lindstrand & S. Selander (Eds.), *Estetiska lärprocesser* (pp. 103–120). Lund: Studentlitteratur.

(2009a). Farvel til "de rigtige svars" pædagogik. In L. Tanggaard & S. Brinkman (Eds.), *Kreativitetsfremmende laeringsmiljöer i skolen* (pp. 27–54). Frederikshavn: Dafolo.

(2009b). How curiosity for facts, explanation and skills can become part of the curriculum. *Nesse Seminar, 20 November.* Brussels: The European Commission.

(2009c) Schools as sites of creativity: Staging creative teaching and learning. *Paper addressed to the Creativity Ambassadors of the EU for 2009.* Malmö: Malmö Högskola.

(2010). Hidden impacts of a cultural migration. Traces of Lewis Coser's transatlantic experiences in his sociological work. In C. Schrecker (Ed.), *Transatlantic Voyages and Sociology* (pp. 239–254). Farnham: Ashgate.

(2011). Homo pedagogicus. Kreativt lärande och pedagogiska språkhandlingar. *Pedagogisk forskning i Sverige, 16*(2), 44–158.

(2012a). Unpacking biographical narratives: Investigating stories of artistic careers in Northern Jutland, Denmark. In K Hackstaff, F. Kupferberg & C. Negroni (Eds.), *Biography and turning points in Europe and America* (pp. 9–40). Bristol: Policy Press.

(2012b). Theorizing turning points and decoding narratives. In K. Hackstaff, F. Kupferberg & C. Negroni (Eds.), *Biography and turning points in Europe and America* (pp. 227–259). Bristol: Policy Press.

(2012c). Från lärarvetenskap till lärandevetenskap. Lärandets gåta och pedagogikens plats i vetenskapssystemet. *Pedagogisk Forskning i Sverige, 17*(3), 222–252.

(2013). Medierat lärande och pedagogisk teori. In L. Amhag, F. Kupferberg & M. Leijon (Ed.), *Medierat lärande och pedagogisk mångfald* (pp. 15–51). Lund: Studentlitteratur.

(2014a). Den udviklende skole. Skolen i morgen. *Tidskrift for skoleledelse, 17*(7): 2–4.

(2014b). Entreprenörskap som problembaserat lärande. S. 73–98 i Bali Lelinge & Pär Widén. *Entreprenöriellt lärande i skolan.* Lund: Studentlitteratur.

(2016). Den fænomenologiske fortæller. In I. G. Bo, A.-D. Christensen & T. L. Thomsen (Eds.), *Narrativ forskning. Tilgange og metoder* (pp. 149–166). Copenhagen: Han Reitzel.

(2017a). Transformative agency as social construction. Overcoming knowledge constraints in science. *Art and Technology. Social Science Information, 56*(3) 454–476.

(2017b). Konst och bilddidaktik. In M. Häggström & A. Marner (Eds.), *Visuell kunskap för multimodalt lärande* (pp. 195–192). Lund: Studentlitteratur.

(2018a). Problemsituationer och kulturella resurser. *Pedagogisk Forskning i Sverige, 23*(1– 2), 3–14.

(2018b). Biography research in the Nordic countries. In H. Lutz, M. Schiebel & E. Tuider (Eds.), *Handbuch Biographieforschung* (pp. 765–776). Vienna: Springer Verlag.

Lagercrantz, O. (1979.) *August Strindberg.* Stockholm: Wahlström & Widstrand.

Lakatos, I (1974). Popper on demarcation and induction. In P. A. Schlipp (Eds.), *The Philosophy of Karl Popper.*(pp. 241–271). La Salle, IL: The Library of Living Philosophers. Volume XIV Book I.

Lakatos, I. (1978). *The methodology of scientific research programmes.* Philosophical Papers Vol. I. (J. Worrall & G. Currie eds). Cambridge: Cambridge University Press.

Lakatos, I. & Musgrave, A. (Eds.). (1970). *Criticism and the growth of scientific. knowledge.* Cambridge: Cambridge University Press.

Lakoff, G. & Johnson, M. (1983). *Metaphors we live by.* Chicago, IL: University of Chicago Press.

Lamarque, P. & Olsen, S. H. (1994). *Truth, fiction and literature.* Oxford: Clarendon Press.

Lampugnani, V. M. (Ed.). (1963/1986). *Encyclopedia of the 20th century architecture.* London: Thames & Hudson.

Langer, S. K. (1948/1958). Philosophy in a New Key. *A study in the symbolism of reason, rite and art.* New York: Mentor Book.

(1953/2008). Feeling and form. In S. M. Cahn & A. Meskin (Eds.), *Aesthetics. A comparative anthology* (pp. 317– 326). Malden, MA. Blackwell.

Lasswell, H. D. (1959). The social setting of creativity. In H. H. Anderson (Ed.), *Creativity and its cultivation* (pp. 203–221). New York: Harper & Row.

Latour, B. (1984/1993). *The pasteurization of France.* Cambridge, MA: Harvard University Press.

(1987). *Science in action. How to follow scientists and engineers through society.* Cambridge, MA: Harvard University Press.

(1990). Drawing things together. In M. Lynch & S. Wolgar (Eds.), *Representations in scientific practice* (pp. 19–68). Cambridge, MA: MIT Press.

(1993). *We have never been modern.* Cambridge, MA: Harvard University Press.

(1998). *Artefaktens återkomst.* Stockholm: Nerenius & Santérus.

(1999). *Pandora's hope. Essays on the reality of science studies.* Cambridge, MA: Harvard University Press.

(2000a). When things strike back: A possible contribution of "science studies" to the social sciences. *British Journal of Sociology, 51*(19), 107–123.

(2000b). On the partial existence of existing and non-existing objects. In L. Daston (Ed.), *Biographies of scientific objects* (pp. 247–269). Chicago, IL: University of Chicago Press.

(2005). *Reassembling the social.* Cambridge, MA: Harvard University Press.

Latour, B. & Wolgar, S. (1979). *Laboratory life. The social construction of scientific facts.* London: Sage.

(1986). *Laboratory life. The construction of scientific facts.* Princeton, NJ: Princeton University Press.

Laudan, L. (1977). *Progress and its problems. Towards a theory of scientific growth.* London: Routledge & Kegan Paul.

(1981a). *Science and hypothesis. historical essays on scientific methodology.* Dordrecht: Reidel.

(1981b) A problem solving approach to scientific progress. In I. Hacking (Ed.), *Scientific revolutions* (pp. 144–166). Oxford: Oxford University Press.

Laudan, R. (1984). *The nature of technological knowledge. Are models of scientific change relevant?* Dordrecht: Seidel.

(1987). *From mineralogy to geology*. Chicago, IL: University of Chicago Press.

(1990). *Science and relativism. Some key controversies in the philosophy of science.* Chicago, IL: University of Chicago Press.

(1996). *Beyond positivism and relativism*. Boulder, CO: Westview.

Laudan, L. & Leplin, J. (1991/2007). Empirical equivalence and underdetermination. In M. Lange (Ed.), *Philosophy of Science* (pp. 248–261). Oxford: Blackwell.

Lave, J. & Wenger, E. (1991). *Situated learning – legitimate periphery participation*. New York: Cambridge University Press.

Lawick-Goodall, J. van (1971). *In the shadow of man*. New York: Dell.

Leaming, B. (1998). *Marilyn Monroe*. London: Weidenfeld & Nicolson.

Leader, Z. (2015). *The life of Saul Bellow. To fame and fortune 1915–1964.* London: Jonathan Cape.

Le Corbusier. (1931/2017). *Towards a new architecture*. New York: Dover Publications.

Lee, H. (1996). *Virginia Wolf.* London: Chatto & Windus.

Leew, R. de (Ed.). *August Strindberg*. Zwolle: Uitgeverij Wanders.

Lennig, A. (2000). *Stroheim*. Lexington, KY: University Press of Kentucky.

Leonard- Barton, D. (1995). *Wellsprings of knowledge. Building and sustaining sources of innovation.* Boston, MA: Harvard Business School Press.

Lepsky, K. (1996). Art and language. Ernst H. Gombrich and Karl Bühler's theory of language. In R. Woodfield (Ed.), *Gombrich on art and psychology* (pp. 1–26). Manchester: Manchester University Press.

Lessing, D. (1994). *Under my skin. Volume 1 of my autobiography to 1949.* New York: HarperCollins.

Lessing, G. (2008). Lacoon. In C. M. Cann & A. Meskin (Eds.), *Aesthetics. A comparative anthology* (pp. 122–130). Malden, MA. Blackwell.

Levin, C. (2008). *Creativity in the school context.* Lund: Department of Psychology, Lund University.

Levin, J. (2002/2003). *Hur universum fick sina fläckar*. Stockholm: Norstedts.

Levinson, J. (2006). *Contemplating art*. Oxford: Clarendon Press.

(2016). *Aesthetics*. Oxford: Oxford University Press.

Lewis-Williams, D. (2002). *The mind in the cave*. London: Thames.

Lindberg, D. C. & Westman, R. S. (Eds.). (1990). *Reappraisals of the scientific revolution*. Cambridge: Cambridge University Press.

Lindström, L. (2007). Gardner om hur vi tänker. In A. Forsell (Ed.), *Boken om pedagogerna* (pp. 212–235). Stickholm: Liber.

Lin, X. (2006). *The art of Chinese painting*. Bejing: China International Press.

Lipset, S. M. (1979). *The first new nation. The United States in a comparative perspective.* New York: W. W. Norton.

Litman, B. l. (1998). *The motion-picture mega industry*. Boston: Allyn and Bacon.

Lloyd, G. E. R. (1968). *Aristotle: The growth and structure of his thoughts.* Cambridge: Cambridge University Press.

(1970). *Early Greek science: Thales to Aristotle*. New York: W. W. Norton.

(1991). *Methods and problems in Greek science.* Cambridge: Cambridge University Press.

(2002). *The ambitions of curiosity. Understanding the world in Ancient Greece and China.* Cambridge: Cambridge University Press.

Long, R. E. (1994). *Ingmar Bergman. Film and stage.* New York: Harry N. Abrams.

Lopes, D. (1996). *Understanding pictures.* Oxford: Clarendon Press.

Lorenz, K. (1966/1996). *On aggression.* London: Routledge.

Lucie-Smith, E. (1999). *Konstnärsliv. 1900-talets stora mästare.* Stockholm: Alberg Bonniers.

Luhmann, N. (1987). *Soziale Systeme.* Frankfurt am Main: Suhrkamp.

(1994). Copierte Existenz und Karriere. Zur Herstellung von Individualität. In U. Beck & E. Beck-Gernstein (Eds.), *Risikante Freiheiten* (pp. 191–200). Frankfurt am Main: Suhrkamp.

(1995/2000). *Art as a social system.* Stanford, CA. Stanford University Press.

Lukes, S. (1972). *Émile Durkheim. His life and work.* New York: Harper & Row.

(1977). *Essays in social theory.* New York: Colombia University Press.

Lumet, S. (1996). *Making movies.* New York: Vintage Books.

Lyell, C. (1830/2009). *Principles of geology. Volume 1.* Cambridge: Cambridge University Press.

Lyell, C (1832/2009). *Principles of geology. Volume 2.* Cambridge: Cambridge University Press.

(1833/2009). *Principles of geology. Volume 3.* Cambridge: Cambridge University Press.

(1863/1970). *The antiquity of man.* London: John Murray.

Lyman, R. L. &. O'Brien, M. J. (1998). The goals of evolutionary archeology. History and explanation. *Current Anthropology, 19*(5), 615–652.

(2002). Classification. In J. P. Hart & J. E. Terrell (Eds.), *Darwin and archaeology. A handbook of key concepts* (pp. 69– 87). Westport, CT: Bergin & Garvey.

Lynn, K. S. (1987). *Hemingway.* New York: Simon & Schuster.

(1997). *Chaplin. His life and times.* New York: Simon and Schuster.

Lynton, N. (1980/1989). *The story of modern art.* London: Phaidon.

Lyon, J. K. (1980) *Bertolt Brecht in America.* Princeton, NJ: Princeton University Press.

Lyotard, J.-F. (1984). *The postmodern condition.* Minneapolis, MN: University of Minnesota Press.

(1994). *Om det sublime.* Copenhagen: Akademisk Forlag.

Maddox, B. (2003). *Rosalind Franklin. The dark lady of DNA.* New York: HarperCollins.

Magalener, M. & Kain, R. M. (1955/1990). *Joyce. The man, the work, the reputation.* New York: Plantin Publishers.

Mailer, N. (1995/1997). *Picasso. Portrait of Picasso as a young man.* London: Abacus.

Makarius, M. (1986/1988). *Chagall. The master works.* London: Bracken Books.

Maland, C. J. (1989). *Chaplin and American culture. The evolution of a star image.* Princeton, NJ: Princeton University Press.

Malcolm, J. (1993). The silent woman. *The New Yorker*, Aug. 23 & 30, 84–159.

Malinowski, B. (1948). *Magic, Science and Religion and Other Essays* (R. Redfield ed.). Glencoe, IL. Free Press.

(1961). *Argonauts of the western Pacific.* New York: Dutton.

Maltby, R. (1994). *Hollywood cinema. An introduction.* Oxford: Blackwell.

Manco, J. (2013). *Ancestral journeys. The peopling of Europe from the first centuries to the Vikings.* London: Thames & Hudson.

Mannheim, K. (1972). *Essays on the sociology of knowledge.* London: Routledge & Kegan Paul.

(1936). *Ideology and utopia.* New York: Harcourt, Brace & World.

Margulis, L. & Sagan, D. (2003). *Acquiring genomes. A theory of the origins of species.* New York: Basic Books.

Markovits, I. (1995). *Die Abwicklung. Eine Tagebuch zum Ende der DDR-Justiz.* Munich: C. H. Beck.

Marshall, A. (1890/1916). *Principles of economics. An introductory volume.* London: Macmillan.

Martin, R. A. (1978). *The theater essays of Arthur Miller.* Harmondsworth: Penguin.

Martindale, C. (1990). *The clockwork muse,* New York: Basic Books.

Marton. F. Hounsell, D. & Entwistle, N. (1984/1986). *Hur vi lär.* Stockholm: Prisma.

Marton, F. & Booth, S. (1997). *Om lärande.* Lund: Studentlitteratur.

Marx, S. (1988). *Mayer and Thalberg. The make-believe saints.* Hollywood: Samuel French.

Mathews, N. M. (2001). *Paul Gauguin. An erotic life.* New Haven, CT: Yale University Press.

Maurois, A. (1956/1985). *Olympio: The life of Victor Hugo.* New York: Carroll & Graf.

(1965/1983). *Prometheus. The life of Balzac.* New York: Carroll & Graf.

May, L. L. (1980). *Screening out the past. The birth of mass culture and the motion picture industry.* New York: Oxford University Press.

May, L. L. & May, E. T. (1982). Why Jewish movie moguls: An exploration in American culture. *American Jewish History*, 72(1), 6–25.

May, R. (1975/1994). *Modet at skapa.* Stockholm: Natur & Kultur.

Mayr, E. (1942/1999). *Systematics and the origin of species from the viewpoint of a zoologist.* Cambridge, MA: Harvard University Press.

(1982). *The growth of biological thought.* Cambridge, MA: Belknap.

(1998). *This is biology. The science of the living world.* Cambridge, MA: Belknap.

(2002). *What evolution is.* London: Phoenix.

(2004/2007). *What makes biology unique?* Cambridge: Cambridge University Press.

McBrien, J. P. (1997). *Pocket guide to Chicago architecture.* New York: W. W. Norton.

McCarthy, D. (1996). *Knowledge as culture*. London: Routledge.

McDougal, D. (2001). *The last mogul. Lew Wasserman, MCA, and the hidden history of Hollywood*. New York: Da Capo Press.

McFall, L. (2002). Advertising, persuasion and the culture/dicotomy dualism. In P. du Gay & M. Pyke (Eds.), *Cultural economy* (pp. 149–165). London: Sage.

McGilligan, P. (1997). *Fritz Lang*. New York: St. Martin's Press.

McKeon, M. (Ed.). (2000). *Theory of the novel*. Baltimore & London: Johns Hopkins University Press.

McLellan III, J. E. & Dorn. H. (1999). *Science and technology in world history. An introduction*. Baltimore: Johns Hopkins University Press.

McQuail, D. (Ed.). (2002). *McQuail's reader in mass commuication theory*. London: Sage.

Mead, G. H. (1934/1967). *Mind, self & society*. Chicago, IL: University of Chicago Press.

Meade, M. (2000/2001). *The unruly life of Woody Allen*. Lanham, MD: Cooper Square Press.

Meecham, P. & Sheldon, J. (2005). *Modern art: A critical introduction* (2nd ed.). London: Routledge.

Meerttin, R. K. (1963b/1973). The ambivalence of scientists. In N. W. Storrer (Ed.), *The sociology of science. Theoretical and empirical investigations* (pp. 383–412). Chicago, IL: University of Chicago Press.

Meldolesi, L. (1995). *Discovering the possible: The surprising World of Albert O. Hirschman*. Notre Dame, IN: University of Notre Dame Press.

Menger, P.-M. (1989). Rationalité et incertitude de la vie d'artiste. *L'Anné sociologique, 39*, 111–151.

(1999). Artistic labor markets and careers. *Annual Review of Sociology, 25*, 541–574.

Menger, P.-M. & Gurgang, M. (1996). Work and compensated unemployment in the performing arts. Exogenous and endogenous uncertainty in artistic labour markets. In V. A. Ginsburgh & P.-M. Menger (Eds.), *Economics of the arts. Selected essays* (pp. 347–381). Amsterdam: Elsevier.

Merton, R. K. (1938/1970). *Science, technology and society in seventeenth century England*. New York: Howard Fertig.

(1942/1968). Science and democratic social structure. In *Social Theory and Social Structure* (pp. 604–615). New York: Free Press.

(1957). Priorities in scientific discovery: A chapter in the sociology of science. *American Sociological Review, 22*(6), 635–659.

(1961/1973). Singletons and multiples in science. In *N. W. Storrer* (Ed.), *The sociology of science. Theoretical and empirical investigations* (pp. 325–342). Chicago, IL: University of Chicago Press.

(1963/1973a). Multiple discoveries and strategic research site. In N. W. Storrer (Ed.), *The sociology of science. Theoretical and empirical Investigations* (pp. 371–382). Chicago, IL: University of Chicago Press.

(1963/1973b). The ambivalence of scientists. In N. W. Storrer (Ed.), *The Sociology of Science. Theoretical and Empirical Investigations* (pp. 383–412). Chicago, IL: University of Chicago Press.

(1968a). The sociology of knowledge. In *Social theory and social structure* (pp. 510–542). New York: Free Press.

(1968b). Karl Mannheim and the sociology of knowledge. In *Social theory and social structure* (pp. 543–562). New York: Free Press.

(1968/1973). The Mathew effect in science. In (Ed.). *The sociology of science. Theoretical and empirical investigations* (pp. 419–438). Chicago, IL: University of Chicago Press.

(1976). *Sociological ambivalence and other essays.* New York: Free Press.

Merton, R. K. & Garton. J (1977). *The sociology of science in Europe.* Carbondale, IL: Southern Illinois University Press.

Middlebrook, D. (2004) *Her husband. Ted Hughes and Sylvia Plath.* New York: Penguin Books.

Migayrou, F. (2015). Eyes within eyes. Architecture and mathesis. In O. Cinqualabre & F. Migayrou (Ed.), *Le Corbusier. The measures of man* (pp. 14–25). Zurich: Scheidegger & Spiess.

Miller, A. (1988). *Timebends. A life.* London: Methuen.

Miller, A. I. (2000). *Insights of genius.* Cambridge, MA: MIT Press.

Miller, D. (2006). *Out of error. Further essays in critical rationalism.* Aldershot: Ashgate.

Mills, H. (1982/1983). *Mailer. A biography.* London: New Englsh Library.

Mitchell, W. J. T. (1994). *Picture theory.* Chicago, IL: University of Chicago Press.

Mithen, S. (Ed.) (1998). *Creativity in human evolution and prehistory.* London: Routledge.

Mizener, A. (1958). *F. Scott Fitzgerald: A biographical and critical study.* London: Eyre & Spottiswoode.

Mokyr, J. (1990a). *The lever of riches. Technological creativity and economic progress.* Oxford: Oxford University Press.

(1990b). *Twenty-five centuries of technological change.* London: Routledge.

(2002). *The gift of Athena: Historical origins of the knowledge economy.* Princeton, NJ: Princeton University Press.

(2009). *The enlightened economy. Britain and the industrial revolution 1700–1850.* London: Penguin Books.

Mol, A. (2010). Actor-network theory. Sensitizing terms and enduring tensions. Kölner Zeitschrift für Soziologie und Sozialpsychologie. *Sonderheft* 50: 253–269.

Monaco, J. (2000). *How to read a film.* Oxford: Oxford University Press.

Monk, R. (1990). *Ludwig Wittgenstein. The duty of genius.* New York: Hafner Press.

Montuschi, E. (2003). *The objects of social science.* London: Continuum.

Moon, C., Miller, W. F., Hancock, M. G. & Rowen, H. S. (Eds.). (2000). *The Silicion valley edge. A habitat for innovation and entrepreneurship.* Stanford, CA: Stanford University Press.

Mordden, E. (1987). *The Hollywood studios.* New York: Knopf.

Morgan, J. (1984/2017). *Agatha Christie. A biography.* London: HarperCollins.

Morell, L. (2004). *Kunstneren som polyhistor. "Den intellektuelle overbygning" i Per Kirkeby's værk.* Aarhus: Aarhus Universitetsforlag.

(2011). Jorn afer Jorn. In J-E. Jørgensen (Ed.), *Jorn International* (pp. 189–194). Aarhus: AROS.

Moszynska, A. (1990). *Abstract art.* London: Thames & Hudson.

Mothersill, M (1986/2008). Beauty restored. In S. M. Can & A. Meskin (Eds.), *Aesthetics. A comprehensive anthology* (pp. 509–520). Malden, MA: Blackwell.

Moulin, R. (1987). *The French art market. A sociological view.* New Brunswick, NJ: Rutgers University Press.

Muhlstein, A. (1984). *Baron James. The rise and fall of the Rothschilds.* New York: Vintage.

Müller, J. E. (1996). *Intermedialität.* Münster: Nodus Publikationen.

Murdoch, I. (1987) *Sartre. Romantic Rationalist.* New York: Viking.

Murray, P. & Murray, L. (1963). *The art of the Renaissance.* London: Thames & Hudson.

Nabokov, V. (2011). The Russian professor. *The New Yorker,* June 13 & 20 : 100–104.

Naess, A. (2007). *När jorden stod stilla. Galileo Galilei och hans tid.* Stockholm: Leopard.

Naremore, J. (1988). *Acting in the cinema.* Berkeley, CA: University of California Press.

Nercessian, N. J. (1998). Kuhn and the cognitive revolution. *Configurations, 6*(1), 87–120.

Nielsen, K. & Kvale, S. (2000). *Mästarlära. Lärande som social praxis.* Lund: Studentlitteratur.

Nietzsche, F. (1968). *The will to power* (W. Kaufmann ed.). New York: Vintage.

Nietzche F. W. (1972). *Således talte Zarathustra.* Copenhagen: Jesperse og Pio.

Nietzsche, F. W. (1996). *On the genealogy of morals.* Oxford: Oxford University Press.

Nietzsche F. (1999). *The birth of tragedy and other writings.* Cambridge: Cambridge University Press.

Nisbet, R. A. (1966). *The sociological tradition.* New York: Basic Books.

(1969/1970). *Social change and history.* London: Oxford University Press.

Nobel, A. (2001). *Hur får kumskap liv?* Stockholm: Carlssons.

Oates, J. C. (2000/2002). *Blonde.* Stockholm: Bonniers.

(2005). *En författares övertygelse.* Stockholm: Wahlström & Widstrand.

O'Brian, P. (1976/2003). *Picasso. A biography.* London: HarperCollins.

O'Brien, M. J. & Lyman, R. L. (2000). Darwinian evolutionism is applicable to historical archeology. *International Journal of Historical Archeology,* 4 (1), 71–112.

O'Brien, M. J., Lyman, R. L. & Schiffer, M. B. (2005) *Archeology as a process. Processualism and its progeny.* Salt Lake City, UT: University of Utah Press.

O'Hear, A. (1982). *Karl Popper.* London: Routledge & Kegan Pauls.

Oldroyd, D. (2009). Geophysics and geochemistry. In P. J. Bowler & J. V. Pickstone (Eds.), *The Cambridge history of science. Volume 6: The modern biological and earth sciences* (pp. 395–214). Cambridge: Cambridge University Press.

Olby, R. (1974/1994). *The path to the double helix. The discovery of DNA.* Mineola, NY: Dover.

 (2009). *Francis Crick. Hunter of life's secrets.* Cold Spring Habor, NY: Cold Spring Harbor Press.

Olivier, F. (1935/1982). *Picasso und seine Freunde.* Zürich: Diogenes.

 (2001). *Loving Picasso. The private journal of Fernande Olivier.* New York: Harry N. Abrams.

Olsen, S. H. (1987). *The end of literary theory.* Cambridge: Cambridge University Press.

Oppenheimer, S. (2003). *Out of Eden. The peopling of the world.* London: Constable.

Orwell, G. (1946/1968). Why I write. In S. Orwell & I. Angus (Eds.), *The collected essays, journalism and letters of George Orwell.* Volume *1: An age like this 1920–1940* (pp. 1–7). New York: Harcourt Brace Jovanovich.

 (1931/1968a). A hanging. In S. Orwell & I. Angus (Eds.), *The vollected essays, journalism and letters of George Orwell. Vol. 1: An age like this, 1920–1940* (pp. 44–48). New York: Harcourt Brace Jovanovich.

 (1931/1968b). The spike. In S. Orwell & I. Angus (Eds.), *The vollected essays, journalism and letters of George Orwell. Vol. 1: An age like this, 1920–1940* (pp. 36–43). New York: Harcourt Brace Jovanovich.

 (1985). *The war broadcasts* (W. J. West ed.). London: Duckworth.

Ostow, M. (1982). *Judaism and psychoanalysis.* New York: Kraw Press.

Papagianni, D. & Morse, M. A. (2013). *The Neanderthals rediscovered. How modern science is rewriting their story.* London: Thames & Hudson.

Parker, I. (2020). The really big picture. *The New Yorker,* Feb. 17 & 24, 48–59.

Parkinson, G. H. R. (1977) *Georg Lukács.* London: Routledge & Kegan Paul.

Parsons, T. (1938/1968). *The structure of social Action I & II.* New York: Free Press.

 (1939/1964). The professions and social structure. In *Essays in sociological theory* (pp. 34–49). New York: Free Press.

 (1964). Introduction. In M. Weber (Ed.), *The sociology of religion* (pp. xix–llxvii). Boston, MA: Beacon Press.

Pasternak, A. (2016). *Lara. The untold love story that inspired Doctor Zhivago.* London: William Collins.

Pauling, L. (1947/1988). *General chemistry.* New York: Dover.

Penrose, R. (1958/1968). *Picasso. His life and work.* New York: Schooken Books.

Perkins, D. N. (1981). *The mind's best work.* Cambridge, MA: Harvard University Press.

 (1995). *Smart schools. Better thinking and learning for every child.* New York: Free Press.

Peters, T. & Austin, N. (1985). *A passion for excellence.* New York: Random Books.

Petrosky, H. (1996). *Invention by design. How engineers get from thought to things.* Cambridge, MA: Harvard University Press.

Pettersson, B. (2001). *Handelsmännen.* Stockholm: Ekerlids Förlag.

Pevsner, N. (1936/1991). *Pioneers of modern design. From William Morris to Walter Gropius.* London: Pelican.

(1943/1990). *An outline of European architecture.* London: Penguin.

Pfeiffer, J. E. (1977). *The emergence of society. A prehistory of the establishment.* New York: McGraw-Hill.

Pfeiffer, J. (1982). *The creative explosion. An inquiry into the origins of art and religion.* New York: Harper and Row.

Pierce, C. S. (1991). *Pierce on signs. Writings on semiotics by Charles Sander Pierce* (J. Hoopes ed.). Chapel Hill, NC: University of North Carolina Press.

Pine II, B. J. & Gilmore, J. H (1998). Welcome to the experience economy. *Harvard Business Review,* July–August, 97–105.

Pine II, B. J. & Gilmore, J. H. (1999). *The experience economy: Work is theatre and every business a stage.* Boston, MA: Harvard Business School Press.

Pinker, S. (1995). *The language instinct.* London: Penguin.

(1997/1999) *How the mind works.* London: Penguin Books.

Plath, S. (1975). *Letters home. Correspondence 1950–1963.* (A. S. Plath ed. and selected with a commentary). London: Faber & Faber.

(1992/2008). *The collected poems of Sylvia Plath.* New York: Harper Perennial.

(2000). *The unabridged journals of Sylvia Plath* (K. W. Kukil ed.). New York: Anchor Books.

Polanyi, M. (1962). *Personal knowledge. Toward a post-critical philosophy.* Chicago, IL: University of Chicago Press.

Polkinghorne, D. (1998). *Narrative knowing and the human sciences.* Albany, NY: State University of New York Press.

Pope, R. (2006). *Creativity. Theory, history, practice.* London: Routledge.

Popper, K. R. (1934/1959). *The logic of scientific discovery.* London: Hutchinson.

(1947/1966). *The open society and its enemies* (vols 1 & 2) (5th ed. rev.). London: Routledge.

(1957/2002). *Historismens elände.* Gothenburg: Daidalos.

(1963). *Conjectures and refutations. The growth of scientific knowledge.* London: Routledge and Kegan Paul.

(1968) Remarks on the problems of demarcation and rationality. In I. Lakatos & A. E. Musgrave (Eds.), *Problems in the philosophy of science* (pp. 88–102). Amsterdam: North Holland.

(1969/1977).The logic of social science. In T. W. Adorno (Ed.), *Positivist dispute in German sociology* (pp. 87–104). London: Heinemann.

(1972). *Objective knowledge. An evolutionary approach.* Oxford: Clarendon.

(1974). Autobiography of Karl Popper. In P. A. Schlipp (Ed.), *The philosophy of Karl Popper.* (pp. 3–83). La Salle, IL: *The library of living philosophers. Volume XIV Book I*

(1994a). *The myth of the framework* (M. A. Notturno ed). London: Routledge.

(1994b). *Knowledge and the Body-Mind Problem.* London: Routledge.

(1998). *The world of Parmenides.* London: Routledge.

(1999). *All life is problem solving.* London: Routledge.

Potter, L. (2006/2008). *Mathematics minus fear*. London: Penguin.

Powdermaker, H. (1950) *Hollywood. The dream factory*. Boston, MA: Little Brown. and Company.

Prideaux, S. (2005). *Edvard Munch. Behind the scream*. New Haven, CT: Yale University Press.

Putnam, S. (1947/1987). *Paris was our mistress*. London: Plantin Publishers.

Ramsay, T. (1926/1964). *A million and one nights. A history of the motion picture*. New York: Simon & Schuster.

Raphael, A. (1994). *Ultimate risk*. London: Corgi.

Rapp, C. (2009). The nature and goals of rhetoric. In G. Anagnostopoulos (Eds.), *A companion to Aristotle* (pp. 579–596). Malden, MA: Blackwell.

Rauterberg, H. (2007). *Und das ist Kunst?* Hamburg: Fischer.

Renfrew, C. & Bahn, P. (2008). *Archaelogy: Theory, methods and practice*. London: Thames & Hudson.

Renfrew, C. & Morley, I. (Eds.). (2009). *Becoming human. Innovation in prehistoric material andspiritual culture*. Cambridge: Cambridge University Press.

Renn, J. (Ed.). (2001). *Galileo in context*. Cambridge: Cambridge University Press.

Repcheck, J. (2003/2009). *The man who found time. James Hutton and the discovery of the earth's antiquity*. New York: Basic Books.

Rewald, J. (1993). *The history of Impressionism*. New York: Museum of Modern Art.

Riazanov, D. (1927/1973). *Karl Marx and Friedrich Engels*. New York: Monthly Review.

Richards, R. J. (2009). Classification in Darwin's origins. In R. J. Richards & M. Ruse (Eds.), *The Cambridge companion to the origins of species* (pp. 172–193). Cambridge: Cambridge University Press.

Richards, R. J. & Ruse, M. (Eds.). (2009). *The Cambridge companion to the origins of species*. Cambridge: Cambridge University Press.

Richardson, J. (1991/1992). *A life of Picasso. Volume I: 1881–1906*. London: Pimlico.

(1996/1997). *A life of Picasso. Volume II: 1917–1917*. London: Pimlico.

(2007/2009). *A life of Picasso, Volume III. The triumphant years 1917–1932*. London: Pimlico.

Ridley, M. (2006). *Francis Crick. Discoverer of DNA*. New York: HarperCollins,

Rihll, T. E. (1999). *Greek science*. Oxford: Oxford University Press.

Ricoeur, P. (1981). Narrative time. In W. J. T. Mitchell (Ed.), *On narrative* (pp. 165–186). Chicago, IL: University of Chicago Press.

(1985). *Time and narrative. Volume 2*. Chicago, IL: University of Chicago Press.

Ritzer, G. (1975). *Sociology – a multiple paradigm science*. Boston: Allyn and Bacon.

(1992). *Sociological theory* (3rd ed.). New York: McGraw-Hill.

Robert, M. (1980). *The origins of the novel*. New York: Harvester Press.

Robinson, D. (1996). *From peep show to palace. The birth of American Film*. New York: Columbia University Press.

(2001). *Chaplin. His life and art*. London: Penguin Books.

Roe, S. (2006/2007). *The private lives of the Impressionists*. London: Vintage.

(2015). *In Montmartre. Picasso, Matisse and the birth of Modernist art*. New York: Penguin Press.

Rogers, E. M. & Larsen, J. K. (1984). *Silicon Valley fever. Growth of high-tech culture*. New York: Basic Books.

Romano, E. (1997). *The Impressionists. Their lives, their work, their paintings*. New York: Penguin Studio.

Romer, J. (2012/2013). *A history of Ancient Egypt. From the first farmers to the great pyramids*. London: Penguin Books.

Roper, R. (2015). *Nabokov in America*. New York: Bloomsbury.

Rosa, S. de (2001) *Writing with Hitchcock*. New York: Faber & Faber.

Rose, F. (1995). *The agency*. New York: Harper Business.

Rosenberg, N. (1976). *Perspectives on technology*. Cambridge: Cambridge University Press.

(1982). *Inside the black box. Technology and economics*. Cambridge: Cambridge University Press.

(1994). *Exploring the black box*. Cambridge: Cambridge University Press.

(2000). *Schumpeter and the endogenity of technology. Some American perspectives*. London: Routledge.

(2010). *Studies on science and the innovation process*. Pistcataway, NJ: World Scientific.

Rosenblum, R. (1986). The demoiselles. Sketchbook no. 42, 1907. In A. Glimcher & M. Glimcher (Eds.), *The sketchbooks of Picasso* (pp. 53–80). London: Thames and Hudson.

Ross, A. (2020). The bristlecones speak. *The New Yorker, Jan*. 20, 46–53.

Ross, L. (1984). *Picture*. New York: Garland.

Ross, S. (2003). Style in art. In J. Evinson (Ed.), *The Oxford handbook of aesthetics* (pp. 228–244). Oxford: Oxford University Press.

Rosten, L. (1941). *Hollywood. The movie colony, the movie makers*. New York: Harcourt Brace Jovanovich.

Rostovtzeff, M. (1966). *Grækenlands historie*. Copenhagen: Jørgen Paludans foalag.

Rothery, D. A. (2008). *Geology*. London: Hodder.

Rothko, M. (2004). *The artist's reality. Philosophies of art*. New Haven, CT: Yale University Press.

Rothman, B. (1977). *Jean Piaget. Psychologist of the real*. Ithaca, NY: Cornell University Press.

Rothman, S. & Lichter, S. B. (1982). *Roots of radicalism. Jews, Christians and the new left*. Oxford: Oxford University Press.

Rowley, H. (2005). *Tête-à-tête. Simone de Beauvoi and Jean-Paul Sartre*. New York: HarperCollins.

Rubenfeld, F. (1997). *Clement Greenberg. A life*. New York: Scribner.

Rubin, J. H. (1994). *Manet's silence and the poetics of Bouquets*. London: Reaktion.

Rubin, W. (Ed.). (1984). *Primitivism in 20th century art.* New York: Museum of Modern Art.

(1989). *Picasso and Braque. Pioneering Cubism.* New York: Museum of Modern Art.

(1994). The genesis of Les Demoiselles d'Avignon. In W. Rubin, H. Seckel & J. Cousins (Eds.). *Les Demoiselles d'Avignon* (pp. 118–144). New York: Museum of Modern Art.

Rudwick, M. J. S. (1972). *The meaning of fossils.* London: Macdonald.

(1996). Geological travel and theoretical innovation: The role of "liminal" experience. *Social Studies of Science, 26,* 143–159.

Ruse, M. (1979/1999). *The Darwinian revolution. Science red in tooth and claw.* Chicago, IL: University of Chicago Press.

(2006). *Darwinism and its discontents.* Cambridge: Cambridge University Press.

(2008). *Charles Darwin.* Malden, MA: Blackwell.

Ruskin, J. (1853/2001). *The stones of Venice.* London: Penguin.

Russell, B. (1957). *Västerlandets filosofi.* Stockholm: Natur och Kultur.

Ryle, G. (1949/2000). *The concept of mind.* London: Penguin.

Säljö, R. (1984/1986). Att lära genom att läsa. In F. Marton, D. Hæuunsell & N. Entwistle (Eds.), *Hur vi lär* (pp. 102–125). Stockholm: Prisma.

(2000). *Lärande i praktiken. Ett sociokulturellt perspektiv.* Stockholm: Norstedts.

(2005). *Lärande and kulturella redskap. Lärprocesser och det kollektiva minnet.* Stockholm: Norstedts.

Sartre, J.-P. (1965). *Anti-semite and Jew.* New York: Schocken.

Sarup, M. (1988). *An Introductory guide to Post-structuralism and Postmodernism.* New York: Harvester Wheatsheaf.

Saussure, F. de (1916/1970). *Kurs i allmän lingvistik.* Stockholm: Bo Cavefors.

Sawin, M. (1995/1997). *Surrealism in exile and the beginning of the New York school.* Cambridge, MA: MIT Press.

Sawyer, R. K. (2006). *Explaining creativity. The science of human innovation.* Oxford: Oxford University Press.

Saxenian, A. (1991). The origins and dynamics of production networks in Silicon Valley. *Research Policy 20,* 423–437.

(1994). *Regional advantage: Culture and competition in Silicon Valley and Route 128.* Cambridge, MA: Harvard University Press.

Saxtorp, J. W. (1982). *Brechts politiske engagement.* Copenhagen: Hans Reitzel.

Shackelford, G. T. M. & Frèches-Thory, C. (2004). *Gauguin Tahiti. The studio of the South Seas.* London: Thames & Hudson.

Sharff, S. (1982). *The Elements of Cinema. Toward a Theory of Cinesthetic Impact.* New York: Colombia University Press.

Schatz, T. (1981). *Hollywood genres: Formulas, filmmaking and the studio system.* New York: Random House.

(1988). *The genius of the system. Hollywood film-making in the studio era.* New York: Faber & Faber.

Schellewald, B. (2017). Searching for traces. Chagall and icons. In K. Helfenstein, & O. Osadtschy (Eds.), *Chagall. The breakthrough years, 1911–1919* (pp. 102–115). Cologne: Verlag der Buchhandlung Walther König.

Schepelern, P. (2000). *Lars von Triers film: tvang og befrielse.* Copenhagen: Rosinante.

Schickel, R. (1996). *D. W. Griffith. An American life.* New York: Limelight Editions.

(2012). *Steven Spielberg – a retrospective.* Bath: Palazzo Editions.

Schjeldahl, P. (2020). The shape of things. Donald Judd in retrospect. *The New Yorker, March* 9, 82–83.

Schlender, B. & Tetzeli, R. (2015). *Becoming Steve Jobs.* London: Sceptre.

Schmitz,M. (1995). *Wendestress. Die psychosozialen Kosten der deutschen Einheit.* Berlin: Rohwolt.

Schnauber, C. (1992). *Spaziergänge durch das Hollywood der Emigranten.* Zurich: Arche Verlag.

Scholes, R. (1981). Language, narrative, and anti-narrative. In W. J. T. Mitchell (Ed.), *On narrative* (pp. 200–208). Chicago, IL: University of Chicago Press.

(1982). *Semiotics and interpretation.* New Haven, CT: Yale University Press.

Schön, D. A. (1983). *The reflexive practitioner. How professionals think in action.* New York: Basic Books.

Scholz, D. & Thomsen, C. (Eds.). (2008). *The Klee universe.* Berlin: HatjeCantz.

Schrödinger, E. (1944/1992). *What is life?* Cambridge: Cambridge University Press.

Schumacher, E. & Schumacher, R. (1978). *Leben Brechts.* Berlin: Henschel Verlag.

Schumpeter, J. A. (1945/1979). *Capitalism, Socialism and Democracy.* London: George Allen & Unwin.

Schuster, P.- K. (2008). The world as fragment. Building blocks of the Klee universe. In D. Scholz & C. Thomson (Ed.), *The Klee Universe* (pp. 15–24). Berlin: HatjeCantx.

Schusterman R. (2003). Aesthetics and postmodernism. In J. Levinson (Ed.), *The Oxford handbook of aesthetics* (pp. 771–782). Oxford: Oxford University Press.

Schutz, A. (1973–75). *Collected papers I–III.* The Hague: Nijhoff.

Searle, J. (1969). *Speech acts. An essay in the philosophy of language.* Cambridge: Cambridge University Press.

(1996). *The construction of social reality.* London: Penguin.

Seger, L. (1992). *The art of adaption: Turning fact and fiction into film.* New York: Holt & Co.

Seligman, K. (1948/1971). *Magic, supernaturalism and religion.* New York: Pantheon.

Server, L. (1987). *Screenwriters. Words become pictures.* Pittstown, NJ: Main Street Press.

Seymour-Jones, C. (2008). *A dangerous liaison.* New York: Overlord Press.

Shapin, S. (1996). *The scientific revolution.* Chicago, IL: University of Chicago Press.

Shapin, S. & Schaffer, S. (1985). *Leviathan and the air-pump.* Princeton, NJ: Princeton University Press.

Sharff, S. (1982). *The elements of cinema. Toward a theory of cinesthetic impact.* New York: Colombia University Press.

Shelden, M. (1991). *Orwell. The authorized biography.* New York: HarperCollins.

Shields, C. (2002). *Jane Austen.* Stockholm: Albert Bonniers.

(2007/2014). *Aristotle* (2nd ed.). London: Routledge.

Shiff, R. (1984). *Cézanne and the end of impressionism. A study of the theory, technique, and critical evaluation of modern art.* Chicago, IL: University of Chicago Press.

Shils, E. (1970). Tradition, ecology, and institution in the history of sociology. *Daedalus, 99*(4): 760–825.

Sikov, E. (1998). *On Sunset Boulevard. The life and times of Billy Wilder.* New York: Hyperion.

Simmel, G. (1964). *The sociology of Georg Simmel. Translated, edited and with an introduction by K. H. Wolff.* New York: Free Press.

Simonton, D. K. (1999a). *Origins of genius: Darwinian perspectives on creativity.* New York: Oxford University Press.

(1999b). Creativity as blind variation and selective retention: Is the creative process Darwinian? *Psychological Inquiry, 10*, 309–328.

(2007). The creative process in Picasso's Guernica sketches: Monotonic improvement versus nonmonotonic variants. *Creativity Research Journal, 9* (4), 329–344.

(2010). Creative thought as blind-variation and selective-retention: Combinatorial models of exceptional creativity. *Physics of Life Review, 7*, 156–179.

(2011a). Creativity and discovery as blind variation. Campbell's (1960) BVSR model after the half-century mark. *Review of General Psychology, 15*(2), 158–174.

(2011b). Big-C creativity in the big city. In D. E. Andersson, Å. E. Andersson & C. Melander (Eds.), *Handbook of creative cities* (pp. 72–84). Northampton, MA: Edward Elgar.

Sjögren, H. (2002). *Lek och raseri. Ingmar Bergmans teater 1938–2002.* Stockholm: Carlsson.

Skidelsky, R. (1994). *The economist as savior. 1920–1937.* New York: Allen Lane.

Skinner, A. S. (1983). *Adam Smith F.R.S.E. (1723–1790).* Edinburgh: University of Edinburgh.

Sklar, R. (1994). *Movie-made America.* New York: Vintage.

Skvorecky, J. (1984). *The engineer of human souls.* New York: Alfred. A. Knopf.

Slide, A. (1970). *Early American cinema.* New York: A. S. Barnes.

Sloan, P. R. (2009) The making of a philosophical naturalist. In J. Hodge & G. Radick (Eds.), *The Cambridge companion to Darwin* (2nd ed.) (pp. 21–43). Cambridge: Cambridge University Press.

Smith, C. H. & Beccaloni, G. (Eds.). (2009). *Natural selection and beyond. The intellectual legacy of Alfred Russell Wallace.* Oxford: Oxford University Press.

Smith, S. (2000). *Hitchcock: Suspense, humour and tone.* London. British Film Institute.

Smith, P. (1995). *Impressionism*. London: Everyman Art Library.

Smith, R. (1980/1994). Conceptual Art. In N Stangos (Ed.), *Concepts of modern art. From Fauvism to Postmodernism* (pp. 256–270). London: Thames & Hudson.

Snodin, M. & Stavenow-Hidemark, E. (1997). *Carl och Karin Larsson. Skapare av ett svenskt ideal*. Stockholm: Albert Bonniers Förlag.

Söderholm, C. (2008). *Svenska formgivare*. Lund: Historiska Media.

Solomon, M. (1995). *Mozart*. New York: HarperCollins.

Solzhenitsyn, A. (1976). *Kalven och egen*. Copenhagen: Gyldendal.

Sommar, I. (2000). *Ødesign*. Stockholm: Wahlström& Widstrand.

Sonesson, G. (1992). *Bildbetydelser. Inledning till bildsemiotiken som vetenskap*. Lund: Studentlitteratur.

Sontag, S. (1966/2013). Against interpretation. In D. Rieff (Ed.), *Essays of the 1960s and 70s* (pp. 10–285). New York: The Library of America.

(1969). *Konst och antikonst*. Stockholm: Pan/Norstedts.

(1977). *On photography*. Harmondsworth: Penguin.

Sørensen, J.-E. (Ed.). (2011). *Jorn International*. Aarhus: Aarhus Kunstmuseum.

Sperling, C. W. & Miller, C. (1998). *Hollywood be thy name. The Warner Brothers story*. Lexington: University Press of Kentucky.

Spoto, D. (1976/1992). *The art of Alfred Hitchcock*. New York: Anchor Books.

(1983/1998). *The dark side of genius. The life of Alfred Hitchcock*. New York: Da Capo.

(2009). *Spellbound by beauty. Alfred Hitchcock and his leading ladies*. London: Arrow Books.

Sprinchorn, E. (1982). *Strindberg as dramatist*. New Haven, CT: Yale University Press.

Spurling, H. (1998/2000). *Den okände Matisse*. Stockholm: Norstedts.

(2003). *The girl from the fiction department. A portrait of Sonia Orwell*. London: Penguin.

(2009). *Matisse. The life*. London: Penguin Books.

Squire, J. E. (1992). *The movie business*. New York: Simon & Schuster.

Staiger, J. (1992). *Interpreting films*. Princeton, NJ: Princeton University Press.

Staiger, J. (Ed.) (1995). *The studio system*. New Brunswick, NJ: Rutgers University Press.

Stangos, N. (Ed.). (1974/1994). *Concepts of modern art. From Fauvism to Postmodernism* (2nd ed.). London: Thames & Hudson.

Stanislavskij, K. (1944). *Mit liv i kunsten*. Copenhagen: Nyt Nordisk Forlag Arnold Busck.

(1967) *En skuespillers arbejde med sig selv*. Copenhagen: Nyt Nordisk Forlag Arnold Busck.

Starko, A. J. (2001). *Creativity in the class room: Schools of curious delight*. Mahwav, NJ: Lawrence Erlbaum.

Stecker, R. (2003). Definitions of art. In J. Levinson (Ed.), *The Oxford handbook of aesthetics* (pp. 136–154). Oxford: Oxford University Press.

Steffensen, E. (2017). *At trække en streg. Per Kirkeby, liv og værk*. Copenhagen: Gyldendal.

Steinberg, S. (1989). *The ethnic myth. Race, ethnicity and class in America*. Boston: Beacon Press.

Steinberg, L. (1988).The philosophical brothel. *October*, 44 (Spring), 7–74.

Stenberg, H. (2002). *Att bli konstnär*. Lund: Sociologiske Institutionen, Lunds Universitet.

Stent, G. S. (1970). *DNA. Daedalus, 99*(4), 909–937.

Sternberg, R. J. (Ed.). (1988). *The nature of creativity*. New York: Cambridge University Press.

(Ed.). (1999). *Handbook of creativity*. Cambridge: Cambridge University Press.

Stevenson, A. (1989). *Bitter fame. A life of Sylvia Plath*. Boston: Houghton Mifflin.

Stinchcombe, A. L. (1965). Social structure and organizations. In J. G. March (Ed.), *handbook of organisations* (pp. 142–193). Chicago, IL: RandMcNally.

Stokes, P. D. (2001). Variability, constraints and creativity. *American Psychologist, 56*(4), 353–359.

Stone, I (1961). *Han som skapade en värld. Roman om Michelangelo*. Stockholm: Forum.

(1934/1987). *Han som älskade livet*. Stockholm: Wahlström & Widstrand.

Strauss, A. (1959). *Mirrors and masks. The search for identity*. Glencoe, IL: Free Press.

Strauss, A. & Glaser, B. (1971). *Status passages*. London: Routledge & Kegan Paul.

Strauss, M. (2004). *Alfred Hitchcock's silent films*. Jefferson, NC: McFarland & Company.

Stringer, C. (2011). *The origin of our species*. London: Allen Lane.

Stringer, C. & Andrews, P. (2005). *The complete world of human evolution*. London: Thames & Hudson.

Strong, B. & Davies, M. (2006/2011a). *History of creativity in the arts, science, and technology, USA Pre-1500* (2nd ed.). Dubuque, IA: Kendall Hunt. 1500

(2006/2011b). *History of creativity in the arts, science, and technology, USA 1500-present* (2nd ed.). Dubuque, IA: Kendall Hunt.

Sturken, M. & Cartwright, L. (2001). *Practices of looking. An introduction to visual culture*. Oxford: Oxford University Press.

Sulloway, F. Jr. (1996). *Born to rebel. Birth order, family dynamics, and creative lives*. New York: Pantheon Books.

Sumner, W. G. (1906/1960). *Folkways*. New York: Mentor Books.

Suppe, F. (Ed.). (1974). *The structure of scientific theory*. Urbana, IL: University of Illinois Press.

Svanholm, J. (2001). *Malerne på Skagen*. Copenhagne: Gyldendal.

Svedjedal, J. (1999). *Skrivaredans. Birger Sjöbergs liv och diktning*. Stockholm: Wahlström & Widstrand.

Swedberg, R. (1990). *Economics and sociology*. Princeton, NJ: Princeton University Press.

Swedberg, R. (Ed.) (2000). *Entrepreneurship.The social science view*. New York: Oxford University Press.

(2012). Theorizing in sociology and social science. Turning to the context of discovery. *Theory and Society, 41*(1), 1–40.

Sweetman, D. (1995). *Paul Gauguin. A complete life*. London: Hodder & Stoughton.

Symons, J. (1987). *Makers of the new. The revolution in literature*. New York: Random House.

Tafdrup. P. (1991/1997). *Över vattnet jag går. Skiss till en poetik*. Stockholm: Ellerströms.

Tan, A.-G. (2007). (Ed.). *Creativity. A handbook for teachers*. Piscataway, NJ: World Scientific.

Taylor, J. R. (1978). *Hitch: The life and times of Alfred Hitchcock*. New York: Pantheon.

(1983). *Strangers in paradise. The Hollywood émigreés 1933–1950*. London: Faber & Faber.

Therborn, G. (1973). *Vad är bra värderingar värda?* Lund: Bo Cavefors.

(1977). *Science, class and society. On the formation of sociology and historical materialism*. London: New Left Books.

Thompson, J. (2006). *How to read a modern painting. Understanding and enjoying the modern masters*. London: Thames & Hudson,

Thompson, K. (1985). *Exporting entertainment. America in the world film market. 1917–1934*. London: British Film Institute.

Thompson, K. & Bordwell, D. (2003). *Film history: An introduction*. London: McGraw-Hill.

Thompson, L. (2007/2008). *Agatha Christie. An English mystery*. London: Geadline.

Thomson, B. (1987). *Gauguin*. London: Thames & Hudson.

(2000). *Impressionism. Origins, practice, reception*. London: Thames & Hudson.

Thomson, B. (Ed.). (1993/2004). *Gauguin by himself*. London: Thames & Hudson.

Thoren, V. (1990). *The lord of Uranborg, A biography of Tycho Brahe*. Cambridge: Cambridge University Press.

Thorstendahl, R. (1966). *Historia som vetenskap*. Stockholm: Natur och kultur.

Thurman, J. (1984). *Karen Blixen. En fortællers liv*. Copenhagen: Gyldendal.

Tidd, J., Bessant, J. Pavitt, K. (1997). *Managing Innovation*. Chicester: Wiley.

Timm, M. (2008). *Lusten och demonerna. Boken om Bergman*. Stockholm: Norstedt.

Tolstoy, L. (1898/1995). *What is art?* London: Penguin Books.

Tomkins, C. (1996). *Duchamp. A biography*. New York: Henry Holt.

(2001). The modernist. *New Yorker, November 5*, 72–83.

(2019). The enchanter. *The New Yorker December 9*, 52–61.

Tøjner, P. E. (2008). Maleri som scene. In M. J. Holm & P. E. Tøjner (Eds.), *Per Kirkeby. Louisiana 2008* (pp. 12–27). Humlebæk: Louisiana Museum of Modern Art.

Tocqueville, A. de (1945). *Democracy in America (vols I & II)*. New York: Random House.

Törnqvist, G. (2009). *Kreativitet i tid och rum*. Stockholm: SNS Förlag.

Trigger, B. G. (1989). *A history of archaeological thought.* Cambridge: Cambridge University Press.

(2003). *Artifacts and iideas.* New Brunswick, NJ. Transaction.

Truffault, F. (1983/2017). *Hitchcock.* London: Faber & Faber.

Tudge, C. (2005). *The tree. A natural history of what trees are, how they live, and why they matter.* New York: Three River Press.

(2008). *The bird. A natural history of who birds are, where they came from, and how they live.* New York: Three Rivers Press.

(2009). *The link. Uncovering our earliest ancestor.* London: Little Brown.

Ullman, L. (2015/2017). *De oroliga.* Stockholm: Bonniers.

Vella, J. A. (2008). *Aristotle. A guide for the perplexed.* London: Continuum.

Veblen, T. (1962). The intellectual pre-eminence of Jews in modern Europe. In M. Lernerr (Ed.), *The portable veblen* (pp. 476–479). New York: Viking.

(1968). *Imperial Germany and the industrial revolution.* Ann Arbor, MI: University of Michigan Press.

Vest J. M. (2003). *Hitchcock and France. The forging of an author.* Westport, CT: Praeger.

Vezin, A. & Vezin, L. (1992). *Kandinsky and der Blaue Reiter.* Paris: Pierre Terrail.

Vincenti, W. G. (1990 /1993). *What engineers know and how they know it.* Baltimore, MD: Johns Hopkins University Press.

Vitoux, F. (1992). *Céline. A biography (ch. 1).* New York: Paragon House.

Vygotsky, L. S. (1971). *The psychology of art.* Cambridge, MA: MIT Press.

Vygotsky, L..S. (1995). *Fantasi och kreativitet i barndomen.Gothenburg: Daidalos.*

(1999). *Tänkande och språk.* Gothenburg: Daidalos.

Wagner-Martin, L. (2003). *Sylvia Plath. A literary life* (2nd ed.). Basingstoke. Palgrave.

Walker, A. (1987). *Vivien. The life of Vivien Leigh.* New York: Grove.

Waller, J. (2002). *Fabulous science. Fact and fiction in the history of discovery.* Oxford: Oxford University Press.

Walther, I. (Ed.). (2005. *Art of the 20th century* (vols I & II). Cologne: Taschen.

Walton, J. (1992). Making the theoretical case. In C. Ragin & H S. Becker (Eds.), *What is a case?* (pp. 121–137). New York: Cambridge University Press.

Walton, K. L. (1990). *Mimesis as make-believe.* Cambridge, MA: Harvard University Press.

Wartofsky, M. W. (1968). *Conceptual foundations of scientific thought. An introduction to the philosophy of science.* New York: Macmillan.

Watson, J. D. (1968/1996). *The double helix. A personal account of the discovery of the structure of DNA.* New York: Touchstone.

(2001). *Genes, girls and gamow. After the double helix.* New York: Vintage.

Weber, M. (1904–1905/1958). *The Protestant ethic and the spirit of capitalism.* New York: Scribners.

(1922/1964). *The sociology of religion (Introduction by T. Parsons).* Boston: Beacon Press.

(1948a). Science as vocation. In H. H. Gerth & C. W. Mills (Eds.), *From Max Weber. Essays in sociology* (pp. 129–136). London: Routledge.

(1948b). Class, status and party. In H. H. Gerth & C. W. Mills (Eds.), *From Max Weber. Essays in sociology* (pp. 180–195). London: Routledge & Kegan Paul.

(1961). *General economic history*. New York: Collier.

(1964). *The theory of social and economic organization* (T. Parsons ed.). New York: Free Press.

Weber, M (1976). *The agrarian sociology and ancient civilizations*. London: New Left Books.

(1980). *Gesammelte Politische Schriften*. Tübingen: J. C. B. Mohr.

(1983). *Gesammelte Aufsätze zur Wissenschaftslehre*. Tübingen: J. C. B. Mohr.

Weber, N. F. (2008). *Le Corbusier. A life*. New York: Alfred A. Knopf.

Weber, R. J. & Perkins, D. N. (Eds.). (1992). *Inventive minds. Creativity in technology*. New York: Oxford University Press.

Wedberg, A. (1959). *Filosofins hisotia. Nyare tiden itll romantiken*. Stockholm: Bonniers.

(1967). *Filosofin genom tiderna. 1660-talet. 1700-talet*. Stockholm: Bonniers.

Weintraub, L. (2003). *Making contemporary art. How modern artists think and work*. London: Thames and Hudson.

Weisberg, R. W. (1993). *Creativity beyond the myth of genius*. New York: W. W. Freeman.

(2006). *Creativity, understanding innovation in problem solving, science, invention, and the arts*. Hoboken, NJ: Wiley.

Welch, E. (1984). *Art in Renaissance Italy*. Oxford: Oxford University Press.

Weldon, F. (2002/2011). *Audo da fay*. Stockholm: Massolit förlag.

Wennberg, A. (2007). *Tänk om der är så? Om Tycho Brahes instrument och vad han kunde gåora med dem*. Landskorna: Kultutnämnden i Landskrona.

Wensierski, H. J. von (1994). *Mit uns zieht die alten Zeiten. Biographie und Lebenswelt junger DDR-bürger im gesellschaftlichen Umbruch*. Opladen: Leske & Budrich.

Wertsch, J. V. (2007). Mediation. In H. M. CJ. V. *The Cambridge companion to Vygotsky* (pp. 178–192). Cambridge: Cambridge University Press.

West, N. (1939/1986). *Græshoppens dag*. Copenhagne: Centru.

White, H. C. (1993). *Careers and creativity. Social forces in the arts*. Boulder, CO: Westview.

White, H. C. & White, C. A. (1965/1993). *Canvases and careers. Institutional change in the French painting world*. Chicago, IL: University of Chicago Press.

(2007). Mediation. In H. Daniels, M. Cole and J. V. Wertsch (Eds.), *The Cambridge companion to Vygotsky* (pp. 178–192). Cambridge: Cambridge University Press.

Whewell, W. (1984). In Y. Elkana (Ed.), *Selected writings on the history of science*. Chicago, IL: University of Chicago Press.

(1989). *Theory of scientific methods* (by R. Butts ed. and Introduction). Indianapolis, IN: Hackett.

White, H. C. &. White, C. A. (1965/1993). *Canvases and careers. Institutional change in the French painting world*. Chicago, IL: University of Chicago Press.

White, L. (1964). *Medieval technology and social change*. Oxford: Oxford University Press.

White, M. & Gribbin, I. (1997). *Einstein. A life in science*. London: Simon & Schuster.

Whitfield, E. (1997). *Pickford. The woman who made Hollywood*. New York: Faber & Faber.

Whitfield, S. (1967/1994). Fauvism. In N. Stangos (Ed.), *Concepts of Modern Art. from Fauvism to Postmodernism* (pp. 11–29). London: Thames & Hudson.

Whitley, R. (1984). *The intellectual and social organization of science*. New York: Oxford University Press.

Whittemore, D. & Cecchettini. P. A. (1976). *Passport to Hollywood. Film immigrants anthology*. New York: McGraw-Hill.

Wickham, G. (1985/1992). *A history of the Theatre* (2nd ed.). London: Phaidon.

Wiener, N. (1993). *Invention. The care and feeding of ideas*. Cambridge, MA: MIT Press.

Wild, J. J. (1992). The origins of soft tissue ultrasonic echoing and early instrumental application to clinical medicine. In R. J. Weber & D. N. Perkins (Eds.), *Inventive minds. Creativity in technology* (pp. 115–141). New York: Oxford University Press.

Will, B. (2000). *Gertrude Stein and the problem of "genius."* Edinburgh: Edinburgh University Press.

Williams, E. (1999). *The million dollar mermaid*. San Diego, CA: Harvest.

Wilson, E. O. (1975/2000). *Sociobiology. The new dynthesis*. Cambridge, MA: Belknap.

(1980). *Sociobiology. The abridged edition*. Cambridge, MA: Belknap.

(1991/2001). *The diversity of life*. London: Penguin.

(2012). *The social conquest of earth*. New York: Liveright.

Wilson, L. G. (1972). *Charles Lyell. The years to 1841: The revolution in geology*. New Haven, CT: Yale University Press.

Wilson-Bareau, J. (Ed.). (1991/1995). *Manet by himself*. Boston, MA: Little Brown.

Wimsatt, W. C. & Beardsley, M. C. (1954/1992). Det intentionella felslutet. In C. Entzenberg & C. Hansson (Eds.), *Modern litteraturteori. Från rysk formalism till dekonstruktion*. (pp. 115–130). Lund: Studentlitteratur.

Winch, P. (1958). *The idea of a social science and its relation to philosophy*. London: Routledge.

Winchester, S. (2002). *The map that changed the world*. London: Penguin Books.

Woodhead, L. (2012). *Shopping, seduction and Mr. Selfridge* (rev. ed.). London: Profile.

Wray, K. B. (2011). Kuhn and the discovery of paradigms. *Philosophy of the Social Sciences, 41*(3), 380–397.

Wright, C. (1978/1984). *The Dutch painters*. London: Orbo.

Wrigley, E. A. (1988). *Continuity, chance and change. The character of the industrial revolution in England*. Cambridge: Cambridge University Press.

Wullschlager, J. (2008). *Chagall. A biography*. New York: Knopf.

Zahner, N. T. (2006). *Die neuen Regeln der Kunst. Andy Warhol und der Umbau des Kunstbetriebs im 20. Jahrhundert.* Frankfurt: Campus.

Zalewski, D. (2009). The background hum. Ian McEwan's art of unease. *The New Yorker, February* 23, pp.46–61.

Zangwill, N. (2001). *The metaphysics of beauty.* Ithaca, NY: Cornell University Press.

Ziman, J. (1996). *Reliable knowledge. An exploration of the grounds for belief in science.* Cambridge. Cambridge University Press.

Zukowsky, J. (Ed.). (1988) *Chicago architecture. Volume 1: 1872–1922.* Munich: Prestel.

# Index

For EU product safety concerns, contact us at Calle de José Abascal, 56–1°,
28003 Madrid, Spain or eugpsr@cambridge.org.

www.ingramcontent.com/pod-product-compliance
Ingram Content Group UK Ltd.
Pitfield, Milton Keynes, MK11 3LW, UK
UKHW020403140625
459647UK00020B/2616